BOOKS BY

THEODORE M. BERNSTEIN

HEADLINES AND DEADLINES   1933, 1961
(with Robert E. Garst)

WATCH YOUR LANGUAGE   1958

MORE LANGUAGE THAT NEEDS WATCHING   1962

THE CAREFUL WRITER   1965

ƒP

THEODORE M. BERNSTEIN

THE CAREFUL WRITER

A MODERN GUIDE TO ENGLISH USAGE

THE FREE PRESS
New York London Toronto Sydney

A LEONARD HARRIS BOOK

The quotation on page 312 is reprinted with the permission of Charles Scribner's Sons from THE SUN ALSO RISES, page 3, by Ernest Hemingway, copyright 1926, Charles Scribner's Sons; renewal copyright 1954, Ernest Hemingway.

The quotation on pages 258-259 is reprinted with the permission of D. C. Heath from SYNTAX (Volume III of A GRAMMAR OF THE ENGLISH LANGUAGE), page 281, by George O. Curme, copyright 1931, D. C. Heath.

THE FREE PRESS
1230 Avenue of the Americas
New York, NY 10020

THE FREE PRESS and colophon are trademarks
of Simon & Schuster Inc.

First Free Press Paperback Edition 1998

Designed by Harry Ford

Manufactured in the United States of America

7 9 10 8

Library of Congress Cataloging-in-Publication Data is available.

ISBN 0-684-82632-1

THIS, TOO, IS FOR BEATRICE

CAREFUL—AND CORRECT

(A title devised to avoid the word INTRODUCTION,
which so many readers find frightening)

WRITING is one art form that can be practiced almost anywhere at almost any time. Normally, you cannot paint in the office, or sculpture in the classroom, or play the piano in a plane or the trumpet on a train. But, given some paper and a writing implement, one can write in any of these places. What emerges will not always be a work of art; yet it could be. At the very least we can introduce clarity, precision, and grace into the most ordinary of our written communications.

People are accustomed to thinking of their everyday writing efforts—the business letter, the thank-you note, the student history exercise, the news story, the advertisement, the press release, the legal brief—as if they were forms in which one merely filled in the blanks. But they need not be that. There is always scope for originality and adroit phrasing, and always need for logical thinking and clear expression. These things do not usually come spontaneously; they require thought and mental discipline. Thus, unless one belongs to that tiny minority who can speak directly and beautifully, one should not write as he talks. To do so is to indulge in a kind of stenography, not writing.

Naturally, there is no guarantee that the well-written brief will win the suit or that the well-written theme will be graded "A," any more than there is a guarantee that good writing will, by itself, make a novel a best-seller. What good writing can do, however, is to assure that the writer is really in communication with the reader, that he is delivering his message unmistakably and, perhaps, excellently. When that happens, the reader takes satisfaction in the reading and the writer takes joy in the writing.

This book is designed as a guide to good written English usage. Only a generation or so ago such a design was a relatively uncomplicated matter. The worst the author expected was some disagreements with his opinions and perhaps an occasional characterization of himself as a dunce. Today, however, he faces not only these hazards but, in addition, challenges to his issuing any pronouncements at all. The challengers say—or seem to say—that no one has any business pronouncing on usage, that the only authority in this field is the unclear, imprecise, and often vulgar voice of the masses.

One or two of these far-out challengers have alluded to compilers of usage as "self-appointed oracles." To this charge I shall have to plead guilty. But it is not really my fault. I tried very hard to get a legitimate appointment, but I could not even find a listing in the telephone directory for an Office of Oracle Appointments. This made me wonder how the challengers had obtained their appointments. I could only conclude that they had not been appointed at all but had assumed office by what they took to be a sort of popular election. Now I am a firm believer in democracy, but I also believe that there are some fields of human activity in which a count of noses does not provide the best basis for law and order.

In the absence, then, of an official appointment as Oracle First Class, whence come the oracular outgivings contained in the following pages? That is a fair question and deserving of an answer. Let it be said at once that the author did not come striding down the slopes of some linguistic Sinai clutching tablets of the law under his arm. Nor did he have an insomniac vision of how to form the Perfect Language. The guides to good usage presented in this book arise from six sources:

First, the practices of reputable writers, past and present.

Second, the observations and discoveries of linguistic scholars. The work of past scholars has, when necessary, been updated. The work of contemporary scholars has been weighed judiciously.

Third, the predilections of teachers of English, wherever—right or wrong, like it or not—these predilections have become deeply ingrained in the language itself.

Fourth, observation of what makes for clarity, precision,

viii

and logical presentation. In some instances such observation brings forth something akin to spit and polish, and just as spit and polish is valuable in the running of a taut ship so is it valuable in the disciplining of writing.

Fifth, personal preferences of the author—and why not? If reputable writers are entitled to personal preferences and the whims of the multitude are often heeded, why should I be left out? After all, it's my book.

Sixth, experience in critical examination of the written word as an editor of *The New York Times,* a newspaper that strives, perhaps a mite harder than most newspapers, for precision, accuracy, clarity, and—especially in recent years—good writing.

In 1958 I brought out a book entitled *Watch Your Language* because, as I said then, a publisher had twisted my arm. Some of that same kind of twisting accounts for the present book, but another kind has presented a more compelling motive. It is the twisting of our language, which is being encouraged by linguists and teachers who find it easier to follow their sometimes benighted charges than to lead them. The issue is not so much "corruption" of the language as it is a withering away of the ability to use it for coherent communication, especially in writing. Ask any college English professor, ask any graduate school dean, ask any industrial personnel manager, ask any editor.

The challengers mentioned earlier are in the camp of the structural linguists. Structural linguistics, which may have had its beginnings a century and a half ago but has come to wide notice only in the last few decades, borrows the methods of science in an attempt to arrive at an objective description of a language. In doing so the structuralist eschews moral evaluations. Questions of correctness, says Professor Samuel R. Levin in a typical structuralist statement, "involve value judgments which the linguist, as structuralist, does not reckon himself qualified to make." [1] Structural linguistics begins with the smallest units of sound ("phones"), classifies them into the smallest *significant*

[1] *College English,* February, 1960.

units of sound (those groups are called "phonemes"), then in turn classifies phonemes into *meaningful* units of sound ("morphemes," that is, words or affixes). From this point the study seeks to identify the structure of grammatical units and then to identify the arrangements and forms of such grammatical units that make up the structure of the language.

In an age in which there is a widespread urge to be scientific—to stand aside and analyze things, classify them, and describe them—no one can argue with the desire to examine language to see what makes it tick. Nor would anyone dispute that the effort has turned up much that is of value. But scrutinizing the language objectively and mechanically is one thing; it is quite another thing to attempt to apply the findings of such a scrutiny to the teaching of speaking and writing, fields in which things other than flat, unevaluated findings come into play. To take an analogy: An objective, scientific study of an automobile might produce findings that the steering gear permits all manner of rational or irrational turning—weaving from side to side and driving in circles as well as normal right and left turns; that pressing the accelerator down to the floor will make the car go like a blind bat out of hell; that one-way signs and red traffic lights in no way interfere with the mechanism or operation of the car. These would all be valid findings, but they would be of only limited help as elements in a course in sane driving. Nor would a study of the driving habits of the populace as a whole be much more helpful. Unreliable statistics gathered by an absent-minded canvasser and programed on an abacus suggest that 87 per cent of drivers ignore a red light at least once a month, that 56.2 per cent cross a solid dividing line at least once per 100 miles, that 71 per cent have at some time driven while intoxicated, that 99 per cent have exceeded the speed limit more than once, and that 100 per cent park illegally at least twice a year. Advice to drive as others do might thus not be the wisest counsel.

It was said at the outset that this book is designed as a guide to good *written* English usage. The word *written* is italicized to emphasize that there is a distinction between spoken language and written language. Much of the heat of the quarrels between the structuralists and what they refer to as the traditionalists could be drawn off if there were greater awareness of that distinction not only in theory but also in practice. Leaders among the structuralists do, indeed, recognize the distinction, but many of the followers either minify it or use it as an instrument for making writing appear to be somehow an inferior human endeavor. Let us look at what some of the cooler heads among the structuralists have said.

". . . speaking and writing are different but interacting activities," says Professor Sumner Ives. "They are not the same, do not follow all of the same conventions, and are not done for the same list of purposes. Neither is finally and fully determinative for the other. No competent linguist would suggest that the teacher of written English should accept in student writing all of the conventions and the same characteristics of style as are customary in speech, even that of the most cultivated." [2]

Professor Paul Roberts tells us:

"It should be noticed that the problem of correctness becomes much simpler when we are careful to discriminate between speech and writing. Usage governs both, but in quite different ways. We must be forever in disagreement among ourselves and with our fellow citizens on what is correct in speech. It depends on who and what and where we are and on who and what and where we want to be. But in writing, and particularly in certain aspects of writing, we can achieve very considerable agreement." [3]

And one more—Professor Henry Lee Smith, Jr.:

". . . the written language is more immediately accessible than the spoken language; the written language has a permanence in contrast to the ephemeral character of speech; the written language is always more rigidly structured, more insistent on precision and clarity by the very virtue of the fact that it must stand alone. For these reasons, if for no others, it should be studied, understood, and mastered. With a real understanding of the difference between the spoken and written language, it

[2] *College English*, December, 1955.
[3] *College English*, October, 1960.

should be obvious that we should never allow our students to write 'just the way they talk' any more than we should try to teach them to talk the way they *have* to learn to write. The failure to see and to understand the distinction between standard colloquial speech and the literary language, and the failure to understand the relationship between speech and writing have been, I am convinced, the chief obstacle in imparting to our students both real literacy and a confident competence in speaking." [4]

But there are hotter heads among the structural or descriptive linguists. Some of them affirm that "spoken language is the language." [5] Others even repudiate the phrase "spoken language"; one of them calls it a "layman's term" and asserts that "the linguist distinguishes between *language* and *writing*." [6] They point out, quite correctly, that the human race has been speaking perhaps for millions of years but has been writing only a relatively short time, that large segments of the race still cannot read or write, and that the individual child learns to speak at an earlier age than he learns to read and write. From these self-evident facts they leap to the conclusions that writing is "less important" than speech[7] and that "the language of today is not to be identified with that found in books but is to be found chiefly on the lips of people who are currently speaking it." [8]

Them conclusions simply ain't got no justification (those words were found on the lips of people). Just what "important" means in this context it is hard to know, but it may be pertinent to ask whether the written Constitution of the United States is less important than the spoken "Fill 'er up," whether the written *Hamlet* is less important than the spoken "Man, I got the blues," or whether the written receipted bill is less important

4 *College English*, January, 1959.
5 *The English Language Arts*, prepared by the Commission on the English Curriculum of the National Council of Teachers of English, 1952, Appleton-Century-Crofts, p. 276.
6 *A Course in Modern Linguistics*, by Charles F. Hockett, 1958, The Macmillan Company, p. 4.
7 *Linguistics and Your Language*, by Robert A. Hall, Jr., 1950, Anchor Books, Doubleday & Company, p. 32.
8 *The English Language Arts*, p. 276.

xii

than the spoken "Okay, bud, now you're all paid up." Undoubtedly, there are situations in which the spoken word is more "important" than the written word and undoubtedly we give and receive more spoken words than written words in this noisy age. But neither is dispensable in a modern civilization; we simply could not carry on our day-to-day activities in a highly organized society without written language, to say nothing of passing on to posterity our law, our literature, and our scientific knowledge.

Once the far-out linguists have accepted the notion that the language of today is to be found on the lips of the people who are speaking it, they find it easy to embrace the corollary that flows from this notion: There are levels of usage and each is acceptable provided it is appropriate to the situation in which it is used and is appropriate to the user. What this means, many of them say, is that we must abandon ideas of right and wrong, good and bad, correct and incorrect. Some go even further and suggest that if one's English is what some of us might shyly term inferior, the only reason to change it is to achieve "social and financial success." [9] In other words, the only incentive for improvement in one's use of English is to be the desire for a coveted job or a better social position. Such materialism and such cynicism are indeed astonishing, and the more so since they spring from members of the teaching profession. Where, in this depressing picture, is the desire for education for its own sake? Where is the ideal of excellence?

The recognition that there are levels of usage is, of course, nothing new; we have always known that different elements of the population employ different kinds of language. (It is interesting to note in passing that many of the same linguists who reject the characterizations "good" and "bad" or "correct" and "incorrect" or "better" and "worse" placidly accept the word "levels," although it implies planes of different elevation, of which some must be higher than others. But the failure to find the precise word is a common deficiency these days.) Although levels of usage have always been recognized, what is new in the contemporary world is the equal blessing bestowed on all of

[9] *Linguistics and Your Language*, p. 29.

them. And implicit in that blind blessing is a reluctance to hurt anyone's feelings or to make him feel inferior. This attitude is puzzling. There are more poor fiddlers than good ones, but no one hesitates to say that there is such a thing as good violin playing. There are more golfers who play in the nineties and above than play in the seventies, but no one hesitates to say that there is a correct way to play out of a sandtrap or a correct club to use on the green. There are more do-it-yourself carpenters who bungle than there are competent professionals, but no one hesitates to say that there is a right way to fashion a tenon and mortise and a wrong way. In none of these fields do ideas of right and wrong seem to be injurious. In language alone are the bunglers blessed.

Those who affirm that there are, indeed, such things as correctness and incorrectness in writing are in danger of being put in the false position of defending a rigid, unchanging code of English. That is not what they are defending. Of course the language has always changed and will always change, and that is well recognized in all camps.

The change in the twentieth century has been quite noticeable but not revolutionary. Visualize the language as three overlapping glass doors. At the right is a narrow one labeled "formal." In the center is a wide one labeled "reputable." And at the left, broadest of all, is one labeled "casual." What has happened is a gradual shift of two of these to the left. The narrow "formal" segment of the language has almost disappeared behind the portion marked "reputable." The stilted, highly stylistic language of other days is restricted today to baccalaureate addresses, to court decisions, to specialized papers in learned journals, and to a few other uses. The broad category "reputable" (the word is used here in its particularized meaning of employed by and approved by skillful users of the language) has absorbed most of the "formal" category and it, too, has shifted to the left to take in more of the "casual" segment than ever before. Reputable speech and writing are more hospitable to colloquialisms and even to slang than in earlier days. The widest category—"casual" —is the relaxed, informal, often slangy, sometimes illiterate de-

xiv

motic converse. It has changed, as the words of the masses always change, but it has moved neither left nor right.

There is no need, then, for argument about the existence, the inevitability, and the desirability of change. There is need, however, for argument about the existence of such a thing as good English and correct English. Let us not hesitate to assert that "The pencil was laying on the table" and "He don't know nothing" are at present incorrect, no matter how many know-nothings say them. Let us insist that *disinterested* be differentiated from *uninterested,* not as a fetish but as a means of preserving a word that is needful. Let us demand that words be placed in a sentence where they logically belong, provided only that they do not defy idiom—and let us not imagine that idioms come into being overnight. Let us do these things not to satisfy "rules" or to gratify the whims of a pedagogue, but rather to express ourselves clearly, precisely, logically, and directly—and to cultivate the habits of mind that produce that kind of expression. Let us, in short, write carefully and correctly.

"We have long preserved our constitution," said Dr. Johnson more than two centuries ago, "let us make some struggles for our language."

ACKNOWLEDGMENTS, EXPLANATIONS, AND SUCH[10]

ALMOST A COLLABORATOR, Bertram Lippman of the English Department of Bayside High School, New York City, shares credit for whatever is right in this book. Whatever is wrong is probably the result of my not having taken some suggestion of his or not having heeded some caution of his. He is a sound grammarian and an effective teacher, but no stuffy pedagogue. His primary contribution to this volume was his tireless research into various knotty questions of usage; his secondary contribution was his counsel on proper conclusions; his tertiary contribution was his zeal for the work—a zeal that often overwhelmed me with more

[10] See page 432.

material than I felt I could use. A happy by-product of his efforts emerged in the preparation of a book of his own in a related field: *Runaway Language* (Macmillan).

Leonard R. Harris, editor-publisher, midwifed this book, as he did two others of mine. Perhaps midwife is not quite the right word, since he was present at the conception and was in attendance throughout the long period of pregnancy. Painstaking but never painsgiving, he edited the manuscript with perception and almost unbelievable attention to detail.

In an acknowledgment in *Watch Your Language* I spoke of Lewis Jordan, news editor of *The New York Times*, as the solid anvil against which much of the material of that book was hammered out. He performed the same function for much of the material of this book, focusing the lights of a practical editor on many dark problems of usage (and for an anvil to focus lights takes a fine talent). He, too, edited the manuscript and contributed many helpful thoughts.

Finally, we sought a reading by a distinguished linguistic scholar, and Professor Mario A. Pei of Columbia University kindly consented to perform the task. Dr. Pei offered some sound correctives and useful opinions. It is not to be assumed that he is in agreement with every position taken in these pages—probably no authority on usage would be. Nor is he responsible for whatever errors may yet linger in the text; his job was that of the attorney general, not that of the precinct detective. For his contribution I am deeply grateful.

* * *

The text contains a substantial number of short entries on the pattern of "Forbid takes the preposition *to*." Their presence in this form probably does not need explanation, but an explanation appears anyway under the heading PREPOSITIONS.

* * *

Reference works cited in the text are, for the most part, indicated by a single name. A list of these abbreviations and the works they refer to follows:

BRYANT: Margaret M. Bryant, *Current American Usage*, New York, Funk & Wagnalls Company, 1962.

CURME: George O. Curme, *Syntax* (Volume III of *A Grammar of the English Language*), Boston, D. C. Heath and Company, 1931.

EVANS: Bergen Evans and Cornelia Evans, *A Dictionary of Contemporary American Usage*, New York, Random House, 1957.

FOWLER: H. W. Fowler, *A Dictionary of Modern English Usage*, London, Oxford University Press, 1926, 1937.

JESPERSEN: Otto Jespersen, *A Modern English Grammar* (in seven parts), London, George Allen & Unwin, Ltd., 1954.

MARCKWARDT: Albert H. Marckwardt, *American English*, New York, Oxford University Press, 1958.

OXFORD: *Oxford English Dictionary*, London, Oxford University Press, 1928.

PARTRIDGE: Eric Partridge, *Usage and Abusage*, Penguin Reference Books edition, Baltimore, Maryland, Penguin Books, 1963.

PERRIN: Porter G. Perrin, *Writer's Guide and Index to English*, Chicago, Scott, Foresman and Company, 1942; and Third Edition, 1959.

STRUNK: William Strunk, Jr., and E. B. White, *The Elements of Style*, New York, The Macmillan Company, 1959.

WEBSTER: *Webster's New International Dictionary of the English Language*, Second Edition, Springfield, Massachusetts, G. & C. Merriam Company, 1959.

WEBSTER III: *Webster's Third New International Dictionary of the English Language*, Springfield, Massachusetts, G. & C. Merriam Company, 1961.

* * *

Other books mentioned in the text are: *The American College Dictionary*, Random House, New York, *The American Language*, H. L. Mencken, Alfred A. Knopf, New York; *Comfortable*

Words, Bergen Evans, Random House, New York; *Familiar Quotations*, John Bartlett, Little Brown and Company, Boston; *The Oxford Book of Quotations*, Second Edition, Oxford University Press, London and New York; *Webster's New World Dictionary of the American Language*, The World Publishing Company, Cleveland; *Words Into Type*, Marjorie E. Skillin and Robert M. Gay, Appleton-Century-Crofts, Inc., New York; *Words on Paper*, Roy H. Copperud, Hawthorn Books, Inc., New York; and *Write It Right*, Ambrose Bierce, The Neale Publishing Company, New York.

* * *

One book from which I have borrowed unashamedly, modifying the opinions of the author in a few instances and parroting his words almost exactly in others, is *Watch Your Language*.

In that earlier work all the examples of bad and good usage were from *The New York Times*. In this volume they are drawn from a variety of publications—chiefly newspapers, since they provide a greater volume of readily available material than any other class of printed matter. The examples are presented exactly as they appeared, except for a few that have been abridged to eliminate irrelevant matter or to make the point under discussion more evident. The only examples fabricated for the occasion are those that bear the evidence of fabrication on their face: the ones that say, "John loves Mary like anything."

T.M.B.

New York, April, 1965

xviii

THE
CAREFUL
WRITER

A MODERN GUIDE
TO ENGLISH
USAGE

A, AN

1. WHICH TO USE. In Old English there was only *an*. But anyone who has ever heard the kid next door wailing that he didn't "wanna" do his homework can reconstruct the process that brought *a* into being over the centuries. The aversion to anything that slows speech, the tendency to slur and elide, weakened the indefinite article *an* before sounded consonants to *a*. So, although *an* continues to be used before a word beginning with a vowel (*an* egg, *an* elephant) or an unsounded consonant (*an* hour, *an* honor), *a* is used before a word beginning with a sounded consonant (*a* giant, *a* huge man). The only problems here come with words beginning with the aspirate "h" or with a "yew" sound. There is a lingering tendency on the part of some American writers to use "an historic document," though they wouldn't be caught even in a British pub saying "an hotel." But the preferred form these days, on both sides of the Atlantic, is "a historic document." A is used also before words beginning with a "yew" sound: "a university," "a European," "a utopia."

A minor complication arises with some abbreviations. Do you write, "He received a M.A. degree" or "an M.A. degree"? Do you write, "a N.Y. Central spokesman" or "an N.Y. Central spokesman"? The test is how people say or read such designations. "M.A." registers with most people as alphabetical letters, not as "Master of Arts"; hence, "an M.A. degree" is proper. On the other hand, "N.Y. Central" is instantly translated by the mind into "New York Central"; it would not be read as "En Wye Central." Therefore, "a N.Y. Central spokesman" is proper.

2. WITH PLURALS. A is used before a plural noun only if it is followed by *few*, *very few*, *good many*, or *great many*. Webster explains that in this construction *few* and *many* were originally singular nouns followed by the partitive genitive (*a few* of the

3

boys). Though *few* and *many* are now plural nouns, the singular article survives.

A kind of journalistic shorthand has brought forth some incongruous combinations of plural nouns and singular articles: "an estimated 40,000 troops and police," "an additional fifteen Senators." What is meant in these instances is "an estimated total of 40,000 troops and police" and "an additional total of fifteen Senators" or, simply, "fifteen more Senators." Logically, they should be so written, but idiom permits the illogical form. Sometimes, of course, what appears to be a plural is actually thought of and construed as a singular. When you write "a round $150," you are thinking not of 150 individual greenbacks, but of a sum of money. Therefore, the singular article is proper and so would be a singular verb: "A round $150 was offered for the vase." Likewise, in "A good 150 miles is the distance from New York to Albany," the singular article and verb are correct because, again, you are thinking not of individual miles but of a unit of distance. *See also* COLLECTIVES.

3. WITH COORDINATE NOUNS. The article should appear before each of the nouns unless they constitute a single idea. Thus, "A desk and a chair stood at opposite corners of the room," but "A desk and chair used by Poe while writing some of his stories were sold at auction." Likewise: "A father and mother [*husband and wife*] were killed in the crash," but "A father and a mother [*unrelated*] were killed in the crash."

ABDOMEN
See BELLY.

ABHORRENCE
Takes preposition *of.*

ABHORRENT
Takes preposition *to.*

ABILITY
Takes preposition *at* (doing); *with* (something).

ABILITY, CAPACITY

The distinction between these words is not always properly made. *Ability* is a more positive quality than *capacity*. A person can be born with either *ability* or *capacity*, but *ability* can be acquired, whereas *capacity* cannot. Thus, a child may have a *capacity* to learn art; after he has studied or practiced he may also have the *ability* to paint.

ABJURE, ADJURE

The Latin prefixes of the two words are opposites, yet the words themselves are often confused. Example: "It disavows all teaching, based on accounts of the crucifixion, that the Jews should be subject to disdain, hatred, or persecution, and it abjures preachers and catechists not to take a contrary position." *Abjure* (with the prefix "ab" denoting away or from) means to put aside, forswear, repudiate, or renounce. *Adjure* (with the prefix "ad" denoting toward or to) originally meant to swear to and now means to command, solemnly direct, or entreat; it was the word intended in the cited quotation. Suggested aid to memory: "b" stands for banish, "d" for direct.

ABOUND

Takes preposition *in* or *with*.

ABOUT

1. IN APPROXIMATIONS. The preposition *about* suggests inexactness; therefore, it is redundant when it is included in a sentence containing other such suggestions. "The crowd was estimated at about 4,000," for example, contains two such other suggestions: the word "estimated" and the round number. Delete *about. See also* AROUND. For *a comment on* AT ABOUT, *see* PREPOSITION PILE-UP.

2. FOR "ON." In police-blotter lingo people usually suffer injuries "about the head" or "about the neck" or "about the legs." This use of the word is not incorrect, but it is not common usage outside police and newspaper circles. Moreover, *about* has

5

the "feel" of proximity to but not contact with. *On* would be the more precise word.

ABSENCE
See LACK.

ABSENTEEISM
Here is an example of how the language infuses new life into dying words. In its older meaning, dating to the early nineteenth century, *absenteeism* referred to a landlord's practice of living away from his estate. When twentieth-century sociologists and students of industrial relations delved into the absence of workers from their jobs because of illness or an intention to embarrass their employers, a word was obviously needed to describe this condition. The old word was seized upon, and the new meaning has become so common that the former one is all but forgotten.

ABSOLUTE
See INCOMPARABLES.

ABSOLUTE CONSTRUCTIONS
These are participial phrases grammatically unconnected with the rest of the sentences in which they appear ("absolute" from Latin *absolvere*, denoting loose or free from). Sometimes they contain a noun or pronoun that is the subject of the participle (*"The sun having risen*, we resumed our journey") and sometimes they do not (*"Speaking of journeys*, did you ever visit Tibet?"). In each example the opening phrase is the absolute; it is grammatically independent of the rest of the sentence. The absolute need not, however, introduce the sentence. It may appear at the end ("When the yacht race would finish none could forecast, *wind and weather being what they are*") or it may appear in the middle ("Yacht races, *generally speaking*, are a bore").

Of the absolute constructions that contain a subject, only two things need be said. First, in speech they are uncommon because they are wooden and tend to sound like translations from

Latin; in writing they are only a little less uncommon and for the same reason. They are sometimes used effectively ("He stiffened at the sound in the dark, *his jaw taut, his eyes unblinking*"), but usually they are better avoided. Surely instead of "*The sun having risen*, we resumed our journey" it is more natural to write, "When the sun had risen, etc." Second, the temptation to writers, compositors, and proofreaders to insert a comma between the subject and the participle must be sternly resisted. The temptation arises from an unthinking assumption that the noun is the subject of the main verb of the sentence rather than of the participle. Fowler observes: " 'The King having read his speech from the throne, their Majesties retired' is the right form; but newspaper writing or printing is so faulty on the point that it would appear nine times out of ten as 'The King, having read his etc.' " Whether or not Fowler's statistical appraisal was correct for his own day, it is a fact that today examples of the erroneous comma are hard to find. Nevertheless, the caution is set down here pro forma.

As to the absolute constructions that do not contain a subject, the writer must make certain that no subject is lurking anywhere else in the sentence; otherwise he may find himself with a dangling participle on his hands. (*See* DANGLERS.) The essence of this kind of absolute construction is that the participle has no specific reference to anyone or anything and none is intended. When we say *considering the circumstances*, we usually don't have anyone in mind who is doing the considering; when we say *given such-and-such a situation*, we don't have the idea that anyone is either giving or receiving. The meaning is generalized and indeterminate. Therefore, we have a true absolute if we say, "Judging by the outcome, Snuffles was the best dog in the show." However, we are in trouble if we say, "Judging by his form, stance, and gait, Snuffles was chosen for the blue ribbon by the officials." In the first instance "judging" does not refer to anyone in particular, but in the second instance it clearly refers to the officials who did the judging. From the syntax of it we have a dangling participle, with the pooch in the position of judging himself.

7

Participles that through idiom have become absolutes (some grammarians describe them as "neo-prepositions") include, in addition to *considering, given,* and *judging,* such words as *concerning, excepting, failing, granted, provided,* and *regarding.* There are also countless idiomatic participial combinations like *generally speaking, beginning in June, taking one thing with another.*

A final caution: Since the absolute construction is syntactically independent, it should not be joined to the rest of the sentence by a conjunction. Here is an example of the error: "Granted the Army looked a little ridiculous in the case of Pfc. Goode, but anyone who has served in the armed forces knows of this type of individual." Not only is the "but" superfluous, but in addition, under the rule that conjunctions must connect like grammatical constructions, it is wrong.

ABSOLUTELY

The word means unconditionally, completely, wholly. It should not be diluted to mean *very* or *yes.*

ABSOLVE

Takes preposition *from* or (sometimes) *of.*

ABSTAIN

Takes preposition *from.*

ABSTRACT (vb.)

Takes preposition *from.*

ABUT

Takes preposition *against* (a wall); *on* (a line).

ACCEDE

Takes preposition *to.*

ACCELERATE, EXHILARATE

You would expect that no one but an illiterate would confuse these two words, but two authorities (Partridge and Evans) testify that the words are, indeed, often confused. It is true that you occasionally hear the gas pedal on an automobile spoken of as the *exhilarator* instead of the *accelerator*, but beyond that the testimony of the authorities will have to be taken on faith. Nevertheless, for the guidance of the confused illiterate who picked this book up by mistake, *accelerate* means to quicken, *exhilarate* to gladden.

ACCIDENT, MISHAP

An *accident* is a chance, undesigned occurrence. It may be good ("a fortunate accident") or bad ("an unfortunate accident") or neutral ("the accident of birth" or "the accident that France and Germany have a common border"). A *mishap*, however, is an unfortunate happening; you cannot have a "lucky mishap." There is, in addition, a distinction between the two words that does not emerge from most dictionary definitions. Whereas an *accident* may be either major or minor, there is no such thing as a "major mishap." An airplane crash in which twenty-three persons were killed could be termed an *accident*, but not a *mishap*. The word is simply too puny to carry such a burden.

ACCIDENTAL PUNS

Outdoors it was a fine day in Washington in the spring of 1959, but indoors small squalls whistled through the Senate chamber. The Senators, debating confirmation of Mrs. Clare Boothe Luce as Ambassador to Brazil, were raking over her long public career. Senator Everett McKinley Dirksen of Illinois, Byronic in appearance and Bryanesque in speech, arose to champion the fifty-six-year-old nominee. He defended her eloquently and then, in a crescendo of rhetoric, asked:

"Why thresh old straw and beat an old bag of bones?"

His sheepish attempts to explain away the fluff were all but lost amid the guffaws from the gallery.

This is an almost classic example of the accidental pun. The preoccupied speaker or writer brings forth what he believes to be a charming brain child and looks around to find an illegitimate brat grinning up at him mischievously. At best it is a minor distraction to those addressed; at worst it is an unwanted chuckle-producer in a serious context. And it is a commoner writing flaw than is generally imagined. Here, from a book directed to intellectuals and written by an unusually careful author, is one example:

"The best of [publishing] firms declare their main function to be the bringing to book of wayward authors. . . ."

From the daily press it is not difficult to cull instance after instance:

"At a public hearing in the school here residents told state highway engineers that they were so proud of their rural homes, little shops, tidy farms, quiet school streets, picket fences, and stone walls that they would fight a $2,500,000 superhighway to the last ditch."

"According to a leading Soviet oceanographer, the abyssal depths of the sea harbor living representatives of ancient species whose fossil remains have still not been found."

"What the French refer to as 'bifteck' may soon become as rare on Parisian tables as a glass of milk."

"Let us say farewell to expressions such as 'Far East,' which orients people in terms of Downing Street. . . ."

"Ironically, the threat of a steel walkout appeared to be a major factor making the price increase possible."

"Mr. Gassmann's score contains no noises of wood-sawing, motor-chugging, or vocal cackling, but creates all its sounds from scratch, by purely electronic means."

"There was a sprinkling of children among those who were baptized."

From a dispatch about the inspection by a party of Americans of a Soviet atomic icebreaker: "Thus, what promised to develop into a somewhat difficult situation was resolved and the ice was broken." And again, alas, in the same dispatch: "Admiral Rickover said the engineers and crew had answered all questions freely once the ice was broken."

From an article about the teaching of mathematics: "The basis of the problem, reduced to its lowest common denominator, is arithmetic, according to those coping with the problem."

From a story about the economic plight of New Jersey egg farmers: "Here most poultry farmers have long put all their eggs in one basket."

From a report of a convention of the American Symphony Orchestra League: "The music heard was an unusual note, for this is a convention devoted mostly to discussion."

Sometimes it is difficult to determine whether the puns are really accidental or, rather, are intentional but ill-advised. The examples concerning the teaching of mathematics and the plight of the poultry farmers are in this category. Either way, however, they should be avoided unless there is a considered desire for a humorous touch *and* the pun is plainly intentional *and* the pun is very, very good, which all puns should be to justify their existence. The intentional but ill-advised pun should be severely eschewed; the accidental pun can be rooted out only by a careful rereading of what has been written. *See also* PUNS.

ACCOMMODATE

Takes preposition *to* or *with*.

ACCOMPANIED

Takes preposition *with* (things); *by* (persons).

ACCORD, ACCORDANCE

Takes preposition *with*.

ACCOUNTABLE

Takes preposition *to* (persons); *for* (acts).

ACCRUE

Accrue is best restricted to legal and financial senses: "Interest accrues on the bonds." Using the word in the general sense of to result or to grow—as in, "Senator Jones expects that votes will accrue from his New England campaign tour"—is not desirable. It is reaching for a synonym and catching affectation.

Accrue takes the preposition *to*.

11

ACCUSE

Takes preposition *of.*

ACCUSED

See ALLEGED, ACCUSED, SUSPECTED.

ACOUSTICS

See -ICS.

ACQUAINT

Takes preposition *with.*

ACQUIESCE

Takes preposition *in.*

ACQUIT

Takes preposition *of.*

ACRONYMS

Acronyms (from *acro*, meaning extreme, plus *nym*, meaning name) are words made up of initials or syllables from a group of words (*radar* from *radio detection and ranging system*), or of first and last syllables of a group of words (*motel* from *motor hotel*). Acronyms have long been a minor conceit of the Soviet Russians, who have delighted, since the early Twenties, in such words as *Amtorg, agitprop, Gosplan, Ogpu,* and *Nep.* During World War II acronyms were taken up by other countries, particularly the United States. From such war terms as *snafu, awol, Wacs, Waves, Spars, Seabees, Shape, Shaef, Cincus,* and *sonar* has sprung a vast progeny of civilian acronyms—or should one say civacs? Some venerable organizations have embraced the acronym so completely that they have abandoned the original words that fathered it; for example, the Hebrew Immigrant Aid Society is now exclusively Hias. Other organizations that obviously selected names (many of them elongated and tortured) that would provide memorable acronyms have likewise cast aside

12

the full names; we now have Care rather than Cooperative for American Remittances to Everywhere, and Action rather than American Council to Improve Our Neighborhoods.

As colorful, easily remembered short-cut words, acronyms without question have become increasingly useful in the language. They have proved particularly helpful in an age of rapidly expanding scientific and technological interests by providing handy nicknames for complicated and sometimes unpronounceable terms.

But one word of caution about the use of acronyms is in order. The apparent stranger at a cocktail party who slaps you on the back with a jovial "Where've you been all these years, you old son-of-a-gun?" is a disconcerting chap. You should know him, you think, but you can't place him for the life of you. Strangers like these occasionally grin at readers out of magazine articles and news stories. Here is an example from a news item. It said that the weekly newsletter of the Committee on Political Education had criticized the Vice President. The seventh paragraph began: "COPE said the Vice President's proposals. . . ." COPE? That name would send any reader groping back up the preceding six paragraphs to try to identify the stranger. An unfamiliar acronym or abbreviation should be properly introduced by a writer immediately after the title to which it refers. Naturally, some names, like UNESCO, are old friends and need no introduction. But watch out for those strangers.

ACTIVE VOICE AND PASSIVE VOICE

First let us define these by illustration. Active voice: "The cat caught the rat." Passive voice: "The rat was caught by the cat." Next let us define them in traditional, grammatical terms. When the subject of the verb is the agent performing an action, and the object is that which is acted upon, the verb is in the active voice. When the subject of the verb is the recipient of the action, the verb is in the passive voice. The verb may thus be thought of as a transmission belt carrying the action from one element to another. When the belt is moving forward, so to speak, the verb is active; when it is in reverse the verb is passive.

Since the active voice is the simpler, more direct form of expression, it characterizes the beginnings of speech not only in the race but also in the individual. The primitive man would be no more likely to say "Hut was burned by fire" in preference to "Fire burned hut" than the infant would be to gurgle "Candy is wanted by baby" rather than "Baby wants candy."

With its greater elementary directness, the active voice is more common than the passive and, what is more important to the writer, conveys greater force, greater speed, greater vigor. In writing, as elsewhere, a straight line is the shortest distance between two points. The active voice strikes like a boxer moving forward in attack; the passive voice parries while back-pedaling. The author of the Declaration of Independence designed that document to present the strongest possible justification of the Colonies' course and to sound a trumpet call to action. In its 1,500 or so words only about a dozen verbs appear in the passive form. Most of the verbs are hard-hitting active forms: "He has plundered our seas, ravished our Coasts, burned our towns, and destroyed the lives of our people." The effect throughout the document is impressive.

The passive voice, used without cause, tends to weaken writing. It also usually requires the use of more words. Which may be another way of saying the same thing. Compare "A good time was had by all" with "Everyone had a good time," or compare "Our seas have been plundered by him" with "He has plundered our seas."

All this is not by any means to suggest that the passive voice is useless and to be avoided. Like the boxer, the writer requires a variety of tactics, and sometimes the parrying blow strikes with telling effect. The passive voice is desirable in the following situations:

1. When the agent performing the action is thought of as too unimportant or too obvious to mention and is less significant than the object of the action. "The mail was delivered at eleven o'clock this morning"; "Jones was indicted for the kidnapping."

2. When the agent performing the action is indefinite or un-

14

known. "Silk hats are not worn these days"; "The Bible was written no earlier than the fourth century."

3. When the intention is to emphasize the doer or the thing done by placing that element at the end of the sentence, which is an emphatic position. "The play was written by Eugene O'Neill"; "We can't drive because our car is being repaired."

4. When the intention is deliberately to avoid strong language, to play it pianissimo. Science and diplomacy, two fields in which equanimity is the advisable attitude, particularly favor the restrained statement: "It has been suggested that 0.06 Gm. (gr.) of mercury salicylate be given three days before each dose of the Tryparsamide"; "The delegation of the Soviet Union is of the opinion that certain positive work has been done"; "At this conference the attitudes of the sides concerning a number of problems have been better explained. . . ."

Since the restrained statement with its abundance of passive voices possesses status because of the relationship to such higher forms of human activity as science, philosophy, and statesmanship, it is natural that some lower forms make use of the device in quest of gilt by association. Thus, the advertiser seeking snob appeal sometimes employs it (". . . certainly, this international affection for Cadillac has never been more soundly based—or more richly deserved—than it is at the present time") and the government functionary, striving to make an important sound, has a fondness for it (and sometimes becomes entangled in unbelievable syntax, as in the instance of the World War II gray-out placards in New York, which began, "Illumination is required to be extinguished . . ."). More on this subject appears under WINDYFOGGERY. *See also* DOUBLE PASSIVE.

Footnote on voice: Within a sequence a switch should not be made from active voice to passive voice or vice versa unless a continuous action is being described, and even then the switch is not entirely desirable. The following sentence, presenting a continuous action, may pass muster: "Senator Eugene McCarthy asked for Senate recognition, was recognized, and said he had found an error in *The Congressional Record*." Yet even here the sentence would be improved by changing "was recognized" to

15

"gained it." The switch in voices in the following sentence, which is clumsy in any event, is not good: "The baby cooed as his paralyzed mother received an award, napped through speeches, was elected mascot, and accepted the stares of admirers with placid contentment." If the transmission belt is suddenly thrown into reverse, the reader is sure to be jarred.

A.D.

Anno Domini means in the year of our Lord, and its abbreviation should not, therefore, be affixed to the name of a century. "The sixth century A.D." would mean the sixth century in the year of our Lord, which is preposterous. Write "the sixth century after Christ" or, better still, just "the sixth century" (it would be understood to mean after Christ unless it was followed by *B.C.—before Christ*). Moreover, the meaning A.D. shows that it should precede the number of the year and should not carry the preposition *in*. Correct: "Arminius died A.D. 21."

AD

Ad for advertisement is in just as good standing these days as *cello* for *violoncello, phone* for *telephone, piano* for *pianoforte, auto* for *automobile, taxi* for *taxicab, plane* for *airplane,* or *bus* for *omnibus.* Use no period and no quotation marks.

ADAGE

"The press secretary facetiously recalled the old adage of the machine politican—'vote early and often.'" Dictionaries (with a single exception) affirm in one way or another that an *adage* is a long-established saying; therefore the "old" is redundant. Incidentally, an expression that someone thought up yesterday is not an *adage*—yet. To put it another way—and this is obvious—"age" is a part of *adage*.

ADAPT, ADOPT

There should not be much danger of confusing these two, but in case there is, here is the distinction: *Adapt* means to take a thing and conform it to one's own purpose; *adopt* means to take a thing and make it one's own as is. A foreign minister who *adopted* his predecessor's policy would employ it without change. If he *adapted* his predecessor's policy, he would employ it with modifications.

Adapted takes the preposition *to* (a use); *for* (a purpose); or *from*.

ADDICTED

When the devotion is to something considered harmful or potentially bad, like narcotics or liquor, *addicted* is proper. When it is to something generally held to be useful or good, use of the word is at best semijocular. If your idea of something humorous is, "I am addicted to opera," then go to it. The rest of us will go our several ways.

Addicted takes the preposition *to*.

AD-DICTION

A castaway on a desert island will go through all conceivable sorts of antics to attract attention and gain succor. An ad man will also do almost anything to attract attention, but he spells his succor differently. Among the things he will do is misuse the English language. But let it not be thought he does not know better. Indeed, he does, but he is not shooting for A's in college; he is shooting for G's in the market place. What he does in his prose is misuse the language skillfully. It may be said that the profession's ad-diction is skillful misuse of English.

Of course, any profession has its second-raters. There was the New York restaurateur who fancied himself qualified to do his own advertising and had printed in gilt letters on his window and in black letters on his menus the slogan, "Like the acrobat it's the turnover that counts." The total absence of grammar is matched only by the ineptitude of the appeal, which suggests that the place is going to throw the food at you and that you had better gulp it and get out in a hurry.

That ignorant misuse of *like* is not to be compared to the conjunctive use that told us about a cigarette that "tastes good like a cigarette should." There the ad man knew what he was doing. He was trying to move his slogan as close to the popular lingo as he could, and if the grammar stirred up an academic flurry, so much the better for his attention-getting—that was lagniappe. Success, however, stimulates imitation, and the results are often unhappy. Look, for instance, at this automobile ad: "Flattens hills like it flattens the floor."

Then there are the odd things the ad men do to verbs. No doubt they can cite obscure dictionary entries to justify *gentling* the smoke by *traveling* it farther, but they surely cannot cite common usage. The same goes for *gifting* a man with a box of underwear. They cannot even summon a dictionary to the defense, however, when they write about pancakes and suggest, "Disappear some butter into the brown hotness of them." What shall be said about an automatic washer that *obsoletes* all others? Or about the ship-line ad that urges you to "swim yourself in shape as we cruise you to Jamaica" and promises that "you'll sun it up in the largest outdoor pool afloat"? In a single day's newspaper one store advertises a *lynx-lavished coat* and another advertises a *fur-lavished greatcoat*. The coincidence is strange, but the word use is even stranger, though who is to say it is incorrect? One can sympathize with James Thurber, who wrote that one morning a woman came chattering into his dreams, saying, "We can sleep twenty people in this house in a pinch, but we can only eat twelve."

There is reason in all this apparent Madison Avenue madness. Usually, more lies behind the linguistic oddities than a bid for attention. Your ad man, however insensitive he may be to good usage, is quite sensitive not only to the meanings of words but also to their connotations, their auras, their capacity for evoking appropriate images. He might have written, for instance, about a "fur-trimmed greatcoat," but surely *fur-lavished* suggests to the susceptible woman that she is going to get a great deal more fur for her money. He could write about shoes or gloves or chairs that were "handmade," but he would rather coin the word *handcrafted* because it suggests greater care, greater skill, greater pride in workmanship, all traceable to "craft" with its subtle suggestion of the old craft guilds.

18

He perhaps goes to an extreme when he writes of *ingeniously engineered boating shoes,* but he knows he is appealing to men, who normally have great respect for anything that is "engineered"—anything except their own demotion. Here we get into the realm of putting on airs, where the most commonplace things are made to seem grand or at least highly desirable. Thus we have "a new concept in girdles," and apartments that are "a new concept in gracious living." (*See* CONCEPT.) We are invited to "open the door to tomorrow" (which turns out to be a new model of a car), or to witness "the dawn of a new day on the road" (a tire). The ad writer not only is putting his best foot forward; he is going into orbit.

In recent years advertising has recognized that the scientific community are the people with status, and has tried to borrow some of their luster by aping their language. The scientists, for reasons of economy of expression and with confidence that their colleagues will understand, often resort to telescoped phrases. Example: "The gear train has a higher speed-reduction ratio." The advertiser's imitation comes out, "faster wheel return," "perma set tuning control," "arrow-straight tracking," "complete range of data transmission systems," "no razor scrape."

Without doubt, all these affectations have some effect on the language. There is not much need to be concerned about the like-a-cigarette-should phrase, because it almost carried with it its own corrective by bringing the disputed grammatical point to the attention of a larger number of people than would otherwise have heard of it. Nor does the peculiar use of verbs need to concern us, because it does not seem to have caught the fancy of ordinary users of the language. The pseudo-scientific telescoping reflects a fairly normal tendency (*see* NOUNS AS ADJECTIVES), although advertising exaggerates it. The effect that is most feared is what might be called, to coin an ad man's phrase, the hot-rodding of the language—the tendency to overstatement, the tendency to depreciate valuable words, and, let's face it, the tendency to misrepresent—ad nauseam. A chronic fever is the surest road to debilitation.

ADHERENCE

Takes preposition *to*.

ADJACENT

Takes preposition *to*.

ADJECTIVES, PLACEMENT OF

Intimate as is the relationship of an adjective to the noun it modifies, the noun sometimes has an even more intimate relationship to another element. "His driving was inexpert of the car" is so inept a sentence that it would never be written. We feel that "of the car" bears a closer relationship to "driving" than does "inexpert." Nevertheless, a writer occasionally cannot bear to have his noun and his adjective parted too long and will turn out a sentence not dissimilar to the inept one quoted. For instance: "Their reaction is furious to commercial hit tunes that try to strike a compromise between jazz and the traditional sentimentalism of the local Tin Pan Alley." If the writer is averse to relegating the predicate adjective to the end of the long sentence —as well he might be—let him reconstruct the sentence. Let him write, for example, "They react furiously to, etc." Rewriting is often the solution to what seems to be an awkward problem.

ADJECTIVES, SEQUENCE OF COMPARATIVES OR SUPERLATIVES

When a sentence contains a series of adjectives that are uniformly in the *more* or *most* form, there is no problem: "The ring he bought was the most beautiful and expensive in the store." But when these forms appear in conjunction with "-er" or "-est" forms, a difficulty sometimes arises: "One of the world's most expensive and rarest waxes is largely responsible for the shine in a shoeshine." Good form and good taste require that in a mixture of this kind the "-er" or "-est" form should come first, and the *more* or *most* form thereafter. Thus, the sentence should

20

read: "One of the world's rarest and most expensive waxes, etc."
Why? One reason is that if the form containing *more* or *most*
comes first, these words tend to carry over to the other form and
you have the effect of a double comparative or double superlative
—"most rarest." Another reason is that, in the interest of cadence
and rhetorical effect, it is well to build from the shorter phrase to
the longer.

ADJECTIVES AS NOUNS

Every once in a while one of Miss Thistlebottom's disciples
enters an objection to the use of *human* as a noun. Although it is
true that the Oxford lists this use as "now joc. or affected,"
Webster manages to accept it with a straight face, and there is
no reason why the rest of us should not do likewise.

The conversion of adjectives into nouns is as ancient as the
language, and is a device that makes for efficiency in expression.
Such conversion has taken place in every field of human endeavor: In medicine we have *cardiacs, prophylactics,* and *seda-
tives;* in the military sphere we have *generals, privates, regulars,*
and *offensives;* in railroading we have *locals, expresses, limiteds,
uppers,* and *lowers;* in journalism we have *editorials, extras,* and
shorts; in meteorology we have *highs* and *lows;* in education we
have *principals* and *majors;* in police work we have *detectives
and operatives;* and in the new jargon of broadcasting we have
commercials, specials, spectaculars, documentaries, and *visuals.*
Even in the field of grammar we have *adjectives, substantives,
accusatives, datives, connectives, expletives,* and *nominatives.*

Then there are a host of adjectives that are used absolutely
—that is, without their implied nouns—and to all appearances
they are actually nouns: *the rich and the poor, the land of the
free and the home of the brave, on one's own.* It should be obvious, then, that there is nothing irregular in the conversion of
human into a noun, and that if it is not accepted universally at
the moment, it certainly will be ultimately. Those who resist its
acceptance must be classed as *conservatives,* if they will pardon
the expression.

ADJECTIVES WITH CONDITION OF HEALTH
See CONDITION OF HEALTH.

ADJURE
See ABJURE, ADJURE.

ADJUSTED
Takes preposition *to*.

ADMISSION, ADMITTANCE
Admittance, the much rarer word, conveys the literal meaning of allowing entry; *admission* carries the meaning of making available certain rights and privileges. The student who gains *admission* to the college of his choice may find a sign on the faculty club door: "*Admittance* to faculty members only."

ADMIT
Takes preposition *of* (a solution); *to*.

ADMITTANCE
See ADMISSION, ADMITTANCE.

ADOPT
See ADAPT, ADOPT.

ADOPT, ASSUME
In the sense of to take to or upon oneself, the words are somewhat synonymous, but with a fine shade of difference. *Assume* often implies pretense, as when one *assumes* a role or a pose. However, one could *adopt* an attitude (take it up as a matter of choice) or *assume* an attitude (pretend it was one's position). See also ASSUME, PRESUME.

ADOPTED, ADOPTIVE
When a married couple *adopts* a child, the child quite obviously is *adopted* and the couple equally obviously is not. The proper designation for the parents, according to Webster, is

adoptive. However, Webster itself in another context gives us this sentence: "Under the Roman law the adopted child came under the potestas of his adopted parent. . . ." Even the dictionary, it would seem, has difficulty in accepting the correct word. *Adoptive* is undoubtedly the correct word, the logical word, the better word to describe the parents, but it is perhaps too proper. And words that are too proper, like girls who are too proper, are not easily embraced.

ADORABLE
See **ATOMIC FLYSWATTERS.**

ADVANCE, ADVANCED
In military parlance an "advance position"—a rather rare phrase—is one from which an *advance* is in progress or in preparation, whereas an "advanced position" is a forward position. Likewise an "advance guard" is one that moves ahead of a main body. There is no such thing as an "advance degree," as in this sentence: "Kenyatta took an advance degree under Bronislaw Malinowski." Make it *advanced.*

ADVANCE PLANNING
A wasteful locution. *Planning* is the laying out of a future course; *advance* is therefore superfluous.

ADVANCE WARNING
See **WARN.**

ADVANTAGE
Takes preposition *of* or *over.*

ADVERBIAL CLAUSE, MISUSE OF
An adverb, an adverbial phrase, or an adverbial clause may qualify several parts of speech, but a noun is not one of them. Yet the error of tying an adverbial modifier to a noun is not infrequent: "As I left my hotel, in the relatively modern part of

Glasgow, I saw one or two innovations since I had last been in town." "Innovations" is, of course, a noun and needs to be modified by an adjective or an adjectival clause, but as it stands it is modified by an adverbial clause beginning with *since*. "Innovations that had been introduced since . . ." would be fine; then you would have an adjective clause, beginning with "that," modifying the noun, and an adverbial clause, beginning with *since*, modifying the verb "introduced."

Another aspect of this matter is the linking of a *when* clause to a noun: "One of the finest scenes in American literature is when the duke, in *Huckleberry Finn*, tries to persuade the king to substitute 'obsequies' for the more original term 'orgies.'" One remedy, as in the previous example, is to make the adverbial *when* clause modify a verb—"one of the finest scenes occurs when. . . ." Another remedy is to convert the clause following the "is" into a noun clause—"that in which. . . ." *See also* WHEN AND WHERE.

ADVERBIAL FORCE IN NOUNS

Phrases such as "a place to live" or "no place to hide" occasionally provoke questions as to their grammatical validity. Must they not be recast, the questioners ask, to read "a place in which to live" or "no place to hide in"? The answer would seem to be, No. Idiom has given the noun *place* in such constructions the force of the adverb *where*. That does not mean that *where* can necessarily be substituted for *place*; it means merely that the notion of *where* is implicit in *place*. And the word is unusual in this respect because the same privilege is not accorded to words of comparable meaning that might be used in such constructions. You could not say, for instance, "a city to live" or "no house to hide."

However, *place* is not unique in enjoying this special status. The privilege is also exercised by *time* ("a time to be born, and a time to die") and by *way* in the sense of method or manner ("that is the way to do it"). Again, you could not substitute other words or even synonyms for *time* and *way*; you could not say, "an era to be born" or "the method to do it." Idiom has bestowed on *time* the adverbial force of *when,* and on *way* the adverbial force of *how.*

These constructions involving *place, time,* and *way* are not the usual modifying phrases that Jespersen terms infinitive post-adjuncts, such as "in time to come" or "the last to leave," because in these there is no need for a preposition, as is suggested in "a place to live." Still less do they resemble constructions in which the infinitive is transitive and the preceding noun or pronoun is the object, as in "a question to consider" or "someone to love." The adverbial use of nouns is rare in English, but not nonexistent. We say, for example, "Let's go home" or "She bought a piece of silk a yard long" or "He works nights." It may be that *place, time,* and *way* are clamoring for admission to the small band.

ADVERBS

Most adverbs end in "-ly," but a good many have two forms: with and without the tail. Examples of those with two forms are *bad, badly; bright, brightly; cheap, cheaply; hard, hardly; loud, loudly; sharp, sharply; slow, slowly;* and *tight, tightly.* In general, the "-ly" forms are favored in reputable writing and the shorter forms in casual language, but this guide is by no means invariable and is, moreover, subject to the whims of idiom. It will not do, for example, to say, "He was sitting prettily" or "Take it easily." (*See* OVERREFINEMENT.) Nor can exception be taken to "Go slow" or "Come close." Where there is a real choice, however— where idiom does not dictate one form or the other—the reputable writer will prefer the "-ly" form; he will modify the following sentences as indicated by the bracketed phrases: "It was hot and humid and the visitors strolled a bit slower [more slowly] than usual"; "Sponsors are going to screen television scripts closer [more closely]"; "They have discovered that they can write small checks cheaper [more cheaply] by using a revolving check credit account."

Occasionally a writer will use an adverb form where an adjective form is required. Here is one illustration: "Baghdad, since the recent unsuccessful putsch, seems to be drawing ever more closely to the U.S.S.R." The "more" is what threw this writer off;

had that word been omitted, he would have seen that Baghdad was not drawing "closely" to the U.S.S.R., but "closer" to it; the verb in this instance is in effect a copulative, or linking, verb with the sense of "becoming."

ADVERBS, PLACEMENT OF

The fear of allowing an adverb to come between the parts of an infinitive often, though not always, has a reasonable foundation. This is discussed under SPLIT INFINITIVE. But some writers, blinded by the split-infinitive obsession, seem determined not to split anything except hairs. Thus, they will not permit an adverb to divide elements of a compound verb. There is no reasonable foundation for this attitude. The truth is that more often than not the proper and natural place for an adverb is between the parts of a compound verb. Here is an improper and unnatural placement: "If the period of the truce were used by the enemy to build up bases the Allied advantage largely would disappear." The proper and natural form is "would largely disappear."

Two other examples will suggest an additional guide for the placement of the adverb: "A broad reorganization of the Immigration and Naturalization Service virtually has been completed"; "The Governor said he was considering seriously asking the Legislature to delay or abandon the inspection plan." Fowler makes the sound point that if the adverb and verb naturally suggest an adjective and noun, they should stand together. In the two examples "virtually completed" suggests virtual completion and "considering seriously" would, in its proper order, suggest serious consideration. Properly, therefore, the sentences should read "has been virtually completed" and "was seriously considering." Notice further how the misplacement of the "seriously" in the second example leads to an ambiguity: Was the Governor "considering seriously" or was he thinking about "seriously asking"?

A more flagrant instance of ambiguity caused by misplacement of the adverb appears in this sentence: "In the past, eleven plans for removing troops gradually have been drawn up by the United Nations." What is meant: gradual removal of troops or gradual drawing up of plans? Obviously, some kind of obsession prevented the writer from saying what he meant to say: "gradually removing troops."

When more than one adverb appears in a phrase, a misplacement sometimes results not in ambiguity but in stylistic ineptitude. To write of "a most strategically placed missile site" is unexceptionable: "most" qualifies "strategically," which in turn qualifies "placed." However, if the phrase were "a most strategically desirable missile site," we would have a different-colored horse. Here "most" does not modify "strategically"; it modifies "desirable." A preferable construction would be, "strategically a most desirable missile site" or "a most desirable missile site strategically." The fault is not uncommon: "Students at the Bronx School are the best intellectually equipped in the city" (make it, "intellectually the best equipped"); "Northeast Airlines, Inc., one of the most financially troubled members of its industry . . ." (make it, "financially one of the most troubled members").

ADVERBS, RELUCTANT

Some words ending in "y" seem to rebel against being adverbs or being turned into adverbs. Whereas *cheery*, true to its meaning, is happy to help out in a sentence such as "He sang cheerily," the word *ugly* kicks and screams when you force it into an adverbial role in a sentence such as "He behaved uglily." Likewise, *funny* resists in a sentence such as "He grimaced funnily." *Masterly*, although designated by dictionaries as an adverb to begin with, has a curious sound when used this way: "He paints masterly." Similarly with *friendly*, as in "He greeted me friendly," and with *kindly*, as in "He smiled kindly." These words have the additional adverbial forms *masterlily*, *friendlily*, and *kindlily*, but, like *uglily*, they are rarely used.

What to do? Well, if a word resists conversion, you may as well give in, because otherwise it will merely sit sulking in its sentence and your reader will convict you of cruelty. The way to give in is to rephrase the passage so that no one will ever know that you and the word have quarreled. Instead of writing "He behaved uglily," make it "He behaved in an ugly way"; instead

27

of writing "He paints masterly," make it "He paints in a masterly manner"; instead of writing "He greeted me friendly," make it "His greeting to me was friendly." A retreat of this kind is better than clumsy bravado.

ADVERSARY, ANTAGONIST, OPPONENT

An *opponent* is merely one who is on the other side in a contest of any kind, whether it be a chess match, a lawsuit, or a football game. *Antagonist* implies more heightened opposition, and is applied to one who with personal antagonism seeks to gain the upper hand. The word *adversary* overlaps both the others, but carries the connotation of one who is in more sustained opposition.

ADVERSE, AVERSE

Adverse means opposed, antagonistic, hostile. It is incorrectly used in the following sentence: "He reads the morning papers and is not adverse to reading about himself." In this example of litotes there is no intention of conveying an idea of hostility; the intention is rather to suggest disinclination. *Averse*, therefore, would be the word to use because it means disinclined, reluctant, loath.

Both words take the preposition *to*. *Averse* may, but rarely does, take the preposition *from*.

ADVISEDLY, INTENTIONALLY

An action taken *advisedly* is one that has been thought out, carefully considered. An action performed *intentionally* is one that is done purposely rather than accidentally. Thus, you might kick a policeman *intentionally*, but probably not *advisedly*.

ADVISER

This spelling is preferred to *advisor*.

ADVOCATE (n.)

Takes preposition *of*. To *advocate* takes the preposition *for*.

28

AEGIS

Having the primary meaning of a shield, *aegis* is not a simple synonym for jurisdiction. Hence, improper: "According to United States law, such devices would undoubtedly come under the aegis of the Federal Drug Administration since other contraceptives do, too." Harking back to its primary meaning, *aegis* still carries with it in its derived meanings some faint notion of protection or at least benevolence.

AFFECT, EFFECT

Despite their quite different meanings, these two words tend to be confused. As verbs, *affect* means to influence or to have an effect or bearing on, and *effect* means to bring about, to accomplish, to execute. Thus, "The two-party coalition effected the passage of the tax program, which will affect almost every taxpayer." For those who have need for such things, a mnemonic device might be: When you mean execute—a word beginning with an "e"—the word you want is *effect*, another word beginning with an "e."

As for the nouns, the wanted word is almost always *effect*. The noun *affect* has a narrow psychological meaning (and is, incidentally, pronounced with the accent on the first syllable).

AFFILIATE (vb.)

Takes preposition *with* or *to*.

AFFINITY

The question that arises with *affinity* is what preposition to use after it. If you think of it as meaning a tie of kinship, sympathy, or attraction, you will use *between*, *with*, or sometimes *to*, and you will discard *for*. And you will be right.

AFFIRM

See SAY AND ITS SYNONYMS.

AFTER THE CONCLUSION OF

A wasteful locution. *After* is normally sufficient.

29

AGENDA

Although a Latin plural (singular *agendum*), *agenda* is now an English singular. Rather than meaning things to be done, it commonly means a program of things to be done, so that it is proper to write: "The agenda was approved by the United Nations Assembly." It is so much a singular that it has its own plural—*agendas*—which is properly used in the sentence "The agendas of two of the Assembly's committees have been adopted." As to the Latin singular *agendum*, it is extinct; no one refers to the next *agendum*, but rather to the next item on the *agenda. See also* DATA.

AGGRAVATE

Commonly, but not by a careful writer, this word is used to mean irritate. Neither the commonness nor the long history of the misuse makes it any better than inept. To irritate is to inflame, annoy, arouse, exasperate. Once a condition has been set up, it can be *aggravated*—that is, made worse, enlarged, enhanced. What is *aggravated* is a condition, not a person. Those who say they are *aggravated* are, most likely, the same persons who say that in the hospital they were diagnosed. *See also* DIAGNOSE.

AGO, SINCE

A review of a recital by a violin-piano team contained this sentence: "It was almost twenty-five years ago since their first joint appearance in New York and twelve since their last." In combination the words *since* and *ago* create a tautology that should be avoided. It is a peculiarly uncomfortable tautology because it entails a reversal of point of view. Both words speak of a past time, but whereas *ago* carries the mind back from the present to the past, *since* carries it from the past to the present. Thus, the mind of the reader of "ago since" meets itself coming back. Proper use of the two words is illustrated in the following sentences: "It was almost twenty-five years ago [not *since*] that they made their first joint appearance"; "It is almost twenty-five years since their first joint appearance."

30

AGREE

Takes preposition *with* (persons); *to* (suggestions); *in* (thinking); *upon* (a course of action).

AIM

Without question, *aim* followed by an infinitive is, if not good British usage, rather acceptable American usage ("I aim to make you my wife, Sue"). Yet, to some, the construction has the dust of the frontier clinging to it. If you are allergic to frontier dust, you will go along with the British usage of *aim at* followed by a gerund ("I aim at making you my wife").

AIN'T

The writer who doesn't know that *ain't* is illiterate has no business writing. The word is not used, of course, in written language except when dialogue is being reproduced, and the writer's ear will tell him how to use it then.

ALIBI

An *alibi* in present-day usage is not merely an excuse; it is frequently an invented excuse intended to transfer responsibility. In this sense there is no other word that serves the purpose. It may be a casualism at the moment, but it will undoubtedly take its place in the standard language. In accordance with BERN-STEIN'S SECOND LAW it is driving the primary, legal meaning into the background. In the legal sense *alibi* means a plea of having been elsewhere than at the scene of an act at the time it was committed. This meaning, too, is served by no other word. Therefore the two meanings are going to have to coexist.

ALIEN

Takes preposition *from* or *to*.

ALL

All is an adjective that sometimes becomes a pronoun, as in, "All I know is what I read in the newspapers," or as in the line from the one-time popular song, "All I want for Christmas is my two front teeth." In both these instances the word is singular. But it may also be plural, as in "All send love to all" or "All were rescued as the ship went down." When *all* is equivalent to *the only thing* or *everything*, it takes a singular verb. Thus, the following sentence is incorrect: "All that the scientists were interested in were the effects of the proton cluster surrounding the path of the cosmic ray particle." But this mistake may be not so much a misreading of *all* as an error of NUMBER (4). *See also* WHAT.

ALL-AROUND

See ALL-ROUND.

ALL AS ADVERB

There is a legitimate place for *all* as an adverb to indicate completeness, as in "all along" and "all hollow." But a modern locution puts it to a completely unnecessary use: "It should not be all that difficult to come by better procedures"; "Castro is not all that important." Sometimes the word order is reversed: "It should not be that all difficult. . ."; "Castro is not that all important." Either way this use of *all* seems more appropriate to spoken language than to written language.

ALL BUT ONE

By what grammarians term "attraction," a noun following *all but one* is singular, and so is a verb following that noun. The attraction, of course, is to the word *one*. This situation makes for what looks like poor grammar, but is good idiom. Thus, all the following are correct: "Mr. Sharkey said he had attended all but one meeting of the City Council"; "Before retiring his oars in 1925, the elder Kelly had won all but one important rowing trophy"; "The police report that all but one child has been rescued."

It should be noted, however, that if the *one* is not followed by a noun, the reinforcement of the singular feeling is lacking and hence the attraction is not strong. The following verb is then plural. Example: "Of the thirteen children all but one were rescued." Likewise a plural noun just ahead of the verb dictates a plural verb: "All but one of the children were rescued." Introducing the "of" phrase, incidentally, is an advisable way to avoid awkwardness. Instead of writing, "All but one gangway was up," it would be more graceful to write, "All but one of the gangways were up." No shame attaches to fleeing from gaucherie. *See also* MORE THAN ONE.

ALLEGED, ACCUSED, SUSPECTED

As adjectives, these words are primarily journalistic property, used—better yet, misused—to designate persons who have tangled with the law. Newspapers speak of *an accused spy, a suspected intruder, an alleged thief.* All are, in a strict sense, improper. A *wrecked plane is* an actual plane that has been wrecked; *a trained soldier* is an actual soldier who has been trained; *an accused banker* is an actual banker who has been accused. But when the journalist writes of *an accused spy,* he does not mean an actual spy who has been accused; he means a person who has been *accused as a spy.* He is using this phraseology as a hedge against defamation.

All three of these journalistic words are, properly speaking, misused when employed in this way because their meanings are distorted. *Alleged thief* involves an additional distortion: You don't *allege* a person, but rather a crime or a condition. Nevertheless, the journalistic need for such a protective qualifier to avoid seeming to impute guilt is so common and so compelling that if this use of *alleged* did not exist, it would be necessary to invent it. So, while acknowledging that the use is not altogether correct, we must recognize that tenure and necessity have established *alleged* in a category similar to *supposed* or *presumed.* However, although *alleged* may enjoy this limited sanction, the ambiguous use of *accused* and *suspected* is best avoided.

ALLEGORY
See RHETORICAL FIGURES AND FAULTS.

33

ALLERGIC

The popular, as distinct from the medical, meaning is "excessively sensitive to certain substances or physical conditions." In this sense it is proper. Beyond this, however, it is also used as a faintly humorous slang word meaning affected by a feeling of antipathy or dislike, as in, "I am allergic to Thackeray." Used thus, it is not in good standing. Even in its proper sense it seems to be susceptible to misuse. For example: "Explaining that he was allergic to hay fever, the guest declined the invitation to ride." Hay fever, of course, results from an *allergy*; the guest might be *allergic* to ragweed, but not to hay fever.

ALLITERATION

See RHETORICAL FIGURES AND FAULTS.

ALL OF

Some syntacticians frown on joining *of* to *all*, except with pronouns, in which instances the combination is clearly necessary. (You cannot say *all us, all it,* or *all them,* but must say *all of us, all of it,* or *all of them.*) Their objection is to what they regard as the illogicality of treating the whole as a part. But as Evans slyly observes, it is hard to see why this is any more illogical than treating *none* as a part, as in the phrase *none of the boys.* Except with pronouns, the *of* is superfluous and the careful writer may wish to omit it on that ground, but its use is well based and cannot be objected to on any other ground.

ALLOWING FOR

See DANGLERS.

ALL RIGHT

Two words. Not *alright.*

ALL-ROUND

In such phrases as *all-round athlete* this form is preferable to *all-around.* Which makes sense when you consider that *around* has the connotation of positions with respect to a center, whereas *round* has the connotation of full or complete, which is what is desired in these phrases.

ALL TOGETHER

"Smith of the Yankees batted in six runs all together." Impossible. He could bat in six runs *altogether* (meaning in sum) as his total for the game, but the most he could bat in *all together* (meaning at one time or in one place) would be four, and it would take a grand slam homer to do that.

ALL TOLD

Told in this phrase has nothing to do with narration; it refers to counting or enumeration, as it does in "The nun told her beads." Thus in describing the tailoring of a garment it would not be correct to say, as one advertiser did, "All told, it took a lot of skill." It would be correct to say, "All told, fifty-two men worked on the garment."

ALLUSION, REFERENCE

An *allusion* is an oblique, indirect mention that does not name the thing specifically, but leaves the identification to the reader or hearer to deduce. A *reference* is a direct naming or description of the thing. The incorrect use of *allusion* appears in this sentence: "Russia eventually may be willing to overlook the destruction of her legation (an allusion to the recent bombing of the Soviet legation in Israel). . . ." There is nothing covert there; it's a *reference*, not an *allusion*. The correct use of the two words appears in this passage: "The Senator, in an allusion to the Administration's budget, said excessive spending must cease. He said too much was being spent on the highway program. This was a reference to the $41 billion outlay for roadbuilding." *See also* RHETORICAL FIGURES AND FAULTS.

ALLY (vb.)

Takes preposition *to* or *with*.

35

ALONE

Alone for *only* is not wrong, but merely affected, in the same way as is *save* for *except*. (*See also* SAVE.) In the sentence, "He is not alone the hardest worker in the company, but also the best," it would be less stilted—and therefore better—to write, "He is not only the hardest worker, etc."

ALONG WITH

See WITH.

ALOOF

Takes preposition *from*.

ALRIGHT

See ALL RIGHT.

ALSO

Except in ordinary speech, the conjunctional use of *also* is frowned upon. In the unpolished sentences of spoken language *also* is sometimes used as the equivalent of "Oh, yes, I almost forgot." We say, "I packed my toothbrush, my pajamas, and a clean shirt; also my swimming trunks." But the writer has no business almost forgetting. His is the duty to plan sentences beforehand, or at least to rework them afterhand. If he finds he has almost forgotten his swimming trunks, he should pack them neatly into the series with the normal conjunction *and*. What is especially deplorable is the practice, common in school compositions, of trying to link sentences and thoughts by the weak connective *also*, which often appears at the head of a sentence: "We played baseball in the afternoon. Also we had a swim." This is not integrated writing; it is simple addition.

ALTERNATE (vb. and adj.)

Takes preposition *with*.

ALTERNATELY, ALTERNATIVELY

The distinction here is that *alternately* carries the meaning

36

of one after the other, whereas *alternatively* carries the meaning of one or the other. The following passage, then, contains an erroneous usage: "In order to keep a closer watch over government information, Sylvester directed that a representative of his office monitor each interview between a reporter and a Pentagon official. Alternately, the official could report the substance of the interview to Sylvester at the end of the day."

ALTERNATIVES

By its derivation from the Latin *alter*, meaning other of two, *alternatives* originally applied (and in the eyes of some strict constructionists still applies) to a choice between two possibilities. However, writers have for a long time used it to mean also a choice among more than two possibilities, perhaps because there is no other single word to convey this meaning; one would have to resort to a phrase, *the other choices*.

Even that phrase, let it be noted, is an inferior substitute because *alternative* and *choice* are not identical in meaning. *Alternative* has a connotation of compulsion to choose. In the sentence, "The alternatives are liberty and death," the implication is that one or the other must be chosen; there is no escape. But in the sentence, "The menu offered a choice of coconut pie or rice pudding," there is no implication that the guest must select one or the other; he can reject them both and get a milkshake at the corner drugstore. Since, therefore, *alternatives* in the sense of a choice among several possibilities fills a want, it may be respectably used in that way, as well as in its stricter meaning.

ALTHOUGH
See THOUGH, ALTHOUGH.

ALTOGETHER
See ALL TOGETHER.

AMALGAM
Takes preposition *of*.

AMALGAMATE

Takes preposition *into* or *with*.

AMATEUR

Takes preposition *of, in* or (sometimes) *at*.

AMBIGUOUS, EQUIVOCAL

The two words have in common the notion of susceptibility of more than one meaning. When a statement is *ambiguous*, the two or more interpretations may be due either to carelessness or to intent. When a statement is *equivocal*, however, the ambiguity is usually considered to be intentional. *Equivocal*, therefore, carries with it nasty overtones that are not normally associated with *ambiguous*.

AMBITION(S)

A person may, to be sure, have more than one ambition. He may, for example, dream of being both well-married and well-heeled. But writers often pluralize the word when it is evident that only a single ambition is involved. For instance: "There are all kinds of splendid types visible, including Kathryn Grant, cast as Mr. Mature's sister, who is a secretary and has ambitions to be a trapeze artist." Vague, analogous sounds undoubtedly crowded in on the writer (as they sometimes do on the common speaker): "has aspirations to be," "has thoughts of being," "has dreams of being," "has designs on being." But the analogy is false because these other words can all be plural manifestations centering on a single goal. (*Aspiration* is a possible exception, but in the sense of *hope* the word is used more often as a plural than as a singular.) For one goal there should be but one ambition, no matter how many dreams there may be.

Ambition takes the preposition *for*.

AMBIVALENT

As a psychological term, *ambivalent* means affected by or creating conflicting or contradictory attitudes. When borrowed for general use, as such specialized words inevitably are borrowed

38

by those who like their learned sound (*see* INSIDE TALK), it is usually misused to mean two-faced, two-sided, double-dealing, two-timing—in fact, almost anything that contains the notion of two. Observe: "Mr. Tobin discusses business deficits as though they were of the same structure as Federal deficits. In the same ambivalent way, Government economists sometimes try to show they are operating on business principles, even while denying the validity of the analogy in general." As applied to the second sentence, *ambivalent* could perhaps be defended, although not solidly, on the ground that conflicting notions are involved. But the writer's misuse of the word is betrayed by his application of it to the first sentence as well; there nothing but two-ness appears.

AMENABLE

Takes preposition *to*.

AMID, AMIDST

The words, both of which have a faintly poetic flavor, mean the same thing, but Americans prefer *amid* and the British prefer *amidst*.

AMONG

Among means in the midst of countable things. When the things are not separable, the word is *in* or *amid* or *amidot*. Therefore, this sentence is incorrect: "Masked firemen groped among the wreckage hours later." "Wreckage" is a mass noun that does not denote countable items. This sentence is likewise incorrect: "Among the recent news emanating from Paris was a provocative item predicting the return of the stocking seam." The item was not found in the midst of one new, a second new, and a third new. In American usage *among* is more common than *amongst*. To the American eye and ear, *amongst* seems to be almost as archaic as *whilst*. *See also* AMID, AMIDST.

AMONG OTHER THINGS

A loose idiom, this one slips so easily from the typewriter

that it sometimes escapes notice, even when its use is patently absurd: "John I. Spreckelmyer of Washington, a government worker who has served, among other things, as a hospital administrator with the Veterans Administration, was present." Surely, Mr. Spreckelmyer would not like to be told that he had served as a "thing." The counsel here is not to abandon the idiom, but rather to use it thinkingly. A precise use is this one: "His attaché case contained, among other things, a pearl necklace and two diamond rings, all believed to have been stolen from the Fifty-first Street apartment."

AMOUNT

Amount applies to mass, bulk, or aggregate. It denotes quantity as distinguished from number. It is correct to write, "A certain amount of care or pain or trouble is necessary for every man at all times," but it is incorrect to write, "The robbers took $120 in United States money from the safe, but left behind a considerable amount of Canadian coins." In this second example, *amount of* would be unexceptionable if followed by "money," or "coins" would be unexceptionable if preceded by *quantity of*.

AMPLE

Ample takes in a little more territory than *enough*, so that the two are not precisely synonymous. If you have *enough* room, you have a sufficient amount to carry on whatever operation you are engaged in; if you have *ample* room, you can spread out a bit.

AMUSED

Takes preposition *at*, *by*, or *with*.

ANACHRONISM

The word is misused in this sentence: "For the humanitarian who went to Poland for the American Relief Commission of the Rockefeller Institute, it is almost an anachronism that he is one of the most decorated men in the country for his combat service." An *anachronism* (root: *chronos*, meaning time) is an error involving a misplacement of time, such as a picture showing George Washington using a telephone. When the element of time is not involved in the incongruity, what is usually meant is an *anomaly* or a *paradox*.

ANALOGOUS

Takes preposition *to*.

ANALOGY

Takes preposition *between* or *with*. See RHETORICAL FIGURES AND FAULTS.

ANAPEST

See FOOT.

AND/OR

Whatever its uses in legal or commercial English, this combination is a visual and mental monstrosity that should be avoided in other kinds of writing. Fortunately it is almost always unnecessary. For example: "The idea abroad that the United States for some years has been drifting about in a leaderless condition, under the inept and/or indolent stewardship of Dwight D. Eisenhower . . . apparently has been demolished by the President in person." If this were made "inept or indolent," it would accommodate observers abroad who thought one thing or the other, and certainly would not exclude those who thought both. However, it must be conceded that there are situations in which a choice of one conjunction or the other will not do the trick. For instance: "The law allows a $25 fine and/or thirty days in jail." The solution here is to write out in plain English, at the cost of just one extra word, what the *and/or* means: "$25 fine or thirty days in jail or both."

AND WHICH

The use of this phrase without a preceding parallel *which*, it will be contended here, is either wrong or usually inadvisable.

(This applies also to *and that* and *and who*, as well as to *but which*, *but that*, and *but who*.) Three examples will suffice to state the case:

1. "The Landrum-Griffin bill, designed to end corrupt labor practices and which are prevalent in the country, was approved by the committee." This sentence, a rather uncommon piece of illiteracy, is clearly wrong. It is wrong not because of the ellipsis of "which is" after the word "bill," but because the expressed *which* does not refer to the same thing as the omitted "which." The antecedent of the expressed *which* is "practices," whereas the antecedent of the unexpressed "which" is "bill." The sentence could be remedied by replacing the "and" with a comma.

2. "Taxicab rides taken within Zone A and which are by far the most numerous will be taxed ten cents each." This sentence is wrong because the two subordinate clauses are not grammatically parallel. The first one (in full it would be "that are taken within Zone A") is a defining or restrictive clause—that is, a clause that is indispensable in defining or explaining the noun to which it refers. The second one, beginning with *which*, is a nondefining clause; it merely conveys additional or parenthetical information, and could be omitted without a material alteration of sense. Two clauses of the same kind—whether defining or nondefining—may be joined by *and* or *but*, but a defining clause and a nondefining clause may not be. The sentence could be remedied by deleting the "and" and enclosing the second clause in commas.

3. "Mr. Hoffa represents the combination of devious dealings and dictatorial, overweening power in some of the leading unions, exposed by the McClellan committee, and which calls for curbs." Granted that there is an ellipsis of the words "which was" ahead of "exposed," this sentence may be grammatically sound: The omitted "which was" in the clause "exposed by the McClellan committee" and the subsequent expressed *which* both refer to the same antecedent, "combination," and both introduce nondefining clauses.

But sound grammar alone does not insure good writing, any more than the mere use of steel insures a smart appearance to your car. Each is an indispensable component that must be fashioned to a desired purpose. Let the reader judge whether the "Mr. Hoffa" sentence, sound though it may be, is not a clumsy concoction and even a momentarily unclear one in which the unheralded *and which* compels a second glance to determine what it refers to. Let the reader also judge whether the insertion of "which was" before "exposed" would not lend a trifle more grace, clarity, and tidiness to the construction.

It may be taken as a rule, applicable in nine sentences out of ten—which should be good enough for any rule—that an *and which* or *and that* should be preceded by a parallel *which* or *that*. The tenth sentence is one in which the nebulous requirements of cadence or euphony suggest omission of the first *which*. Following is an example (in this instance the omitted pronoun is a "that" and the expressed pronoun is a *whose*): "Mr. Hughes insisted that what the members of the House needed was 'a newspaper we can agree is informed and whose news is beyond question.'" A "that" after "newspaper" would be perfectly proper, but it would produce a slight bump in the road.

The advice here, however, is to concentrate on the nine more usual sentences. A writer can always foresee, if perhaps a speaker cannot, an approaching *and which*, and should announce it with a preliminary *which*. Not to do so is to be careless and untidy—in nine instances out of ten. The offense is no less serious than a man's appearance in dinner clothes with a cuff link missing from one shirt sleeve.

As a conclusion to this discussion a specimen so rare as to be of purely laboratory interest may be presented. The specimen, from a translation of a Freud monograph, is an instance of a missing cuff link from the other shirt sleeve: "I once interested myself in the peculiar fact that peoples whose territories are adjacent, and are otherwise closely related, are always at feud with and ridiculing each other." Make it "and who are otherwise closely related."

ANENT

A forget-'em word. "He consulted the dean anent his

studies" suggests an attempt to be pretentious. Like most such attempts, it turns out to be as tasteless as a gold toothpick. Use *about, concerning,* or *regarding.* In the same category is *re* or *in re,* meaning in the matter of ("Re your letter of the 13th inst.," etc.). Leave this one to the lawyers.

ANGRY

Takes preposition *with* or *at.*

ANIMADVERT

Takes preposition *upon.*

ANNOYED

Be annoyed takes preposition *by; feel annoyed* takes preposition *at* or *with.*

ANOTHER

The word is often misused for *more, others,* or *additional.* A typical newspaper example: "The port directly employed 250,000, with another 150,000 indirectly employed." *Another* means one more of the same kind. In the sentence quoted it would be correct only if the second figure were the same as the first. *See also* OTHER.

ANTAGONIST

See ADVERSARY, ANTAGONIST, OPPONENT.

ANTECEDENT

Takes preposition *to.*

ANTERIOR

Takes preposition *to.*

ANTICIPATE, EXPECT

By its derivation, *anticipate* embraces the idea of "doing something" before or in connection with a coming event. The "doing something" involved in *anticipating* need not be taken so literally as to mean the performance of an overt act; it may simply connote an advance accommodation of the mind or the senses, even involuntarily, to the coming event. *Expect* means merely to look toward the coming event. When one says, "I am expecting a good dinner tonight," he means only that he is looking ahead and that a good dinner is in the cards. When one says, "I am anticipating a good dinner tonight," he means (assuming he knows how to use words properly) that his mouth is watering and that a glow of happiness has already begun to suffuse him. To *expect* an attack by the enemy is to look ahead to it; to *anticipate* an attack by the enemy is not only to look ahead to it, but also to dispose one's forces to meet it.

ANTICLIMAX

See RHETORICAL FIGURES AND FAULTS.

ANTIPATHY

Takes preposition *to, toward,* or *against.*

ANTITHESIS

See RHETORICAL FIGURES AND FAULTS.

ANXIOUS, EAGER

Both words convey the notion of being desirous, but *anxious* has an underlay of faint apprehension. In speech *anxious* is used indiscriminately to cover the meanings of both words. We say, "I am anxious to get my operation over with" and "I am anxious to go to the baseball game tomorrow." A chief reason for this practice is that although *eager* would be the proper word to use in the second sentence, it is more a writer's word than a speaker's word. Aside from the casualism "eager beaver," the word is not frequently used in spoken language. In writing, however, both words are common, and since they are, the careful writer will discriminate between them, reserving *anxious* for the situation in which some anxiety is involved.

45

ANY AND ALL

A hackneyed phrase, and wasteful. "Democratic strategists have made determined efforts to divorce their campaign from any and all national implications." Vote for one.

ANYBODY

One word, unless you are talking about a body: "The police were convinced a murder had been committed, but could not find any body."

ANY MORE

Adverbially, this phrase has the meaning of now or hereafter or further. It is properly used, however, only with an outright negative statement ("We don't see each other any more"), or with one that has a negative connotation ("We scarcely ever see each other any more"), or occasionally with a question ("Do you see him any more?"). With an affirmative statement, it is an unacceptable though not uncommon casualism: "The Little Gallery is exceedingly regretful about last week's ad about how we're going to be closed on Saturday instead of Monday any more"; "What's the matter with the world any more?"

ANYONE

One word except when it means any particular person or thing—as in, "He read three novels, but did not like any one of them."

ANYPLACE

A casualism for *anywhere*.

ANYWAY

One word when it means *in any case*, as in, "Whether it rains or shines, the game will be played anyway." Otherwise two words, as in, "The doctor did not regard the illness as in any way serious."

46

ANYWAYS

Illiterate.

ANYWHERES

Illiterate.

APART

Takes preposition *from*.

APATHY

Takes preposition *toward*.

APOSTROPHE

See PUNCTUATION.

APPEND

Takes preposition *to*.

APPORTION

Takes preposition *to*, *among*, or *between*.

APPRECIATE

Since the strict meaning of the word, used transitively, is to evaluate truly, some contend that it should not be used to convey thanks or as an expression of high evaluation, as in the sentence, "I appreciate your efforts in my behalf." Nevertheless, the word is never used in a downgrading sense, but almost always in an upgrading sense. It thus has come to have more than the neutral meaning of mere evaluation; it connotes "to esteem highly." Webster goes a step farther and gives the definition "to be grateful for." With this there can be no real quarrel.

APPREHENSIVE

Takes preposition *of* (danger); *for* (persons).

APPROVE

Takes preposition *of*.

APPROXIMATE

Takes preposition *to*.

APROPOS

Takes preposition *of* or no preposition.

APT, LIABLE, LIKELY

These three words, though close in meaning, have distinctions that are worthy of attention. *Apt* means having an inherent tendency, customarily inclined, or naturally fit. *Liable* means open to or exposed to something unpleasant or disadvantageous. *Likely* means probable or expected. To illustrate the three words (and perform a public service in the process): "Teen-agers are apt to speed on an open road. If they do they are liable to be arrested. Then they are likely to be sorry." In casual speech, *liable* is often used in place of *likely*—as in, "We are liable to go to the ball game tomorrow"—but a careful writer will not tolerate this misuse.

ARBITRATE, MEDIATE

They are not interchangeable. *Arbitrators*, acting as judges, hear evidence. Then they make an award. They have no power —and, in fact, no right—to mediate. *Mediators* act as go-betweens and try to work out an agreement, but lack the authority of ultimate decision.

ARCING, ARCKING

Both words are unpleasant visually. A reader who comes upon, "The spacecraft will have to be shot out over a long arcing course," is sure to be puzzled by the word momentarily. He may also be puzzled by *arcking*, but at least he will know how to pronounce it. Insertion of the "k" has precedents in *picnicking* and *politicking*. The vote here goes for *arcked* and *arcking*, but an even stronger vote goes for avoiding the words altogether.

ARDORS FOR RIGORS OR TRAVAIL

The misuse of *ardor* as a noun meaning something that is

48

arduous would seem to be unlikely. Yet here are two examples from a distinguished newspaper: "But nothing at the show suggests the exorbitant cost of chocolates and the ardors of shopping . . . that plague the Soviet housewife"; "Khrushchev Is Resting. Takes Day Off From Ardors of Hungarian Visit." Here we have a rare situation, in which we can observe the process of BACK FORMATION—the coining of a nonexistent word from an actual word erroneously supposed to be derived from it. The actual word is *arduous*, and the writers wrongly presumed it was derived from *ardor*, which is nonexistent in the presumed meaning. There is not the slightest connection between the two words. *Arduous* means difficult or laborious. But *ardor* means warmth of passion.

ARGOT

See INSIDE TALK.

AROMA

An *aroma* is a pleasant smell, and except jocularly cannot be used to denote an unpleasant one. Wrong: "The houses are near one of Inverness's distilleries, and a spokesman for the residents said the aroma was at times unbearable." Make it *odor* or *smell*.

AROUND

Around for *about*, in the sense of approximately, is casual usage. Therefore, in written English, "about three o'clock" is preferable to "around three o'clock." *Around* is likewise casual in the sense of *from place to place* or *here and there*—as in, "The candidate campaigned around the state, speaking in major cities." In this sense, though, it is establishing itself.

ARRIVE

Takes preposition *at* or *in*.

ARTICLES, OMISSION OF

Some latter-day writers present us with affected sentences like this: "Main feature of the combined first floors of the new building will be a spacious hospitality area." It may be fairly asked what they would do if the sentence were inverted—whether they would write, "A spacious hospitality area will be main feature of the combined first floors of the new building." Beyond doubt the answer is, No. They would put a *the* ahead of "main feature"—and probably, one supposes, knock out the *a* at the beginning of the sentence.

Whence cometh this affectation? *Time* magazine had much to do with spreading it, but *Time* did not originate it. It may be surmised that once upon a time a newspaper editor looked over his paper as it came fresh from the press, noting to his horror that every story on the front page began with the word *the*. He acted decisively. He ordered that thereafter no story was to begin with *the*. It may even be conceded that his intention was not wholly bad. He may have been striving to jolt his writers out of the melancholy monotony of story after story written to the same pattern of similarly constructed sentences. (If this guess is correct, it may account for the equally monotonous procession of stories beginning, "Running for Mayor on a tax-reform platform, Henry Jones had his hair cut today.") In any event, some of our mythical editor's disciples went out into the wide world. They carried his rule with them. Indeed, they went him one better. They decided that not only must no story begin with *the*, but in addition no sentence must begin with *the*.

At some point in this stage of the disfigurement of the language the school of Luce writing entered the picture. The effect was most damaging because a magazine that circulates in the millions cannot fail to influence impressionable young writers and equally impressionable young advertising men with their ears constantly cocked for the new and the "smart," no matter how hideous it may be. The result of all this is sentences like these: "Cause of the disturbance was the proposed wedding between . . ."; "Outcome of some of the conventions can be gauged in advance . . ."; "Reason, he said, was to 'avoid inflationary trends'. . . ."

Nor is the beginning of the sentence the only point attacked by this cancer; nouns in the middle of a sentence now occasionally suffer the loss of their articles, too: "Borough lines, color

50

lines should be invisible, nonexistent, when we are looking for a way to improve education of our children." Why not "the education"? Or, "At the same time most of the more than fifty American scientists interviewed in preparation of this series doubt that . . ."; here the omission of *the* before "preparation" causes the use of an apparently wrong preposition. It should be either "in preparation for" or "in the preparation of," and the meanings are noticeably different.

But it is the initial article of the sentence that is the main target of the pernicious modern attack. When the writer is tempted to lop it off, he should ask himself whether he would as readily delete the other articles in his sentence. Would he write, "Main feature of combined first floors of new building will be spacious hospitality area"? Obviously not, unless he were writing a telegram or a headline. When an article is normal before a noun, it is as necessary as a tail to a puppy, and amputating it hurts. Ask any pup. Above all, remember what the Bible says: "If I forget 'the,' O Jerusalem, let my right hand forget her cunning."

A special journalistic eccentricity causes the frequent omission of *the* before the word "police." A reporter will write, "Mr. Kleme told police that . . . ," although he wouldn't dream of phrasing it that way in his conversation. It is true that in certain contexts the article may be omitted. It is proper to write, "Police are necessary in a big city," just as it is proper to write, "State and church are kept separate under our concept of government." But outside that sphere of extreme generality it is not idiomatic to drop the article. The word *police* should be thought of as parallel to the word *army*. In the same way as you say *the army* or *soldiers* you should say *the police* or *policemen. See also* PERSONNEL *and* NUMERALS WITH COLLECTIVES.

ARTIFACT

By definition an *artifact* is an object of human making. The word "human" is tautological in the following sentence: "Some time this afternoon the small human artifact named Pioneer IV will soar past the moon."

AS

1. SUPERFLUOUS. A not uncommon locution is this: "As cold as it was, he wore no overcoat." The inclusion of the first *as*, strangely enough, is a reversion to older English. Jespersen says it "is now obsolete." And well it might be, as far as logic and necessity go. The first *as* is an adverb of degree, but here no question of degree is involved; the second *as* is not part of the usual *as . . . as* combination ("as cold as an iceberg"), but is a conjunction equivalent to *though*. The best modern usage dispenses with the first *as*.

2. NECESSARY. As a footnote, here is a sentence by a writer who may have misunderstood the principle involved: "Grand Central Terminal was busy as a beehive last night." Here another *as* is indeed needed, to answer the question, How busy? "As busy as a beehive." *See also* LIKE, AS.

AS BAD OR WORSE THAN
See INCOMPLETE ALTERNATIVE COMPARISON.

AS FAR AS
A fairly common error that accompanies this phrase (and *so far as*) is omission of the verb in the clause the phrase introduces, as in this sentence: "The bikini was originally called the 'atome' by M. Heim, and the sky was the limit so far as advertising it." As *far as* and *so far as* may be regarded as prepositions when the words mean "to" or denote the extent of an action and are followed by a noun, as in "I will go as far as Times Square but no farther." However, when the words mean, to quote Fowler, "within what limits a statement is to be applied," the words constitute a conjunction and must be followed by a verb. Thus, in the sentence cited it should be "so far as advertising it was concerned."

AS IF, AS THOUGH
They are interchangeable. As *though*, on its face, seems illogical. Take the sentence, "He looks as though he were ill."

Supplying the obvious ellipsis, we get, "He looks as he would look though he were ill"; *though* does not seem to make sense in this context. The answer is uncomplicated and ancient: An old meaning of *though* is *if*, which is now obsolete except in the expression *as though*.

ASPIRATION

Takes preposition *toward*, sometimes *after*.

ASPIRE

Takes preposition *to*, *after*, or *toward*.

ASSASSIN

An *assassin* is one who either kills or tries to kill treacherously. Thus, the phrase "would-be assassin" is meaningless, unless perhaps the writer is referring to someone who is toying with the idea of attempting a killing. An *assassination*, of course, is an actual killing; therefore it is proper to speak of an "attempted assassination" if the deed does not succeed.

ASSENT

Takes preposition *to*.

ASSERT

See SAY AND ITS SYNONYMS.

ASSESS

The idea of value underlies this word both in its derivation and in its proper use. It means to apportion in the nature of a levy of some kind, or to impose a fine or tax or charge. It does not mean merely to impose, and is thus misused in the following sentence: "Death sentences are rare and are usually assessed only in aggravated cases." In another sense the word means to evaluate, as in, "He assessed the situation calmly."

ASSEVERATE

See SAY AND ITS SYNONYMS.

53

ASSIMILATE
Takes preposition *to* or (infrequently) *with*.

ASSIST
In sense of *be present* takes preposition *at;* in sense of *help* takes preposition *in* or *with*.

ASSOCIATE (vb.)
Takes preposition *with*.

ASSUME, PRESUME
The senses in which the paths of these words cross are not very different. It may be said, however, that to *assume* is to pose a hypothesis, to take something for granted without any evidence, whereas to *presume* is to suppose something to be true, to believe it to be a fact. Thus, when Stanley said, "Dr. Livingstone, I presume?" he was expressing his belief founded on the circumstances; he didn't say, "I assume," to set up an argument in the jungle. *See also* ADOPT, ASSUME.

ASSURE
Takes preposition *of*.

AS THE CROW FLIES
This is a battered figure of speech, particularly in these days when planes fly straighter than any crow ever did. Why not say *by air* or *in a straight line?*

AS THE RESULT OF
The phrase is usually inexact. For example: "Two persons were killed and three injured as the result of a collision of two cars on Highway 9 this morning." Obviously there were other results: The cars were damaged, the road was probably blocked, and perhaps an ambulance driver was called away from an interesting poker game. What was meant in the sentence was *a result of* or *one result of*.

54

AS THOUGH
See AS IF, AS THOUGH.

AS TO
The question to ask oneself about these words is, Are they necessary? Often they are not; often a more precise preposition would serve better. In the sentence "His hearers were in doubt as to his meaning" the preposition *about* would be sharper; in the sentence "There was some question as to his ability to pay" the preposition *of* would be less loose.

The phrase *as to* is a useful device, however, to introduce for immediate attention an element that otherwise would find its place farther on in a sentence: "As to taxes, the President has not yet decided whether to ask for an increase."

A dictum that *as to* should be used in preference to *as for* is a sheer superstition that seems to have been conceived by Ambrose Bierce. *As for* has been used reputably and continuously since the days of Shakespeare and King James. As a matter of fact, it is difficult to conceive of Bierce or anyone else throwing in his poker hand and saying, "As to me, I'm going home." *See also* QUESTION WHETHER.

ASTONISH
See SURPRISE, ASTONISH.

ASTONISHED
Takes preposition *at* (disapproval); *by* (approval).

AS WELL AS
Because of a duality of both meaning and grammatical nature, this phrase gives rise to problems that are not easily resolved. The problems may be crystallized under four headings.

1. THE FORM OF THE VERB THAT FOLLOWS THE PHRASE: The difficulty here is that *as well as* is, technically at least, a conjunction meaning *and not only*, but at the same time has the force of

55

a preposition meaning *in addition to* or *besides*. If it is a conjunction, the form of the verbs before and after it should be identical. By this reasoning the following sentences would be incorrect: "It is indubitably the case that businesses go into debt, as well as obtaining [read *obtain*] equity capital, for the purposes of modernization and expansion"; "Goldberg and Heller want to go further and increase Government spending as well as backing [read *back*] tax revision even if this means more deficits." Fowler is emphatic in maintaining that the phrase must be treated as a conjunction, with the same form of verb fore and aft. Jespersen, on the other hand, says that "in recent times the combination 'as well as' is not infrequently treated as a preposition with a gerund." Fowler's view seems the more reasoned, but Jespersen's the more realistic. In view of respectable modern usage it would be rash indeed to label the foregoing quoted sentences incorrect. Yet the careful writer would be justified in taking the position that the constructions that are the more logical grammatically are preferable. Having thus straddled the main issue, we may now add a postscript that is more positive: When the *as well as* phrase begins a sentence the prepositional treatment is usually inescapable. "As well as taught and studied, Plato wrote books on philosophical problems all his life" is impossible; idiom demands, "as well as teaching and studying." In this and other respects the phrase is similar to RATHER THAN.

2. THE NUMBER OF THE VERB THAT FOLLOWS AN "AS WELL AS" SUBJECT: Do you say, "John as well as Jane were late for dinner," or, "John as well as Jane was late for dinner"? The singular "was" is preferable in such an instance, and the "as well as Jane" would be set off by commas. Aside from the grammar of the construction, it is obvious that there is a principal subject (John), as well as a subordinate one (Jane); the subordinate subject should not be placed on the same plane as the principal one.

3. THE PERSON OF THE VERB THAT FOLLOWS AN "AS WELL AS" SUBJECT: Do you say, "He as well as I am not feeling well," or, "He as well as I is not feeling well"? Again the principal subject would govern and the subordinate subject would be set off by commas: "He, as well as I, is not feeling well." Categories 2

and 3, it will be noted, seem to reinforce the feeling that *as well as* has the force of a preposition; in both instances it does not act as a coordinator, but rather has the force of *besides* or *in addition to*. However, category 4 will restore the balance.

4. THE CASE OF THE PRONOUN FOLLOWING "AS WELL AS": It should be the same as the case of the noun or pronoun preceding the phrase: "You, as well as I, have been elected"; "They have elected you, as well as me." In each instance the conjunctional nature of the phrase is unmistakable: "You have been elected, as well as I [have been elected];" "They have elected you, as well as [they have elected] me."

AT, IN

The force of idiom is nowhere more plainly exhibited than in the almost whimsical choice that users of English make between these two words. How, one might ask, can one newspaper say that a man was appointed consul general *in* Melbourne and another say that he was appointed consul general *at* Melbourne, and which is right? The answers are that there are no rules about the matter and that both are right.

Partridge quotes Dr. Pearsall Smith as laying down a guide to the effect that *in* is applied to large cities and countries and *at* to smaller places. That does not take us very far, and in view of the Melbourne example one wonders whether it is a safe guide even for the short distance it does take us. Webster is more comprehensive. It tells us that when reference to an interior is prominent, *in* is used ("look for a book in the library") and when a place is regarded as a mere local point, *at* is more common ("meet a friend at the library"). It goes on to say that *in* is used before countries or districts and *at* before business houses, public offices, institutions, etc. (But "He has a job in the State Department" is just as common as "He has a job at the State Department.") Finally, Webster tells us that *in* is used if the town or city is regarded as an including area marked by destination or permanency of occupation or familiar association, and *at* if it is regarded as merely a point, as on a trip or on a map or at a remove from the speaker. Here again, however, there are exceptions. A

57

train or a plane could equally well arrive *in* or *at* New York, its destination. A ship, on the other hand, rarely arrives *in* a place, but rather *at* a place. Perhaps here there is a notion of reaching a place, as contrasted with reaching it and proceeding into it.

It should be clear by now that no all-inclusive guide to *at* and *in* is possible. That does not mean that the two words are simply interchangeable; you could not say, for example, that "fish live at the sea." What it does mean is that the choice of one word or the other is a matter of idiom. If English is your native tongue, you will know which word to use. If it is not, no precise, comprehensive guide is available to help you.

ATHLETICS

See -ICS.

ATOMIC FLYSWATTERS

In slang, especially American slang, there is a tendency to go to extremes. At the extreme of understatement a Cadillac may be referred to as a *heap*; at the extreme of overstatement a girl may be referred to as a *queen*. The understatements far outnumber the overstatements, probably because they contain the wry humor of disparagement, which seems to be a feature of slang. In casual speech, apart from slang, there is a tendency to overstatement, and unfortunately the tendency carries over to writing—even to the writing of authors who, except for special reasons, wouldn't permit the intrusion of slang or any other low expressions into serious writing. Thus: "He has certainly been ignorant of a lot of wrongdoing within his department, at a frightful cost to the consumer public"; "The French are not terribly pleased with the Americans"; "The reception visitors from the United States have been accorded in Moscow has been nothing short of fabulous." The tendency is to use powerful words to convey quite moderate meanings, to unleash atomic weapons to kill flies—and that rhetorical figure itself comes close to doing the same thing.

In speech, where this kind of misuse is more common than in writing, we use the strongest words of the language with abandon. A play is *terrific* (no idea of terror) or it is *dreadful* (no idea of dread), a restaurant is *fantastic* (no idea of unreality) or it is *horrible* (no idea of horror). The trouble with this practice is that the "bad" meanings of the words tend to drive out the "good" meanings (*See* BERNSTEIN'S SECOND LAW). It's enough to make strong words weak.

The dilution has gone so far that many of the powerful words have now become mere intensives, so that they appear in such contradictory contexts as "awfully good" and "terribly nice." It is doubtful whether the misusers of these words have ever paused to think what the words mean. The suggestion here is that they do so. To raise an alarm, the following list, surely incomplete, of words often used as atomic flyswatters is offered for examination: *adorable, awful, colossal, disgusting, divine, dreadful, fabulous, fantastic, fearful, frightful, great, horrible, sensational, stunning, terrible, terrific, weird.*

ATTEMPT (n.)

Takes preposition *at*.

ATTENDED

Takes preposition *with* (things); *by* (persons).

AT THE PRESENT TIME

There is nothing wrong with this phrase except that it is a mark of uneconomical writing. It can always be shortened to *at present* or *now*. Often it can be omitted altogether, as in this sentence: "At the present time the Administration is preparing a bill that would give the Atomic Energy Commission authority to sell this property."

AT THIS TIME

A wasteful locution. It means *now*.

ATTORNEY, LAWYER

Lawyer, the general term, designates one who practices law. *Attorney* refers to one who is designated by another to transact business for him; an *attorney* may or may not be a *lawyer*, al-

59

though usually he is. Strictly speaking, therefore, a *lawyer* is an *attorney* only when he has a client. It may be that the desire of *lawyers* to appear to be making a go of their profession has accounted for their leaning toward the designation *attorney*. Another reason undoubtedly is their belief that *attorney* is more elegant.

Two other terms applied to members of the legal profession are *counsel* and *counselor*. *Counsel* means one who gives legal advice, and the word is employed mostly within the profession and in court. *Counselor*, which means the same thing, is used in court as a quite proper designation, in rural circles as an honorific, and among lawyers themselves as a half-humorous term of address.

AUDIENCE

Strictly speaking, an *audience* is a group of hearers, although its meaning is sometimes extended to a group whose principal activity is seeing, as the *audience* at a circus. The word is incorrectly used, however, in the headline, "Fire Draws Audience." Likewise, the onlookers at sports events are not termed *audiences*.

AUDIT

As a verb used in the sense of to hear, *audit* has no excuse for being. Only novelty-hunters would write, "After auditing the President's speech before the United Nations, the *Chicago Daily News* editorialized . . ." or, "Your husband ought to be man enough to audit such a story without hysteria." With *listen to* and *hear* available, there is no use for *audit* in this sense. Aside from its normal meaning of to inspect and verify (an account), *audit* has only one other meaning, and that a specialized one: to take a college course without receiving academic credits.

AUGMENTED

Takes preposition *by* or *with*.

AUTARCHY, AUTARKY

In the sense of economic self-sufficiency, *autarky* is the bet-

60

ter spelling. The etymologies of the two words are set forth more clearly in *Webster's New World Dictionary* than in most other dictionaries. *Autarchy,* meaning absolute rule, has as its root *archos,* first or ruler. *Autarky,* meaning economic self-sufficiency, has as its root *arkeein,* to achieve, endure, suffice.

AVENGE, REVENGE

A simple distinction can be, but is not always, made between the two words. *Avenge* means to mete out punishment for a wrong done, with the idea of restoring the balance of justice. *Revenge,* a meaner word, denotes retaliating resentfully for a wrong done, with the idea of obtaining satisfaction. *Vengeance* and *revenge* are the comparable nouns.

AVER

See SAY AND ITS SYNONYMS.

AVERAGE

See MEAN, MEDIAN, AVERAGE.

AVERSE

See ADVERSE, AVERSE.

AVERT, AVOID

"The second war was different," said a recent British Prime Minister. "I don't think anything could have avoided it." Not true. Switzerland *avoided* it (i.e., kept clear of it, shunned it). The Prime Minister meant to say that he did not think anything could have *averted* it (i.e., prevented it, warded it off).

AWAIT, WAIT

Either one is transitive: "He awaited [or *waited*] his orders." But only *wait* is intransitive: "She waited while he went into the shop." *Wait on* is proper in the sense of standing ready to serve ("The steward waited on the passengers"), but is dialectal in the sense of to wait for ("I'm waiting on you to deal the cards"). A Southerner overheard in a Florida restaurant obviously was

61

unaware of the proper meaning of *wait on*. Asked by his companion whether the waiter had yet given him the check, he replied: "I'm waitin' on him."

AWFUL

See ATOMIC FLYSWATTERS.

AWHILE

The meaning of *awhile* is for a period; the "for" notion is part of the meaning. Consequently it is redundant to write, "She rested for awhile." What you can properly write is, "She rested awhile," or "She rested for a while."

B

BACK AND FORTH

After the verb *see-saw,* the phrase is almost redundant and entirely wasteful: "In sixteen ballots taken in the General Assembly the Chinese delegate and the Japanese delegate see-sawed back and forth." Delete *back and forth. See also* REMAND BACK.

BACK FORMATION

The phrase refers to a nonexistent word coined from an actual word erroneously supposed to be derived from it. For instance, *burglar* has the appearance of a word meaning one who *burgles;* actually, however, *burglar* is an ancient word and *burgle* is a nineteenth-century jocular coinage from it. Likewise, someone theorized that *locomotion* was derived from a verb *locomote* and this back formation was coined, although there was no more reason for the supposition than there is to suppose that *motion* is derived from a verb *mote.*

Some back formations are purely jocular—*burgle, butle, emote, sculpt*—but undiscerning writers take them seriously. Other back formations hang in an equivocal state between partial and full acceptance *enthuse, donate, commentate.* Still others have gained full acceptance—*diagnose, scavenge, laze, drowse.* As is true of many slang and casual words, ultimate acceptance depends largely on whether there is a genuine need, either in meaning or in flavor, for the word that has been *backformated* (and there you have one, freshly minted for the occasion). *For a back formation caught in the act, see* ARDORS FOR RIGORS OR TRAVAIL.

BACK OF, IN BACK OF

Various authorities hold various opinions about these two phrases, ranging from Partridge, who scorns them both, to Evans, who clutches them both to his more generous bosom. In view of the differing points of view, an examination of the phrases may be interesting if not especially rewarding.

Let us look first at the words that may be applied to directions relative to a three-dimensional figure. These words are: (1) *atop* (and perhaps *above*, although this does not necessarily imply proximity), (2) *below* or *beneath*, (3) *beside* or *alongside*, (4) *before*, and (5) *behind*.

Of these single words, two are not entirely serviceable: *atop* because it is unusual, almost poetic, and *before* because it is sometimes ambiguous, as in the sentence, "When the band struck up the anthem, the girl stood before the boy" (does *before* here mean direction or time?). These two have therefore developed alternates in the form of phrases: *on top of* and *in front of*. It is reasonable to assume that analogy led, or misled, to the phrase *in back of*. Let it be noted in passing that for *top* and *front* the alternatives had to be prepositional phrases, since these words are nouns, whereas there was no such necessity in the case of *back*, since *back* is an adverb as well as a noun—one could say, "He moved back of the white line," although one could not say, "He moved front of the white line." *Back of*, therefore, should be at least as worthy as *in back of*, although Webster labels the first as "*colloq., U.S.*," and accepts the second as standard usage. The fact seems to be that both phrases are now acceptable in American speech, although both have dubious standing with our British cousins.

The careful writer, however, will conclude that neither phrase says anything that the single, terse word *behind* does not say just as well, and he will not needlessly put himself on the defensive—by writing, for example, "Get thee in back of me, Satan."

BAD, BADLY

In response to the inquiry "How do you feel?" the reply might be, commonly, colloquially, and carelessly, "I feel badly," or, in careful, proper English, "I feel bad." "Feel" is a copulative verb, equivalent in meaning to "am," and therefore is followed by an adjectival form (*bad*), not an adverbial form (*badly*). The unknowing, who are frightened by their misapprehension of

64

grammar into the OVERREFINEMENT of "This is strictly between he and I," are likewise frightened into "I feel badly."

Now there are those who argue that "feel" is not always a copulative verb, but sometimes is an intransitive verb of emotion, and who therefore would have us say, "I feel badly about having lost my watch." But the argument does not stand up, as can be established by substituting synonyms after "feel." You would say, "I feel sorry [not *sorrily*], rueful [not *ruefully*], distressed [not *distressedly*] about having lost my watch." The only occasion on which "feel" would be followed by an adverb is when the word following the verb is intended to denote degree rather than quality—in other words, when it actually modifies the verb rather than the subject. Thus, we would say, "I feel badly [i.e., *intensely*] the need for enlightenment on this subject," just as we would say, "I feel strongly about this."

BALANCE

In the sense of rest or remainder it is classed in Webster as colloquial and in the Oxford as commercial slang. Nevertheless, it would seem to be a legitimate extension of the bookkeeping term when there is actually a parallel to bookkeeping—that is, when two amounts are involved. It would thus seem to be un-exceptionable to say, "His check was $8. He gave the waiter a $10 bill and told him to keep the balance." This usage, however, would be dubious: "He was told to give up smoking for the balance of his life."

BALDING

"At the age of forty-seven, he is small, slight, and balding." There is no need for such a word. Why not *baldish*? Because, the writers for a certain magazine that loves the word might reply, *balding* implies becoming bald, whereas *baldish* refers to a static condition. However, the scientific evidence is that a man who is *baldish* is getting bald, too. But even if this were not so, how can those magazine people tell by looking at a man whether he is in a static condition or in the midst of a continuing process? Does he bald before their unusually discerning eyes? If they insist on stressing the continuing process, they can say his hair is *receding* or *thinning*, which words at least come from legitimate verbs. By the way, did you ever hear anyone say the word *balding*? Or have you only seen it in print?

BANDIT
See ROBBER, THIEF, BURGLAR.

BANQUET
See FUNCTION.

BASED
Takes preposition *on*, *upon*, or *in*.

BASED ON
A latter-day tendency is to use *based on* as if it were an absolute participle like *considering* or *given*: "Based on future prices today for October delivery, Cuba will pay about $1.5 million for the shipment." This could be corrected to, "Based on future prices . . . estimates are that, etc." Another example: "Once fully certified—based on [make it *on the basis of*] at least four years' carefully observed performance in the classroom—the new teacher would be licensed to teach anywhere in the United States." Some day *based on* may become an absolute phrase; but as of now, unless it has a clear and present subject, it must be classed as a DANGLER.

BASIC
Fowler considered *basic* an "upstart" word used to convey a pinch of the up-to-date and the scientific. He suggested substituting *fundamental*. Whatever may have been true in Fowler's time, it cannot now be said that *basic* is an upstart. Indeed, it is well established.

Starting from a source quite similar to that of *fundamental* —although starting much later—*basic* is pursuing a similar course and now has a derived meaning beyond the specialized one of pertaining to a base or essence. Nor can anyone be blamed for preferring it to the more ponderous *fundamental*. One can, perhaps, object to applying to it a comparative degree as in this passage: "Their cultural likenesses are more basic than their differences." And one can certainly object to placing it in absurd company, as in a sentence about maximum teachers' salaries that spoke of "the present basic top," or in a sentence about "the basic ceiling for savings bank interest." But these are questions of misuse, not of use.

BASIS

Takes preposition *of* or *for*.

BASTION

It is not just a strong point or a fortress; it is literally a structure jutting out from a main fortification—or, by extension, a fortified outpost. Therefore, it would be incorrect to write, "Planes bombed the Red bastion, twenty miles behind the front."

BATHOS

Bathos (from the Greek, meaning depth) is used to speak of dull, low matter-of-factness, or of an absurd descent from the sublime to the ludicrous. A stanza from Byron illustrates this second meaning:

> When a man hath no freedom to fight for at home,
> Let him combat for that of his neighbors;
> Let him think of the glories of Greece and of Rome,
> And get knocked on the head for his labors.

Bathos is not the kind of word you would use in conversation with the butcher boy, but it has a place in literary language. The adjective is *bathetic*. *Bathos* is unrelated in meaning to *pathos*.

BAY WINDOW

See BELLY.

B.C.

See A.D.

BEAUTY

"The beauty of such stations is that a pilot can pick up the signal beamed on any one of the 360 compass headings and use it to navigate." *Beauty* has to do with the senses or aesthetic appreciation. As used here, it is purely a casualism, just one step above "the beauty part."

BE BEING

Partridge devotes much effort and space to arguing the correctness of this combination plus a past participle, as in the sentence, "I should not be being disturbed all the time by rushed jobs if I had independent means." He contends that there is a difference between "I should not be being disturbed all the time" and what seems like the obvious escape hatch: "I should not be disturbed all the time." His contention is that the *be being* version suggests a continual act or recurring state of things, whereas the other version suggests a continuous state.

All this may be conceded without conceding that the *be being* construction is anything but a graceless combination of words. Partridge's victory is Pyrrhic. If a writer desires this slightly different shade of meaning, would he not do better to recast his sentence to sidestep the awkwardness? Could he not write, "Rushed jobs would not be disturbing me all the time if I had independent means"? Instead of "He will be being hanged about this time," would it not be better to write, "They [or "The executioner"] will be hanging him about this time"? The pedestrian who steps in front of a speeding car may well have the right of way, but why argue the case from a hospital bed?

BECAUSE

See FOR (2) *and* REASON . . . IS BECAUSE.

BECOMING (adj.)

Takes preposition *to* or *in*.

68

BEFIT

See FIT.

BEHALF

The distinction between *in behalf of* and *on behalf of* is one that a good writer recognizes instinctively, though he may never have seen it set forth formally. *In behalf of* means for the benefit of, or as a champion or friend: "The money was raised in behalf of the strikers in Georgia." *On behalf of* means as the agent of or in place of: "The lawyer entered a not guilty plea on behalf of the defendant."

BEING AS HOW

See HOW.

BELLY

To say that *belly* is the proper, nontechnical word for that portion of the body between the chest and the hips is not to insure that it is going to be used. The common evasions are *abdomen*, which is a scientific anatomical word, and *stomach*, which properly applies only to one organ within the *belly*. *Paunch*, which originally meant *belly*, now is usually restricted to a protuberant one. This is often called a *pot-belly*, to which, strangely enough, there seems to be less aversion than to *belly* itself. Nevertheless, slang euphemisms have been coined for the abdominal overhang, too: *corporation* and *bay window*, for example. When viewed from the two extremes of the coarse slang *guts* and the arch babytalk *tummy*, the term *belly* seems a fine old word. Perhaps the time is not distant when it will return to common usage, just as *leg* returned from *limb*-o. *See also* EUPHEMISMS.

BELOW

It's often superfluous, as in this sentence: "He stands on his twenty-fourth-floor terrace and watches the crashing girders as they fall to the ground below." *Below* is where ground usually is.

69

BEREAVE

Takes preposition *of*.

BERNSTEIN'S SECOND LAW

Until now Bernstein's Law has designated a statement, known throughout the civilized world, of a property common to such articles as cuff links, dimes, table-tennis balls, and caps of toothpaste tubes. Stated in its simplest, nay its only, form, it affirms: "A falling body always rolls to the most inaccessible spot." Practically, this means that if you drop a cuff link, it is useless to look at the open floor area near your feet. The only thing to do is to get down on all fours, preferably with a flashlight, and peer under the bed.

Henceforth this principle will have to be known as Bernstein's First Law, for now there is a Second Law. The new one is a kind of Gresham's Law applied to words. Gresham's Law, it will be recalled (just as Sir Thomas Gresham recalled it from an earlier formulator), states that "bad money drives out good." This is true of words, too, but the two laws differ in important respects. When a bad currency drives out a good one, the good money at least retains its value and, indeed, sometimes gains in value, whereas the bad currency remains bad.

When a bad word drives out a good one, however, different things may happen. First, the good word most often depreciates in value, although it may hold its own; it never, however, gains in value. Second, the bad word, like the bad currency, may remain bad, but often it appreciates to the level of the good word and sometimes even becomes more valuable than the word it displaced. Stated more succinctly but not more clearly, Bernstein's Second Law holds: "Bad words tend to drive out good ones, and when they do, the good ones never appreciate in value, sometimes maintain their value, but most often lose in value, whereas the bad words may remain bad or get better."

The term "bad words," as used here, refers to secondary meanings that diverge from the true or primary meanings of words, and that come into use because of ignorance, confusion, faddishness, or the importunities of slang.

When such powerful words as *awful, dreadful, fearful,* or *horrible* are used as mere commonplace expressions of disapproval, the primary meanings of the words are displaced and depreciated. (*See* ATOMIC FLYSWATTERS.) At the same time the new meanings remain debased, so that there is a gross loss all around. When *enormity* is widely used in contexts where *enormousness* is meant, the useful genuine meaning of the word tends to become lost and no one is the gainer. The same is true of such manhandled words as *disinterested, glamour, publicist,* and *transpire.* And, of course, there are countless more.

In another category are "bad words" with real utility that drive out "good words" with little or none. There is no need for *fruition* in the meaning of gratification in the use or possession of something, because the occasions for its use are rare and because *pleasure* or *gratification* will usually serve. But there is need for *fruition* meaning coming to fruit. *Internecine* in the sense of deadly—its original sense—is a redundant word in the language, but *internecine* referring to mutual destruction or fratricidal strife is useful. It is a rare occasion when a writer would wish to use *shambles* in its traditional meaning—a place of slaughter—but frequently he would have use for it in the more recent meaning of a scene of chaos. All these are instances of bad words that drive out good ones and then gain in value.

In a final category are bad words that all but drive out good ones, but do not quite do it and so simply coexist with them. The noun *alibi* in the casual sense of an excuse is a prevalent word, but it also holds its own in its true meaning of a plea of having been elsewhere, undoubtedly because it is indispensable in jurisprudence. *Connive* as a casualism meaning to conspire or finagle is pressing hard the primary meaning of the word of shutting one's eyes to wrongdoing, but the primary meaning survives and is likely to continue to do so.

It would be absurd to deplore without qualification the tendency of bad words to drive out good ones. This tendency is one of the ways in which the language grows and becomes more responsive to the writer's and the speaker's needs. Dip into the dictionary casually and you will find word after word—probably they add up to a majority—in which the present-day meaning is a derived or secondary one rather than a rigid rendering of the root of the word. *Decide* today does not mean to cut off; *down* does not mean off the hill; *mass* does not mean a barley cake or a kneading; *piano* does not mean something soft and smooth; *secret* does not mean something put apart. Words, like trees, grow from their roots.

What may well be deplored is the displacement of good words by bad ones to no purpose, or to the detriment of the good ones. It is in this field that the operation of Bernstein's Second Law should be resisted. It is in this field that the language can lose precision and vitality.

BESIDE, BESIDES

Beside means at the side of; *besides* means in addition to or other than. Thus, in the following sentence the usage is incorrect: "Beside Harriman, Hogan, and Crotty, the candidates chosen by the convention were. . . ." In the following sentence both words are used correctly: "Besides John, only James stood beside me in my trouble."

BETTERMENT

Although it is synonymous with *improvement, betterment* is not used interchangeably with that word. It is generally confined to social welfare work, in which it suggests an easing of the lot of unfortunates. At least you would not speak of a "betterment of the student's grades," nor of the "betterment of a piece of real estate."

BETWEEN, AMONG

If Miss Thistlebottom taught you in elementary school that *between* applies to two things and *among* to more than two, she probably knew what she was doing: She was making things easy for herself. It is simpler to lay down a rule than to try to stimulate discriminating thinking, particularly in a school class that ranges from blockheads to eggheads.

Among, to be sure, applies to more than two things, but the relationship it expresses is usually a rather loose one. When three or more things are brought into a relationship severally and reciprocally, *between* is proper. In the following passage *between* would be better than *among:* "Apart from discussions among Washington, Paris, and London on the prospective conference. . . ." The idea of two is inherent etymologically in the word *between,* but so is it inherent in the discussions here referred to: The meetings were being held by Washington and Paris, by Paris and London, by London and Washington. Similarly, to speak of a treaty *between* nine powers would be completely proper and exact. When the relationship is looser, *among* is the proper word: "War reparations were distributed among the nine victorious powers."

BETWEEN AND FROM

A single noun following *between* is plural: "The house lies between 104th and 105th Streets"; "Pupils mature rapidly between the sixth and eighth grades." A single noun following *from* is singular: "The tract runs from 104th to 105th Street" (i.e., from one street to another street); "John was promoted from the seventh to the eighth grade."

BETWEEN EACH (EVERY)

"His nose ran and he sneezed between nearly every shot during the first round of golf he ever played in Scotland." This construction is defended by a minority of grammarians on the ground that there is here a "natural ellipsis"; in full the phrase would be "between nearly every shot and the next one." It is possible to cite writers of standing who have used the construction. Nevertheless, logic and a feeling for orderliness rebel against it, and they have a right to be heard in an age that tends to turn its back on precision. The careful writer will make it "between nearly every shot and the next" or, better still, "after nearly every shot."

BETWEEN YOU AND I

Just as one swallow doesn't make a drunkard, so an isolated instance or so of bad grammar culled from even the most gifted writers does not constitute a valid authentication for that particular misusage. Thus, it is idle to pretend that *between you and I* must be a legitimate construction because Shakespeare used it in *The Merchant of Venice,* or because it can be found elsewhere, lonely and loose. The greatest writer may have committed a grammatical offense because he was preoccupied, or because he was negligent, or because he had in mind a reason that is obscure to his readers now, or merely because he had a bellyache.

Most of those who say or write *between you and I,* Shakespeare excepted, are guilty of OVERREFINEMENT. They have been corrected when they used "It is me" or "You and me ought to get together," and have become gun-shy about the word "me." In addition they are confused because the word "you" is the same in the objective case as it is in the nominative; therefore, although they would not dream of saying or writing *between him and they* or *between her and we* or *between us and she,* the phrase *between you and I* does not sound bad to them. But bad it is, and indefensible grammatically. *Between* is a preposition and it is followed by the objective case: *me.* To say *between you and I* is a needless, pointless, and ignorant exception to a good rule.

BI-

Bimonthly means every two months, and nothing else. *Biweekly* means every two weeks, and sometimes something else: twice a week. *Biannual* means twice a year. *Biennial* means every two years. Without question, man's communication with his fellow man would be improved if *semi-* were used to mean half and *bi-* were reserved to mean two.

BIAS

A *bias* is a mental or emotional state that predisposes one for or against something. It is misused in this headline: "Meany Tells Group Here That Hill 'Smears' Labor in Saying Unions Practice Bias." What was meant, of course, was *discrimination.* Since that is a long word and *bias* a short one, there is a journalistic tendency to abuse the short word—not only for brevity in

74

headlines but also as a variation to avoid repetition. (*See* MONO-LOGOPHOBIA.) Perhaps if we all live long enough, someone will coin a reasonably short word for headline writers—something like *segrex*, which is the Latin root of segregation.

Bias, by the way, may be for or against; in this respect it differs from *prejudice*, which is a preconceived attitude that is almost always against. *Bigotry*, a synonymous word, is a stubborn, intolerant adherence to one's own belief.

BID

In addition to meaning proclaim, command, offer, or make a bid (as in, "to bid for votes"), the word *bid* has also reassumed an older meaning—to ask pressingly—as in the headline "President Bids Both Parties Aid in His Farm Plan." Obviously, it is the headline writers, with their love for and need for the short word, who have reinstated this meaning.

In most uses the past tense is *bade* and the participle *bidden*, but when the meaning is to offer as a price, the past tense and participle are both *bid*. In the trite phrase *bid fair*, the past tense is *bade*, so that this sentence is incorrect: "This little man Dancer bid fair to be a little dandy."

BID IN

Many a writer who would not dream of shaking some stuff onto his apple pie before determining whether it was talcum powder or powdered sugar will be just that undiscriminating in picking up and using a phrase. "The Lincoln letter was bid in at $1,100 by the Carnegie Book Shop of New York"; undoubtedly, the writer heard the phrase once and thought it had a fine technical sound. Alas for him, it has a specialized meaning: to top the highest bid of a bona fide customer in the interest of the owner of the item. It does not mean merely to acquire through a bid. That talcum powder doesn't taste very good.

BIGOTRY
See BIAS.

75

BISECT

Bisect means to cut in two. Incorrect: ". . . the modernization of the four roads bisecting the big park." Four roads would not cut the park in two; make it *intersecting*. As an obvious corollary, don't say "bisect in two."

BLAME ON

Blame on always has been and remains a casualism, no matter how many educated people have used it carelessly. A distinguished newspaper writes editorially: "Professing profound respect for the United Nations . . . he expressed regret that it has not yet achieved all its purposes, and blamed this not on the Soviet abuse of the veto, which he defended, but on the majority powers." What is here being *blamed*—i.e., censured, accused, reproved—is not "this" but "the majority powers." Just as you cannot *censure on*, so you cannot *blame on*. The remedy is to find substitutes—forms of *attribute to* or *lay to*—or to change the construction, making it *blame for* or *put the blame on.*

BLASÉ

Takes preposition *about.*

BLATANT, FLAGRANT

The words overlap a little in that they both suggest attention-calling. In *blatant*, however, the emphasis is on noise: it means brawling, clamorous, noisy, loudly obtrusive. *Flagrant*, from a Latin root meaning to burn, denotes flaming into attention, glaringly wicked, notorious. In short, *blatant* means obnoxiously loud, and *flagrant* means openly evil or scandalous. It would not be precise in a medical article to speak of "this blatant misdiagnosis"; *flagrant* would be the word to use here. It is proper, however, to speak of the turbulence and confusion in a Parliament caused by "blatant electioneering on all sides."

BLAZON

It means to display prominently; it does not mean to mark

out by chipping pieces of bark off trees, as the writer of the following sentence thought: "New York City has blazoned a trail in developing forward-thinking programs for the mentally retarded." The word wanted here, of course, is *blazed*.

BLEND
Takes preposition *with*.

BLEND WORDS
See CENTAUR WORDS.

BLOC
The cause of quick clarity is advanced by using this spelling rather than *block* to refer to a grouping of organizations or members thereof. Not only has the meaning of the word *bloc* a European origin, to which the French spelling is appropriate, but in addition *block* has enough burdens to carry without its having this additional one imposed on it.

BOAST
Takes preposition *of* or *about*.

BOAT
Strictly speaking, a *boat* is a small vessel, restricted in range and usually propelled by oars or sails or an outboard motor. Strictly speaking, then, you would not write (though you might say) that you were "going to Europe by boat," nor, in referring to a liner, would you say, "The boat was making eighteen knots."

Large or seagoing craft are *ships* or *vessels*. *Boat* does appear, however, in some compounds that do not refer to very small craft: *pilot boat, ferryboat, PT boat, gunboat*.

BOOST
In its nontechnical senses, *boost* should be one of the forget-'em words, along with *hike*. "The United Steelworkers executive board is giving its top officers a healthy pay boost." Pure slang.

(So, by the way, is *healthy* used in this way. And thus does a writer, infected by one germ, fall prey to others.) "The rate hikes provided these increases. . . ." A *hike* is a tramp and a tramp is a bum and bum is the word for *hike*.

See also RAISE, RISE.

BORDER
Takes preposition *on* or *upon*.

BOSS
Although it has been in the language for more than a century, *boss* is still labeled by most dictionaries as "colloq." or slang. Its most nearly standard uses are in the senses of a political leader or of a workman's superior. In other senses it is a casualism that should be used with caution in reputable writing. To speak, for example, of a "real estate boss" or an "atomic physicist's boss" is flatly slangy.

BOTH
1. BOTH . . . AS WELL AS. The *as well* part of the phrase *as well as* means virtually the same thing as *both*. An example of redundant usage: "It is feared such an impression might produce ill will both in the United States as well as in Formosa and Seoul." Either delete *both* or change *as well as* to *and*.

2. OTHER REDUNDANCIES WITH "BOTH." In effect, *both* means the two together, and it is sometimes used redundantly when the two-together idea appears elsewhere in the sentence. This is a defect in style. In the sentence, "Both puppies look alike," the *both* should be replaced by *the* or *the two*. In the sentence, "The two are good friends and both worked together at the New York Stock Exchange," the *both* should be replaced by *they*. A more subtle illustration of the same defect occurs in this sentence: "Both Christmas and Hanukkah came on the same day." Either delete *both* or change "the same day" to "December 25."

3. BOTH . . . AND. This pair follows the law of CORRELATIVE

CONJUNCTIONS. Whatever appears after the first member of the team must be exactly paralleled grammatically by what appears after the second member—a noun in the first position must be matched by a noun in the second position, a verb must be matched by a verb, a prepositional phrase must be matched by a prepositional phrase. Two sentences will illustrate the common errors in the use of *both . . . and*.

First: "He will advise the Soviet Premier of his intention to report everything said both to the President and the Secretary." Here the *both* is followed by a prepositional phrase, but the *and* is followed by a noun. This may be corrected in one of two ways: make it either "to both the President and the Secretary" (a noun now follows *both* and another noun follows *and*) or "both to the President and to the Secretary" (prepositional phrases now follow *both* and *and*).

Second, and more serious because the misplacement is worse: "Even the men in the class had to admit that both from the viewpoint of economics and history, the age-old restrictions are disappearing." In this illustration the lack of parallelism almost distorts the meaning, or at least impedes its quick comprehension. Make it either "of both economics and history" or "both of economics and of history."

In these examples, as in so many others, correct grammar produces greater clarity and certainly greater orderliness.

BRAND

Originally a mark burned into a keg or an animal to identify the maker or owner, *brand* is now a commercial term signifying the product of a particular manufacturer, or the kind or quality of a product. It has been extended—at first the extension was semihumorous—to denote a sort or class of anything, as in "Smith's brand of Republicanism." But there is no need for this kind of extension; many other good words say the same thing.

BREAK

Takes preposition *with* or *from*.

BREAKDOWN

Breakdown, used in the sense of *itemization,* is, like *crash program* or *task force,* a FAD WORD. There is nothing wrong with it any more than there is with your favorite armchair—except the tendency, as with the chair, to overuse it so that it begins to show signs of wear. The reason for its fad lies, no doubt, in its faint aura of science—the science of statistics—or its association with the exalted institution of commerce. It means merely a separation into component parts. For this meaning and variations of it several words are available: *analysis, classification, examination,* and others.

Here is an example of the vogue use: "Labor organizations were advised today that their annual financial reports must carry a breakdown of individual expenses of officers and employees." All that is meant in this context is a *listing* or *itemization.* But *breakdown* seems to sound more impressive—or does it? *See* IN-SIDE TALK.

BREAKTHROUGH

Another FAD WORD, this one is beloved of military men and scientists, and hence also of those who wish to sound like them. *See* INSIDE TALK.

BRING

The verb *to bring,* when it denotes physical movement at all, denotes it in the direction of the speaker or writer. The sentence, "The Communists were reported to have brought troops into Tibet," would be proper news writing in *The Early Tibet* (that's the bulldog edition), but would be improper in an article written in New York for *The Times.* The movement opposite to *bring* is *take,* but that verb would not do in the sentence cited. It would have to be *moved* or *sent* or *dispatched.*

When no movement is implied, *bring* may properly be used in the sense of to produce, as a result. It is so used in this sentence: "The plan for changes in Federal grants to states for the needy would bring improved benefits to several large categories."

BRING TO A HEAD

When you stop to think of it, which is what some writers never do when a cliché presents itself, this phrase is rather repulsive: To bring to a head means to suppurate, or to cause pus to form. Substitutes are not plentiful, but there are a few: *to bring to a climax, to bring to a boil* (this is a different kind of boil), *to crystallize, to reach a crisis, to precipitate*.

BRING TO AN END

A wasteful locution. *End* by itself suffices. Variations on this one are *come to an end* and *put an end to*.

BROADCASTED

If you think you have correctly forecasted the immediate future of English and have casted your lot with the permissivists, you may be receptive to *broadcasted*, at least in radio usage, as are some dictionaries. The rest of us, however, will decide that no matter how desirable it may be to convert all irregular verbs into regular ones, this cannot be done by ukase, nor can it be accomplished overnight. We shall continue to use *broadcast* as the past tense and the participle, feeling that there is no reason for *broadcasted* other than one of analogy or consistency or logic, which the permissivists themselves so often scorn. Nor is this position inconsistent with our position on FLIED, the baseball term, which has a real reason for being. The fact—the inescapable fact—is that there are some irregular verbs.

BULK

There are those who would forbid the use of *bulk* to mean the major part, and restrict it to meanings involving volume or mass. However, Hallam spoke of "the bulk of the nation," and Hamilton of "the great bulk of the citizens of America," and Addison of "the bulk of a people." Isolated uses or misuses of a word by even the greatest of writers are not necessarily significant except to prove a precedent, but they may help to reinforce a sound reason. The reason in this instance is that *majority*—the alternative to *bulk*—seems to suggest counted numbers rather than the broad generalization conveyed by *bulk*.

BULLET

Two ballistic misses are contained in these two sentences: "The fifteen-year-old boys are accused of having stolen 3,000 rounds of small-caliber bullets . . ."; "Young Buchanan told the police he had wounded himself when he hit a bullet with a rock." First, a *round* is a unit of ammunition; therefore it would be better to write, "3,000 rounds of small-caliber ammunition." Second, a *bullet* is merely the lead missile at the end of the *cartridge*; therefore the boys stole *cartridges*, not *bullets*, and Buchanan could not have wounded himself by hitting merely a *bullet* because there is nothing explosive about a *bullet*.

BUREAUCRAT

Despite the efforts of some political scientists to clothe it in neutrality, the word *bureaucrat* is—in the English-speaking world, at least—a term of derogation. Most dictionaries are content to describe a *bureaucrat* as one who insists on following inflexible routines. According to *The American College Dictionary*, he does this "without exercising intelligent judgment." That is the closest any of the dictionaries comes to catching the pejorative overtones of a word that is almost always used pejoratively. A *bureaucrat* is all the things the dictionaries say he is, but in addition he is a disagreeable fellow, often one who narrowly tries to arrogate power to himself. Thus, the term is not neutral; it is a loaded word. And so is *bureaucracy*.

BURGEON

It is a common misconception to think of *burgeon* as if it meant to expand or mushroom. What it means is to bud or sprout. One cannot always determine whether the word is being misused because the meanings often overlap, but there is no doubt that the following is a misuse: "The four million people of Hong Kong are still getting water only eight hours a day because of the burgeoning population." The population of Hong

Kong is not budding; it has been growing for a long, long time.

BURGLARIZE

Unlike many -IZE words, this one fills a real need—a need that can otherwise be taken care of only by a cumbersome phrase (rob by burglars, break into and loot, etc.). Therefore, although it is labeled "colloq." by some dictionaries, it may be used without qualm, and indeed with confidence that the "colloq." will vanish in time.

BURGLARY

Burglary is a specialized kind of robbery, the essence of which is a breaking into and entering of a place with the intent to commit a felony. No breaking, no *burglary*; it is then just plain robbery. *See* ROBBER, THIEF, BURGLAR.

BUSINESS

"Mr. Danaher has been in the law business in Washington and Hartford. . . ." A profession should not be called a *business*. Would you say that your family doctor was in the medical *business*? *See also* OCCUPATIONS.

BUT: CONJUNCTION OR PREPOSITION?

The question posed in this article is illustrated by the alternative sentences. "Everyone but I received a gift" and "Everyone but me received a gift." In the first sentence *but* is used conjunctively and the "I" is the subject of an elliptical clause, which would perhaps read "but I did not." In the second sentence the *but* is used prepositionally, as the equivalent of *except,* which is always a preposition. The question is, Which is "right"?

One answer is that neither is wrong. But let us explore further. Webster says: "In modern English the uses of *but* followed by nouns and pronouns are regarded by most writers as conjunctive, although use as a preposition before pronouns is still prevalent in the spoken language, especially when the pronoun is in the final position." Fowler says: "It is true that the conjunctional use has prevailed owing partly to the mistaken notion that No-one knows it b. me is the same sort of blunder as It is me; but it has prevailed, in literary use, & it is in itself legitimate; it would therefore be well for it to be universally accepted."

We have here a confident statement by Webster and a sighing wish by Fowler. Nevertheless, the fact seems to be that throughout the annals of writing, including the present, there has been nothing but vacillation. Even one of the most famous of the *but* quotations has not been free of the indecisiveness. Both *The Oxford Dictionary of Quotations* and *Bartlett's Familiar Quotations* present the famous line as follows: "The boy stood on the burning deck, whence all but he had fled. . . ." But Bartlett carries this footnote: "The first American edition of Mrs. Hemans's *Poems* (1826) gave this line 'whence all but him had fled.' English editions and subsequent American editions seem evenly divided between 'but him' and 'but he.' The last edition published while Mrs. Hemans was still living and presumably approved the contents (Blackwood, Edinburgh, 1829, P. 243) gives 'but he.' "

In the face of this confusion, what guides can be given to the writer? Two suggest themselves. The first is endorsed by most authorities; the second is offered as a recommendation that has reason and some weight of usage behind it.

1. When the pronoun ends the sentence, put it in the objective case, considering *but* to be a preposition. For example: "Everyone received a gift but me"; "Nobody was in sight but him." This usage is completely defensible grammatically. In addition it has a feeling of rightness about it since, except for sentences containing copulas ("It was she") and inverted constructions ("Where is he?"), the final noun in a sentence is normally in the objective case.

2. When the pronoun appears elsewhere in the sentence, it is grammatically attracted to the noun to which it is linked by the *but*, and may thus be put in the same case as that noun. For example: "No one [nominative] but I [nominative] had the combination to the safe"; "To no one [objective] but me [objective]

did he give the combination to the safe." And, of course: ". . . whence all [nominative] but he [nominative] had fled."

BUT, MEANING ONLY

Curme tells us: "In older English the negative *ne* often stood before the principal verb: 'He *nis* (= *ne is*) but a child.' By the later omission of *ne*, as in 'He is *but* a child,' the old conjunction *but* has acquired the meaning of *nothing but*, and is now often felt as an adverb with the force of *only* and thus can now as an adverb be used where it was once not used in older English. . . ." It is thus completely correct to write, "The Soviet Government can but welcome such a statement." What is not correct is to precede the *but* with a negative and thus in effect produce a double negative, as in "It won't cost but a few dollars." Make it "It will cost but a few dollars" or "It won't cost more than a few dollars."

BUT, MEANING OTHER THAN, ETC.

Some grammarians have been critical of the use of *but* as it appears in this sentence: "Dr. Adenauer will not be at the summit conference, a fact that cannot help but wound his pride." They contend that it is "crude and unidiomatic English" and argue for making it ". . . cannot help wounding his pride." Whether or not the *but* construction was "crude and unidiomatic" at one time, it is usual and acceptable today. A point to notice, however, is that this use of *but* is inherently negative, so that to follow it with another negative is to pervert the meaning, as in "Who knows but that five years from now the Soviet bloc may not collapse?" Delete the "not."

BUT HOWEVER

A redundancy that verges on illiteracy. "It's clear today, but however it may rain tomorrow." Choose one.

BUT THAT

See AND WHICH.

BUT WHAT

But what for *but that* is a casualism that is disapproved in good writing. "He said that hardly a day goes by but what [make it *but that*] a similar request is not made of some local prosecutor."

BUT WHICH, BUT WHO

See AND WHICH.

BY MEANS OF

A wasteful locution. Usually *by* is sufficient.

BY NATURE

Often a wasteful locution. "She is graceful by nature" means "She is graceful."

C

CABLEGRAM

" 'For God's sake, keep the Senator on the ticket,' said a cablegram signed by the master and officers of the American ship *Sea Gallant* off the Japanese coast." A *cablegram* is a message that travels by cable. It is most unlikely that the *Sea Gallant* dragged a cable all the way across the Pacific; she used her radio, and sent a wireless message.

CALCULATE

Used properly, *calculate* means to determine by computation ("The pilot calculated that the plane would reach Los Angeles by 6 P.M.") or to prepare a deliberate plan ("His strategy was calculated to trap his opponent's rook"). The word is misused, however, when its intended meaning is to think or suppose, as in, "I calculate we will have spaghetti for dinner." *See also* FIGURE *and* RECKON.

Calculate takes the preposition *on*.

CALLIGRAPHY

Used properly, *calligraphy* does not mean merely handwriting. The first part of the word comes from the Greek, meaning beauty, and the whole word means beautiful handwriting. Therefore, *poor calligraphy* is self-contradictory and *beautiful calligraphy* is redundant.

CALLUS, CALLOUS

The noun is *callus* ("He had a callus on his foot"); the adjective is *callous* ("They showed a callous disregard for law").

CAN, MAY

Whatever the interchangeability of these words in spoken or informal English, the writer who is attentive to the proprieties will preserve the traditional distinction: *can* for ability or power to do something, *may* for permission to do it.

CANNOT

The one-word form is preferred unless the writer desires to put special emphasis on the *not*. An example of such emphasis is contained in the following sentence: "This company can tolerate human mistakes; it can not tolerate sabotage." Such instances, however, are not common. Uncommon, too, is this misuse: "When a painter cannot only exhibit, but also win a prize for what is no more than a piece of unrelieved black canvas, it is time to ask, 'Who's loony now?'" The error here arises from failure to notice that the auxiliary verb, which attaches to both "exhibit" and "win," is *can*, not *cannot*. The *not* is linked to "only."

CANNOT HELP BUT

See BUT, MEANING OTHER THAN, ETC.

CANTILEVERED VERBS

A cantilever is a projecting beam or other building element supported at only one end. To the layman who looks, for instance, at a theater balcony that has no supporting pillars, the cantilever is sometimes a source of wonderment, perhaps even of uneasiness: What in the name of Newton holds it up? In present-day English usage there are some verbs that seem to require support at both ends but get it at only one, and likewise create a feeling of uneasiness. They range from those that are readily acceptable, like *communicate*—"The function of language is to communicate"—to others that are used casually and perhaps semihumorously, like *cope*—"She simply couldn't cope."

The class includes a few transitive verbs for which intransitive meanings have been invented because they are necessary; for example, *publish* used in this sense: "Nine newspapers did not publish during the strike." It also includes some verbs that normally would be followed by a reflexive pronoun—and probably still should be—as in this sentence: "It has taken him some

88

time to adapt [himself], in view of his handicap, to his surroundings in New York."

Eugene O'Neill no doubt had much to do with the present-day proliferation of cantilevered verbs; it was he who introduced one to a wide audience in 1922 when he had the character Yank in *The Hairy Ape* shout repeatedly that people thought he didn't *belong*—without any supporting pillar in the form of a prepositional complement. Psychoanalysis, of course, uses cantilevered verbs as a kind of shorthand; analysts will say that a patient *identifies* or *relates* or does not *adjust*. Laymen tend to pick up this kind of jargon (*See* INSIDE TALK) and, whether useful or not, it becomes popular. It can be safely predicted that many of the cantilevered verbs that originate in psychoanalysis will become so dog-eared at the hands of the intellectuals and pseudointellectuals that they will be discarded for popular use, just as no intellectual would be caught using "inferiority complex" these days. But others will no doubt remain to enrich the language. Whether the tendency to coin cantilevered verbs will persist, one knoweth not.

CAN'T SEEM

From the meanings of the words, the phrase *can't seem* is obviously illogical, as in the sentence "The Governor can't seem to make up his mind." Yet Evans finds it acceptable as an Americanism and Webster finds it acceptable with no qualification at all. Illogical or no, it is clearly idiomatic and in reputable use.

CAPABLE

Takes preposition *of*.

CAPACITY

See ABILITY, CAPACITY. *Capacity* takes preposition *for* (ability) or *of* (volume).

CAPITALIZATION

What follows is by no means an exhaustive compilation of rules for capitalization, but rather a selected list of items in this category that might on occasion puzzle a writer. There is no need, for example, to set forth so obvious a rule as the one that requires a capital at the beginning of a sentence or the one that calls for a capital at the start of each line of poetry (unless the poet has indulged an eccentricity). In some other instances it would be futile to try to provide rules because book, magazine, and newspaper publishers establish their own house style rules and insist on them.

1. *Proper nouns.* Every proper noun—which means the name of a particular person, place, or thing—is capitalized. Normally this would not be a point that would bother a writer, but an element of confusion was introduced with the appearance of Webster III. For some obscure, almost masochistic, reason that dictionary bound itself into a no-capital straitjacket. It capitalizes no word (except God), but tells us that such terms as "january," "new york," and "saint andrew" are *usu cap. Usu cap?* They are *alw cap.*

Proper nouns or adjectives that are applied to common things often tend to lose the capital: *arabic numbers, boycott, diesel engine, klieg lights, manila envelope, paris green, venetian blind, watt.*

2. *Statement after a colon.* If the statement following a colon is a complete one, it begins with a capital. Sometimes for emphasis an incomplete statement begins with a capital, too, as in, "The answer: No."

3. *Titles.* A title preceding a name is always capitalized. (*But see* COINED TITLES.) A title following the name of a governmental official or an ecclesiastical dignitary is also capitalized, but there is no universal rule about other titles following a name: Most publications prefer "John Jones, president of the Stabbem Switchblade Knife Co.," but some capitalize "President" in such an instance.

4. *Headings, titles of books, etc.* In captions of this kind the general practice is to capitalize nouns, pronouns, and verbs and all other words of four or more letters. Also capitalized are *No, Nor, Not, Off, Out, So, Up,* etc. Words of fewer than four letters are capitalized if they are part of a verb phrase, as in,

"Dropped In," "Held Up," "Went Along." The verb of an infinitive phrase is capitalized, as in, "to Be," "to Have." In compound adjectives both words are capitalized: "Two-Headed," "Light-Fingered." But compounds containing a prefix and fractions are set thus: "Re-enter," "Two-fifths."

5. *Names of the Deity.* Such appellations are capitalized, and so are the appropriate personal pronouns *He, Him,* and *His,* but not usually the relative pronouns *who, whom,* and *whose.*

6. *Direct questions.* Whether enclosed in quotation marks or not, a direct question begins with a capital: "The visitor wanted to know, 'Where is the action?' " "Through the centuries philosophers have been asking, What is man?"

7. *Scientific terms.* Names of species are generally set in lower case, but the names of all divisions higher than species are capitalized: "Falco columbarius," "Blatella germanica."

CAREEN, CAREER

The two words are sometimes confused. *Careen* (rhymes with lean) means to tilt or heel over: "The yacht careened sharply at the first buoy." *Career* means to move at high speed: "Out of control, the car careered into a group of children."

CAREFUL, CARELESS

Takes preposition *with* (an object); *of* (value); *about* (small things).

CARTRIDGE

See BULLET.

CASE

The word is not so much misused as overused or used unnecessarily. "In some cases refugees went without food for days" translates more tersely into, "Some refugees went without food for days." *Case* often forms the nucleus of a foggy phrase, which can either be dropped or replaced by something more specific. Examples: "In the case of the Democrats these factors may align a number with Republicans in opposition to some Administration proposals"; make it, "These factors may align a number of Democrats, etc." "These places probably now constitute a minority of all the legislative districts in the state rather than a majority, as was the case not too many years ago"; make it, "as was the fact" or "as was true." When a writer is tempted to use a phrase containing *case*, he would do well to consider (a) whether the phrase is necessary at all, and (b) if it is, whether a more exact word can be substituted for *case*.

CASUALISMS

A certain amount of confusion, almost all of it unnecessary, has attached itself to the word *colloquial*. It means, dictionaries agree, of the nature of or pertaining to conversation, and a *colloquialism*, according to Webster III, is "an expression considered more appropriate to familiar conversation than to formal speech or formal writing. . . ." The confusion arises from the assumption by some who consult dictionaries that colloquial language is "incorrect" language. The truth is that it may or may not be "incorrect."

In any event, Webster III decided to abandon the label "colloquial" for the informal expressions of the spoken language, and thus abandoned something that has been a fixture of lexicography for generations. The editor in chief, Dr. Philip B. Gove, lists as one of the features of the dictionary "the recognition (by not using at all the status label *colloquial*) that it is impossible to know whether a word out of context is colloquial or not." To determine how specious this reason is, all one need do is think of some words that are normally tagged "colloquial" and then try to imagine a context that would make them anything but colloquial. What context could conceivably modify the colloquialism of *stuck-up, noggin, done in, yeah, a dog's age, falsies, gab, the likes of, scads, on the bum,* or *snoot?* And there are easily hundreds more.

It is perhaps significant that Prof. Sumner Ives of Syracuse University, in a review he was commissioned by the G. & C. Merriam Company to write for their new Webster dictionary, omits any mention of this reason. Instead, although he was not a member of the editorial board, he undertakes to offer a reason of his own: ". . . a great many persons have taken the label 'colloquial' to indicate some departure from the highest standards, contrary to the intention of the editors who affixed this label. Hence *Webster's Third New International* does not use this label." Parenthetically, an interesting question arises here. If "a great many persons" think *colloquial* indicates a departure from the highest standards, why doesn't the new dictionary—which elsewhere is so solicitous about the misconceptions of people—include this one among the definitions of the word? After all, "a great many persons" think *flaunt* means *flout*, and the dictionary has seen fit to legitimize their error.

Another apologist for the dictionary, however, does not seem to hold with the notion of making concessions to those who cannot understand plain words when they read them, or who do not take the trouble to read them. Speaking of usage labels in an article in *The Union College Symposium*, Dr. Patrick E. Kilburn writes: "The Third Edition contains a comprehensive set of 'Explanatory Notes' defining the principles upon which the dictionary is compiled: what is to be done if many people are dunderheaded enough to presume that they are able to use so sophisticated a system as an unabridged dictionary without knowing what the operating rules are? If I drink wood alcohol in spite of the manufacturer's plainly affixed label that 'serious gastric disturbances will ensue if taken internally,' who is to blame?" Parenthetically again, when we encounter colloquialisms in the new dictionary we have wood alcohol with no label at all.

If we go along with Dr. Kilburn's thesis that users of the dictionary have an obligation to know the operating rules—and that is not unreasonable—then Webster III might well have retained the label "colloquial," along with the sentence that appeared with the definition of the word in Webster II: "Colloquial speech may be as correct as formal speech." That would take care of Professor Ives's reason for dropping the label. It would not take care of Dr. Gove's, but Professor Ives has already taken care of Dr. Gove's reason by ignoring it (which is just about the kindest way to treat it). But let us go on to other matters.

The words *colloquial* and *colloquialism* may have outlived their usefulness, for two reasons. The lesser of the two is the one mentioned by Professor Ives: that the words have become subject to misinterpretation. If everyone could be induced to read and accept the fine print—the words just quoted from Webster II—this reason would not count for much. But the fact is that "a great many persons" do not read the fine print, and, further, that a great many of those who do either ignore it or cannot overcome their preconceptions and so continue to misinterpret the words. The second reason is that the expressions now dubbed "colloquial" are not always characteristic of conversation these days. Indeed, many colloquialisms are hardly ever uttered; they usually appear only in writing: such words as *hike* (increase), *tycoon, sheepskin, sleuth,* and *straphanger,* and such sports writers' terms as *hickory* (bat), *squared circle, four-bagger,* and *circuit blast.* More important, over the last generation or so writing has become more informal than it ever was before. The area of highly formal writing has shrunk considerably; it is now confined to such things as state papers, articles in learned publications, commencement addresses (and by no means all of those), legal documents, court decisions, and prefaces to dictionaries. Other writing has been quite hospitable to so-called colloquialisms; it has become more informal, more relaxed, more familiar, more casual.

This is not to say that it has become the same thing as spoken language. Written language is bound to command more carefully wrought structure, more precise use of words, more deliberate clarity of thought than the spontaneous outgivings of speech. But writers in recent years have found that they can communicate their thoughts more easily and comprehensibly at the familiar casual level than at the rather alien formal level. Thus, contractions such as *don't, won't,* and *can't,* usually classed as "colloquial," often appear in good writing along with such colloquialisms as *boss, brainwash, boom and bust, face the music, freeze* (prices), and *skulduggery.* In short, many expressions previously thought of as characteristic of conversation—i.e., colloquial—now normally appear in writing. The word *colloquial* is therefore too restrictive and perhaps even misleading. A better word would be *informal,* but that has the disadvantage of seeming to pit these expressions against others that are *formal.* Perhaps the best word to apply, then, is *casual,* in the sense of relaxed, easy, familiar. And an expression that is casual may be termed a *casualism.* Those, at any rate, are the terms employed in this book.

And now for the fine print. The designation *casualism* does not imply that the expression is necessarily unsuitable for serious writing. It is not a red light; it is an orange light. There are, of course, gradations of casualisms: *falsies* is low and unacceptable in most contexts. In most places where the term casualism has been used, an effort has been made to indicate whether the light is red or orange.

CATEGORY

Although this word has come to be almost synonymous with any *division* or *class,* the careful writer will reserve it for matters concerned with science or philosophy. It means a division in a scheme of classification. A particularly loose usage is illustrated by this passage: "The program's work has been less effective—partly, no doubt, because the best American playwrights . . . have been too expensive. I suspect that conditions in this category will improve soon." Whether *category* in that sentence applies (a) to the absence of American playwrights from the program's work or (b) to their costliness or (c) to the playwrights themselves, only the author of the passage can say. But no one of the three possibilities would constitute a *category* in any precise sense.

CAUSE

To write, "The medical examiner said the cause of death was suicide," is not to make an error in grammar but to fail to think clearly. "Suicide" was the nature of the death, or the verdict in the case; the *cause* of death was poison or a bullet or a knife or something else that proved to be lethal.

95

A different kind of error involving *cause* is to write, "The cause of the fire was due to a short circuit." The *cause* was the short circuit, or the fire was *due to* the short circuit. The example is tautological. *See also* REASON . . . IS BECAUSE *and* DUE TO.

CAUTION

Takes preposition *against*.

CELEBRANT

A *celebrant* is one who participates in a religious rite, and not at all the type who is celebrated in this New Year's Day head-line: "Celebrants Attack Four Patrolmen Here." A fellow who tosses down a shot of Scotch, tosses caution to the winds, and tosses his hat into the air is a *celebrator*.

CELEBRATED

See FAMED.

CENTAUR WORDS

From the earliest times the workshop of language has echoed to the sounds of saws and hammers fabricating new words. A common method of manufacture has been to take a root or root word—say, happy—and nail a suffix to it (happi*ness*) or nail a prefix to it (*un*happy) or join all three elements (*un*happi*ness*).

But at the same time, outside the workshop in the green linguistic pasture (which is here brought into being to avoid mixing the metaphor), a process of crossbreeding has been accomplished occasionally. Let us suppose a new atmospheric condition arises in cities situated in valleys whereby a combination of smoke and fog blots out the sun. People find it troublesome to keep saying, "Man, that was some smoke and fog we had today," and so some ingenious amateur linguist coins the word *smog* and everybody is relatively happy groping about in the overcast. Philologists term the process here employed "crossbreeding," "blending," or "contamination," and the words produced by the process they term "blends," "blend words," or "portmanteau words" (this last designation comes from a line in Lewis Carroll's

96

Through the Looking Glass: "You see it's like a portmanteau
. . . there are two meanings packed up into one word").

Well, not many youngsters these days know what a portmanteau is. Moreover, a characteristic of these coined words is
that they usually combine the front end of one animal with the
rear end of another—like a centaur, the mythological beast that
combined the head, arms, and trunk of a man with the body and
legs of a horse. A more descriptive term for the coinages, therefore, might be *centaur words*, and since there are so many designations in the field already, one more cannot hurt.

Centaur words come into being for a variety of purposes.
They may arise from a felt need to bracket two existing things
(*splutter*, apparently from splash and sputter). They may be designed to label a new condition, as in *smog*. They may be coined
to name a new artifact (*transistor*, from transfer and resistor).
They may be devised to label a new field of knowledge or endeavor (*genecology*, from genetics and ecology). They may be
used to reduce a mouthful to a morsel (*neosone*, for neomycin
and cortisone). They may be made up as names of new industrial
organizations (*Digitronics*, from digital and electronics). They
may spring into being as short nicknames for cumbersome titles
(*BuDocks* for the Navy's Bureau of Yards and Docks). They may
be fabricated as the trademarked names of products (*Dicta-
phone, Pantogs, Permafit, Supp-hose*). They may be produced as
minor conceits of periodicals or columnists (*Time* magazine's
cinemorsel, Winchell's *infanticipating*). Or they may be tossed
off ad hoc just for the hell of it (from *Time*: "A darkly handsome
young Italian . . . falls suddenly, Mediterribly in love with the
blonde beauty, and the girl falls instantly, Americandidly in love
with him"). Children not infrequently come out with these coinages, sometimes inadvertently and sometimes intentionally. Little
Jonathan, four years old, rushed to the window at the sound of
fire apparatus and exclaimed, "Hey, Mom! Look at the siren-
gines!"

From the days of the *gerrymander* in the early nineteenth
century, centaur words have proliferated in America, more so
perhaps than anywhere else. The war-born fondness for the short-

cutting and telescoping of words has been greatly accelerated by the scientific explosion since World War II. Without the device of blending it would hardly have been possible to provide an adequate, usable vocabulary for the many new things and thoughts that have come into being in that period. As a force in the growth and adaptation of the English language, centaur words have been the subject of entirely too little attention. Albert H. Marckwardt, in *American English,* is one of the few scholars who have recognized their importance. Others tend to treat them as mere semihumorous tricks. Many centaur words are, of course, just that. Winchell's *apartache, Time*'s stumbling *cinemactress,* and Clare Boothe Luce's *globaloney* do not, to be sure, show signs of immortality. On the other hand, *guesstimate* and *happenstance,* though semihumorous, do shows signs of survival as informal words because they are useful. So does *brunch,* despite its archness and despite its slangy flavor. And then, of course, there is *mixaphor* . . . (*See* METAPHORS AND MIXAPHORS.)

CENTER AROUND

"The strikers are at odds over their actual grievances, but these appear to center around the vacation provision of the contract." The verb *center* means to be collected or gathered to a point. Therefore, one may use *center on, center in,* or *center at,* but should not use *center around.* If one has a particular fancy for the word *around,* he should precede it with *revolve, rotate, cluster,* or some similar word.

CEREMONIAL, CEREMONIOUS

Both, of course, have to do with *ceremony,* but *ceremonious* often has the connotation of standing on it. *Ceremonial* applies to things; *ceremonious* applies to persons or things, and when it applies to persons, it usually means pompous, punctilious, overpolite.

CHAIN REACTION

The vogue of this phrase exemplifies how the ignorant or

the half-knowing pounce upon words that have an up-to-the-minute appearance and flog them out of shape. (*See* INSIDE TALK.) The phrase does not mean a great quantity, as the writer of the following sentence seemed to think: "The comedian's un-rehearsed fall set off a chain reaction of thousands of telephone calls to the TV station." *Chain reaction* means a process in which a cause produces an effect that in turn becomes a cause and so on.

CHAIR

Used as a verb, *chair* is a FAD WORD: "The Pakistani delegate chaired the Security Council meeting." It is probably only a step from this kind of usage to saying that a British conductor podi-umed the New York Philharmonic Orchestra or that a visiting pastor pulpited the church, or, when a Nebraska Senator took the floor, that he floored the Senate. Nouns do become verbs, but not overnight; they have to pass tests of necessity and service-ability, and they only win acceptability slowly. *See* NOUNS AS VERBS.

CHAPERON

The dictionaries spell both the noun and the verb without a final "e" (although Webster adds that *chaperone* is often used for a woman *chaperon*). There seems to be no good reason to defy the dictionaries.

CHARACTER

Loosely employed and often unnecessarily employed, *charac-ter* is losing strength by erosion. A single example will illustrate both evils: "The housing is of a shoddy character." First, *charac-ter* is here being used to mean merely kind, sort, nature, or qual-ity, and in this sense it is a casualism. But, second, the word is quite unnecessary; all the writer is trying to say is, "The housing is shoddy." It is not true that *character* should be applied to per-sons rather than things—a painting or a government can have qualities that could be designated by the word. But *character* might well be reserved for distinctive qualities or the sum of them. As the name for an eccentric person, *character* has been in use for almost 200 years, but it is still either slang or casual usage.

CHARACTERISTIC

Takes preposition *of*.

CHARGE

Takes preposition *with*.

CHASTENED

Takes preposition *by* or *with*.

CHIDE

Takes preposition *for*.

CHILDISH, CHILDLIKE

The only concern here is what these words mean when applied to adults. In that context *childish* is usually a derogatory word: "She is interested only in childish pleasures"; "The older he gets the more childish he becomes." On the other hand, *childlike* usually has a favorable connotation: "She has a childlike simplicity"; "He retains a childlike interest in the wonders of nature."

CHINAMAN

No, unless you are referring to a maker or seller of porcelain. The proper word for a native of China is *Chinese*.

CHORD

See CORD, CHORD.

CIRCLE AROUND

Often, but not always, this phrase is redundant, and when it is the *around* should be deleted. In the sentence, "All day thousands circled around the bier," the *around* contributes nothing. However, in the sentence, "Hostile Indians circled around the stockade," the *around* does contribute something: the idea of movement. "Hostile Indians circled the stockade" would leave the reader in doubt about whether the Indians were standing still or moving. *See also* CENTER AROUND.

CIRCUMSTANCES

Authorities agree that *in the circumstances* and *under the circumstances* are both correct, though not interchangeable. *In the circumstances* refers merely to existing conditions, and implies a continuing state of affairs ("There was a great desire for the status conferred by a college degree, and in the circumstances educational institutions were swamped by applicants"). *Under the circumstances* refers to conditions that impel or inhibit action, and implies a transient situation, long or short ("Under the circumstances, I can only submit").

CITE

Follow this word with a noun, not a noun clause. Wrong: "Mr. Thompson cites that New York has some 32,000 middle-income units." You could say "Mr. Thompson cites the fact that . . . ," or you could find a different verb—for example, *observes, notes, points out,* or *says.*

CIVILIAN CLOTHES

A civilian is one who is not in the armed forces, or, by legitimate extension, one who is not in any force—such as the police and the fire department—that is organized and disciplined in somewhat the same manner as the armed forces. The extension should not be stretched so that such groups as a baseball team or a theatrical troupe become noncivilian. Thus, when a baseball game or a play is over, the players or the actors do not change to *civilian clothes;* they change, perhaps, to street clothes.

CLAIM

Used in the sense of assert, the word *claim* is, as Mencken observed, newspaper jargon. Alas, it has found its way into other kinds of writing, too. Wrong: "Mr. Casper claimed that a college degree was a business necessity." The verb *claim* should not be used as a synonym for say, assert, or declare except when there is at issue an assertion of a right, a title, or the like.

CLASSIC, CLASSICAL

It would be well if *classic* were reserved to mean of the topmost class or standard, and *classical* to mean pertaining to the Greeks or Romans or to other well established systems of bygone days. The meanings are sometimes confused, but need not be. It would also be well if sports writers were to think twice before designating home runs, ski jumps, annual games, and long basketball goals as *classic*. The overuse tends to cheapen the word.

CLAUSES USED INDEPENDENTLY AS SENTENCES

A housewife may decide to serve rack of lamb or she may decide to have the butcher cleave it apart so that she can serve it as lamb chops. A similar choice sometimes confronts the writer. He may decide to present a long and complex thought in a single sentence. Or, as with the sentence you are now reading, he may decide to break up the thought and serve part of it separately, beginning the new sentence with a conjunction. Sentences beginning with *and, but,* or *or* are acceptable provided the practice is not overdone. Indeed, nothing that is overdone is ever acceptable, be it language or lamb chops.

Technically, but only technically, a coordinating conjunction should link clauses within the same sentence. The objection to starting a sentence with such a conjunction is, therefore, a technical one, having more to do with punctuation and strict grammatical construction than with meaning or clarity. Those who advance the objection do not boggle at substituting adverbs having the same meaning for the offending conjunctions: *moreover* for *and, nevertheless* for *but, alternatively* for *or*. The objection serves no useful purpose except as a warning against indulging in the practice to such an extent that it appears to be an affectation.

More conspicuous and therefore somewhat more subject to

objection is the construction in which a sentence begins with a relative pronoun that lacks an antecedent in the same sentence. For instance: "Peter De Vries's large and dedicated audience may feel itself somewhat in the role of a spouse gallantly enduring the retelling of a too-familiar joke. Which is not surprising, since. . . ." Many writers make a stylistic practice of this construction to achieve raciness, jocularity, or a colloquial flavor. But a writer of taste will not indulge in the practice very often, lest it lose its effect through commonness.

CLEAR

Takes preposition *of*.

CLICHÉS

When Archimedes's bath ran over and he discovered something about specific gravity, he was perhaps justified in sprinting into the street without his clothes and exulting. But that does not mean that every kid who sees his Saturday night bath overflow is justified in dashing outdoors naked shouting, "Eureka!" The distinction here is somewhat akin to that between the coiner of a bright phrase and the mere echoer of that phrase. It is the echoing that turns the phrase into a cliché—that is, an overworked, commonplace expression—and the echoer should realize that he has no claim to originality.

This is not to say that all clichés should be avoided like, shall we say, the plague. It is no more possible—or desirable—to do that than it is to abolish gravity. Many of today's clichés are likely to be tomorrow's standard English, just as many of today's standard words were yesterday's metaphors: *thunderstruck, astonish, cuckold, conclave, sanguine,* and thousands of others that form a substantial part of any dictionary. Moreover, the cliché is sometimes the most direct way of expressing a thought. Think of the circumlocution that is avoided by saying that someone has a *dog-in-the-manger attitude.* To attempt to write around a cliché will often lead to pompous obscurity. And for a writer to decide to banish all clichés indiscriminately would be to hamstring—yes, *hamstring*—his efforts.

103

There are many varieties of clichés. Some are foreign phrases (*coup de grâce; et tu, Brute*). Some are homely sayings or are based on proverbs ("You can't make an omelet without breaking eggs," *blissful ignorance*). Some are quotations ("To be or not to be, etc."; "Unwept, unhonored, and unsung"). Some are allusions to myth or history (*Gordian knot, Achilles' heel*). Some are alliterative or rhyming phrases (*first and foremost, high and dry*). Some are paradoxes (*in less than no time, conspicuous by its absence*). Some are legalisms (*null and void, each and every*). Some are playful euphemisms (*a fate worse than death, better half*). Some are figurative phrases (*leave no stone unturned, hit the nail on the head*). And some are almost meaningless small change (*in the last analysis, by the same token*).

Just as it would be unwise to try to banish all clichés, so it would be impossible to discriminate among these various classes, discarding some and accepting others. All that is possible is to set forth several cautions.

1. When a writer finds a phrase of the "small change" category rolling from his typewriter, he should ask himself whether it really has meaning in the context of his writing. The danger is that the phrases are often set down thoughtlessly. When he writes *in this connection*, he should ask himself whether the phrase is necessary at all. When he writes *few and far between*, he should ask himself if he really means that, or if *few* would not be sufficient. When he writes *it stood him in good stead*, he should ask himself whether he does not mean simply *it was valuable*. In short he must scrutinize thoughtfully every phrase that eases itself almost mechanically onto the paper.

2. Borrowed wit is like an old joke, and both can be pretty dreary. The man who tacks a printed sign "THIMK" to his office wall or puts a paperweight in the form of a No. 8 pool ball on his desk is, for all his raucous laughter, a sad fellow. In the same way the writer who says something is *of the common or garden variety* or speaks of the *inner man* is not being scintillating. If the writer cannot be witty on his own, let him not try to be witty at all.

3. If the writer thinks he must use well-worn quotations he

should at least be sure he is quoting correctly. He should not speak of GILDING THE LILY or of *the hoi polloi*.

4. If it is not advisable to rule out all clichés, the writer may be expected to know what he is doing when he uses them and to make clear to the reader that he knows what he is doing. In using a cliché the writer assumes among his readers a community of expression, of allusions, and of reference. If he assumes too much of such a background, his allusions may be abstruse or recondite. If, on the other hand, he wishes to feel sure his allusions will be understood, he risks being trite. The way out of this dilemma is the use of a sophisticated manner of delivering the cliché that takes advantage of the community of background and at the same time shows that the writer knows that his phrase is a cliché. This manner seems almost to put quotation marks around the cliché. It says, for example, "The delegates to the conference seem unable to see the disarmament forest for the weapons trees" or "The President's attitude is the familiar one of viewing more in sorrow than in anger." What is important for the writer to avoid is the delivery of clichés as if he had just discovered them.

Actually we could not avoid the use of clichés even if we wanted to. The very word cliché is in a sense a cliché—its original meaning is stereotype. And writers on the subject inevitably find themselves using in their discussions words like *coinage, freshminted,* and *hackneyed,* all of which are in this same sense clichés. The important thing, however, as must be clear by now, is not to avoid the cliché, but rather to use it only with discrimination and sophistication, and to shun it when it is a substitute for precise thinking.

CLIMAX

Whether the forces of righteousness can ever overhaul the hordes who misuse *climax* in the belief that it means apex or acme is dubious. Indeed, Webster has already given up the chase, though the Oxford has not. Let it be said, at least for the record, that *climax,* which comes from a Greek word meaning ladder, refers to an ascending gradation, not to the last or the highest or the best of a series. (*For a similar misuse, see* CRESCENDO.) It should also be obvious, from the derivation of the word, that it cannot be applied to the lowest point in a sequence, as it is in this sentence: "The drop in popularity of the larger engine reached its climax last September, when sales of the 'eight' fell to a three-year low." *See also* RHETORICAL FIGURES AND FAULTS.

CLIMB DOWN

Climb down would seem to be half-contradictory, but it is accepted in good literary usage. The extremists who gainsay this will ultimately have to alight from their high horse. *Climb down* fills a need by suggesting more active effort than the essentially passive *descend* or *come down*. If *climb down* is approved, it might seem to follow that *climb up* must also be approved. But here we have tautology aggravated by wastefulness. The writer who values terseness will usually omit the *up*.

CLOSURE, CLOTURE

The practice of closing debate in a parliamentary body by putting the matter to a vote originated in 1882 in the British House of Commons. Although occasionally at first the British used the French *clôture* to designate the practice, there is no more reason to use it today than to use *envoyé* for *envoy* or *programme* for *program*.

COALESCE

Takes preposition *with*.

COHORT

The misuse of *cohort* to denote an individual is common: "Before the students sheepishly returned to their dormitories they had brought about the arrest of two of their cohorts." This misuse can result only from bad guessing. Having in mind such words as *costar*, *coauthor*, and *cotrustee*, in which the prefix "co-" has the meaning of *with*, the bad guessers apparently decide that a *cohort* is a *hort* who is *co* with another *hort*. And what is a *hort*? That they don't bother to find out. Actually the "co-" in *cohort*

106

is not a prefix at all. The word comes from a Latin word meaning an enclosure. It was originally applied to a division in the Roman army, and now means a company or band, as in, "a cohort of Yale students."

A similar group word that bowed to a like misuse is *commando*. Borrowed from South Africa during World War II, it originally meant a force of hit-and-run raiders, but persistent and widespread use of the word to mean a member of such a striking group ultimately gave it that secondary meaning. Why, it may be asked, has not the same thing happened to *cohort?* The answer probably is that although *commando* was widely applied to one person ("My brother was a commando at Dieppe"), *cohort* almost never is so applied; the misusers rarely say, "He was a cohort of mine." *See also* MINION.

COINCIDE
Takes preposition *with*.

COINED TITLES
To designate someone as "West 135th Street scrubwoman and subway rider Anna Johnson" may seem somewhat ridiculous, but it is no more ridiculous than what appears currently in news magazines and newspapers. Apparently inspired by *Time* magazine and abetted by news agencies, the practice of converting ordinary descriptive phrases into titles has become widespread "Governor" is a fine, legitimate title; "convicted bookie" prefixed to a man's name is a coinage that is as bogus as a three-dollar bill. Sometimes legitimate titles are combined with illegitimate ones to produce mouthfuls of this kind: "Ohio Supreme Court Judge and former trial lawyer James Garfield." What is gained by such inversion of the normal word order, "James Garfield, Ohio Supreme Court Judge and former trial lawyer"? All that results is awkwardness. And incidentally, the ridiculous titles produce bastardized typography. It is customary to capitalize titles preceding names, but our present-day title coiners cannot bring themselves to capitalize "convicted bookie" or "former trial lawyer," and thereby they confess their sin.

COLLECT

Since *collect* means bring together, it should be obvious that you cannot *collect* one thing. Yet apparently it is not obvious: "I collected a pressure lamp and we went down the narrow path which we had cut through the dense bush from the camp to the river"; "Jim Coates came in and collected the third out"; "Prince Charles, decked out in a black riding hat, sweater, and jodhpurs, collected a pony from the paddock and practiced in a far corner of the field." You can, of course, *collect* a pony in the sense of bringing it under control, but apart from that specialized meaning the only animal you can *collect* is a chicken in parts.

COLLECTIVES

Whether to treat collective nouns as singular or plural is a continuing source of perplexity. The British seem to resolve their doubts in favor of the plural; the Americans seem to resolve theirs in favor of the singular. Both should resolve them in favor of good sense.

If the idea of oneness predominates, treat the noun as a singular. ("The number of accidents is larger this year"—because *number* is thought of as *total*.) If the idea of more-than-oneness predominates, treat the noun as a plural. ("A great number of accidents are preventable"—because *number* is equivalent to *many*.) With *number* or *total*, incidentally, a simple rule is possible: preceded by *the*, it is singular; preceded by *a*, it is plural.

Good sense would suggest that the following sentence be changed: "A variety of water, shore, and marsh birds is attracting large numbers of nature lovers to the Jamaica Bay Wildlife Refuge." The key question to be asked here is, To what are you directing the reader's attention—the idea of *variety* or the idea of *birds?* Clearly in this instance it is *birds*, and the phrase *a variety of* is virtually equivalent to *many*. Hence the verb might better be *are*. *Variety* could be the dominant idea—and the verb singular—if the sentence were of this type: "The variety of shore birds at Jamaica shows that food of many kinds is available."

Couple is another word that sometimes presents a problem

108

of number. It does not seem sensible to say, "The couple was married"; marriage is the joining of two persons, not something that is done to an already existing unit. Nor does it seem logical to say, "The couple was arrested in separate apartments." It is difficult to see how a writer could go wrong by treating *couple* as a plural, although treatment as a singular could be defensible sometimes.

When *majority* means simply "most of," it would be preferable to regard it as a plural rather than write, "The French people have repeatedly shown that a majority of them is in favor of the Defense Community."

The term *per cent* is another one that is susceptible of being construed as either a singular or a plural. Often the decision is made on the basis of what grammarians call "attraction"—the number of the verb is determined in such an instance not by *per cent* itself but rather by the noun following it, to which the verb is attracted. Here in a single sentence are two different but correct uses: "About twenty per cent of the hospital's quota of residents and internes is unfilled, and more than ninety per cent of the filled posts are manned by graduates from foreign countries."

In all these matters good sense is the key. And it suggests a rule that is violated in this headline: "Negro Couple Clings to Their Home." Rule: Once you have made a proper choice, stay with it. *See also* NUMERALS WITH COLLECTIVES.

COLLIDE

A frequent misuse: "Mr. Smith was changing a flat tire when a second car collided with his automobile." When two things *collide* they strike or dash against each other, i.e., both are in motion. A parked car cannot be one of the objects in a collision.

The phrase *in collision*, by the way, has become a journalistic fixture: "Two light planes were in collision over a suburban area of Lincoln today." The clumsy phrase in place of the simple *collided* apparently originated in the distant past in a half-understood caution: to wit, that if you were to say that one plane or car collided with another, you might be seeming to place the blame and thereby inviting a libel suit. From that point some editors jumped to the conclusion that *collided* was a dirty word, not to be used in any circumstances. A safe position but a ridiculous one.

COLLOQUIAL
See CASUALISMS.

COLON
See PUNCTUATION.

COLOSSAL
See ATOMIC FLYSWATTERS.

COMBINE
Except when it refers to a piece of farm machinery, *combine* is an American casualism that most often carries with it the suggestion of something illegal or fraudulent. "A combine of pharmaceutical companies to fix prices" is fair enough usage; "a combine of pharmaceutical companies to underwrite the costs of cancer research" is substandard usage.

COMMA
See PUNCTUATION.

COMMANDO
See COHORT.

COMMISERATE
Takes preposition *with*.

COMMON
See MUTUAL.

COMMUNE
Takes preposition *with*.

COMPARATIVELY
See RELATIVELY.

COMPARE TO, COMPARE WITH
The choice of *to* or *with* to follow *compare* is not a matter of indifference. When the purpose is to liken two things or to put them in the same category, use *to*. When the purpose is to place one thing side by side with another, to examine their differences or their similarities, use *with*. The choice of the preposition was erroneous in each of the following examples: "The economy can be compared with [*to*] a runner who is coasting to get his second wind for another sprint"; "Compared to [*with*] the $4,900,000,000 the Administration has proposed for foreign aid, the cost of the overseas reactor program will be small." Since *compare to* is most often involved in figurative constructions, whereas *compare with* is the more literal, everyday phrase, the uses calling for *with* far outnumber those calling for *to*.

COMPATIBLE
Takes preposition *with*.

COMPENDIUM
Probably because of its massive sound, together with the suggestion of all-inclusiveness that the prefix "com-" calls to mind, *compendium* is one of the words that many use but few know. Far from meaning a large work containing everything but the family dishwasher, it means a brief summary or complete outline. The following phrases show clearly that their authors had no idea of the true meaning of the word: "A whole compendium of new departures in American diplomacy . . ."; "a compendium of all that is linguistically offensive." The adjective *compendious* similarly means concise or abridged.

COMPLACENT
Takes preposition *toward*.

111

COMPLECTED

To say "Señor Covarrubias was a plump, dark-complected man" is to use a dialectal word. Most likely *complected* is a BACK FORMATION—that is, a nonexistent word coined from an actual word erroneously supposed to be derived from it. If *connection* is derived from *connect* and *inflection* is derived from *inflect*—the reasoning probably went—*complexion* must be derived from *complect*. However, the root of *complexion* is the same as the root of *complex*. "A dark-complexioned man" is better.

COMPLEX

See INSIDE TALK.

COMPOUNDS, HOME-MADE

A trick of writers who strain to dazzle their readers is to coin odd participial compounds that have the appearance of normal ones. Here are three examples: "Obviously, Walt Disney and his colleagues don't believe in laurel-resting; they are hard at work. . . ."; "Where foliage spreads into the tropical Ituri Forest live obscure savage tribes and arrow-hunting pygmies"; "One Governor called the Republican candidate ignorant, a hip-shooter, and other uncomplimentary things."

Let's take a look at *laurel-resting*. In appearance it is similar to *broad-jumping*, *fly-casting*, and *bird-watching*, but there is a difference: *Laurel-resting* derives from "resting *on* one's laurels," and that intrusive preposition is the difference.

Take it as a wet-blanket-on-throwing guide that no such compounds should be constructed where a preposition that is an intimate part of the phrase must be left out of the coined compound. Thus, although it may be acceptable to speak of a "rail-splitting President" or a "side-splitting comedy," it is not acceptable to speak of a "conclusion-jumping woman."

Some existing compounds may seem to violate this guide, but actually they do not. The basis for *tightrope walking*, for instance, is not "walking on a tight rope"; the phrase is rather a simple adjective-noun combination like *lake fishing* or *ice skat-*

ing. One that does violate the guide but has become established is *baby sitting.*

COMPRISE

Comprise has the meaning of contain, embrace, include, and comprehend. Thus this usage is incorrect: "He also gave the names of the four books that comprised the body of Roman law." The whole *comprises* the parts, not the reverse. What is wanted in the example cited is *composed, constituted,* or *made up.* Also to be avoided is "comprised of." *See also* INCLUDE.

COMPULSIVE

See INSIDE TALK.

CONCEPT

The tendency among some groups, particularly social workers, teachers, and advertising writers, to make the lesser seem the greater and to enfold the commonplace in the mantle of science or philosophy has had a debasing effect on the word *concept.* Everything from a program for feeding the poor to a new design for a girdle is designated a *concept.* A typical instance is the advertising for a residential development, which boasts that the buildings constitute "a brand new concept in apartment planning." What is usually intended by the misusers is merely *idea, notion, thought, design, program,* or some other less high-flown word. A *concept* is, primarily, an idea that results from drawing a generalization from particulars. An astrophysicist, noting the red shift in the spectrums of distant stars, develops the *concept* of an expanding universe. The word should be used cautiously and precisely.

CONCERN

A *concern* is a business or manufacturing organization, not a professional one. Therefore it is incorrect to say, "Mr. Duff is a member of a law concern in Washington, D.C." Make it *law firm* or *law office. See also* FIRM *and* BUSINESS.

113

CONCERNING
See DANGLERS.

CONCLAVE
Based on the Latin *clavis*, meaning key, *conclave* denotes, strictly speaking, a secret or closed meeting. It should not be used to mean an ordinary convention, as in this sentence: "The meeting of the week was the Standard Oil Company of New Jersey conclave." There are plenty of other words for a plain pow-wow: *meeting, convention, conference, get-together, reunion, parley, assemblage, colloquium, palaver,* and *Kaffeeklatsch*.

CONCUR
Takes preposition *with* (persons); *in* (a measure); *to* (an effect).

CONDITION OF HEALTH
This note is addressed almost exclusively to headline writers, who, because of space limitations, are virtually the only ones who fall into the error now to be exposed: "Legislator Hurt in Crash Is Grave." Well, why wouldn't he be? The headline raises a question about the use of adjectives describing a person's state of health. Some adjectives are definitely ambiguous. One head-line, reporting the aftermath of a fall, says, "Queens Man Is Still Critical," and another, telling about a speech, says, "Stevenson Is Critical." Some adjectives are unambiguous: *healthy, well, ill, sick*. Others could be ambiguous, but usually are not: *better, improved, worse*. The ones to watch out for are those that can be, and often are, ambiguous. In this list are *grave, critical, serious, fine, good,* and *satisfactory*. They should never appear unattended by *condition* or *health*. It must be remembered that when some persons are critical, it's an indication they are well—present company not excepted.

CONDUCIVE
Takes preposition *to*.

114

CONFIDE

Takes preposition *in.*

CONFIDENT

Takes preposition *of.*

CONFORM, CONFORMITY

Take preposition *to* or *with.*

CONGENIAL

Takes preposition *to* or (older) *with.*

CONJUNCTIONS

See CORRELATIVE CONJUNCTIONS, LAW OF.

CONNECTION

See IN CONNECTION WITH.

CONNIVE

Associations of sound often lead the unwary into thinking a word means something quite different from its true meaning. *Livid* suffers misuse because its sound suggests *vivid; enervate* suffers similar misuse because its sound suggests *energy.* The word *connive* gets a double dose of such abuse. First, some writers vaguely associate it with *cunning,* and give us such phrases as "a conniving rogue" and "conniving crooks." Second, some writers (probably the same ones) associate it with *conspire* or *contrive,* and write such sentences as, "Far from conniving against the nomination of the Vice President, he likes him."

The truth is that *connive* means neither of these things. It comes from Latin and French words meaning to wink or shut the eyes, and it means to wink at or shut one's eyes to an irregularity or to something one does not like. It is often followed by *at,* as in, "The police were accused of conniving at gambling in Harlem." Oddly enough, so widespread is the ignorance about this word that it is often avoided in contexts in which, as in the fore-

115

going example, it would be the proper and precise word. In its place one will usually find *winking, blinking* and, yes, sometimes *nodding.*

For the senses in which *connive* is misused there are, of course, plenty of serviceable words: *conspire, scheme, plot,* and even that earthy word, *finagle.* And for the sense in which *conniver* is misused there is the good old word *contriver,* meaning a plotter or schemer. It was good enough for Shakespeare, who has Cassius say, in *Julius Caesar,* Act II, "We shall find him a shrewd contriver."

CONNOTE

See DENOTE, CONNOTE.

CONSENSUS

If it is remembered that the root of this word is the same as the root of *sense,* and that it means a feeling together, *consensus* will be neither misused nor misspelled. It has nothing to do with *census,* which means a counting of people. *Consensus* denotes general agreement. The idea of opinion is built into it; therefore "consensus of opinion" is a pleonasm, and although the phrase is in general use, the careful writer will reject it as he would any other wasteful redundancy.

CONSENT

Takes preposition *to.*

CONSEQUENT

Takes preposition *to, on,* or *upon.*

CONSIDER

Dictionaries give "believe" or "suppose" as subsidiary meanings for *consider,* but it is well to reserve the word for situations involving real mental activity of pondering or thinking over. Example of an undiscriminating use: "In an off-the-cuff reaction, the Mayor considered the report to be unjustified, but he acknowledged he had not had a chance to read it."

CONSIDERING

See DANGLERS.

CONSISTENT

Takes preposition *with*.

CONSIST IN, CONSIST OF

Consist of is used to introduce the component parts, as in, "The play consists of a prologue and three acts." *Consist in* is used to define or to set forth an identity, as in, "The drama of the play consists in the visual contrast between his wretched old age and the images of romance evoked by the tape recording."

CONSONANT

Takes preposition *with*.

CONSUMMATE

The adjective is a superlative word; it means supreme or complete. The meaning does not always seems to be clear to those critics who link it so lavishly to such words as "artist" and "artistry."

CONTACT

There is much to be said for *contact* as a verb. It can replace longer phrases, such as *get in touch with* or *look up*, or single words, such as *meet, find,* or *phone.* In some circumstances it may be desirable to avoid the specific terms. If you say to your friend, "Contact me next week," you may wish to leave to him the option of phoning, calling at your office, sending you a letter, or lying in wait on your front lawn. Unfortunately, it is usually not used so. Most often it is seized upon by those lovers of the FAD WORD who would rather be up to the minute than specific. Deprive your businessman of *contact* and he would be unhappy, but deprive your practiced writer of *contact* and he should be able to make out very well. The verb will undoubtedly push its way into standard usage sometime. Do you think you can wait?

117

CONTAGIOUS, INFECTIOUS

Contagion comes from a Latin word meaning a touching, and a *contagious* disease is one communicated by contact. An *infectious* disease is one communicated by air or water, and it may or may not be *contagious*.

CONTEMPORARY

The word is not an out-and-out synonym for *modern* or *present-day*, as the writer of this passage imagined: "An anti-Jeffersonian charge by Justice Samuel Chase in 1803, reprinted in this collection, was one count in his impeachment by a Jeffersonian Congress. . . . More contemporary items in the collection include papers by Justices Hugo Black and Robert H. Jackson." What *contemporary* means is existing at the same time. It can be used to mean *modern* if no time or person of another period is mentioned, because then the implication is "contemporary with us." Thus, in the absence of mention of any past date or person, "contemporary painting" would mean painting of our day; but if Leonardo were mentioned relevantly, it would mean painting of his day. In the light of this explanation it should also be obvious that you cannot use "more" (in the sense of to a greater degree) ahead of *contemporary*.

CONTEMPTUOUS

Takes preposition *of*.

CONTEND

Takes preposition *with* or *against* (enemies); *about* (issues).

CONTINUAL, CONTINUOUS

Continual means over and over again. *Continuous* means unbroken. The following is a misuse: "When McSorley's finally closes its swinging doors, the oldest place in town that has reportedly been continually in the business will be Pete's Tavern." The meaning here is obviously not again and again. Mnemonic device: *Continuous* ends in *o u s*, which stands for one *uninterrupted* sequence.

118

CONTINUE ON

Pleonastic. Omit the *on*.

CONTRACTUAL

Spelled thus, not *contractural*.

CONTRARY

In the trite phrase "to the contrary notwithstanding," some writers occasionally omit the "notwithstanding." For example: "Controversy to the contrary, the books do acknowledge this gin to be the original base of a classic Martini." Without the "notwithstanding," the phrase says merely "controversy to the opposite effect," and so is meaningless. What the writer intends is to introduce the notion of "despite" or "although there is," but he has not done it. Here is an instance of false economy. *See also* CONVERSE, REVERSE, CONTRARY, OPPOSITE.

CONTRAST

Takes preposition *to* (opposite); *with* (different).

CONVERSE, REVERSE, CONTRARY, OPPOSITE

Converse denotes oppositeness. But beyond that, it declares a transposition of the important members of a proposition or statement: for example, the *converse* of "All radicals are crackpots" would be "All crackpots are radicals." The *contrary* of the statement would be "Not all radicals are crackpots" and the *opposite* of it would be "No radicals are crackpots." As Fowler points out, the *contrary* does not exclude the *opposite*, but includes it as its most extreme form. The most general of the words denoting oppositeness is *reverse*, which could include all the others. It is the word to use unless the writer has a special purpose in mind and a precise knowledge of the meaning of the alternative word he has selected.

CONVICT

Takes preposition *of*.

119

CONVINCE, PERSUADE

The words mean slightly different things, and the difference may have something to do with the fact that *persuade* is sometimes followed by an infinitive, whereas *convince* never is. This sentence is improper: "Three unidentified persons who had taken the girl to the airport futilely tried to convince her to take her seat on the plane." *Persuade* would be the proper word in that construction. *Convince* may be followed by an *of* phrase or a *that* clause, but not by a *to* infinitive. *Persuade*, on the other hand, may be followed by any of them.

The reason for the nonuse of an infinitive after *convince* may be merely, as one writer has suggested, that it "flouts idiom." But perhaps the reason for the idiom itself lies in the meanings of *convince* and *persuade*. *Convince* has the meaning of to satisfy beyond doubt by argument or evidence appealing to the reason. *Persuade* has the meaning of to induce or win over by argument or entreaty appealing to the reason and feeling. With *convince* there is a static situation, which does not in itself suggest a consequent action. With *persuade* a shifting is brought about from one position to another, often with the implication of action to come—and hence another verb form, which may be an infinitive. Whether this excursion into the dark origins of idiom makes sense or no, the fact remains: no infinitive after *convince*.

Winston Churchill, with his sure feeling for words, suggested the distinction between these two when he was contrasting the wartime powers of Roosevelt and Stalin with his own: "They could order; I had to convince and persuade."

CORD, CHORD

There is enough confusion between these two words to warrant some elucidation. First, let us dispose of the musical term *chord* because it is an outsider. It is not based on the same root as the others, but is derived from *accord*; a *chord* in music is an *accord* of sounds. The other meanings of the two words are all derived from the Latin *chorda*, meaning catgut, and have to do with a string or tendon or with something that substitutes for a string, as a line in geometry. Some are spelled *chord*—the *chord* of an arc and the *chords* of a truss in engineering and of an airfoil design in aeronautics. In American usage, however, most of the other words are spelled *cord: vocal cord, umbilical cord, spinal cord, cord of wood.* Thus, for the American reader this sentence needs correction: ". . . it requires only a pair of eyes to gaze at the sky and vocal chords with which to utter a forecast." Vocal *chords* are possible, but they could not be produced with only one pair of eyes present.

CORPORATION
See BELLY. *See also* FIRM.

CORRELATIVE CONJUNCTIONS, LAW OF

Correlative conjunctions are those that are used in pairs: *both . . . and, either . . . or, neither . . . nor, so . . . as, not only . . . but (also), whether . . . or.* The law, which like most laws is occasionally broken for a noble purpose, simply states that such conjunctions should connect two of the same thing—that is, elements of the same grammatical value and in parallel form. This is merely the equivalent of saying that you should not harness a horse and a dachshund to a plow, nor design the façade for a building with three Doric columns on one side of the entrance and one Corinthian column on the other. An example of this kind of imbalance is the following sentence: "This implied not only reductions in officer personnel, but among enlisted men as well." Observe that the *not only . . . but* teams a noun ("reductions") with a phrase ("among enlisted men"). It is illogical and untidy. Correlative conjunctions may connect nouns ("The curriculum includes both economics and history"), adjectives ("Tomorrow is expected to be either cloudy or rainy"), phrases ("There will be reductions not only in officer personnel but also among enlisted men"), or clauses ("I don't know whether the meat is tough or my knife is dull").

The law of correlative conjunctions could be expanded to apply to all conjunctions, i.e., conjunctions should connect elements of equal grammatical weight. But the emphasis here is on the correlative conjunctions because the pitfalls and the errors

121

are more numerous in this area. (*However, see* AND WHICH.) What it all adds up to is that symmetry, logicality, tidiness produce greater lucidity. *See also* BOTH . . . AND *and* NOT ONLY . . . BUT (ALSO).

CORRESPOND

Takes preposition *to* or *with*.

COUNCILOR, COUNSELOR

A *councilor* is a member of a council. A *counselor* is one who gives counsel.

COUNSEL, COUNSELOR

See ATTORNEY, LAWYER *and* OFFICER.

COURSE

The phrase *the course of,* when used in place of *during,* is a wasteful locution; it can always be omitted. "In the course of a news conference" translates into "in [or *at* or *during*] a news conference" with no loss.

CRAFT

1. The advertising fraternity has decided that *craft* is a verb, and so we find the participial adjective *crafted* cropping up in such contexts as this: "Treat the man on your gift list to a finely crafted alligator belt." Most of us will find no use for such oddly crafted words.

2. The plural of *craft* in the sense of vessels or airplanes is *craft,* not *crafts.*

CRASH PROGRAM

See FAD WORDS.

CRASS

Perhaps because it has a sound suggestive of coarse and gross, the word *crass* is often employed to mean those things. Dictionaries agree that this meaning is "rare." Actually the word essentially means stupid, and with its overtones it means bluntly, grossly, insensitively stupid. Unless one knows what a writer has in mind, it is difficult to convict him of a misuse of the word. Nevertheless, the circumstantial evidence of guilt is often strong: "The diversions include a liaison with a married man she loathes, vacuous nights and days in poker parlors and strip-tease joints, and, finally, a blatantly crass faith healer's congregation. . . ." Did the writer mean stupid? Hardly. Again: "They have showed the boy's disgust with his mother after his working-class father died and she squandered the bit of insurance a crass employer paid." It is hard to say what this writer intended, but it is even harder to imagine that he meant stupid.

CREDIT

Although dictionaries give ascribe as one meaning of the verb *credit*, in good usage the connotation is a favorable one. *Credit* should not be used for the ascribing of unfavorable things, as in this sentence: "The society seeks to clear the name of Richard, whom history credits with the slaying of two young princes and other killings and crimes."

CRESCENDO

It is a rising or an increasing, not a loud point, as the writer of the following sentence apparently thought: "The Soviet 'Hate America' campaign has reached a new crescendo of violence and volume." The meaning and loose use of the word are not dissimilar to those of CLIMAX.

CRITERIA

The singular is *criterion*, but occasionally a speaker or a writer will misuse *criteria* as if it were a singular noun, as the following passages illustrate: "I am merely pointing out that one criteria of success, namely that of making a profit, is applied by critics of the small magazine and is not applied when examining other cultural institutions"; "A spokesman for Consolidated Edison in New York compared its personnel to the United Nations', saying: 'We have people of all races so long as they have talent. We need outstanding people and that is the only criteria.'" Similar errors are made with *data, media, strata,* and *trivia*. On the other hand, *see* AGENDA.

CULMINATE

A single passage will serve to expose two fairly common distortions of this word: "Nothing is known of the operation except that the charge was placed 200 feet underground. It culminated a series of three explosions in the same district." The first point to notice is that the transitive use of this verb is generally considered exceptional. The second point is that *culminate* does not mean to finish or to be the outcome or result. It means to rise to the highest point, usually after a series of steps.

Culminate takes the preposition *in*.

CURDLED CLICHÉS

A few writers are in trouble from the minute they take pen in foot. They are the type who not only set down a cliché with a flourish that suggests they have just invented it, but also lack the wit to get it straight. Samuel Goldwyn, the film impresario, has been represented as the prototype of the cliché-twisters and has been credited with such gems as, "That's the way with these directors, they're always biting the hand that lays the golden egg." But Goldwynisms always seem contrived. They always bear the faint imprint of the press agent. It's difficult to visualize the man actually saying, "A verbal contract isn't worth the paper it's written on," or, "Why name your son John? Every Tom, Dick, and Harry is named John." The curdled cliché under discussion here is spontaneous, as well as thoughtless. Nor is it exclusively a malapropism, which is a ridiculous misuse of a word, as in, "Our new executive was born in an orpheum asylum" (also a Goldwyn production, by the way). The curdled cliché may be a malapropism, but often it is a different form of distortion.

Let it be confessed at once that the length of the article devoted to the exposure of this fault is out of all proportion to the prevalence of the fault itself. Fortunately, those who are addicted to it confine their efforts at communication mostly to speech; the only writing they usually attempt is the composition of a letter applying for the job as bkpg mach opr or the affixing of a signature to a multimillion-dollar film contract. Still, an experienced writer can nod now and again. Witness: " 'Even a cat can look at a king,' as Dick Whittacker said." First, the writer got Dick Whittington confused with somebody—G. Whittacker, perhaps. Second, Master Whittington never said anything like that. Witness further: "The program is designed to breach the gap between crowded institutions for the aged and the rising proportion of aged in the population." Bridge, anyone?

The curdled cliché results from a single-barreled effort and a double-barreled deficiency. The effort is directed toward seeming to be knowing, toward trying to be better than one's peers and equal to one's betters, and it flops. It is the tennis novice attempting the gallant leap over the net and falling on his face. The double-barreled deficiency resides in the fact that on the one hand the perpetrator fails to grasp the meaning of the individual words in the cliché, even though he has a glimmering of the meaning of the phrase as a whole, and that on the other hand, he suffers from a bad ear—a defect that causes him to say, "It's a fragment of your imagination," rather than "a figment." Some people have almost a genius for this sort of thing, and they provide an untapped and apparently unfailing source of drollery. Well, not exactly untapped, because what follows is, for the most part, a conscientious record, set down over an extended period, of the unconscious oral outgivings of a certain newspaperman, who of necessity must be nameless. If some of them seem unbelievable, it can only be repeated that this is a conscientious record:

I racked my brains back and forth over that problem.
Senator Long lowered the whistle on McCarthy.
It's in the lap of the cards.
Those guys have been harping on me.
It's an enigma on Russia's escutcheon.
The politicians are out cementing their fences.
The agency won't pay any attention to him; he's just a once-

in-a-moon customer.
That organization is going to the pot.
It happened in my old ballywhack.
I don't know; it's hydroglyphics to me.
That hits it right on the nutshell.
The Senator's got 'em over a wheelbarrow.
There was no talking to them; they got up in their high hat.
He raised a hellabaloo.
*The monsignor at the communion breakfast got off on a tan-
   dem on politics.*
They're trying to hurry to get under the gun.
*We better act right away because our competitors might
   jump into the gun.*
He's a stiff shirt.
He needs some money to tidy him over.
A bunch of legislative bills were dropped into the hamper.
*I'm not sure about this article, so look at it with a jaundiced
   eye, will you?*
We were sitting there like a shooting duck.
They're riding on a tantrum bike.
He muffed the boat.
The prisoner gave a facetious name.
I was so tired I couldn't keep my head open.
I was smoking like a chain.
She blew the rug out from under my sails.
He better watch out; he's skating on thin ground.
I looked every place—all over the sun.
It's a shut-and-dried case.
It's a confused picture; it doesn't make head or sense.
He dashes in and out like a whip of the will.
He was left out in the lurch.
He's upper crust—one of the high polloi.
They're cutting my throat behind my back.

It may well be argued that no writer who heeds what he is
doing would be guilty of offenses as absurd as these. Probably so.
But writers are not always alert. How else explain that one

reports "beetles are ravishing trees" and that another says "praise is being languished on someone"? Writing cannot be done by ear or by rote: It calls for clear and careful thought. He who disregards this warning is skating on mighty thin ground.

CURED
Takes preposition *of*.

D

DACTYL
See FOOT.

DAILY

Here is a really unimportant curiosity. Since *nightly* means by night, as well as every night, you would expect that *daily* would mean by day, as well as every day. But no—at least according to the dictionaries. They restrict the meaning of the word to the sense of every day. By this standard it would be improper to write: "Daily and nightly, Christine is raised aloft to the Madison Square Garden ceiling by a rope attached to a ring in which her hair is entwined." You would have to make it, "Each day and each night. . . ." Perhaps the reason for this curious state of affairs is that *daily* (by far the more frequently used word) has through usage become identified exclusively with the idea of every day.

DANGLERS

Your elementary-school teacher may have approached this subject with a contrived sentence: "Roaring down the track at seventy miles an hour, the stalled car was smashed by the train." She really didn't need to make up an example, because examples are all around us; they are as abundant as slipshod writers. Moreover, they are often just as amusing as her fabrication: "Lying astride the Quebec-Labrador boundary, a prospector looking for gold found the ore in what is known as the Labrador Trough." Or, "As reconstructed by the police, Pfeffer at first denied any knowledge of the Byrd murder." Or, "Small and sallow, her huge dark eyes and mane of hair were her only real beauties." Or, in an ad that spoke of George Washington's clothing, "Although sixty-one years old when he wore the original suit, his waist was only thirty-five."

The fault in all danglers is the failure to put modifiers in close contact with the elements they are supposed to modify. It was not the stalled car that roared down the track, but the train. It was not the prospector that was lying astride the boundary, but the Labrador Trough. The train and the Trough should follow immediately after the participial phrases that modify them. In some instances not only is the contact between modifier and modified element not close; it does not even exist, because the element to be modified simply is not there. Pfeffer was not reconstructed by the police; it was the case or the story, which exists nowhere except in the writer's mind. It was not her eyes and hair that were small and sallow; it was she herself, but she is reflected only in the possessive pronoun "her," and that is not good enough.

English has lost most inflections—those grammatical forms indicating changes in such things as tense, gender, and number—which in many other languages are signposts pointing to relationships between words. This loss is actually in many ways an emancipation, but the freedom should not be interpreted as liberty to run riot. Indeed, the loss of inflections makes the language dependent on word order for intelligibility and style. Danglers are a flouting of clear, logical word order.

Danglers come in many shapes. They may be participles, present or past. (Here is a remarkable specimen in which two of them appear in the same sentence: "Unbeaten thus far this year, the victory was his seventh in a row and his tenth since last dropping a decision last September.") They may be appositive phrases ("A Phi Beta Kappa graduate of Dartmouth, Pat Weaver's head is said to burst with ideas"). They may be clauses (see the earlier George Washington sentence). They may be simple adjectives ("The Avenue of the Americas is duplicating this miracle, in lesser pace and scope, but still exciting." What does "exciting" modify?) And, as the examples have illustrated, danglers may appear at the head of a sentence or elsewhere.

There is one class of what appear to be danglers to which

exception cannot be taken. These are participles (present or past) that are of indefinite reference and that by idiomatic use have passed over from the status of participles to that of prepositions or conjunctions. Such a participle has no noun that it modifies, and none is expected. Examples are: *Generally speaking, speaking of, provided, considering, judging, concerning, failing, given, granting, owing to* (*see* DUE TO), *allowing for,* and stock phrases like *putting two and two together* and *getting down to brass tacks.* (*See also* ABSOLUTE CONSTRUCTIONS.) A question might here be raised concerning the distinction between phrases like these last two and the one cited earlier, "As reconstructed by the police. . . ." The distinction rests on two tests: Does the reader expect a noun that the phrase modifies? Is the phrase common enough to be considered an idiom? The police phrase fails on both counts.

DASH

See PUNCTUATION.

DASTARDLY

The essence of this word is the quality of cowardice. A *dastardly* act is not merely a vicious one, but in addition one that involves a mean avoidance of danger. Thus, a super-thug who orders a rival rubbed out is probably doing something *dastardly,* but the trigger man who risks his neck in the actual shooting is probably not doing something *dastardly,* no matter how reprehensible his act may be.

DATA

The use of *data* as if it were a singular noun is a common solecism: "London Psychiatrist Asserts Data Is Lacking to Prove Soviet Superiority." The Latin singular—*datum*—is not in use; when the singular is required, it is usual to write "one of the data" or "one item in the data." It may be asked, If AGENDA, which is also a Latin plural, has become an English singular, why has not *data* done the same? The connotations of the words provide the answer. *Agenda* has departed from its original meaning of things to be done, and now means a program of things to be done. Its singular force is so strongly felt that the word has developed its own plural—*agendas. Data,* on the other hand, has retained its meaning of things or facts. Its plural force has been strong enough so that no need has been felt to give it a plural of its own—no one has yet suggested writing, "These datas are convincing." All of this does not overlook the fact that some respected and learned writers have used *data* as a singular. But a great many more have not. Whatever the future may bring, at this time the use is still a solecism.

DEAD BODIES

Tautological: "They said many dead bodies, mostly of children, were seen floating on the water." In this sense bodies means corpses. You wouldn't speak of live bodies, would you?

DEADLY, DEATHLY

Deadly means lethal or death-dealing, as in "a deadly poison." *Deathly*, in modern usage, means resembling death, as in "a deathly silence" or "a deathly complexion."

DEBAR

Takes preposition *from.*

DECIDE

Takes preposition *on* or *upon;* in legal terminology, also *for* or *against.*

DECIMATE

Although the word literally means to take a tenth part of, it may legitimately be used by extension to mean to destroy a considerable part of. Any further extension, as in the following sentence, is improper: "In the film a nuclear war has caused fall-out that has completely decimated life in the Northern Hemisphere." The "completely" betrays that what the writer meant was *annihilated.* With *annihilated,* by the way, "completely" would be redundant.

DECLARE

See SAY AND ITS SYNONYMS.

DEFAMATION

See LIBEL, SLANDER.

DEFECT (n.)

Takes preposition *in* (an artifact); *of* (a person).

DEFEND

Takes preposition *from* or *against*.

DEFICIENT

Takes preposition *in*.

DEFILE (vb.)

Takes preposition *by* or *with*.

DEFINITE, DEFINITIVE

Definite means precise or exactly delimited. *Definitive* means final or beyond argument. A *definite* statement is one that is explicit; a *definitive* statement is one that is not challengeable.

DEGREE

The phrase *to a degree* originally had the meaning of to the last degree, that is, to the utmost. Now, however, it means merely in moderate measure. In this sense it is somewhat analogous to the phrases *to an extent* and *up to a point*. All three emphasize limitation. Both *degree* and *extent*, it should be noted, often are used in wasteful locutions. The writer who sets down "He was ill to a serious degree" means no more than "He was seriously ill"; and the writer who sets down "The program was broadened to a great extent" means merely "The program was greatly broadened."

DEIPNOSOPHIST

One who is good at dinner-table conversation is a *deipnoso-*

phist (from the Greek *deipnon*, meaning a meal, and *sophistes*, a wise man). There is no reason for this entry unless it is to point out that with a word like that to describe himself, even an amateur *deipnosophist* is off to a flying start. *See* OMPHALOSKEPSIS.

DELAY, POSTPONE

A sentence saying that an aim of the Soviet Union was "delaying and, if possible, postponing the United States armament of West Germany" serves to direct attention to the fine distinction between these synonymous partners. Both contain the idea of a putting back in time. *Delay*, however, has the flavor of to impede or hinder, whereas *postpone* has the meaning of a more formal putting off to a later time.

DELUSION, ILLUSION

A *delusion* is a false belief, one that often entails some peril. An *illusion* is a false perception. *Illusion* is much the milder word. If you watch the magician "saw a woman in half," you are observing an *illusion*; if you think he really did it, you are suffering from a *delusion*.

DEMANDING

Takes preposition *of*.

DEMEAN

There are two words *demean*. One, usually reflexive, means to conduct or behave (oneself). The other means to lower or degrade, as in this sentence: "These are just some of the League's demands which would further demean the actor's status at a time when he is seeking greater dignity and some measure of security." The second word is objected to by many lexicographers on the ground that it is catachrestic, that is, a word wrongly used for another (in this instance, *debase* or *degrade*). The argument is made that the "mean" part of the word has misled users into thinking that the original word *demean*, which is related to mere *demeanor*, had something to do with debasement.

133

Now, if this had happened yesterday or ten years ago or even twenty-five years ago, the purists might be justified in manning the ramparts against the new barbarian. However, the Oxford tells us that it happened around 1601. That is one element that changes the look of the matter: An attempt to roll back three centuries of usage is quixotic. More important, however, is the fact that nowadays the word is more often used—and understood—in the sense of debasement than it is in the sense of comportment. There is ample precedent for the legitimization of words of illegitimate origin, and this word has surmounted its bastardy.

DENOTE, CONNOTE

Perhaps the simplest way to mark the distinction between these two words is to say that *denote* means, *connote* implies. To *denote* is to furnish a plainly comprehensible sign or, when applied to words, to furnish a factual, exact definition. To *connote* means to suggest in a secondary or attributive way; when applied to words it embraces all the overtones, flavors, and suggestions that are not explicit in the purely minimal dictionary definitions.

DEPEND

In the sense of to be contingent, the word *depend* requires the preposition *on* or *upon*. An erroneous casual construction is exemplified by, "The Yankees are expected to win, but it depends whether Ford is able to pitch."

DEPLORE

Originally *deplore* meant to lament or bewail; then it came to mean to regret deeply. It still means to regret deeply, but it usually also carries with it an undertone of disapproval. To say that "The President deplored the tactics of Congress" is to say not only that he regretted them but also that he frowned upon them. Incidentally, as Partridge points out, *deplore* governs a thing or quality, not a person—so that, for example, the President could not *deplore* the Congressmen, although he could *deplore* their tactics.

DEPRECATE, DEPRECIATE

Depreciate almost never is misused; *deprecate* almost always is. "I hope you won't mind if I respectfully call your attention to the implication of superiority in your use of terms," Dr. Peale wrote to Mr. Kennedy. "By the phrase 'non-Catholic' it seems to me that you are actually deprecating the majority of people in this country." What Dr. Peale obviously had in mind was *belittling* or *disparaging*, and that is what *deprecate* means. It is the opposite of *appreciate*, meaning to value (highly). The root of *deprecate* is *precari*, meaning to pray. *Deprecate* means "to pray against," hence that you wish whatever it is would go away, hence that you disapprove.

DEPRIVE

Takes preposition *of.*

DERIVE

Takes preposition *from.*

DEROGATE

Takes preposition *from.*

DEROGATION

Takes preposition *of, from,* or *to.*

DEROGATORY

Takes preposition *to, from,* or (rarely) *of.*

DESERTS

Deserts, as in "just deserts," has nothing to do with pastries or sundaes topped with whipped cream, and therefore it is not spelled *desserts*. It derives rather from the same root as *deserve*. *Deserts* are those things that are deserved—appropriate rewards or punishments.

DESIROUS

Takes preposition *of.*

DESIST
Takes preposition *from.*

DESPAIR
Takes preposition *of.*

DESPOIL
Takes preposition *of.*

DESSERTS
See DESERTS.

DESTINED
Takes preposition *to* or *for.*

DESTITUTE
Takes preposition *of.*

DESTRUCTIVE
Takes preposition *of; to* (injurious).

DETER
Derived from the Latin root *terrere,* meaning to frighten, *deter* conveys the notion of preventing or discouraging something through fear. It follows that the word is applied to persons or perhaps animals, but not to things. You would not write, therefore, that "the Government deterred the sale of an unused hospital."

DETRACT
Takes preposition *from.*

DEVELOP
See DISCOVER, DEVELOP, INVENT.

DEVIATE
Takes preposition *from.*

136

DEVOLVE

Takes preposition *from* or *upon*.

DIAGNOSE

A common misuse: "He was diagnosed as suffering from high blood pressure." You *diagnose* the condition, not the patient.

DIALECT

There is such a thing as false condescension—like patting a midget on the head in the belief that he is a small boy. A form of it is the attempt to represent dialect by misspellings that merely render the normal pronunciations of words. Is "sez" different from "says," "kum" different from "come," "croocial" different from "crucial," "wimmin" different from "women"? What kind of dialect, if any, do those spellings suggest?

From a broader point of view dialect is a touchy problem. Unless a writer has an exceptionally well attuned ear he should not attempt it. He may assume that residents of Brooklyn say, "a poil from an erster," but anyone who has heard the Brooklyn tongue in action knows it is closer to "a pay-ul fum an erster." Aside from the danger of error, there is the danger of suggesting class, social, or racial snobbery. The danger may be slight in fiction writing, but it is real and present in other writing, particularly in newspaper writing. A writer with a good ear can get around all these pitfalls and can suggest dialect by using normal words normally spelled, relying entirely on choice of words and peculiarities of construction. A reporter covering a campaign tour of New York's East Side by Nelson Rockefeller communicated all the flavor of dialect by having characters in his news story say, "For Rockefeller he gives discounts" and "Can I put 'Hello' in the bank?" and "I should live so long." That is a more foolproof and more satisfactory way of conveying dialect.

DICKENS

See MUTUAL.

DICTION

There are those who would confine *diction* to the meaning of choice of words or manner of expression. This is, indeed, its principal meaning. But since the word traces back to a Latin root meaning say, the use of *diction* to refer to mode of speaking or enunciation is wholly proper and well established.

DICTUM

In nine instances out of ten *dictum* is a perfectly proper word to use for an authoritative pronouncement. The tenth instance is one in which the word appears in a strictly legal context; there it has, in the minds of lawyers at least, a different and specialized meaning. The technical legal meaning denotes a court's opinion on something that is a side issue in a case. The following sentence, then, contains an inadvisable usage: "The committee's report was apparently designed to soften the impact of reapportionment on sparsely populated upstate counties while conforming to the Supreme Court's 'one man, one vote' dictum." A better word here would be *ruling* or *principle*.

DIFFERENT

1. "Describing the bribery plot, the prosecutor said that two different men had approached Mr. Jones in his room at the Plymouth Hotel." Naturally the men were *different*; they always are. What was meant here in place of this common solecism was that two men approached Jones on different occasions or for different purposes.

2. *Different* is frequently used superfluously. Whereas it might be useful to say, "Two different versions of the murder were presented to the jury"—since two versions could be the same in substance—it is unnecessary to include *different* in a sentence such as, "Three different brands of cigarettes were served at the dinner."

3. An error of number sometimes arises after *different*: "The ruble has a quite different value inside the Soviet Union and in the outside world." Make it "quite different values" or "a quite

138

different value inside the Soviet Union from what it has in the outside world."

DIFFERENT FROM, DIFFERENT THAN

Any writer who wishes to confine himself to *different from* will never be wrong, and—particularly if he has a closed mind on the subject—he need read no farther. There is no argument about *different from*. There is, however, considerable argument about *different than*, and the argument rages despite the acknowledged fact that eminent writers of the past and the present have used the locution. Before setting forth a conclusion let us examine the contentions of the *than* school.

A popular spokesman of the structural linguistic permissivists, who normally show scant respect for the connection between logic and grammar, resorts to logic to defend *different than*. Conceding that *than* may be used only with the comparative form of an adjective ("We may say greener than but not green than"), this spokesman argues that *different*, though it looks like a positive form, "has the standing of a comparative adjective." To support this, he says that *different* can be qualified by degree words, such as *much, far, a great deal*, whereas the positive form of an adjective cannot be. A glance at Webster under the word *far*, for example, disputes this statement immediately; the dictionary presents these examples: "The day is far spent" and "He was not far wrong." The adjectives *preferable* and *apart* can also be qualified by degree words, as can many participial adjectives: *advanced, limited, divided, disunited, discussed*, etc. Indeed, the spokesman himself, in another context, mentions a group of words—*anterior, inferior, senior, superior*—that can be qualified by a degree word, *much*. He says these are actually comparatives, but do not have the English comparative form. One might think that, according to his lights, they would be analogous to *different*. Happily, however, he does not suggest the locutions *inferior than* or *superior than*.

But the essence of the matter is this: Does *different* really have the standing of a comparative adjective like "greener"? Let us see. When you say, "The grass is greener than the leaves," there is an ellipsis of the words "are green." Likewise: "The man is wiser than the boy [is wise]." But in the sentence, "Boys are different than girls," what omitted words are understood—"are different"? Obviously absurd. The only situation in which *different* has the standing of a comparative adjective is one in which it is made a true comparative in the same way any other adjective is—as in, "Lemons are different from oranges, but apples are more different than lemons [are different]."

So much for the forces of logic. In other quarters the argument is advanced that *different* has a "semantic identity" with *other*—which, of course, is followed by *than*. However, *different* just as often has a semantic identity with *dissimilar* and *unlike* and almost as often with *distinct*, none of which words are followed by *than*. Finally, we encounter the almost mystical argument that, well, *different* is "felt" to be a comparative and, by golly, if it isn't one it ought to be. Undoubtedly, it is such reasoning—or unreasoning—that produced the slogan of a certain interstate trucking corporation that has proudly painted on the tailboards of its trucks: "Faster than rail, regular than mail."

Is *different than* completely swept aside, then? Not quite. Let us first examine how practiced writers use it. Evans quotes three of them: "See that you use no word in a different sense than it was used in a hundred years ago" (Walter Page). "It has possessed me in a different way than ever before" (Cardinal Newman). "How different things appear in Washington than in London" (John Maynard Keynes). Here are three more: "In Pakistan, Afghanistan, and Turkey the name Ike has a familiar ring, sounding little different than does the twang of a Midwesterner to an Easterner"; "Easter is calculated by the Russian Orthodox Church in a slightly different manner than in the West"; "The bidding of a hand in rubber bridge might be different than in tournament bridge." There is a common denominator in all these sentences. Evans has pointed it out and drawn a tenable conclusion from it. "In the examples just given," he says, "*than* introduces a condensed clause. It could not be replaced by the single word *from* but would require *from that which* or even more words. There is no doubt that the best writers and speakers generally prefer *than* to an elaborate construction such as *from that which*."

Starting from the premise that *different* should normally be followed by *from*—a premise that holds firmly when the next element in the sentence is a noun or a pronoun ("Boys are different from girls"; "My opinion is different from his")—we yet may allow exceptions, and be tolerant of *than,* when what follows *different* is a clause. Insistence on *from* would produce in the Cardinal Newman sentence quoted in the foregoing paragraph some such monstrosity as this: "It has possessed me in a different way from the way in which it ever before did." There is no need to try to "explain" the use of *than* in such instances either logically or grammatically; it is sufficient to say that the word is a useful device to avoid awkwardness, cumbersomeness, and elaborate wastefulness with words. It may be that rules are not made to be broken, but neither are they made to enslave. To insist on *different from* regardless of the clumsiness it sometimes produces would be to let the horse ride the horseman.

Addendum: Even when a writer has dutifully preceded a noun with *different from,* in accordance with the premise stated at the start of the preceding paragraph, he is not necessarily safely home. Here is a writer who is still wandering around in the dark: "The attitude among these Ivy Leaguers is much different from people elsewhere." The sentence as written contrasts "attitude" with "people," which is not the intention. Make it, ". . . different from that of people elsewhere." Again: "Heart muscle requires different substances from brain tissue." This one seems to be contrasting "substances" with "brain tissue." What is meant is, "Heart muscle requires different substances from those required by brain tissue." (The original sentence, by the way, as one in which "brain tissue" is part of a condensed clause, would be appropriate for the use of *different than.*) But the point that is being made in this addendum is that there is more to writing than good usage and good grammar; these provide no safe refuge for the foggy thinker.

141

DIFFERENTIATE

Takes preposition *from*, *between*, or *among*.

DIFFER FROM, DIFFER WITH

Every man *differs from* (is unlike) his neighbor, but every man does not necessarily *differ with* (disagree with) his neighbor. That is the present-day distinction between the two phrases. But it should be pointed out that *differ from* may also be used to denote disagreement, especially if the nature of the disagreement is thereafter specified: "The Republican candidate differs from his opponent in favoring a tight-money policy." Here, too, however, *differs from* is equivalent to *is unlike*.

DILEMMA

As is, or should be, evident from the "di" at the beginning of *dilemma*, there is something twofold about the word. A *dilemma* is a situation entailing a choice between two distasteful alternatives. The word is carelessly used, however, when all that is under discussion is a problem: "The question is basically the common suburban dilemma: Should construction of apartments be allowed in one-family areas?" Preferable words: *predicament, problem, plight, quandary, difficulty, question.*

DIMENSIONS

See PROPORTIONS.

DIRECT, DIRECTLY

Direct is both adjective and adverb; *directly* is adverb alone. As adverbs the two sometimes have distinctive meanings and sometimes meanings so close that the choice is left to idiom or inclination. For the sense of without delay or immediately, *directly* is invariable: "You will go to your room directly after dinner." For the sense of exactly or precisely, *directly* again is the correct word: "He trained his field glasses directly on the target." For the sense of without detours or without interruption, either word is used, although *direct* with its crisper sound is often preferred to convey the meaning more effectively: "Direct [or, less good, *directly*] from producer to consumer"; "The oil Arab has jumped direct [or *directly*] from the camel to the Cadillac, entirely missing the stagecoach, the train, the tram, and the Model T Ford." When the sense of the needed word is clearly adverbial (for example, answering such questions as "How?" or "To what degree?"), the more obviously adverbial form, *directly*, is used: "He was made directly responsible for the program"; "The defendant was linked directly with the conspiracy."

DIS-

In word formation the easy way is not always the simple way. The prefix "dis-," denoting reversal, removal, or negation, provides an example. Embark means to go aboard a vessel. When it was necessary to convey the reverse of this action, our forefathers simply affixed a "dis-" in front of the word and gave us *disembark*. That was the easy way, but it was not a simple, direct approach because it produced a word that really means to un-go-aboard a vessel or something like that.

Many such words have become firmly embedded in the language, and there is little we can do about the situation. It is not suggested here that the situation is calamitous; still, the little we can do might well be done. In the first place, as opportunities offer for coining needed words of this variety we can avoid the easy way and take the simple way. For instance, it is necessary to get people off planes as well as ships these days. Therefore, why write, "The Secretary almost became a bore upon the topic from the instant he disemplaned"? With a simple word like *deplane* available, why select the complicated, awkward *disemplane?* In the second place, when two words of this kind exist side by side, it might be well to choose the simpler, shorter one—*dissociate* rather than *disassociate, disfranchise* rather than *disenfranchise, unbosom* rather than *disembosom, dethrone* rather than *disenthrone, untwine* rather than *disentwine, unravel* rather than *disenravel, disburden* rather than *disemburden, discumber* rather than *disencumber,* and, to be sure, *deburk* rather than *disembark.*

DISAPPOINTED

Takes preposition *in, with, by,* or *of.*

DISAPPROVE

Takes preposition *of.*

DISCOMFITURE, DISCOMFORT

Discomfiture has nothing in common with *discomfort* except a resemblance in sound and appearance. Yet it is often used as if it had a resemblance in meaning, too: "For the Communist rulers of Kerala State, this morning's development was pure balm; it spared them the discomfiture of an immediate parliamentary debate." *Discomfiture* means complete defeat, overthrow, rout. *Discomfort* means lack of comfort, uneasiness. If you suffer *discomfiture,* you most certainly suffer *discomfort,* too, but the reverse is not necessarily (or even usually) true.

DISCOURAGE

Takes preposition *from.*

DISCOVER, DEVELOP, INVENT

A thing that is *discovered* was already in existence but unknown. It is erroneous, therefore, to write, "Ameripol SN synthetic rubber was discovered by Goodrich-Gulf scientists." A synthetic is *invented* (i.e., created or concocted) or, if a basic formula was already known, *developed* (i.e., expanded, perfected, brought to a more advanced, or at least different, state).

DISCRIMINATION

See BIAS.

DISENGAGED

Takes preposition *from.*

DISGUSTING

See ATOMIC FLYSWATTERS.

144

DISINTERESTED

If one is *disinterested* in a situation he is neutral and has no selfish interest in its outcome. For some reason, however, many writers seem to be uninterested in using it correctly: "Up to now the private manufacturing industry in electronics has been fundamentally disinterested in U.H.F. because of the economic uncertainties involved." The word wanted here is *uninterested,* which means lacking interest. A judge may or may not be *uninterested* in a case, but he must be *disinterested.*

DISPENSE

Takes preposition *with* or *from.*

DISPOSSESS

Takes preposition *of* or *from.*

DISQUALIFY

Takes preposition *from* or *for.*

DISSATISFIED

Takes preposition *with.*

DISSENT

Takes preposition *from.*

DISSIMILAR

Takes preposition *to.*

DISSOCIATE

Takes preposition *from.*

DISTASTE

Takes preposition *for.*

DISTILL

Takes preposition *from* or *out of.*

145

DISTINCTIVE, DISTINGUISHED

Distinctive emphasizes the quality of being noticeably different and recognizable; *distinguished* emphasizes the quality of being outstanding or eminent.

DISTINGUISH

Takes preposition *between, from,* or (rarely) *into.*

DISTINGUISHED

See DISTINCTIVE, DISTINGUISHED.

DISTRUSTFUL

Takes preposition *of.*

DIVED

See DOVE.

DIVERT

Transitive only. Therefore this usage is improper: "The ship diverted from its course to pick up the captain of a French freighter." Use *veered, departed, turned, went off,* or *was diverted.*

DIVEST

Takes preposition *of.*

DIVIDE

Takes preposition *between* or *among.*

DIVINE

See ATOMIC FLYSWATTERS.

DIVORCE

Takes preposition *from.*

DOC

See MEDIC, MEDICO.

DOCK

If it isn't something in which a prisoner stands, a *dock* is the space between two piers or a space cut into the shore line for the use of ships. Only in loose, casual usage is it a *wharf*. So the ship goes into a *dock*, but the passengers go onto a *pier* or *wharf*.

DOMINATE, DOMINEER

Take preposition *over* (or none).

DONE

The headline, "Ecuador Rail Line Done," illustrates an improper, casual use of *done*. The word should not be used in good writing to mean finished or completed. It is proper to say, "The roast is done," but this does not mean it is finished; it means the roast is sufficiently cooked.

DOPE

See DRUGS.

DOTE

Takes preposition *on*.

DOUBLE DUTY

Double duty is a phrase that may be applied to constructions in which a single word is made to serve two purposes. Example: "The Army, which now regards organic aviation as integral as the rifle and bayonet. . . ." Notice that the first *as* is bigamously wedded both to "regards" and to the second *as*. Another example: "Winston Churchill in *Triumph and Tragedy* raises a question as to what extent these powerful pressures affected Mr. Truman." The *to* looks backward to *as* and forward to "what extent."

Concerning a similar instance, a newspaper reader wrote to an editor complaining that he had been cheated out of another "to." "I want my other 'to,' " he added. "I hope I am not wrong in asking you, whom I have decided to address this letter, which you may or may not reply, to, to, to."

147

Making one word do double duty is somewhat like hanging a picture on the wall to hide a crack. But not exactly like it, because the writers of such constructions don't know there is a crack, or else are not aware that they are hanging a picture. (*For a reverse error, see* FEATHERBEDDING.)

Another kind of double duty involves the use of a single term in two different senses. Take, for instance, this bifocal sentence: "Kwame Nkrumah, born in the mud-hut village of Nkroful in 1909, is pronounced as if it were spelled Qua-meh En-Kroomah." First, Nkrumah is treated as a person ("born . . . in 1909"), then, when the sentence proceeds, as a name ("pronounced as if . . ."). A similar solecism appears in the following passage from Gibbon: "The Bulgarians, a name so innocent in origin, so odious in its application, spread their branches over the face of Europe." A variation of the fault is evident in this passage: "He talked about the 'wonderful' building program going on in every city he had seen. The building is going on all right, but it is quickly and poorly constructed by unskilled workers with inferior materials." Notice that in the second sentence of the passage "building" first means a program or process, then abruptly becomes a structure, although the heedless writer probably did not mean even that but rather the total of all structures. Eternal vigilance is the price of good prose.

DOUBLE GENITIVE

The question is sometimes asked whether this construction is justified: "He had often been a guest of Mr. Goldfine's." The answer is, Yes. What is termed by some the *double genitive* seems to be a hoary idiom in English. Of course, sometimes it even affects the meaning. For instance, "A picture of Mr. Goldfine" means one thing; "A picture of Mr. Goldfine's" means something entirely else. Grammarians have argued over the origin and nature, but not the validity, of the double genitive with the fervor of hot-stove league fans rehashing a World Series play. They don't even agree on what it is or what to call it. Of them all, Jespersen seems to be the canniest. By his analysis, the "of" in such phrases is "an empty word" meaning "who is" or "which is," and this makes possible the joining of words that it is difficult or impossible to join otherwise. Thus, in the phrase cited the meaning would be "a guest who is Mr. Goldfine's." The analysis is of little concern or utility to anyone except a historical grammarian, but for those who are interested it may be found in *A Modern English Grammar*, Part III, page 15 ff. It may be added that when a pronoun is involved the genitive is invariably "a friend of his," never "a friend of him."

DOUBLE NEGATIVES

Two classes of these constructions may be noted. One is the common, gutter variety: "Don't give me no butter on my toast." This is indisputably bad grammar and vulgar talk. So if the kid says, "I ain't got no pencil," give him one across the mouth and tell him to go out and steal a pencil. The other class of double negatives is what might be termed the fringe class. It comprises deliberate double negatives designed to produce understatement ("Adultery is not infrequent among this tribe") and various constructions that are not all clearly double negatives but that exercise a certain fascination for the savants. ("No, no," or "He would not confess, not even when he was tortured.")

Miss Thistlebottom used to say in P.S. 10 that the trouble with double negatives was that two negatives make an affirmative. This is not true, linguistically, anyway. When you say something is not infrequent you are not quite saying that it is frequent. Moreover, if her reasoning were followed out three negatives would turn the statement back into a negative and four would make it affirmative again. Is that what we mean when we say, "Never, never, never, never"? But, anyhow, who's counting? "No, no," "never, never," and the like are not double negatives but merely repetition of a thought. Similarly in the "He would not confess" sentence the clause "not even when he was tortured" is really a separate thought that finds itself included in the sentence almost by an accident of punctuation. Those grammarians who justify this "double negative" sentence certainly would not condone it if the sentence were inverted: "Not even when he was tortured would he not confess." This should demonstrate that the "tortured" phrase is really not part of the original sentence at all but an independent thought added for emphasis. What they are justifying, then, is not a double negative. Would it be a triple negative if the sentence read, "He would not confess, no, not even when he was tortured"? Obviously not. These fringe instances are not of much concern to the writer. It is only the gutter variety that is likely to bring him condemnation, and if he does not know enough to avoid that fault, he should be in another line of work. *See also* NOT, SUPERFLUOUS.

DOUBLE PASSIVE

Some double passives are merely awkward, or expressions of gobbledygook: "Illumination is required to be extinguished."

Others, however, are downright ungrammatical as well as maladroit: "The runaway horse was attempted to be stopped by the policeman"; "Breezy Point is planned to be converted into a huge, privately financed community." Fowler notes the false analogy between constructions of this kind and the superficially similar construction in, "The man was ordered to be shot." He observes that the active forms from which they are derived are quite dissimilar. In one instance it is: "They ordered the man to be shot." Here "man" is one of two objects of "ordered," the other being the phrase "to be shot," and "man" can therefore be made the subject of the passive verb "was ordered." In the Breezy Point sentence, however, the active form would be: "They planned to convert Breezy Point, etc." Here "Breezy Point" is the object of "convert," and bears no grammatical relation to "planned." It therefore cannot be made the subject of "planned" when that verb is turned into the passive voice. To do so is to create one of what Fowler rightly terms "monstrosities . . . as repulsive to the grammarian as to the stylist."

DOUBT

The selection of the conjunction to introduce a clause after *doubt* or *doubtful* is a matter of idiom. In negative statements *that* is used: "I do not doubt that he is honest"; "There is no doubt that the bill will be passed." In such instances, be it noted, the expressions indicate confidence; no actual doubt is involved. In positive statements, however, where real doubt is being expressed, the following clause is introduced by *whether* or *if*: "The Attorney General doubts whether a conviction can be obtained"; "It is doubtful if the company can remain solvent." (Some grammarians frown on "if" when used in this way, but it is not improper. *See* IF, WHETHER.) Even in positive statements *that* may be used when, as in the earlier examples, the intention is to express unbelief rather than uncertainty of opinion: "The Attorney General doubts that the law is constitutional." *See also* BUT MEANING OTHER THAN *and* BUT WHAT.

DOUBTFUL, IN DOUBT

On the face of it, these two expressions would seem to mean the same thing: uncertain. But an overtone that is not disclosed in dictionaries makes *doubtful* the stronger of the two. If we say, "The patient's recovery is in doubt," the meaning is that the doctors are not sure whether he will recover. If we say, "The patient's recovery is doubtful," the usual understanding is that recovery is unlikely.

DOUBTLESS

See SIMULTANEOUS.

DOVE

In popular speech *dove* is widely used as the past tense of *dive*. Undoubtedly the word is based on the analogy of the past tense of *drive*. But notice that such analogies often are not pursued to a logical conclusion; no youngster has ever been heard to say, "I have diven into the pool ten times so far." In writing, at least, this usage is improper: "The plane dove into the ground and all were killed." Make it *dived*.

DRAMATICS

See -ICS.

DREADFUL

See ATOMIC FLYSWATTERS.

DRENCH

Takes preposition *with*.

DRUGS

A *drug* is anything used as a medicine. Most narcotics are *drugs*, but all *drugs* are not narcotics by any means. Pharmacists object, with some justice, to the use of *drugs* as a synonym for heroin, morphine, cocaine, or hashish. It is true that the word is widely used in this sense and that it also appears in such compounds as *drug fiend, drug addict,* and *drug peddler*; still, precise usage would give the preference to *narcotics* in each instance. *Dope*, by the way, is slang when used as a synonym for *narcotics*.

DRUNK

1. As a noun *drunk* is slang: "Because so many drunks lived in the village, it acquired a bad name." Make it *drunkards*.

2. As an adjective *drunk* is used predicatively: "He was drunk." But it is not used attributively, that is, preceding the noun it modifies: "The actor was convicted of drunk driving." Make it "drunken driving." Evans thinks that *drunken* when used attributively and applied to persons "seems a little archaic and poetic." As in that quaint phrase "drunken bum," eh?

DUE TO

The controversy over this phrase can be summed up in two illustrative sentences: 1. "His fall was due to the icy sidewalk." All grammarians and practiced writers agree that this usage is correct. *Due* is an adjective and it here modifies a noun, "fall." 2. "He fell due to the icy sidewalk." Strict grammarians object to this usage on the ground that the adjectival character of *due* is here disregarded, and the phrase treated as if it were a prepositional phrase. Curme says: "The preposition *due to* is not more incorrect than the preposition *owing to* . . . but it is not yet so thoroughly established in the language."

Although that was written in 1928, it is still true. There is something curious about the situation, however. It seems likely that for every *owing to*, five *due to*'s are written or spoken. Why, then, should *owing to* have gained admittance into the language so readily while *due to* still has to fumble to produce its credentials? Probably the same quality that accounts for the relatively infrequent use of *owing to* explains its readier acceptance: it has a more dignified, a faintly stilted, sound to it. There can be little doubt that *due to* used as a prepositional phrase will ultimately become thoroughly established in the language. But the careful writer, who does not wish to be suspected of negligence, will in the meanwhile use *because of*, which has a less casual flavor and is above suspicion grammatically. This, then, is in the nature of a progress report. *Due to* in the sense of *because of* still has not made the grade, though it will make it.

DUE TO THE FACT THAT

A wasteful locution. Substitute *because*.

DUTCH UNCLE

"The Commissioner delivered a stern Dutch uncle talk yesterday." A *Dutch uncle* is one who reproves with great severity; hence, his talk is always stern; hence, we have here a redundancy.

DWELL

Takes preposition *in, at,* or *on.*

DYSPHEMISM

See RHETORICAL FIGURES AND FAULTS.

153

E

EACH

The word is, of course, singular. When it is the subject of a sentence it takes a singular verb: "Each of the defendants is subject to a five-year sentence." When it is merely an adjunct to a plural subject, however, the plural subject remains in control and the verb is plural. Thus this sentence is incorrect: "Mr. Siemer and his wife each is subject to sentences of five years in prison." It should be "are subject to."

So much for the number of the verb. The number of a later noun depends on whether the *each* comes before or after the verb. If it comes before the verb, the noun remains in the plural: "They each are subject to sentences of five years." If it comes after the verb, the noun becomes singular: "They are each subject to a sentence of five years."

Whether *each* is placed before or after the verb depends in turn on how much stress you wish to put on the separateness and distributiveness of the elements. When you want to hit the separateness hard, you place the *each* after the verb. *See* BETWEEN EACH (EVERY).

EACH OTHER

1. AS A PRONOUN. This sentence is improper: "This fall the President and the Premier will visit each other's country." *Each other* is regarded as a reciprocal pronoun, plural in its meaning; in the genitive it is equivalent to *their*. Therefore it should be "each other's countries." In a different construction you would say, "Each will visit the other's country," but that, to repeat unashamedly, is a different construction.

2. EACH OTHER VS. ONE ANOTHER. Whatever may be said (and much has been) for and against restricting *each other* to two and *one another* to three or more, it must be acknowledged that many writers do not draw such a distinction.

154

The use of *each other* for more than two is not common; still it does occur: "In addition to ending a decades-long dispute among the four states as to each other's rights to Delaware water. . . ." More prevalent is the use of *one another* for only two: "He said Washington's action had been particularly damaging to the delicate relations between India and Pakistan at a time when the two countries had been developing a more friendly approach to one another." Strict grammarians argue against using *one another* for two, and for restricting it to three or more. But they have not had their way in the past and are not likely to have it in the future.

EAGER

Takes preposition *for, after,* or *in; see also* ANXIOUS, EAGER.

EASY, EASILY

Except in some colloquial expressions like "take it easy," the use of *easy* as an adverb is classed as illiterate. "Do your Christmas shopping easy at Blum's" will pass no muster. *See* OVERREFINEMENT.

ECLECTIC

Eclectic pertains to what is chosen from sources here, there, and everywhere. The stress is not on the quality of selection but rather on the fact of free borrowing. Thus the word is not synonymous with *discriminating* or *fastidious*.

ECONOMICS

See -ICS.

-ED

The discussion here concerns nouns that are made into the chief components of compound adjectives. Is it a *middle-sized* room or a *middle-size* room; is it a *four-engined* plane or a *four-engine* plane? The question, be assured, is of no real importance, but from time to time inquirers raise it. These inquirers are entitled to an answer. But they will get none here—only more talk.

No answer is possible because in this field the language submits to no rules. You can scrutinize whole categories of words and sometimes imagine you have hit upon a principle, but as soon as you do, the next word you think of constitutes an exception. It is a baffling and frustrating business, full of inconsistencies and anarchy. One can speak of a *barefoot* boy (with or without cheek of tan), but never of a *barehead* boy; one can speak of a *blackface* comedian, but if he is a double-dealer he is *two-faced*; a car may have *left-hand* drive, but justice is always *even-handed*. Once you embark on these treacherous seas, no matter how well-intentioned you are, your voyage is ill-omened, even if you carry with you a four-leaf clover.

According to dictionaries, the suffix "-ed," when used to make adjectives out of nouns, means "possessing or provided with or characterized by." That explains what it means, but does not explain when it is used. It may be said in general (but don't enter this in the rule book) that most nouns formed into adjectives take the "-ed." That generalization is set down here only because it seems to be easier to compile a list of normal adjectives with the "-ed" than one of adjectives without it. It may also be said— and this is said with far more trepidation—that when the meaning of the adjective is "consisting in whole or in overwhelmingly predominant part," the "-ed" is often not used, and this seems to be the modern tendency. Thus we have *three-room* apartment, *loose-leaf* book, *twelve-tone* scale, *three-ring* circus, *white-wall* tires, and *paperback* book.

Then there are words that may be written either way: *teen-age(d)* boy, *two-tone(d)* car, *hard-surface(d)* road, *long-sleeve(d)* shirt, *horn-rim(med)* glasses, *honey-color(ed)* dress, and *stocking(ed)* feet. (As to those feet, there are people who, perhaps with reason, discern a distinction: *stocking* feet merely notes the absence of shoes; *stockinged* feet calls attention to the presence of stockings.)

The nearest one can come to a rule—and it is almost certain that as soon as these words are in print they will have to be eaten —is that if the nounal adjective applies to an animate creature, it takes the "-ed"; thus: *four-legged* animal (as contrasted with an inanimate object, a *gate-leg* table), *two-headed* calf, *tow-headed* boy, *cross-eyed* girl, *red-winged* blackbird, *yellow-bellied* sapsucker (and all other compound-adjectival birds), *flat-chested* woman, *lantern-jawed* man, *left-handed* pitcher, and *light-fingered* pickpocket.

As a concluding note to an inconclusive discussion, an example may be cited to demonstrate that writers sometimes do not realize that they are dealing with such compound adjectives and do not quite know how to handle them: "With different size constituencies and different length terms, differing collective attitudes would develop, he forecast." To begin with, both compound adjectives require hyphens. Next, although "different size" is acceptable, "different-sized" would be better, in accordance with the first non-rule set down in this article. Finally, "different length," whether it has a hyphen or no and whether it has an "-ed" or no, will not make a comfortable adjective, and the writer should not have attempted it. It is simply a matter of idiom or sound. And perhaps that observation truly sums up everything that has gone before.

-EE

The suffix "-ee" is properly applied to a noun in a passive sense to indicate the person or thing to which something is done. In recent years, however, a tendency has arisen to use the suffix indiscriminately—to use it even when there is already a perfectly good word to express the desired thought.

Trainee is fine; he is a person to whom something is being done. He is being trained. *Refugee* seems to be an ancient enough malformation to be respectable; in addition, there is no other word to convey the idea. This latter consideration applies also to *escapee*. *Fugitive* could be a substitute in most senses, but it has a faintly pejorative connotation (probably because of its common use in the phrase "fugitive from justice") that makes it undesirable as a designation for, let's say, one who has made his way from a country of tyranny to a land of freedom. *Escapist* won't do because the psychologists have taken that over, and *escaper* does not strike the modern ear as right.

On the other hand, why should an oddity such as "Another returnee from overseas was . . ." be used? "Person returning" or merely the word "returning" would serve here. Webster assigns various statuses to "-ee" words. It finds *standee* and *invitee* colloquial, *civilizee* rare, and *quizzee* standard. These sometimes mysterious designations are not always helpful. The best guide is to avoid "-ee" words that sound odd and to eschew coining needless ones, particularly if they are malformations.

EFFECT

See AFFECT, EFFECT.

EFFETE

A very inaccurate digital computer indicates that for every time *effete* is used in its proper meaning of barren, unfertile, spent, or exhausted, it is used a hundred times improperly to mean soft, foppish, weak, or effeminate. For example: "Professional football certainly is not getting effete. What a television documentary portrayed as 'The Violent World of Sam Huff' is just as violent as it always was." The writer obviously thought *effete* somehow contrasted with violent. Not so. Another example: "And since tea and coffee receptions were too effete for West Virginia, it was all right to call receptions an 'ox roast' in the northern part of the state, a 'weenie roast' in the southern part." Effeminate? Elegant? Foppish?

EGOISM, EGOTISM

Egoism refers to a tendency to view matters as they bear upon oneself. *Egotism* refers to the practice of referring excessively to oneself in discourse. Fowler thought he saw signs that *egoism* was ousting *egotism* even in the popular senses. The converse seems to be true, so that *egoism* is now confined largely to philosophical contexts.

EH?

As an interjection expressing mildly surprised inability to comprehend, *Eh?* serves here to categorize examples of the writing of something not really meant, or the failure to write something that was meant, or, simply, errors in logic. The lesson they display is that good writing is good thinking translated into visual form. To put it another way, clear thinking is an indispensable prerequisite to clear writing. The examples, it is believed, will illustrate the theorem.

From a sports report: "No Chicago player got farther than second base and that was John Goryl, who doubled in the fifth with one out." Goryl, then, was the "no player."

From another newspaper article: " 'It is not that these people will not or cannot read English; they just won't,' Mr. Lovick said." It's not that they won't, it's just that they won't.

From an automobile ad: "If nothing will satisfy you, this motor car will." What this says is: If nothing is what it takes to satisfy you, we have a great hunk of nothing for you.

From a book on newspaper editing: "In any of these processes, care should be taken that no fact is eliminated that would cause a wrong impression to be conveyed." Be sure to retain every misleading fact.

From a news report: "They contend that any affirmative word on a new car—still nine months away from dealers' showrooms, if at all—would jeopardize current buyer interest." "If at all" what?

From another news report: "Of 789 British doctors who died in a twenty-nine-month period, they said, death was attributed to lung cancer in thirty-five cases and contributed to death in a thirty-sixth case." There's no denying that death does make a great contribution to death.

From still another news report: "The extract was injected into several mice, which died within two to six minutes. Given smaller doses, the mice recovered." Rodent resurrection.

And from a popular book on politics, this specimen of confused presentation: "Not since 1944 has any Democratic candidate (Franklin D. Roosevelt) received a majority of the popular vote (51.7 per cent)."

It may be argued that in some of these instances a reader would grasp the meaning and not give the faults a second thought. But there are careful readers as well as careless writers, and to them the faults would be set down as black marks in the authors' records. The writer is duty-bound to give a second thought to what he is doing if he is to qualify as a craftsman.

EITHER

1. *Either* normally means one of two. It has been used occasionally over the years to designate one of more than two, as in "either past, present, or future," but this must be regarded as abnormal usage.

2. *Either . . . or* is disjunctive; that is, the words connect by separating, not by joining. That makes this sentence incorrect: "The disk jockey could not be reached for comment at either his New York or Stamford homes." *Either* refers to one *or* to the other one; therefore: "either his New York or Stamford home."

3. *Either . . . or* as correlative conjunctions should connect two of the same kinds of grammatical elements in parallel form. (*See* CORRELATIVE CONJUNCTIONS, LAW OF.) Two examples of misuse will suffice. In each instance a virgule (/) indicates where the *either* should go. "The Ambassador allowed the presumption that the message / was either from the President or had been sent at his direction"; "Nonresidents would be able / to claim either the flat ten per cent deduction up to $1,000 or to itemize their deductions in full."

4. *Either*, even when it seems to have the meaning of *both*, is followed by a singular verb: "Either of the men is qualified for the job." *For the number of the verb after* either . . . or, *see* NUMBER.

EITHER FOR EACH OR BOTH

" 'It might be better,' Mr. Gilbert said, 'to compare some of the good things on either side of the Atlantic.' " Though not wrong, *either* used in this way is at best slightly formal, at worst faintly archaic.

EKE

Eke has Anglo-Saxon roots meaning to increase or add. When you *eke* something out, you add to it or supplement it, as "The teacher eked out his income by working as a part-time waiter." What is *eked out* is the original stock or supply, not the thing that results. In short, *eke out* does not mean squeeze out, as the following sentence suggests: "After a series of fits and starts yesterday the stock market eked out a gain." Still less does *eke* mean what one sports writer had in mind: "Sherman's club eked past weak Pittsburgh and Washington before the offense started to hold its own."

ELAPSE

As a noun, *elapse* is obsolete, archaic, or rare, depending on which dictionary you consult. The general idea is that the word should not be used as it is here: "Elimination of tariffs would not be effected until elapse of a five-year period of gradual reduction." The noun is *lapse*. *Elapse*, of course, is properly used as a verb: ". . . until five years of gradual reduction had elapsed."

ELDER, OLDER

Older may be used in a comparison of any old things, whereas *elder* is restricted to a comparison of persons. In addition, *elder* has less to do with absolute age than with relative age. An *elder* brother may be two years old. *Elder*, in other words, is an indication of seniority. These days *elder* is less used than *older* in virtually all situations. It is mandatory, however, in the phrase "elder statesman."

ELEGANT

Although not so much misused (or even used) as it was a generation or so ago, *elegant* is still overused as a word-of-all-work for designating something especially good. It means fastidiously tasteful, or graceful in a refined and appropriate way, usually with overtones of richness. To speak of "an elegant cut of roast beef" or "an elegant day" is to despoil the word.

161

ELIGIBLE

Takes preposition *for*.

ELLIPSIS SLIPS

Ellipsis in grammar permits the omission of a word in part of a sentence if it can be supplied or understood from a neighboring part of the sentence. In "His life was short and his time ill spent" the "was" that has been omitted from the second clause is readily supplied by the reader. An *ellipsis slip* results when the word to be supplied is not in the same form (number, gender, tense) as in the construction from which it is understood. "Irwin made a great leaping catch for the final out of the seventh when the bases were filled and Wilhelm pitching." Here there is a change in number; the word to be supplied is "was," not the "were" of the expressed compound verb. Fowler and Evans agree that in sentences of a simple pattern (an example from Fowler is "He is dead, & I alive," and an example from Evans is "I was young, they old"), the change in number can be understood along with the word itself. That is to say, they agree that this kind of ellipsis is permissible. The writer will have to decide, however, whether what is permissible is always advisable; whether, let's say, the gain in precision by the insertion of the proper word does not outweigh the economy or dramatic quality achieved by its omission.

Probably the most common ellipsis slip occurs with the use of compound verbs where the two expressed auxiliaries do not both match the one expressed main verb. Examples: "Every Presidential campaign is 'historic' because its outcome can and often has shaped the course of history"; "The United States has not and does not shirk this responsibility"; "Turning in a false alarm has and may result in homicide." There can be little argument that these should be written, "can shape and often has shaped," "has not shirked and does not shirk," and "has resulted and may result." Another type of ellipsis slip—the "as good if not better than" variety—is discussed under INCOMPLETE ALTERNATIVE COMPARISON.

ELOPE

Elopement does not have the marriage act built into it; *elope* means only to run off with an intention of being married. Therefore if a couple were married after an *elopement,* it is well to say so lest you leave them in a state of unmarried sin.

ELSE

See OTHER (AND ELSE).

ELSE'S

The only question that might arise about this word—and it's hard to see why it should in this day and this age—is whether the possessive inflection is affixed to *else* or to the pronominal word coupled with it. That is, do you say (and write) "someone's else girl" or "someone else's girl"? The answer is obvious. It doesn't make sense but it does make good idiom: You say "someone else's girl." The two words are so closely coupled that they are thought of as a compound pronoun.

EMANATE

Takes preposition *from.*

EMBARK

Takes preposition *in, upon,* or *on.*

EMBELLISHED

Takes preposition *with.*

EMERGE

Takes preposition *from.*

EMIGRATE

Takes preposition *from.*

EMOTE

A BACK FORMATION that, take it from Webster, is jocose. It

has no place in an unjocose context like this: "Although Miss Booth appears to be mismated, she transcends the stereotyped situations by sensitive emoting and timing."

EMPHASIZE

Sometimes the bare definition of a word in the dictionary does not quite catch overtones the word may carry in actual use. For example, *emphasize* is defined as meaning to give emphasis to, to stress. Yet it conveys more than that, and the additional connotation is one of particular concern in journalistic writing, in which an ideal is objectivity. After *emphasize* the reader tends to supply the idea that what is being *emphasized* is "the fact that," as in this sentence: "The Secretary emphasized that the program was designed to stimulate state and local programs, and not to supplant them."

The same connotation clings to the word *stress*. In the head-line, "Soviet Deceitful, Envoy Stresses," the tendency is to accept as fact what is being *stressed*. The compound verb *to point out* raises a similar problem; what is *pointed out* obviously is something that exists. In all these instances, considerations of impartiality and objectivity indicate the use of verbs of mere saying, or verbs that suggest allegation.

ENAMORED

Takes preposition *of* or *with.*

ENCROACH

Takes preposition *on* or *upon.*

END

Takes preposition *with* or *in.*

ENDED, ENDING

"The State Department's Office for International Exchange reported today its activities for the six months ending last June 30." Although it must be acknowledged that this is common usage, the preferred usage—preferred because more logical and more precise—would make it *ended*. When the period is one completed in the past, *ended* is the better word. What we have here is an ellipsis: "the six months [that were] ended last June 30." *Ending* is proper for a period to be completed in the future: "the six months [that will be] ending next June 30." Evans and Partridge disagree, maintaining that *ending* may be used for past periods also. Evans cites the example, "If you will refer to the inventory for the year ending March 31, 1915, you will find, etc." He calls this a historical present, as does Partridge. However, it is difficult to reconcile this with Evans's description of what the historical present is: "Occasionally we use a present tense in describing a past event in order to make the action more vivid. This is called the historical present, or the dramatic present. It is acceptable when what is being told is really extraordinary, as in 'I opened the bathroom door, and what do I see but a camel!' " On Evans's own definition one may be pardoned for swallowing the camel but straining at the 1915 inventory.

ENDOWED

Takes preposition *with*.

END RESULT

The faddists, borrowing from the mathematicians, are inundating us with *end results*; e.g., "The end result of segregation and lack of compulsory education for Africans is . . ." and "It is a collection of his speeches loosely strung together by a brief directing narrative; the end result is surprisingly readable and quite informative." An *end result* is conceivable in the working out of a mathematical problem in which there are intermediate results, but in plain English an *end result* is simply a *result*. *For similar pretentious phrases, see* MATHEMATICAL TERMS *and also* FAD WORDS.

ENGAGED

Takes preposition *in* or *upon*.

165

ENGINEER

See SCIENTIST.

ENHANCE

To *enhance* is to increase or make greater. Although it is usually used in favorable contexts ("his prestige was enhanced," "the benefaction was enhanced"), it is not uncommonly used in unfavorable contexts as well ("the offense was enhanced," "the injury was enhanced"). Fowler makes an additional observation about the word; it applies, he says, only to things, not to persons.

ENORMITY

Authorities on usage are virtually unanimous in reserving *enormity* for the idea of wickedness or outrageousness and in employing *enormousness* to mean great size. Here is a common misuse: "The sobering scientific appreciation of the enormity and complexity of the problem involved in manned orbital flight was reflected in the statements of the head of the Space Task Group."

ENTER

Takes preposition *on, upon,* or *into.*

ENTHRALLED

Takes preposition *by.*

ENTHUSE

A great many good writers condemn this verb or eschew it, which comes to the same thing. As a BACK FORMATION from *enthusiasm,* it is one that has not won full acceptance. Most dictionaries term it colloquial.

ENVIOUS

Takes preposition *of.*

ENVY, JEALOUSY

One might almost say that these two words are used as if they were interchangeable. Thus in an advertisement: "Jealous because she dresses better . . . but pays less? Don't envy her. Follow her to Ohrbach's." Sometimes the words are used as if one were a more intense form of the other: "There, within a stone's throw of the sea, he makes his home, and his description of how he does this makes one move from envy to downright jealousy." The words are scarcely synonymous, however. *Envy* means discontented longing for someone else's advantages. *Jealousy* means unpleasant suspicion, or apprehension of rivalship.

It was said at the outset of this item that one might almost say that the two words are used as if they were interchangeable. The reason for the "almost" is that one of the two words is used hardly at all; in common speech *jealousy* has just about driven out *envy*. This is about as unreasonable as deciding to do without pepper, that salt is enough.

EPIDEMIC, EPIZOOTIC

To speak of an *epidemic* of coughing sickness among harness horses, for example, is to indulge in a loose usage. *Epidemic* comes from *epi* (in or among) and *demos* (people). The word for a disease that is widespread among animals is *epizootic*.

EPITHET

An *epithet* is an adjective or phrase describing a characteristic quality of a person or thing. It is not a pejorative word, because an epithet may be either good or bad: *Peter the Great, yellow-bellied coward*. Still, a great many writers and readers think of it as a disparaging word. Which may be why *epithets* are usually "hurled."

EPITOME

If a writer speaks of "the very epitome" of something or other, you can be fairly sure he does not know the meaning of the word. Likewise, if in writing of a collection of photographs of Hindu art he says, "Here is the sap of life at its epitome," it is an odds-on bet he thinks *epitome* means quintessence or something similar. More often, however, the word is used dubiously, like this: "The grand parade was the epitome of regal ostentation."

In such instances the writer is perhaps entitled to the benefit of the doubt. For those who may be uncertain about the word, let it be said that *epitome* does not mean acme or height or greatest or living end; it means a kind of summary or condensation, or a part that is representative of a whole.

EPOCH

Properly speaking, *epoch* denotes the beginning of a new period, a turning point. Again properly speaking, *era* is the period started by an *epoch*. The evidence is, however, that very little proper speaking goes on these days when *epoch* is used. Although most of us would refer to the period of development of atomic fission as "epoch-making," few of us, it is to be feared, would refer to that period as an *epoch*, which, properly speaking, it was. It would be well to make the distinction between *epoch* and *era*, but probably the distortion of *epoch* has gone too far to be reversible.

EQUAL

See INCOMPARABLES. *Equal* takes preposition *to*.

EQUALLY AS

As means to the same degree, or *equally*. Therefore *equally as* is redundant. It is condemned by Fowler as an "illiterate tautology." The condemnation would embrace a sentence such as this: "We stand second to none in defending freedom of the press, but there are other freedoms . . . that are equally as important." The remedy here is to drop the *as*. You could, of course, drop the *equally*, but the result would be less emphatic than is obviously desired. This is because *as* is a pallid word.

Since it is pallid, writers often wish to lend additional stress to the idea of equality, and do it by coupling another word or phrase to *as*, and writing *just as*, *quite as*, or *every bit as*. The question then arises whether these emphasizers, which seem to be equivalent to *equally*, are not as redundant with *as* as *equally* itself. The answer is in the negative, as can be demonstrated by the fact that with none of them can the *as* be omitted. You cannot write, "freedoms that are just important" or "quite important" or "every bit important." ("Quite important" would be good English, but of course the meaning would be somewhat different.) With *equally as*, however, it is immaterial, except so far as emphasis is concerned, which word is dropped.

EQUATE

"Grateful though we are for the colorful account of WAPE, Jacksonville, in your Aug. 24 issue, there are certain statements made that simply do not equate the facts." *Equate* does not mean to equal, as this writer seemed to think; it means to make equal or to express as equal. Therefore, it is followed by *with* or *to*.

EQUIVALENT (adj.)

Takes preposition *to* or (sometimes) *with*.

EQUIVALENT (n.)

Takes preposition *of*.

EQUIVOCAL

See AMBIGUOUS, EQUIVOCAL.

ERA

See EPOCH.

ESCAPE

From a news story: "Two prisoners were foiled last night in their movie-script plan to escape the Tombs." *Escape*, as an intransitive verb, means to break free, and is followed by *from* or *out of*. As a transitive verb, not followed by a preposition, it means to avoid, evade, or elude ("he escaped punishment"). The prisoners sentence should be served with a preposition.

ESPECIAL, SPECIAL

If a distinction is to be made between these two words, it is that *especial* has the meaning of outstanding; *special*, the mean-

169

ing of particular in contrast with general. The distinction is not generally being made, however, because *special* is sweeping the whole field. In the adverbial forms *especially* is holding its own, as in, "The Soviet Union is believed to have some military superiority, especially in the field of missiles."

ESSENTIAL (adj.)

Takes preposition *to*.

ESSENTIAL (n.)

Takes preposition *of*.

ESTIMATED

Takes preposition *at*.

ESTIMATION

As a fancy variant for opinion or judgment, the word *estimation* suffers dilution. *Estimation* involves a rough calculation or measurement. To say, "In my estimation the film was poor," is to stretch the word and make it do duty for a better-suited one.

ESTRANGED

Takes preposition *from*.

ETC.

Et cetera and its abbreviation (meaning "and other things of the same kind") is acceptable in technical writing, provided the sampling from the list makes clear what the other things are that are designated *etc*. In any other kind of writing, however, the use of the term might suggest either that the writer was too lazy to supply the missing items or that he was not quite sure what they were. In any event, *etc*. has no place in writing that has any literary pretensions. The use of *and etc*. or of *etc., etc.,* of course, constitutes a display of ignorance—ignorance, at least, of the meaning of *et cetera*.

ETERNAL

See INCOMPARABLES.

EUPHEMISMS

A *euphemism* is a word or phrase that affords a way of getting around saying something unpleasant. The thing for the writer to decide when the question of employing a euphemism arises is, Which is the more unpleasant: the mealy-mouthed phrase or the unpleasant thing itself?

Euphemisms are not fig leaves, intended to hide something; they are diaphanous veils, intended to soften grossness or starkness. When their purpose is to avoid vulgarity or the arousing of disgust, they have a legitimate place in good writing. It may be preferable to write that a man and woman "spent the night together" than to set forth in detail just how they spent it. And then there is the tabloid headline about the man transformed by surgery into a girl: "Doctors Say Christine Can't Date Yet." That word "date" is about as far as a newspaper could go and stay this side of outright vulgarity. It must be recognized, however, that from the minute the veil of a euphemism is manufactured it begins to wear thin. Consider the transition from "toilet" to W.C. to *washroom* to *bathroom* to *lavatory* to *powder room* to *rest room* and so on, undoubtedly ad infinitum. (Consider also, by the way, the absurdity committed by the Peace Corps girl who wrote home from Nigeria, "Everyone except us . . . goes to bathrooms in the streets.") Constantly changing mores outrun euphemisms and make it necessary to go on producing new veils.

When the purpose of a euphemism is not to avoid vulgarity but rather to skirt the fringes of emotion, the writer will usually be well advised to veto the euphemism. The phenomenon of death, which has in all its aspects become encrusted with euphemisms, is a case in point. Not only does the ordinary person shy away from the stark yet dignified words of this phenomenon, saying that someone has *passed away* or *gone to his rest* instead of saying that he has died, but also those who make a business out of death are untiring in their efforts to give their business the appearance of something pleasant. The *undertaker* (the word itself is an ancient euphemism) is now a *mortician, burial* is almost always *interment,* and the *coffin* is invariably referred to as a *casket.* It is interesting to note the lengths to which the death people will go to get their euphemisms accepted. They have agitated unceasingly to persuade the press to drop the word *coffin* and to substitute *casket.* They have even come up with the notion that *coffin* is inaccurate since a *coffin* is wedge-shaped and present-day burial chests are not. There is nothing in etymology or history to support this notion. Nevertheless, they have apparently persuaded the Webster people that there is, because the Webster dictionary modified its definition of *coffin* not many years back so that it now includes the phrase "commonly wedge-shaped." The whole effort is self-defeating, however, for if the death people should win the skirmish over *coffin* versus *casket,* it will be only a matter of time before they will have to cast about for a euphemism to replace *casket.* Our grandchildren will perhaps be placed in *demise chests* and *restituted* by *mortifiers.*

If a writer needs further guidance about the use of euphemisms, let it be noted that it is the less intelligent and less educated who are most addicted to these linguistic evasions. These are the people who say someone has *passed on,* who refer to every man as a *gentleman* and every woman as a *lady,* who say a pregnant woman is *expecting,* and who say an intoxicated fellow is *a little under the weather.* ("Intoxicated" was itself once a euphemism, having lost its literal meaning of to be poisoned.) Such genteelism is passing, and with it are passing a good many euphemisms. *See also* RHETORICAL FIGURES AND FAULTS.

EX-

The peculiarities of this prefix are of more concern to headline writers than to the rest of us. In the dim past some reputable editors evidently decided that the prefix "ex-" must be attached only to the principal noun of a phrase. Thus we get "Waldorf Ex-Headwaiter Admits Tax Evasion," or, still sillier, "Tax Ex-Official Held." Any day now one may expect to read a headline about a "Bathing Ex-Beauty."

The reason for the decision of the old-time editors is clear, if not cogent: If the prefix is attached to the modifier it might seem to qualify only that word rather than the whole phrase. Fowler criticizes "the ex-Tory Solicitor-General" as meaning the man formerly was but no longer is a Tory. But the trouble with hooking the prefix to the noun is that this, too, seems to exclude part of the phrase from the qualification of "ex-." An extreme example might be "female ex-impersonator," which would falsify the fact. Either way the difficulty lies in the illogicality of coupling the "ex-" to the part when the intention is to couple it to the whole.

Obviously we have here a dilemma. In most writing the dilemma can be gotten around by using *former* instead of "ex-," but not so in headlines or in quoted speech. One solution—and one that is recommended here—is the frank coinage of a word *ex* that would require no hyphen; we then would say "Ex Tax Official Held." For souls not bold enough to accept this solution the best advice is to affix the prefix "ex-," with the hyphen, ahead of the entire phrase. All the evidence is that it is a baseless superstition to believe that "ex-" may be hooked only to the principal noun.

EXAGGERATION
See RHETORICAL FIGURES AND FAULTS.

EXCEPT

Let the grammarians who maintain that *except* is a conjunction ("No one was admitted except I") and those who maintain that it is a preposition governing an objective case ("No one was admitted except me") battle it out. The writer may comfortably sit it out on the sidelines, un-neutrally taking the side of the prepositionists, and he will be in an unassailable position. He may write without challenge, "No one was admitted except me."

As to *excepting*, the word *except* has all but displaced it. *Excepting* is used, indeed is almost mandatory, in negative constructions: "All branches of government, not excepting the

White House, were involved in the problem." Otherwise *except* is the word. *See also* BUT: CONJUNCTION OR PREPOSITION?

EXCEPTION

Takes preposition *to, from,* or *against.*

EXCLAMATION POINT

See PUNCTUATION.

EXCLUDE

Takes preposition *from.*

EXCLUSIVE

Takes preposition *of.*

EXCUSED

Takes preposition *from* or *for.*

EXHIBIT, EXHIBITION

An *exhibit* is an item or collection of items in an *exhibition.* A misuse: "A pictorial exhibit of Bolshevism's forty-year record was opened yesterday."

EXHIBITIONISM

See INSIDE TALK.

EXHILARATE

See ACCELERATE, EXHILARATE.

EXONERATE

Takes preposition *from* or *of.*

EXPECT

See ANTICIPATE, EXPECT. *Expect* takes preposition *of* or *from.*

EXPECT FOR SUPPOSE OR BELIEVE

"I expect you did not do your homework" or "I expect you don't like my cooking" is common in speech but uncommon in good writing. Fowler found the idiom "so firmly established in the colloquial use that if . . . there is no sound objection to it, the period of exile is not likely to be long." This was one of Fowler's bad guesses; after two-score years the idiom is still classed by most dictionaries as "colloq." or "dial.," and careful writers still avoid it.

EXPEDITE

"They backed the commissioner in the view that the plan should be expedited quickly." Delete "quickly"; the word *expedite* means to accelerate or quicken.

EXPEL

Takes preposition *from*.

EXPERIENCED

Takes preposition *in* or *at*.

EXPERT

Takes preposition *in*, *at*, or *with*.

EXPERT

See SCIENTIST.

EX POST FACTO CONSTRUCTION

The term is used here to describe elements of a sentence that are incongruous because they are written from the point of view of hindsight. If that description is not clear, the illustrations will be. "John declared that the general had personally persuaded the dead soldier to re-enlist in the Army eight months ago." (A dead soldier wouldn't be much good to any army.) "Mrs. Michaelis's body had been savagely battered, apparently with a bloodstained chunk of concrete." (The concrete wasn't bloodstained until after the battering.) "Mrs. Cox was passing the wrecked store at

393 Bridge Street when the truck swerved from its course, hit a parked car, and smashed into the store." (It wasn't a wrecked store when she was passing it, but only after the truck hit it.) Legitimate uses of anticipatory words or phrases are classed grammatically as "prolepsis." (*See* RHETORICAL FIGURES AND FAULTS.) Illegitimate uses—illegitimate because faintly ludicrous—constitute the ex post facto construction and should be avoided.

EXPRESSIVE

Takes preposition *of.*

EXTENT

For To an extent, see DEGREE.

EXTRACT

Takes preposition *from.*

EXUDE

Takes preposition *from.*

F

FABRICATE

In its nontechnical sense *fabricate* means to invent or devise falsely. Therefore, "falsely" introduces a redundancy in this sentence: "Mr. Abakumov falsely fabricated this case."

FABULOUS

See ATOMIC FLYSWATTERS.

FACED

Takes preposition *by* or *with*.

FACE UP TO

Here is an example of how the English language has been adapted to meet a need. The verb *face*, in one of its definitions, means to confront boldly or resolutely. But it also means other things, predominantly to stand in front of. Now, finding yourself in front of something is one thing, but finding yourself in front of something with the compulsion to prepare to act is something else. The word *face* would certainly convey the first idea, but it would not necessarily convey the second.

Look, for instance, at this sentence: "There is a rising conviction among the Germans that the United States Administration is determined to make them face unpleasant prospects." The implication there is that the United States is going to make things unpleasant for the Germans. That, however, was not the intent of the sentence, which, let it now be revealed, actually contained the phrase *face up to*. With that phrase the intent is quite different; it means that the United States is determined to make the Germans prepare to do something about the unpleasant prospects. The word *face* by itself is not sufficient to convey this thought, but the later expansion *face up to* is; there can be no doubt of the meaning.

The following sentences bring out clearly that *face* alone, despite dictionary definitions and its original meaning, would not suffice to deliver the intended meaning: "The nation's business and industry are beginning to face up to the grim possibility of a nuclear war"; "Eisenhower is reluctant to come to grips with a political opponent or face up to a troublesome situation"; "The model is a Negro and the writer is white, and they face up to the fact that a happy ending for them in his native Maine would be difficult." There is no disputing that *face* by itself can mean to meet boldly and prepare to do something. But the fact of usage is that it also can mean merely to confront, and that something more is needed to convey the idea of girding the loins.

Adding what may be termed "tails" to the verb *face* to satisfy this need is by no means the same thing as superfluously adding tails to a verb without gaining even the shadow of a different meaning—as has happened with *head up*, for example, which means nothing different from *head*. *See* VERB TAILS.

FACT

The fact or *the fact that* is often a wasteful locution. It can also be a loaded phrase when it seems to accept as fact what is rather a contention or an allegation. Here is a sentence that combines both faults: "The Soviet Premier reiterated the fact that his country was peace-loving." Another instance, this one merely of waste: "He recalled the fact that Columbus discovered America."

The phrase cannot invariably be eliminated, however. With some verbs a noun clause is not sufficient: "The Governor did not relish the fact that a union leader would be his opponent." Likewise the phrase is necessary after a preposition: "The Mayor's attention was directed to the fact that his budget was the largest yet."

FACTOR

It is not so much that *factor* is incorrectly used; it is difficult to misuse a word that has so broad a meaning as this: one of the elements that contribute to a result. It is rather that it is overused —used when a more precise word would be better, or used when the thought could be expressed more concisely by omitting it altogether. Instead of writing, "Mr. Ehrenburg's essays constitute a re-examination of the factors of greatness in Chekhov's art," it might be better to replace *factors* with *components, ingredients, elements,* or some other less tawdry word. And, to take an example from Strunk, instead of writing, "Air power is becoming an increasingly important factor in deciding battles," it might be better to write, "Air power is playing a larger and larger part in deciding battles."

FACTS

"No matter what the true facts of the situation are, the Arab world seems. . . ." Delete "true"; there are no such things as false facts, except, according to the dictionaries, "loosely," and these turn out to be *allegations* or *suppositions.*

FAD WORDS

Not long ago members of the New York State Legislature (of all people) rebelled at Governor Rockefeller's repeated use of *task force* to describe his special study groups. Every committee, panel, or investigative body he appointed seemed to be designated a *task force.* The use was symptomatic of a present-day desire for supercharged writing, in which writers pounce upon any piece of jargon they can find in specialized fields and convert it into a fad word. Thus, nothing is increased or accelerated or intensified any more; it is *stepped up.* Nothing is detailed; it is *spelled out.* Nothing is gradually reduced; it is *phased out.* Skill is no longer skill; it is *know-how.* Now, there is nothing wrong with an occasional use of such a term when it fits the context. What is wrong is peppering pages with such words. And what is particularly objectionable is a thoughtless, inappropriate use, as in a news story that began: "A crash program to assist the New Haven Railroad was announced yesterday." If there's anything a railroad does not need, it's a *crash program.* The plea here is not for flat writing; it is rather against hot-rod writing. Let's kick off a drive against it. Let's begin the countdown. Some of the fad words that are discussed separately are *allergic, balding, breakdown, breakthrough, chain reaction, kudos, marginal, spell out, target, trigger. See also* INSIDE TALK.

FAIL

Used precisely, *fail* presupposes a goal, an intention, a requirement, or an expectation. The word is not properly used to express a mere "not" idea, as in the following sentence: "India has thus far failed to break off relations with China because of reported anxiety that a breach might lead to an aerial bombardment of Indian positions and even Indian cities." Likewise it would not be proper to write, "Conservationists have charged that DDT is poisonous to many forms of wildlife and fails to break down into harmless chemical components over long periods." In these instances "has not broken off" and "does not break down" should be substituted for the *failed* construction.

Fail takes preposition *in, at,* or *of.*

FAILING

See DANGLERS.

FALLACY

A *fallacy* is not merely an error, but a particular kind of error: one that results from improper reasoning, faulty logic. The word derives from a Latin term that means deceptive, and a *fallacy* is a kind of mistake that has a deceptive appearance of correctness. If a gambler reasons that a coin tossed repeatedly will turn up half heads and half tails, and that since it has come up heads twenty times in a row the next toss therefore must be a tail, he is guilty of a *fallacy*. But if he then bets his whole stake on a tail in the next toss, he is guilty of a *mistake* arising from the *fallacy*. If that does not make clear the distinction between a *fallacy* and an error, it at least should be a warning to gamblers. (By the way, the twenty-first toss was also a head.)

FAMED

To write of "Paul Engle, famed Iowa poet" is not to write incorrectly, but rather to raise the question whether the writer has for some reason gone out of his way to avoid the customary word *famous*. *Famed* is the participle of the verb to fame. In general there is nothing wrong with using a participle as an adjective, but there might be some question when, as in this instance, an adjective from the same root already exists. *Celebrated*, originally a participle, has independent existence as an adjective, but no other adjective from the same root coexists.

FANTASTIC

See ATOMIC FLYSWATTERS.

FARTHER, FURTHER

The general preference is to restrict *farther* to ideas of physical distance and to use *further* for everything else. This, then, would be improper: "The Thor's production prototype was farther advanced than that of the Army." Fifty years hence writers probably will not have to worry about this distinction, because it looks as if *farther* is going to be mowed down by the scythe of Old Further Time.

FASCINATED

Takes preposition *by* (person); *with* (thing).

FASCINATION

Takes preposition *for*.

FATAL

See INCOMPARABLES.

FATAL, FATEFUL

If writers would ignore the small area in which these two words overlap in meaning, and would concentrate instead on the meanings in which they are distinct, there would be less confusion of the two. *Fatal* in its distinctive meaning applies to that which leads to death or destruction. *Fateful* in its distinctive meaning applies to that which leads to great consequences, good or bad.

FAVORABLE

Takes preposition *for, to,* or *toward.*

FEAR (n.)

Takes preposition *of.*

FEARFUL

See ATOMIC FLYSWATTERS.

FEASIBLE FOR POSSIBLE

Feasible means that something can be done; *possible* means that something can happen. Improper: "A feasible explanation of the burglary is that the thief was seeking secret documents."

FEATHERBEDDING

The article DOUBLE DUTY describes situations in which a single word is subjected to overwork by being compelled to carry the burden of two meanings, as is the word *to* in this sentence: "He was uncertain as to whom he was indebted." This is sweated labor. But the reverse situation occurs sometimes, a situation in which two workers sign in to do the job of one. This is featherbedding. Example: "It is becoming increasingly clear that in the judgment of many persons, in the industry as well as out, that television has not yet found the way to direct sponsorship of programs without serious effect on the medium's over-all content." (Delete one *that.*) "Were those correspondents right who said it was better to take a chance on getting back to the free world rather than risk the arrival of the Soviets?" ("Better" makes "rather" superfluous.) No ignorance produces errors of that kind; the cause is forgetfulness, sheer carelessness. The cure is obvious and simple: The writer, once he has set down his sentences, must turn editor and examine them critically.

182

FEATURE

Originally, Webster labeled the verb *feature* as "Colloq. U.S." Fowler feared the verb would make its way into popular use, which, he thought, would be a pity. His prediction has proved correct, his disapproval unjustified. The word has made a place for itself and it is in some contexts almost indispensable. The supermarket that is "featuring pig's knuckles this week" surely should not be expected to say that it is "giving special prominence to pig's knuckles this week." Like all newcomers, however, *feature* should not be embraced too avidly or crushed with affection.

FEED

Takes preposition *on* or *off*.

FEMININE ENDINGS

As women have made their way in growing numbers into more and more fields that used to be posted "Men Only," the tendency has been to drop the many suffixes that set them apart. For instance, *authoress* is a rare word these days, and *doctoress* is as good as extinct. *Negress* and *Jewess* usually give way to Negro and Jew, and *chairlady* and *forelady* (or *-woman*) quite often give way to chairman and foreman. Offsetting this disappearance of the feminine ending is a modern "cute" tendency to invent some new ones, such as *usherette* and *farmerette* and *strippeuse*. A few feminine endings have held their own: *actress*, *heroine, confidante*. But the tendency, as has been noted, is to avoid the feminine form—in writing, that is.

FEVER

See TEMPERATURE.

FEW

In the phrase "a few," *few* plays the role of a noun and therefore the article preceding it is appropriate. The same noun role is played by *many* in "a good many" or "a great many."

FEWER, LESS

The general rule is to use *less* for quantity and *fewer* for number. Thus: "The building has less floor space than the Empire State, yet it contains no fewer than 1,200 offices." There is one oddity about *fewer:* Whereas it is fine to write, "The Liberals won three fewer seats than in the previous election," you run into idiom trouble if you reduce the number to one; you cannot say "one fewer seats," nor can you say "one fewer seat." The only escape hatch is "one seat fewer." The only other problem about *fewer* is to distinguish whether it is quantity or number that is being spoken of. For instance: "Not many of these buildings are fewer than thirty years old." The thought here is not of individual years but of a period of time; therefore, *less.* Another example: "Some professors earn fewer than $7,500 a year." Make it *less.* The thought is not of separate dollars but of a sum of money.

FEW IN NUMBER

See **IN NUMBER, IN SIZE.**

FIEND

A *fiend* is a devil or wicked creature. As used in phrases like *opera fiend, autograph fiend,* or *dope fiend,* the word is slang. Probably the first of this breed was *dope fiend,* applied to one who was "crazy" for narcotics or crazed by them. From that point it was just a short hop, skip, and jump to one who was "crazy" for opera or autographs or golf or artichokes. Perhaps an echo of the word *fan* had something to do with the spread of the word. In any event, *fiend* is not standard usage in this sense.

FIGURATIVELY

See **LITERALLY.**

FIGURE

Like **CALCULATE** or **RECKON,** the verb *figure* means to count in numbers or to reach a conclusion based on a computation. To use it as a synonym for *suppose* or *think,* as in "I figure it ought to be a good show," is improper. Worse still is the slang expression "it figures," meaning "it is (or was) to be expected," as in the sentence "It figures that Ackerman is not above larceny."

FILIBUSTER
See HIJACK.

FINAL
See INCOMPARABLES.

FINE
As an adverb, *fine* is classed by Webster as dialectal and colloquial. So if you write, "He is behaving fine," you are not writing good.

FINE WRITING
Strangely enough, in this phrase "fine" has come to mean almost the reverse of its usual meaning of superior or refined. *Fine writing* is ornate or overblown, hence, bad writing.

FIRE
"Thirteen were still on the U.N. payroll Dec. 17, but two were due to be fired yesterday." Common in everyday speech, *fire* in the sense of to discharge or dismiss is slang, inappropriate in shaped writing.

FIRM
A *firm* is a partnership, which has no standing in law as an entity distinct from its members in the way that a *corporation* is a legal person. The brevity of the word constantly tempts headline writers to use it—and often they use it erroneously. Acceptable synonyms when a *corporation* is meant are *concern* and *company*. See also CONCERN.

FIRST, FIRSTLY
Over the years there has been much firing back and forth over these words, but one gets the impression that the antagonists have been firing blanks. Some have objected for obscure reasons

to the word *firstly*. Yet all have sanctioned *secondly, thirdly, fourthly,* plus what is almost invariably designated as *etc.* (Whether the *etc.* covers *forty-thirdly* or *eight-hundred-seventeenthly* nobody ever says.) If there is going to be quarreling over whether to use *first . . . secondly* or *firstly . . . secondly* —although Heaven only knows why there should be—perhaps the obvious and simplest way to handle a series is *first . . . second* (both of which words, by the say, are as much adverbs as are *firstly, secondly*). This solution, incidentally, takes care of *forty-thirdly*. Surely a *first . . . second* listing is in no way inferior to a *one . . . two* listing, about which no one has ever fired a shot.

FIT

Except in casual speech, the past and perfect tenses are *fitted*. This, then, is unacceptable: "Nothing has quite fit the popular image of the Soviet Union. . . ." Treat *befit* similarly.

FIX

A hole-in-the-wall shop in a ramshackle, now-demolished building fronting on Columbus Circle in New York used to bear this arrogant sign: "Handy Harry. He Can Fix Anything." He could, too. In the linguistic world the word *fix* itself has become a sort of Handy Harry. It serves a variety of uses and it can almost cover up a great many shortcomings, including a writer's sloth or his inability to find the precise word he needs. Does your cuckoo clock require repairing? You *fix* it. Are you thirsty for Martinis? You *fix* them. Do you wish to find your exact position at sea? You *fix* it. Does your face need lipstick and powder? You *fix* it. Do you wish to make easy money betting on a basketball game? You *fix* it. Is your hair disarrayed? You *fix* it. Are your negatives completely developed? You *fix* them. Are you deciding on the date for the club's next meeting? You *fix* it. And so on and so on, including an assortment of noun uses of the word to mean a predicament, a navigational position, or an unethical prearrangement (*See* "Quotation marks" *in article,* PUNCTUATION). Some of these examples are standard primary meanings of the word *fix*. These primary meanings, as can be deduced from the Latin root of the word (which means fasten), all contain the sense of establishing, securing, giving stability, or rendering definition. Most of the examples, however, are casual uses that are quite common, especially in America. Whether they are to be used in good writing will depend on the desired flavor of what is being written or on whether a substitution for *fix* will result in stilted circumlocution. In cases of doubt the writer will be well advised to fix on a precise, non-nebulous word rather than on *fix*.

FIXATION
See INSIDE TALK.

FIXIN'S
"Turkey and all the fixin's." Twice a year—at Thanksgiving and Christmas—newspapers throughout the land trot this one out (a turkey trot, perhaps?) and the sorely beset reader might well ask, "Gee, Maw, does we-all have to eat them thar warmed-over clichés agin this year?"

FLAGRANT
See BLATANT, FLAGRANT.

FLAIL, FLAY
Those who are addicted to SONIC WRITING occasionally write *flay* when they mean *flail*; e.g., "Who is to stay that ham-like hand when it flays away?" The word *flay*, in its primary definition, means to tear the skin off. It is, incidentally, the darling of many headline writers who probably do not know that. As a verb, *flail* means to whip or flog, usually with a swinging motion like that employed in using a *flail*.

FLAIR
If *flair* were to be employed in its primary sense, it would apply mainly to bloodhounds, because it means originally a sense of scents. As with most words, we may allow extensions of the original meaning and accept *flair* to mean inborn discernment.

187

Thus, "Fidel Castro returned to the Premiership with his flair for drama" is proper if what is meant is his instinctive feeling for what is dramatic. It is less than precise if what is meant is his liking for the dramatic. Alas, the word is used too often as if it meant flourish, talent, or mere aptitude.

FLAMMABLE

Identical in meaning with *inflammable*, the variant *flammable* has for some years been pushed forward by fire underwriters. They argue—and no doubt with justice—that non-philologists in the population, on picking up a can of cleaning fluid labeled *inflammable*, believe the fluid will not burn and may thus be compelled to learn philology the hard way. These elements of the population, it is contended, think of words like *active* and *inactive* or *capable* and *incapable* and never give a thought to other meanings of the prefix "in-," as in *incarcerate*, *incise*, or *inflame*. If it will save a single burned eyelash, by all means let's have *flammable* (or even *flameable*, as one fuel company in Florida writes it).

FLANK

Since a *flank* in an animal is the fleshy section between the ribs and the hip, and in a human being is the outside of the thigh, there can be in any creature only *two flanks*. When the word is carried over into military or any other terminology, this same two-ness applies. You cannot have three *flanks*, as this sentence suggests: "The United States officials insisted that Soviet armored cars, which had flanked the convoy on three sides, be removed."

FLATLY

Almost always superfluous, *flatly* tends to slip into sentences before such verbs as *refused* or *rejected*, usually because the writer thinks of it—if, indeed, he thinks about it at all—as an intensifier. Sometimes the word fits the facts, more often it does not. In "The United Nations General Assembly flatly refused tonight to take up the problem of colonialism by a vote of seventy-two to five," the word is redundant since it means positively or plainly or in a manner to rule out argument—and the vote makes all this clear. On the other hand, if a case went to the Supreme Court, which threw it out in a ten-word ruling, it would be proper to say, "The court flatly denied the appeal."

FLAUNT, FLOUT

Of these two, *flout* is almost never misused, whereas *flaunt* is misused about half the time. *Flaunt* means to wave or make a boastful display. *Flout* means to scoff at or treat with contempt. First, a specimen of the rare misuse of *flout*: "Don't those beautiful movie people, who flout their private lives to the world like adolescents, ever intend to grow up?" Now for the more common error; in each of the following examples *flout* is the word that was meant: "I hope that no parents, by their examples, will teach their children to flaunt the law"; "The Secretary charged the South Korean Government with 'unilateral action' flaunting the authority of the United Nations Command"; "Officially, ordinary crime was a capitalist monopoly and could not exist in a Marxist state. Even in greatly exaggerated fictional form, to say it did exist was to flaunt the ruling ideology." Perhaps it will help those who are confused by these two words to keep in mind that one who is defiant of authority is, to mint a word, a *floutlaw*.

FLAY

See FLAIL, FLAY.

FLIED

You won't find it in most dictionaries, but *flied* is the past tense of *fly* in one specialized field: baseball. You could not say of the batter who hoisted a can of corn to the center fielder that he "flew out"; you must say he *flied out*.

FLOUT

See FLAUNT, FLOUT.

189

FOLK, FOLKS

Folks is a casualism, as in the sentence "Single folks topped the list, with 70.8 per cent having headaches." Even without the "s" it is considered archaic or arch or both, and therefore is not suitable for general straightforward writing. The odd usage "He is just folks"—meaning that he is simple and unpretentious—is a cut or two lower in the linguistic scale.

FOND

Takes preposition *of.*

FONDNESS

Takes preposition *for.*

FOOT

In verse a *foot* is a combination of syllables making up a metrical unit. The five most common feet in English verse are the *iamb* or *iambus* (‿ᐟ as in the word "omit"), the *trochee* (ᐟ‿ as in the word "writing"), the *dactyl* (ᐟ‿‿ as in the word "ignorance"), the *anapest* (‿‿ᐟ as in the word "understand"), and the *spondee* (ᐟᐟ as in the words "bad breath"). Memorize this stanza, noting its cadences, and you will always know which is which:

> IAMBUS, *King of all the North,*
> *Sucking* TROCHEES, *ventured forth.*
> *Galloping* DACTYLS *emerged from their nest,*
> *But he struggled and conquered this* ANAPEST.
> SPONDEE!

FOR

1. AS A LOADED WORD. The innocuous-appearing little word *for* can, in some circumstances, be a side-taking or loaded word, putting the writer in the position of characterizing or expressing an opinion when neither is his intention. For example: "He was criticized for meddling at a time when East-West diplomatic re-

lations hung in the balance." Or: "Continued criticisms of the British Government for following a 'soft' approach to the Soviet Union. . . ." In these contexts *for* is equivalent to a *because* phrase, and thus seems to accept as fact what is being criticized. This was not the intention of either writer. Correcting the fault may require a little circumlocution. In the first example make it "for what was said to be meddling" or "as a meddler," and in the second example make it "asserting that it is following a 'soft' approach." The extra words are necessary if the statements are to be impartial.

In a comparable and quite common situation in newspaper writing it is all right to say that a man was *indicted for murder* of his grandmother because the murder, regardless of who committed it, presumably is a fact, but it may be dangerous to say he was *indicted for murdering* his grandmother since the *for murdering* (read "because he murdered") and the grammar of the sentence connect the man with the murdering. This may seem like a fine point, but fine points can draw blood.

2. FOR, BECAUSE. *Because* has all but superseded *for*; writers seem to feel that *for* is faintly archaic, or at any rate not so strong a word as *because*. Still, if a choice has to be made between the two, the distinction between them may be set forth as follows: *Because*, a subordinating conjunction, introduces a direct cause-effect relationship between what follows it and what precedes it ("It is a good play because it was written by Shakespeare"). *For*, a coordinating conjunction, introduces a less direct relationship and usually tacks on to the original statement some substantiation or explanation ("It is a good play, for it contains pathos, humor, and high drama").

FOR, PLUS SUBJECT OF AN INFINITIVE

The point at issue here concerns such constructions as "I want for you to phone me tomorrow"—that is, those in which the "for, etc." is the object of a verb. No question arises when the "for, etc." modifies a noun or an adjective; it is entirely proper to write, "There is no requirement for students to take a swimming test," or, "He was reluctant for his daughter to take up an acting career." But when the "for, etc." is the object of a verb, some doubt crops up despite the growing use of the construction in spoken language.

Evans says: "In the United States *for* is now standard English when it introduces the subject of an infinitive that is being used in place of a *that*-clause. But it is not acceptable when the infinitive is not being used in this way. For example, we do not say *I want that you should come* and therefore *I want for you to come* is also unacceptable." With the latter part of this passage it is easy to agree. The first part, however, is dubious. A perfectly good sentence with a *that*-clause would be, "The doctor advised that he walk two miles a day." But it would not be proper to transform that into, "The doctor advised for him to walk two miles a day." Similarly, "I request that you leave" does not properly translate into "I request for you to leave." And there is a faintly dialectal quality about this sentence: "American policymakers apparently did not mean for their hints to be taken literally."

One present-day linguist affirms that this type of construction is a regionalism prevalent in the South and Southwest. Even educated people in those sections certainly use the construction in everyday speech, but it is doubtful whether many of them use it in shaped writing. The careful writer would do well to avoid it.

FORBID
Takes preposition *to* (infinitive).

FOREIGN
Takes preposition *to*.

FOR FREE
"The drivers will pay their transportation to Stanford, but will have the run of the inn for free." The phrase *for free* is semi-humorous slang, perhaps originally used by semiliterates who did not realize that *free* is not synonymous with *nothing* but with *for nothing*.

FORMIDABLE

In its derivation *formidable* contains the idea of fear, and the primary meaning of the word is arousing dread or alarm or, more broadly, awe. The French, who have the same word, have stretched theirs so that it also means tremendous or great. Perhaps under their influence, writers of English have used the word loosely to mean merely large or impressive. Thus we read that "the number of Americans who visit Italy each year is formidable." The word need not be limited to the notion of fear-inspiring, but it should be confined to contexts in which the desire is to suggest either apprehension ("a formidable opponent") or awe ("formidable learning") or at least difficulty ("a formidable task").

FORMULATE

To say "The President is trying to formulate a judgment on the China question" is to use a pretentious and inaccurate word for a simple one—*form*. *Formulate* means to work out as a formula, and its applications are more in the fields of science or mathematics than in the field of general writing.

FOR THE PURPOSE OF

A wasteful locution. "The meeting was called for the purpose of examining housing proposals." Why not *to examine?*

FORTUITOUS, FORTUNATE

Fortuitous means happening by chance. *Fortunate* means marked by good luck. *Fortuitous* is often misused when *fortunate* is intended, as in this passage about an astronaut who was troubled by droplets of water bouncing weightlessly around inside his capsule until he scooped them into his handkerchief: "This proved to be a fortuitous procedure, for the astronaut found the dampened handkerchief convenient for mopping up dust and wiping his face."

FOUNDED

Takes preposition *on, upon,* or *in.*

FOUNDER

"Five persons were rescued from the schooner *Amberjack*, which foundered and apparently sank in heavy seas yesterday." If the ship *foundered*, it did not "apparently" sink; it did sink, because that is what *founder* means—it has a built-in sink.

FRACTION

Used to mean a small part, *fraction* is, as Partridge says, infelicitous, and, as Webster says, colloquial. These designations should be quite enough to warn the careful writer, even aside from the technical and not necessarily pertinent objection that ninety-nine one-hundredths, though a *fraction*, is no small part.

FRANKENSTEIN

Frankenstein was the fictional physiology student who constructed the monster, not the monster itself, as many seem to think: "One would like to know what will happen when the politicians get through, and what would have happened had they not created a Frankenstein." The error, through long and repeated use, has won wide acceptance not only in the movies and on television, but also in Webster. Nevertheless, it is still an error, on a par with a MISQUOTATION like "gilding the lily." If you don't mind misquoting, you will not mind misusing *Frankenstein*, but if you do care, you will use *Frankenstein('s) monster* or perhaps will turn to another word, like *golem* or *robot*.

FREEDOM

Takes preposition *from* or *of*.

FREUDIAN TERMS

See INSIDE TALK.

FRIEND

Takes preposition *of* or *to*.

FRIENDLY

Takes preposition *to* or *toward*.

FRIGHTENED OF

A casualism when used as a synonym for *afraid of*—as in, "The Katangese officials have been frightened of outbreaks." *Frightened* takes the preposition *at* or *by*.

FRIGHTFUL

See ATOMIC FLYSWATTERS.

FROM

For number of a single noun following *from, see* BETWEEN AND FROM.

FROM HENCE, FROM WHENCE

Hence means from here or from now. *Whence* means from which place or from which position. Notice that both words contain the idea of *from*. It is therefore tautological to repeat that idea in this way: "Mr. Praeger, as orderly and meticulous as Vienna, from whence he came, said that. . . ." Despite the fact that *from whence* has occasionally been used by good writers, it is a pleonasm and is best avoided.

FROWN

Takes preposition *at, on,* or *upon*.

FRUGAL

Takes preposition *of*.

FRUITFUL

Takes preposition *in* or *of*.

FRUITION

Commonly, but erroneously, associated with fruit, the word *fruition* means enjoyment or pleasurable possession of something. Here is a precise but uncommon use of the word: "He was happy in the fruition of his extensive library." And here is an imprecise but common use of the word: "The efforts of a New Jersey man to have an American hospital built in Poland are nearing fruition." In this situation the writer faces the unusual choice of being precise but probably unclear, or being imprecise but understood. He may be helped out of his dilemma by the fact that Webster has recognized the inexact meaning—realization or fulfilment—as a standard one. *See* BERNSTEIN'S SECOND LAW.

FUGITIVE

Takes preposition *from.*

FULL

Takes preposition *of.*

FULSOME

It does not mean full, copious, or bounteous, as the writer of this passage seemed to think: "Shai K. Ophir, a first-rate mime, offered last night a display of a fulsome repertory." It means overfull and offensive because of insincerity; repulsive, odious. It most often appears—and appears incorrectly, of course—in the phrase "fulsome praise."

FUNCTION

1. One of the meanings of the noun is a formal, ceremonial event. To term a luncheon of the Tuesday Afternoon Bridge and Bingo Club a *function* is to be ostentatious and slightly vulgar. This same organization always refers to its annual fried-chicken-and-ice-cream dinner as a *banquet*—and when it does the same stricture applies.

2. Another sense of the noun refers to the duty or course of action that customarily or habitually goes with an office, calling, or operation. It is not normally a one-time thing, as a professor seemed to think when he opened his speech with these words: "It is my function here to indicate something about the basic trends which are vitally affecting every sector of America now. . . ." A *function* is a built-in activity. What the professor meant was *duty* or *purpose* or *mission* or *task.*

FUNNY

Only in casual language does *funny* mean odd or peculiar; in serious communication it is restricted to the meaning of humorous or mirth-provoking. It is particularly inappropriate in this kind of context: "Funniest of all is that five days after the Chancellor left town on a trip to the United States and Japan, his usually docile Cabinet broke out into a public controversy." On the other hand, it is quite appropriate in an informal context, as in Adlai Stevenson's droll remark after his 1952 defeat for the Presidency: "A funny thing happened to me on the way to the White House."

FURTHER

See FARTHER, FURTHER.

FUSED PARTICIPLE

See GENITIVE WITH GERUND.

GALORE

Sure, and it's a fine broth of a word—in its place. Its place is not good, serious writing. Usually an adverb meaning abundantly, and usually appearing after a noun, it is classed in American usage as a casualism. It may be used for jocular or breezy or slangy effect, just as the imported word *kosher* may be, but *galore*, a Gaelicism, is inappropriate in a passage like this: "Task forces galore—composed of earnest-minded but often naïve intellectuals—are trying to delineate reforms in well-written phrases."

GAMBIT

In chess the word refers to an opening move in which a piece is sacrificed to obtain a strategic advantage. Derivatively, it means a concession to get things started. It does not mean any opening move, or merely a maneuver in the course of a game, or a negotiation, or what not. If a lad wooing a lass invites her to dinner, it is not a *gambit*; if he in addition invests his hard-earned pay in orchids and champagne in the hope of a later return, it is.

GAME

See OCCUPATIONS.

GANTLET, GAUNTLET, GAMUT

Two of these you run and the other you throw down: A *gantlet*, originally a form of military punishment in which the culprit sprinted between two files of men who beat and belabored him, is one thing you run. Webster III to the contrary notwithstanding, a *gauntlet* is not the same thing; it is a glove, which in days of chivalry was thrown to the ground to signify a challenge. A *gamut* is a series of musical notes—specifically, a scale—and that, too, is something you run.

198

Gauntlet is the one word of the three that gives rise to error
—such errors as these: "In black, buttoned to the chin, bearing
a reticule, Mrs. Moody ran the gauntlet"; "Residents of the
Katangese capital ran a gauntlet of fire in crossing the street."
The practice in this country has been to keep the distinct spellings of *gauntlet* and *gantlet*, which have entirely different deriva-
tions, and the practice seems to be a good one.

GENDARME

To speak of "Paris gendarmes grappling with rioters" is to
use an inaccurate designation for a Parisian policeman. French
cities have policemen, villages and other small communities have
what we would call constables, and the rest of the countryside
is policed by *gendarmes,* who are thus equivalent to our state police. Facetiously, Americans sometimes refer to any French
policeman—indeed, any policeman anywhere—as a *gendarme,*
but it is neither correct nor, if truth be told, funny.

GENDER

Gender is a grammatical term, denoting (in English)
whether words pertaining to a noun or pronoun are classed as
masculine, feminine, or neuter. It is not a substitute for *sex* (but,
then, what is?). Indeed, in some foreign languages *gender* often
disregards sex. In German, for example, *Weib,* the word for
woman, is neuter; in French *plume,* the word for pen, a sexless
article, is feminine. To use *gender* as if it were synonymous with
sex is an error, and a particularly unpardonable one in scientific
writing, as in this example: "The treatment given the newborn
is dependent not only on the degree of medical skill but also on
such massive variables as gender, social position of the parents,
and the number of children in the family, to name only a few."

GENERALLY SPEAKING

See DANGLERS.

GENITIVE WITH GERUND

Fowler hurled some of his strongest language against what

he dubbed the fused participle. To make his case he cited three sentences, and analyzed them, as follows:

1. Women having the vote share political power with men.
2. Women's having the vote reduces men's political power.
3. Women having the vote reduces men's political power.

In the first, he said, the subject of the sentence is *women*, and *having* is a participle, a kind of verbal adjective. In the second the subject is the verbal noun or gerund *having*, and *women's* is a possessive case attached to that noun. The grammar in these two is normal. In the third, the subject is neither *women* (since "reduces" is singular) nor *having* (for if so, *women* would be left in the air without grammatical construction), but a compound notion formed by fusion of the noun *women* with the participle *having*. It is from this jerry-built construction that Fowler derived the term "fused participle," although it is fairly clear that *having* in the third sentence is being used as a gerund, rather than as a participle. And it is this jerry-built construction that he advised writers to avoid as corrupting, indefensible, cumbrous, vulgar, and a bad thing.

Undoubtedly Fowler had a point. But his condemnation was too sweeping, too absolute. Moreover, his case might have been stronger had he not rested it—as he need not have—entirely on a technical grammatical ground.

A writer who would try to follow Fowler's dictum by saying, "The eggs were shipped without one's being broken," should turn in his typewriter. Fowler himself, in correcting some fused participles, bestowed his blessing on these passages: "Which will result in many's having to go into lodgings" and "It is no longer thought to be the proper scientific attitude to deny the possibility of anything's happening." Few writers with a feeling for idiom would be willing to accept those locutions. Tacking an "'s" on to a noun is not always the way to avoid a fused participle, especially in view of the tendency in English not to use the possessive case for nouns denoting lifeless things (*See* POSSESSIVES).

There are other situations in which a genitive form is not possible: Some pronouns and other words of a pronominal character, and some adjectives that occasionally take the form of nouns, do not have a genitive form. Here are a few examples cited by Jespersen: 'He had every day a chance of this happening"; "He wouldn't hear of that being possible"; "We are mortified at the news of the French taking the town from the Portuguese"; "No fear had they of bad becoming worse."

In still other situations the subject of the gerund is a group of words for which a genitive form would be awkward if not impossible. More examples cited by Jespersen: "He would not hear of Mrs. Mackenzie and her daughter quitting his house"; "The cause of some part of mankind being black"; "There would be no harm in a lady of rank taking notice of a poor gentleman."

It will be noticed that the foregoing paragraphs have the tone of exceptions to a general practice, and that is the intention. That, indeed, is also the tone of discussions of the subject by both Curme and Jespersen. At the start of his section on "Subject of the Gerund," Curme says: "Like a verb, a gerund may have a subject, but, like other verbal nouns, its subject is in the genitive. . . ." His ensuing discussion is devoted in the main to instances in which the genitive is not or cannot be used. Jespersen begins his extensive study of "Subject of the Gerund" by saying, "The subject of the gerund is naturally expressed by the genitive case or a possessive pronoun . . . ," and later on he speaks of "the grammatical tendency to use the genitive." It seems evident that the genitive with the gerund was almost invariable from the days of Old English until the beginning of the eighteenth century, when instances of the accusative or nominative as subject of the gerund began to appear. But anything except the genitive is still a deviation, albeit sometimes a legitimate one, from the tradition of the language. Along with innovations in usage, this tradition is subtly but positively passed on from generation to generation and it cannot be disparaged or brushed aside as irrelevant.

Had Fowler rested his case on historical as well as grammatical grounds it would have been stronger. Grammatical objections can sometimes be overcome. For one thing, idiom has a way of thumbing its nose at grammar. In defiance of grammar and logic, idiom treats "more than one" as a singular subject;

in the same way it usually regards "none" as a plural. For a second thing, grammatical objections can be overcome in part by inventing new grammar. You simply call the fused participle a "nexus" (Jespersen) and all is explained—or is it?

What guides, then, can be offered to the sensitive writer about this construction? One general guide, which flows from the history of the language, is to use the genitive with the gerund whenever it is possible: "He had never given a thought to its [not *it*] being illegal"; "There is speculation upon the possibility of Mr. Chaplin's [not *Chaplin*] being barred from the United States and of his [not *him*] being excluded from making any more films in Hollywood"; "There is no fear of the Cabinet's [not *Cabinet*] being endangered before the National Assembly votes on the accords."

When the genitive does not seem to be possible, a slight reconstruction of the sentence—frequently accompanied by improvement—is a possibility that should be examined: "A case could be made for different objectives in news presentation being handled differently [different handling of different objectives]"; "There is no chance of any of them going hungry [that any of them will go hungry]"; "This is one of several steps taken by the Secretary to prevent the ceiling on expenditures being broken again next year [prevent the ceiling on expenditures from being broken again next year]."

Despite all diligent effort, however, the writer will find that some "fused participles" will simply have to remain fused. The classes of exceptions have already been indicated, and here are some additional examples: "The cry of outrage over girls as young as thirteen years old plunging to their deaths from windows of the burning building has never been stilled"; "We have been unable to find any trace of anyone answering this description having been in this country recently"; "The shock felt at Frenchmen killing Frenchmen in Algiers was reflected in Parisians' faces as they scanned newspapers"; "He said that he was not writing his memoirs and that he strongly disapproved of persons active in public life doing so"; "What are the odds against that happening?"

Obviously, Fowler's condemnation of this fused construction takes in too much territory. Still, it is hard to take issue with him when he says that it is corrupting English style. Those who see nothing wrong with "I hate my best friend losing his job" or "They arriving late is inexcusable" are corrupted beyond hope of salvation. Such avoidable uses are gauche and offensive to anyone with sensitivity about usage. We can agree with Fowler when he says, "Every just man who will abstain from the fused participle (as most good writers do, though negative evidence is naturally hard to procure) retards the progress of corruption."

GENTLEMAN

See LADY.

GET

The verb *get* has a multitude of meanings, a great many of them casual or slang. Along with FIX, it is one of the handiest, if not always the best adapted, tools of the language. This statement suggests that, just as a carpenter would not find the handle of a screwdriver the best implement for driving a nail, so the writer about to use *get* would do well to see whether he has a more serviceable word in his kit. A few examples will demonstrate the ubiquitousness of the word.

1. "Before the insect season gets under way, homeowners are advised to be armed against the invasion. Among the many booklets available from the Department of Agriculture is one outlining how to get rid of wasps. You can get it free from the Department's Office of Information." The phrase *gets under way* translates with commendable economy into *begins*. *Get rid* is not so readily replaceable, although *eliminate* or *wipe out* is available; nevertheless it exemplifies the use of *get* as a colorless copula (or linking) verb, other instances of which would be *get tired, get sick, get clear, get started*. In the phrase *get it free*, the word *get* is merely a weak synonym for *obtain*.

2. "He got into the union at the age of fifteen and got married five years later." The first *got* is perhaps meaningful; it sug-

gests more of an effort than *entered* or *joined*. But the second *got* is a gaucherie. Ambrose Bierce is not to be taken as the last word on words; still he has a point when he says in *Write It Right* that if *got married* is correct, "we should say, also, *got dead* for *died;* one expression is as good as the other." There are those who contend that to use "was married" would make it impossible to distinguish the action from the resulting state, but this is a quibble because in almost all cases, as in the one above, the context makes the meaning clear. The exceptional instance might be one like the sentence quoted by Curme, "He is married now, but I can't tell you when he got married," or like this one: "She has been married so often you might think she enjoys just getting married, not being married." Such exceptions, however, are rare.

3. "When he gets talking fast the words start to fall over one another." This is akin to *get going* or *get started*. All are casual usages and are not good enough for reputable writing. Remedies would be "When he starts talking fast" or "starts to talk fast" or "is talking fast."

4. "This country has got to meet the challenge of communism." In the sense of must, compelled, or obliged, *got* is again classed as casual. Still, because of its usefulness, nay, irreplaceability, for the purpose of strong emphasis, it is more likely than most other casual uses of the word to gain literary acceptance. To see how it adds force, compare *has to meet, must meet,* and *has got to meet.* There cannot be much doubt that *got* in this sense has simply got to win approval. *See* GOT VS. GOTTEN.

GETTING DOWN TO BRASS TACKS
See DANGLERS.

GILD THE LILY
"In fact, instead of gilding the lily it lampblacks the stove." The line from Shakespeare that is misquoted more often than it is correctly quoted is from *King John,* and reads: "To gild refined gold, to paint the lily. . . ." *See also* MISQUOTATION.

GIVEN
See DANGLERS.

GLAMOUR
A FAD WORD that is seldom used in its pristine sense of magic, *glamour* (and that spelling is preferred to *glamor*) primarily means deceptive charm or enchantment. As used by advertising writers and press agents, it seems to mean everything from prettiness to a resplendent aura of romance. It is even applied to weapons of destruction: "The Polaris submarines are the glamour weapons of the armed forces." Slangily, it is used in such phrases as *glamour stocks, glamour boy, glamour pants,* and *glamour puss.* Whether the primary meaning can be recaptured is uncertain, but it should be recognized that present-day uses are debasing a word that is not easily replaceable.

GLEAN
Literally, to *glean* is to collect in bits what has been left by the reaper. By metaphorical extension it means to collect bits with great effort. By improper further extension it is misused to mean merely to gather. Example: "From an interview with Mr. Humhal of Vienna, I glean the following. . . . Faultless cut and fit does not suffice, the proof of good tailoring is seen in the wearing. . . ." *Glean* is not a simple synonym for *learn, find, acquire, deduce, collect, derive, obtain, garner,* or *get.*

GLOW
Takes preposition *with.*

GOLEM
See FRANKENSTEIN.

GORGEOUS
Properly used, *gorgeous* applies not to a person but to the adornment of a person. This is an improper use: "It does not take Hogan long to make the discovery that the newly arrived girl is

gorgeous." A peacock could be described as *gorgeous* because of its plumage, and the girl could be described as *gorgeous* if the reference was to her plumage. But as a synonym for *beautiful* or *splendid*, the word is slang.

GOT VS. GOTTEN

Some writers on usage tend to esteem British English above American English, and for them only *got* is legitimate and *gotten* is cast into outer darkness. But British English is not necessarily superior (or inferior, either) to American English. It is not evident that "chemist's shop" is in any way better than "drugstore," that "in hospital" is better than "in the [or *a*] hospital," or that "pub" is better than "bar" (indeed, nonlinguistically it may well be inferior). The two branches of the language are like two broad roads running side by side in the same direction; in some places one may be on a higher level, in other places the other may be on a higher level, but in most places they proceed on the same level. In its use of *gotten* in addition to *got* American English may well have the advantage. Let Marckwardt furnish evidence:

"British English has but one past participle for the verb *got*, namely the form *got*. American English has, in addition, the form *gotten*, which no speaker of British English ever uses in the first place, and which many Britons assume, moreover, to be the only American form. . . .

"In fact, most Americans regularly make a very precise distinction between *got* and *gotten*. 'We've got ten thousand dollars for laboratory equipment,' means that the funds in question are in our possession—we have them. 'We have gotten ten thousand dollars for laboratory equipment,' means that we have obtained or acquired this particular sum of money. Few Americans would have the slightest question about the difference in the meaning of these two sentences. . . ."

Marckwardt explains that *get* early developed *got* or *gotten* as its past participle, but that in England *gotten* seems not to have continued in use beyond the middle or late part of the seventeenth century, while Americans have continued to use it up to the present. Thus Americans have been able to make the distinc-

206

tion between *have got* and *have gotten,* which the British cannot do in precisely the same way.

Now that all this has been explained, attention should be directed to Marckwardt's phrase, "no *speaker* of British English." What is clearly under consideration in the whole passage is spoken English rather than written English. Both *have got* and *have gotten* are appropriate to spoken language, but usually are inappropriate to written language. In *have got,* indicating possession, the *got* is obviously superfluous and the phrase would be presented in writing as *have* or *own* or *possess. Have gotten* might occasionally be useful in written language, particularly when the verb does not take an object—as in, "The $29,500,000 duckling industry has gotten together as the Long Island Duck Farmers' Cooperative, Inc." Here it is a matter of indifference whether *got* or *gotten* is the word. In most instances, however, a more precise verb would be used: "He has gotten [received] his just deserts"; "He has gotten [obtained] what he was after"; "She has gotten to be [become] familiar with the rules of the society"; "He has gotten [bought, acquired, stolen] a new car." *See* GET.

GRADUATE

A superstition clings to this verb. The superstition is that you must not say, "He graduated from college," but must say, "He was graduated from college." Actually the forms are equally correct in American usage (the Oxford even designates the second form as "now rare exc. U.S."). The superstition may have arisen from the fact that it is incorrect to say, "He graduated college." It is easy to imagine how some foggy-minded schoolmarms may have associated this acknowledged crime with the completely innocent, "He graduated from college."

GRANTING

See DANGLERS.

GRAPPLE

Takes preposition *with.*

GRATEFUL

Takes preposition *to* (persons); *for* (benefits).

GREAT

See ATOMIC FLYSWATTERS.

GRIEVE

Takes preposition *at, for,* or *after*.

GROOM

Although *groom* for *bridegroom* is in common usage, there are those who regard the word as unrefined in this sense, perhaps because of its association with a manservant who cares for horses. For what it is worth, the objectors do have etymology on their side. *Bridegroom* comes from the Anglo-Saxon *bryd* (bride) and *guma* (man). In the sixteenth century, either deliberately or confusedly, the second part of the word became *grome* (groom).

GUTS

See BELLY.

GYMNASTICS

See -ICS.

H

HAD

A peculiar use of *had* is illustrated by this sentence: "The surveyors had firecrackers tossed at them by the children, and guns fired over their heads, and then found that the air had been let out of their tires." Lint pickers sometimes object that if you say "I had my hair cut," which expresses causality on the part of the subject, then to say "The surveyors had firecrackers tossed at them" expresses a similar causality and means that the surveyors instigated their own torment. Webster tells us, however, that one meaning of *have* is "to suffer or experience from an exterior source; as, he had his leg broken." Thus, the use is legitimate. But all that is permissible is not necessarily advisable. In some situations in which a sentence might seem slightly ludicrous even to non-lint pickers a reconstruction is advisable. Example: "He had his hair cut and then had his arm broken."

HAIL, HALE

First, there is *hail*, which is what you do to the chief, your friend, or a taxicab. Second, there is *hale*, which derives from *haul*, and that is what the policeman does to the robber when he escorts him to the police station. Third, there is the adjective *hale*, which is what a man is when he is also hearty. Numbers 1 and 3 give little trouble. However, Number 1 is often erroneously substituted for Number 2: "It is also common knowledge that the conditions that the committee has found in the unions, which have been, or are scheduled to be, hailed before it, are not usual." It should be *haled* (i.e., *hauled*). As a footnote to all this, the idomatic phrase is *hail* (not *hale*) *fellow well met*. The phrase has to do with the ease of greeting a person, not with the state of his health.

HALF

There are still some diehards who object to cutting a melon

in half or slicing a deficit *in half*. They insist that the melon must be cut *in halves* or *in two* and that the deficit must be sliced *by half*. However, *in half* is well-established, and any attempts to outlaw it must be classed as OVERREFINEMENT.

HAMSTRING

The word, meaning to disable or cripple, refers to the cutting of the *hamstring*, a tendon in the back of the knee. Therefore, it has nothing to do with the stringing of a ham, as Fowler points out. Further therefore, according to Fowler, the past tense should not be that of the word string; i.e., it should not be *hamstrung*, but should rather be *hamstringed*. However, what should be is not always what is. The acceptable and prevalent past tense is *hamstrung*, and a writer who uses *hamstringed* must be prepared to answer a great deal of sneering and abusive mail.

HANDCRAFT

"These shoes are handcrafted from the supplest of leather." A case of AD-DICTION. *See* CRAFT.

HANKER

Takes preposition *after* or *for*.

HAPPEN

See TAKE PLACE, OCCUR.

HARA-KIRI

From the Japanese *hara*, meaning belly, and *kiri*, meaning cut, *hara-kiri* is the proper spelling. "Hara-kari" is one incorrect variant and "hari-kari," which probably was associated in the popular mind with Harry Carey, an old-time movie cowboy, is another. Incidentally, when the Japanese refer to ritual suicide, they do not often use *hara-kiri*; they say *seppuku*.

HARDLY

1. Like *scarcely*, the word *hardly* is equivalent to a negative. Therefore, as with any other negative, avoid doubling up on it,

as the writer of this sentence did: "The Governor drove through the city without causing hardly a ripple." *See* DOUBLE NEGATIVES.

2. *Sooner,* as a comparative, is followed by *than* ("No sooner had the car passed than the bomb exploded"), but *hardly,* which is not a comparative, is not followed by *than,* but rather by *when.* "Hardly had the car passed when [not *than*] the bomb exploded."

HARD PUT

Hard put and *hard put to it* are equally good as idioms. Although *hard put to it* is perhaps more common, there can be no quarrel with *hard put,* since *put* by derivation has a meaning of pushed, thrust, or pressed. Therefore: "He was hard put [pressed] to give an answer."

HEADQUARTERS

It can be used as a singular, but its use as a plural is far more common.

HEALED

Takes preposition *of* (disease); *by* (agency).

HEALTHY, HEALTHFUL

Strictly speaking, *healthy* applies to good physical condition, whereas *healthful* applies to something that is conducive to that condition ("Jones is healthy because he takes healthful exercise"). *Healthy,* however, is so robust that it is pre-empting both meanings and it is hardly a solecism any longer to say that "Jones takes healthy exercise." Footnote: *Healthy* to mean large or vigorous is pure slang, as in, "The United Steelworkers executive board is giving its top officers a healthy pay boost," or in, "The heedless writer got a healthy kick in the pants for misusing healthy."

HEAR TELL

See TELL (2).

211

HEART (TO TAKE)

Takes preposition *from* or *at*.

HECTIC

In its original meaning *hectic* pertains to a wasting physical condition like consumption. In that meaning it has not had much utility for the ordinary writer. But because of its connection with fever it has been taken up in a broader sense to mean at first feverish and now fully packed and excited, as in, "After a hectic day the President did not get to bed until well after midnight." In this sense there is no other word that quite suffices. *Excited* or *exciting* falls short of the mark because it lacks the sense of something doing every minute; *feverish* rather overshoots the mark in one way by suggesting too much heat and passion, and undershoots it in another way—the same way that *excited* does. *Hectic*, a vogue word in Fowler's day, has won its way to respectability. *See* BERNSTEIN'S SECOND LAW.

HELP BUT

See BUT, MEANING OTHER THAN, ETC.

HENCE

See FROM HENCE, FROM WHENCE.

HERSELF

See HIMSELF (HERSELF, MYSELF, ETC.)

HIJACK

Occasionally a word that has outlived a contemporary meaning is not discarded but rather put to use in an extension of that meaning or in a different one altogether, much as a pirate would convert his empty grog bottle into a candleholder. That is what happened to the word *filibuster*. Originally it meant a freebooter, and was applied to adventurers who plundered Latin American coasts, and, later, to interventionists who incited rebellion in certain Latin American countries. When the situations that had given rise to the word subsided, *filibuster* was retained in the language with a different meaning: political procrastination by a minority to block a piece of legislation.

The word *hijack* has a similar history. It came into use in the Twenties, meaning to steal bootleg liquor or other contraband in transit. But when Prohibition expired, the word did not expire with it; it was found to have a utility not provided by any other word. Decades later it was still being used to describe the taking over by an armed band of a ship at sea, the diversion by force of a plane in flight, and the stealing of a truck carrying merchandise. It could be defined now as meaning to steal or otherwise take over illegally a conveyance—land, sea, or air—or its contents while in transit. The nouns are *hijacking* and *hijacker*. All are considered casual, but since they are not readily replaceable they are likely to become standard ultimately.

HIKE
See BOOST.

HILARIOUS
Often *hilarious* overstates what the writer intends to say (unless the writer is in the advertising business, in which case the overstatement is intentional). *Hilarious* does not mean merely mirthful; it means noisily so. For the television show to be *hilarious* the average watcher must be guffawing most of the time.

HIMSELF (HERSELF, MYSELF, ETC.)
"At the meeting, he said, were himself, his wife, and Mr. Jack." Make it *he*. "He said his daughter, Mrs. Clifton Daniel, and her family would spend the holidays with Mrs. Truman and himself at Independence, Mo." Make it *him*. The "-self" words are used for two purposes: for emphasis ("I'll fix it myself"; "The others were hesitant but he himself had no qualms") and reflexively, to turn the action back on the grammatical subject ("She dressed herself quickly"; "He makes himself inaccessible"). In the latter sense the words are reflexive pronouns.

213

HINDER

Takes preposition *from.*

HINDRANCE

Takes preposition *to.*

HINGE

The proper preposition to follow this verb is *on* or *upon.* A *hinge* is a joint on which a member hangs (*hinge* is related to hang) or on which it turns or swings. The preposition *about* (or *around*) is a misuse, as in this sentence: "Professor Tobias begins by explaining that most definitions of the border line between highly advanced apes and primitive men hinge about what he calls a 'cerebral Rubicon.' " *See also* CENTER AROUND.

HINT

Takes preposition *at.*

HISTORIC, HISTORICAL

That is *historic* that figures in history; that is *historical* that pertains to history. A house that was built in Southampton, L.I., 300 years ago by one of the founders of the town is not "the historical salt-box home," but "the historic salt-box home." *Lust for Life* is a *historical* novel (based on the life of an actual person), not a *historic* novel. The shorter form of pairs of this kind (*historic-historical; economic-economical; comic-comical*) is generally the more important or more significant.

HITHERTO

The meaning of *hitherto* is until now, but it is sometimes erroneously used to mean until then. For instance: "In his effort to save the government and the Union, Lincoln pushed the powers of the Presidency to a new plateau high above any conception of executive authority hitherto imagined in this country." The word *previously* would have made the sentence correct. Another example, referring to a building erected in 1862: "Mr.

214

Stewart spent the hitherto unheard of sum of $2,750,000 to construct the six-story building." Make it *theretofore* or, still better, reword the sentence. *Thitherto* is a possible but strained substitute.

HOBSON'S CHOICE

The meaning of this phrase is that you get no choice at all. It traces back to the sixteenth century and a Cambridge stable-keeper named Thomas Hobson, whose rule was that each customer must take the horse nearest the door or no horse at all. It is therefore incorrect to use the phrase as if it meant the kind of choice involved in a dilemma, as in this sentence: "But how long, in Berlin, must we rely on this cruel Hobson's choice between honoring pledges and eviscerating the world?"

HOLOCAUST

The *caust* part of the word means burnt, and the whole word means fiery destruction entailing loss of life. It is not merely a synonym for *disaster* or *catastrophe*.

HOME, HOUSE

It is a tribute to the unquenchable sentimentalism of users of English that one of the matters of usage that seem to agitate them the most is the use of *home* to designate a structure designed for residential purposes. Their contention is that what the builder erects is a *house* and that the occupants then fashion it into a *home*.

That is, or at least was, basically true, but the distinction has become blurred. Nor is this solely the doing of the real estate operators. They do, indeed, lure prospective buyers not with the thought of mere masonry but with glowing pictures of comfort, congeniality, and family collectivity that make a *house* into a *home*. But the prospective buyers are their co-conspirators; they, too, view the premises not as a heap of stone and wood but as a potential abode.

There may be areas in which the words are not used interchangeably. In legal or quasi-legal terminology we speak of a "house and lot," not a "home and lot." The police and fire departments usually speak of a robbery or a fire in a *house,* not a *home,* at Main Street and First Avenue. And the individual most often buys a *home,* but sells his *house* (there, apparently, speaks sentiment again). But in most areas the distinction between the words has become obfuscated. When a flood or a fire destroys a community, it wipes out not merely *houses* but *homes* as well, and *homes* has come to be accepted in this sense. No one would discourage the sentimentalists from trying to pry the two words apart, but it would be rash to predict much success for them.

HONOR
Takes preposition *with, by,* or *for.*

HOPE
Takes preposition *for* or *of.*

HOPEFULLY
A common misuse of this word is illustrated in the following sentences: "The sixteen astronauts are negotiating a $3,000,000 contract to sell to a publishing company their personal stories—including, hopefully, the account of a visit to the moon"; "Hopefully, two-thirds of this cost would be covered by Federal grants." This solecistic use probably arises from a false analogy. You can use adverbs like *fortunately* or *luckily* in this way. They mean "in a fortunate or lucky manner," and in the kind of construction cited would be equivalent to "it is fortunate that. . . ." But *hopefully* as used here does not mean "in a hopeful manner," nor is it equivalent to "it is a hopeful thing that." The intended meaning is "it is hoped that" or "if hopes are realized," and these phrases should be used. The Germans have a word that covers the intended meaning—*hoffentlich.* And in English we can take care of a somewhat similar situation with *regrettably* (in a manner that calls for regret) as contrasted with *regretfully* (in a manner full of regret). But regrettably *hopefully* is not equal to the burden sometimes placed upon it. What is needed is a word like *hopably,* which is not here being nominated for the job.

HOPEFUL OPTIMISM

"Peking's confidence is based on hopeful optimism." Is there any other kind? Delete "hopeful."

HORRIBLE

See ATOMIC FLYSWATTERS.

HOUSE

See HOME, HOUSE.

HOUSEWARES

"Houseware Show Called a Success," said the headline. At first thought you would expect *houseware* to be correct because we have such things as *chinaware, copperware, dinnerware, earthenware, hardware, tinware,* and *leatherware.* However, *ware* refers to a collection of a single class of articles or articles having a quality in common, which holds true for the categories listed. *Housewares,* however, are a miscellany of articles; hence the plural form is correct, the singular is not.

HOW

An adverb, sometimes used conjunctively, *how* means in what way or manner. That meaning is important to keep in mind in examining the ways in which the word is used and misused. It is one thing—and standard usage—to say, "He told us how he had spent his vacation." The implication there is that the vacationist related his experiences. It is quite another thing—and not standard written usage—to say, "He told us how he had gone on a vacation during the heat wave." Unless the vacationist described the packing of his luggage, the trip to the airport, the charm of the plane stewardess, and his arrival at his destination, that sentence is substandard casual usage. What is meant is not *how* but *that.* Here is a similar misuse: "He said he saw no way how the company stood to benefit from the loan." This could be corrected either by writing, "He said he did not see how," or by changing the *how* to *in which.*

One step below *how* misused for *that* is *as how* ("He told us

217

as how he had gone on a vacation"). Still more vulgar is *seeing as how* or *being as how*. These locutions are so obviously illiterate that a knowing writer occasionally uses them in the belief that they will lend a comic effect. Let the reader judge the validity of that belief: "As much as it staggered our credulity, seeing as how we hadn't yet done our annual midyear reflection upon the films of the last six months, we had to concede that the young lady was oppressively correct."

HOW COME?

Although common in spoken language, *how come?*—meaning why? or in what manner does it happen?—is out of place in good writing. Perhaps the nearest approach to it in literature is Shakespeare's occasional use of *how chance*, as in this line from *A Midsummer Night's Dream*: "How chance the roses there do fade so fast?" But to cite this use as legitimatizing *how come?* would probably make even Shakespeare turn over in his hallowed grave.

HOWEVER

When the word *however* is properly placed in a sentence it throws contrasting emphasis on what precedes it. The two *howevers* in the following passage illustrate the point: "Mr. Wilcox said that the United States 'would prefer' that the Soviet declaration be considered in the Political Committee. He did not say, however, how the United States would vote. However, it was learned later that both the United States and Britain would 'go along' with consideration of the Soviet proposal by the Assembly itself." Notice that the first *however* establishes the contrast between what Mr. Wilcox did not say and the statement in the first sentence of what he did say. The second *however* points to the contrast between what he did not say and what was learned later. This one could also be properly placed after "later," but it is probably better where it is so as to signal the contrasting statement at once. Incidentally, if your elementary-school teacher told you never to begin a sentence with *however*, forget it. The governing consideration should always be simply this: Which ideas are to be contrasted? May Mrs. Phillips of P.S. 10 rest in peace.

Sometimes it is difficult to find just the right place for *however*, and sometimes when this difficulty arises the tendency is to place it too late in the sentence. An account of a speech by the Secretary of State quoted him on the virtues of the framers of the United States Constitution, and then went on: "Delegates at the 1945 San Francisco organizational conferences of the United Nations, of whom he was one, however, were ignorant of the atomic bomb." The contrast intended here is between the framers of the Constitution and the San Francisco delegates. But the placement of the *however* erroneously throws the contrasting emphasis on "of whom he was one." The *however* could be placed after "United Nations," although it is usually better not to delay for so long its appearance in the sentence. Alternatively it could stand at the head of the sentence, thus establishing the contrast between the ideas of the two sentences. Again, may Mrs. Phillips rest in peace.

HOWEVER FOR HOW

"However can the company meet its obligations?" is casual usage and is not employed in good writing. Make it *how*. When the *ever* is fully adverbial, however, it may appear in a sentence with *how* but not joined to it and usually not even adjacent to it: "Since the company is losing more money each year, how can it ever meet its obligations?"

HOWEVER WITH BUT

But however is a redundancy, as is *but nevertheless*. Vote for one in each instance.

HUMAN

See ADJECTIVES AS NOUNS.

HURT

"The department's 37,500 offices do not hurt from want of business." This archaic-sounding use of *hurt* is described by the Oxford as "now only colloq."

HYPERBOLE

See RHETORICAL FIGURES AND FAULTS.

HYPHEN

See PUNCTUATION.

I

IAMBUS
See FOOT.

-ICS
Words ending in the suffix "-ics" (*acoustics, politics, tactics, gymnastics*, etc.) are regarded as either singular or plural, depending on meaning. When the word is being treated as a subject or science, it is construed as singular ("Tactics is among the subjects taught at West Point"). When the word denotes practical activities or qualities, it is construed as plural ("The tactics of the Battle of Gettysburg are studied at West Point"). The distinction is not always easy to determine. Should it be "Politics was his lifelong avocation" (that is, politics as an art or subject for study) or "Politics were his lifelong avocation" (that is, politics as a day-to-day activity)? Often the context will suggest which is proper, but if doubt persists it is probably better to resolve it in favor of the singular. And, when the predicate noun is in the singular, as it is in the sentence just cited, the tendency is to treat the "-ics" word as a singular also. Incidentally, economics is almost always construed as singular, perhaps because it is difficult to think of it in the sense of practical activities.

IDENTICAL
Takes preposition *with* or *to*.

IDENTIFY
Takes preposition *with*.

IDEOLOGY
Undoubtedly a vogue word used by the windy, the pompous, and would-be up-to-the-minuters, *ideology* must nevertheless be accorded a respectable place in modern English usage because there is no word to take its place as the counterpart or secular

parallel of religion. Evans gives the word an accurate definition when he writes: "While it is true that in its strictest sense the word is a philosophical term meaning the science of ideas, most linguists now feel that usage has established it as a standard term for the body of doctrine, myth, and symbols of a social movement, institution, class, or large group or such a body of doctrine, etc., with reference to some political and cultural plan, together with the means of putting it into operation." By this definition, communism and fascism are *ideologies*. On the other hand, urban renewal, the thinking behind advertising, and programs for block parties are not. Extension of the word to cover such things as these is to be shunned.

IDIOM

See LO, THE POOR IDIOM.

IF, WHETHER

Whether is the normal word used to introduce a noun clause: "They asked whether we would attend the dinner." However, *if* is well established in this role in most constructions. It, too, may be used to introduce noun clauses after such verbs as *see, ask, learn, doubt,* and *know.* Nor is this usage a recent deviation, as some grammarians seem to suggest. The Oxford quotes from the King James Bible of 1611, "Hee sent foorth a doue from him, to see if the waters were abated" (Genesis viii, 8). *If* is not used in this way, however, when the noun clause begins the sentence, because it tends to throw the reader off the track by suggesting a condition, as in this example: "If we were coming to dinner was the object of his inquiry." Likewise, *if* should not be used where it opens the door to ambiguity, as in the following sentence: "The President asked to be informed if his bill was in trouble in the Senate." Does it mean "at whatever time" his bill was in trouble or *whether* his bill was in trouble now? *See also* DOUBT.

IF AND WHEN

"Senator Dempsey's design, which the Administration without doubt will strongly resist if and when active resistance becomes necessary, is all too apparent." Try dropping *and when* out of this cliché and see whether there is any difference. Similar clichés that do not even whimper under amputation are *unless and until* (cut off "and until") and *when, as, and if* (cut off "when, as, and" unless you are a member of the bar, and even then you might consider doing so).

IF NOT

Usually perfectly clear in spoken language, *if not* becomes a tantalizing ambiguity in written language. This sentence illustrates the point about written language: "The proposed taxes would be levied primarily, if not exclusively, on New York and Pennsylvania residents." It is not possible to tell whether the phrase "if not exclusively" means "perhaps exclusively" or "but not exclusively." A speaker would leave no doubt about what was meant; his intonation and emphasis would make his intention clear. If he said, "The proposed taxes would be levied primarily, if not ex ^{CLU} sively on, etc.," he would mean "perhaps exclusively." On the other hand, if he said, "The proposed taxes would be levied primarily, if not exclusively, on, etc.," he would mean "but not exclusively." This illustration brings out one of the several elements that make written language a thing distinct from spoken language. There is no opportunity in writing to indicate a rise or fall in tonal register, and very few ways to indicate stress. The solution to the present problem should have become evident in its very discussion: If you mean *perhaps*, say so; if you mean *but not*, say so.

ILK

The political orators and writers of letters to the editor who cannot speak of this country without calling it "these United States" are the ones who are most fond of the phrase "of that ilk." For example: "The people will not be satisfied with a Symington, a Johnson, or others of that ilk. They sense that the hour demands youth. . . ." *Ilk*, of Scottish derivation, means roughly the same in name or place: When a Scotsman speaks of "MacNeil of that ilk" what he means is "MacNeil of MacNeil." Obviously, then, you cannot speak of "similar ilk," as in this sentence: "The menu is slightly more inspired than those of many other restaurants of similar ilk." Originally as a mild drollery and now as a weary cliché, but always erroneously, *ilk* was and is used to mean kind, class, breed, or stripe. Strangely, its users seem to regard it as a word of disparagement, but that is as much of a mistake as to think of a Scot as a farthing-pincher. *Ilk* should be added to the list of forget-'em words.

ILLUSION
See DELUSION, ILLUSION.

IMAGE
In the sense of a public feeling about an industry, a person, a corporation, or a product, *image* is a FAD WORD and a form of AD-DICTION. And its customary use is often inaccurate. The essence of the word *image*, which comes from the same root as imitate, is the idea of likeness or true representation. But this is not always what the pitchmen mean when they speak of an *industrial* (or *corporate*) *image*. They often talk of changing or improving the *image*, but what they have in mind almost never involves changing or improving the industry or the corporation itself. This is much like setting out to change your reflection (or image) in the mirror without doing anything to yourself. Nonetheless, the advertising and public relations people do seem to pull off the trick. That merely demonstrates that they are not really doing anything to the *image*, but doing something rather to the public mind; they are either creating an illusion or removing one.

The fad for *image* will probably fade. But if it does, you may be sure that the busy brains of Madison Avenue will be equal to producing a new fad.

224

IMMIGRATE

Takes preposition *to* or *into*.

IMMURED, INURED

There is no reason why these words should be confused, except that they sound somewhat alike, but they sometimes are misused: "The Green Bay Packers, as immured to the elements as Eskimos, rode over the New Yorkers with the inexorability of a snowplow." From the Latin *murus*, a wall, *immure* means to wall in or imprison. *Inure*, the word needed here, means to accustom or habituate.

Immure takes the preposition *in* or *within*. *Inure* takes the preposition *to*.

IMPACT

A strong word, *impact* is in danger of losing some of its power at the hands of the kind of faddists who are always reaching for the flame thrower to light a cigarette. *Impact* denotes a forceful impingement, a collision, a violent communication of force. Often it is used when all that is intended is *effect* or *influence*, as in this example: "One of the questions raised by the Mayor's attack on the Governor is its impact on their collaboration to give New York City voters an opportunity to vote on a new charter this year."

Impacted is a piece of government lingo that has come into use in recent years. It is used in the phrase *impacted areas* to mean those areas containing heavy concentrations of Federal workers or military personnel. Considering that *impacted* means forced closely together, the governmental usage is not too wide of the mark.

IMPATIENT

Takes preposition *at, of, with,* or *for*.

IMPEACH

Takes preposition *for* or *of*.

IMPENETRABLE
Takes preposition *to* or *by*.

IMPERSONATE
Redundancy results from this kind of misuse: "Milton Berle will impersonate the part of Jerry Biffle." Since *impersonate* means to act the role of, Berle will either "impersonate Jerry Biffle" or "act the part of Jerry Biffle."

IMPERVIOUS
Takes preposition *to*.

IMPLEMENT
As a verb, *implement* means to carry out or furnish with the means for carrying out. There is nothing wrong with it except that it is a fancy word for a plain idea and that in recent times it has become a FAD WORD, beloved especially of officialdom. "The military, particularly in the Army, appeared to be pressing for permission to implement at once the entire contemplated build-up." In that sentence the word "build-up" (also a proper one except that it, too, is faddish) betrays the kind of thinking that brought forth *implement* in the same series of words. What could just as well have been written here by a plain man who had never been influenced by the Pentagon is ". . . permission to make the entire contemplated increase at once." The put-into-practice sense of *implement* appears in this sentence: "Officially, the Government was pressing ahead to implement the Administration's new space communications policy." Before using *implement* it would be well to consider the possibilities of *execute, carry out, fulfill, make, accomplish,* and *achieve. See* WINDY-FOGGERY.

IMPLICIT
Takes preposition *in*.

IMPLY, INFER
The common error is to use *infer* when *imply* is meant:

226

"Bishop Russell emphasized that he did not mean to infer that all American families were 'going to pieces.' " Rarely is an error made the other way round—the use of *imply* for *infer*. Still it does happen: "Asked if he meant that the Russians were bluffing, the Secretary said at a news conference that that was 'a fair implication.' " *Imply* means to suggest or say indirectly. *Infer* means to deduce or conclude from facts or indications. The *implier* is the pitcher; the *inferrer* is the catcher. There are conceivable situations in which it would not be possible to tell whether *infer* had been correctly or incorrectly used. For instance: "Just because I eat spaghetti with a screwdriver are you inferring that I am nuts?" It would be difficult to tell here whether the speaker meant, "Are you suggesting?" or "Are you deducing?" In most such instances, however, the implication would be, and it would be correct to infer, that the speaker was guilty of a solecism. Particularly if the speaker ate spaghetti with a screwdriver.

IMPOSE
Takes preposition *on* or *upon*.

IMPRACTICABLE, IMPRACTICAL
These two words have distinct meanings, and the distinction is worth preserving. *Impracticable* means not feasible, not capable of being carried out. *Impractical* means not valuable in practice. Of course an "impractical fellow" is not one who is not valuable in practice, but rather one who eats spaghetti with a screwdriver (*cf.* IMPLY, INFER just above). *See also* PRACTICABLE, PRACTICAL.

IMPRESS
Takes preposition *on, with, into,* or *upon*.

IMPRESSED
Takes preposition *by* or *with*.

IMPROVE
Takes preposition *on* or *upon*.

IN

See AT, IN.

IN, INTO

"He dived in the river and swam toward the struggling woman." If he dived *in* the river, he was already in the water before he performed the action; *in* denotes merely position. The required word here is *into*, which denotes movement to an interior position. Verbs of motion usually take *into*, and this is true when they are used figuratively as well as when they are used literally ("He threw his hat into the ring"; "A new element has been injected into the discussion").

INACCESSIBLE

Takes preposition *to.*

INCENTIVE

Takes preposition *to* or *for.*

INCIDENTAL

Takes preposition *to* or *upon.*

INCLUDE

A sports article said that seven baseball players (now of fond memory) would return to New York from Pittsburgh, then continued: "The seven included Antonelli, Williams, Maglie, McCall, Grissom, Wilhelm, and Castleman." There are seven names in that list. The word *include*, however, usually suggests that the component items are not being mentioned in their entirety. If all are being mentioned, it would be better to write "The seven were . . ."; or, if there is an irresistible urge for a fancy word, to use *comprised. See also* COMPRISE.

INCOMPARABLES

When Orwell wrote that "All animals are equal but some are more equal than others," one would have thought the bite of his sarcasm sufficient to destroy the arguments of those who try to justify the use of the comparative and superlative degrees with words that express absolutes. But the arguments persist—as do the misuses. "Perhaps one of the most unique of Austrian exports is . . ."; "Nothing is more fatally dangerous to the G.O.P. . . ."; "His rule of the party is more absolute than that of any of his predecessors."

It is not necessary or desirable to draw up a long list of words that do not seem to admit of comparison, because if one goes hunting for such words he will find himself in a philosophical predicament and a literary straitjacket. He will find himself questioning quite innocent words: A thing is either smooth or it is not smooth (he will find himself saying), therefore how can one thing be smoother than another? One need not go looking for absolutes, but when they are obvious, they should be inviolable. It is not only a matter of logic, but also a matter of preserving words that are not replaceable. If we allow the literary unwashed to determine that "more unique" is correct usage, the meaning of *unique* becomes eroded. What word will we then have to convey the meaning of "the only one of its kind"? Shall we have to coin another word for this idea—"scrumpish," for example? If we do, you can be sure that it will not be too long before the unwashed are using "more scrumpish," and then we shall have to coin still another word. There are not many words in the category of absolutes that require conservation measures, but the few there are should be diligently protected against erosion. A modest list might include *absolute, equal, eternal, fatal, final, perfect* (despite the Constitution's "more perfect union"), *supreme, total, unanimous,* and *unique.*

INCOMPLETE ALTERNATIVE COMPARISON

This term is exemplified by the following sentence: "Many families and single lodgers are resettling in other slums, as bad or worse than those marked for obliteration in the current slum-clearance programs." *Worse* is completed by *than,* but how about *as bad?* It stands there in frustrated isolation. It cries for completion. One way to correct this, and a rather formal way, is to make it "as bad as or worse than." Another and perhaps more graceful way is to complete the *as bad* immediately with an *as*, going right on to the word *those*, and tacking the *or worse* on at the end of the sentence.

Here is a sentence in which the first suggested remedy cannot be applied: "And certainly passive resistance can be used with as much or more justification against Moscow than it was against London." What *can* be done is to make it ". . . with as much justification against Moscow as it was against London, or with more justification." Or a simpler form with no perceptible change in meaning might be "at least as much justification against Moscow as it was against London." One way or another, such constructions should be tidied up.

INCONGRUOUS
Takes preposition *with*.

IN CONNECTION WITH
The phrase *in connection with* is a soft, all-purpose compound preposition. To many writers it has an impressive sound; they feel sure it will divert attention from their failure or inability to choose a more precise preposition. Examples of its misuse can be heaped up, but one will suffice: "There was a certain amount of good-natured needling between the Governor and the Mayor in connection with the respective contributions of state and city to solving the city's problems." All the writer meant there was *about*. Incidentally, his weakness for the impressive sound is betrayed also by the vacuous "a certain amount of" and the superfluous "respective."

Of course, the phrase *in connection with* has its legitimate occasions. For example, a news story telling of a United States proposal concerning underground atomic explosions said: "This proposal was made in connection with the United States suggestion for a phased approach to an atomic test ban." The two proposals were actually linked—they were connected; therefore *in connection with* was proper. Addendum: watch out for the phrase *in this connection*. It can usually be amputated painlessly.

INCONSISTENT

Takes preposition *with*.

INCORPORATE

Takes preposition *with* or *into*.

INCREDIBLE, INCREDULOUS

Incredible means unbelievable; *incredulous* means unbelieving, skeptical. From these definitions the error in the following not uncommon misuse should be obvious: "The incredulously rude Khrushchev is the leader of a political philosophy so devious that even the sanctity of the American Embassy in Moscow has not escaped its espionage."

INCULCATE

Takes preposition *on*, *upon*, or *in*.

INDEFINITELY

Although *indefinitely* means without known or prescribed limits, the advertising fraternity has conditioned us to think of it as meaning for a long, long time. Of course, it could also mean for a short, short time. But when the ad man says, "State Emblem Water is sealed in glass to last indefinitely," he does not intend to suggest that it may go bad in five minutes—or perhaps five years; he means to imply that it will be good for an eternity. If that is the connotation that has clustered about the word, so be it. But what, pray, does "more or less indefinitely" mean, as in, "Some top Government economists have a genuine hope that the present expansion can be kept going more or less indefinitely"? And what did the short-order chef mean when he said, "These frozen French fries will keep almost indefinitely?"

The word *limited* has been similarly twisted. It means within bounds, but the advertisers want you to think it means brief or short. When they say, "for a limited time only," they mean you had better get on your motorcycle and "act now!" Again, the word *nominal* does not mean small, as the advertisers

231

would sometimes have you believe, but rather in name only. Therefore, as Evans says in his *Comfortable Words,* "a nominal fee is not merely a low fee, but one so low, compared to what might be expected, that it can be regarded merely as a token payment. If a charge, however small, is a reasonable charge for what is done or given, it is not nominal."

INDEPENDENT

Takes preposition *of.*

INDIVIDUAL

Except in one circumstance, the use of *individual* to mean a person is either jocular (though only wearily so) or contemptuous. It is neither of those in this sentence: "It is the impression of some individuals in the trade that earlier plans for a Weaver-Caesar operation have been virtually abandoned." The single exception is when it is desired to distinguish the one referred to from a class or a different category, as in: "The plan was to award German corporations as well as individuals a part of the assets." *See also* PEOPLE, PERSONS.

IN DOUBT

See DOUBTFUL, IN DOUBT.

INDULGE

Takes preposition *in* or *with.*

INDULGENT

Takes preposition *to* or *of.*

INFECTIOUS

See CONTAGIOUS, INFECTIOUS.

INFER

See IMPLY, INFER. *Infer* takes preposition *from.*

INFERIOR

Takes preposition *to.*

INFESTED

Takes preposition *with.*

INFILTRATE

Takes preposition *into.*

INFILTRATION

Takes preposition *of.*

INFINITIVE, PERFECT

See SEQUENCE OF TENSES.

INFINITIVES

Let it be acknowledged at once that the questions to be raised under this title cannot be settled by rules, but can be settled only by feeling, by ear, by taste—which are probably other ways of saying by idiom.

1. "An expanded rural development program is proposed to assist farms in the low income areas attain a higher standard of living." The question here is whether the bare infinitive "attain" is proper or whether the so-called sign of the infinitive—*to*—must be included. Anyone with feeling, ear, and taste for English will agree that the *to* must be included. In present-day English the *to* form is used in an overwhelming majority of instances and thus is normal. Omission of the *to* is exceptional, and the exceptions are summed up succinctly by Evans as follows:

"In modern English the infinitive without *to* is used after *do, let* and the regular auxiliary verbs such as *will, can, must;* after *bid, dare, feel, hear, make, need, see,* in the active voice but not in the passive; in certain constructions or with certain senses of the word after *have, help, find, come, go, run, try;* and occasionally after other verbs meaning 'see,' such as *behold, mark, observe.*"

Difficulties arise when a writer tries to use analogy to force words into this category of exceptions. If "help farms attain" is correct, he apparently reasons, why shouldn't "assist farms attain" also be correct? There is no rule to answer such a question. The answer is simply that usage and idiom frequently demolish analogy.

2. "This quality to better itself again and again is the essence of *McCall's* astonishing circulation rise. . . "; "Remember Mr. Deeds, the Vermont Yankee whom people considered mad because he had the crazy idea to set up a collective farm with a large inheritance he received?" The difficulty here is the use of an infinitive where idiom calls for a gerund—"quality of bettering" in the first example and "idea of setting up" in the second. Again there is no rule that will steer a writer around such treacherous rocks; he must navigate by idiom. Fowler gives this much guidance: "There is very little danger of [in?] using the gerund, but much of using the infinitive, where the other would be better." He also warns that the perils of analogy lurk here, too: "The use of the infinitive is often accounted for, but not justified, by the influence of analogy; because *able*, or *sufficient*, or *adequate, to perform* is English, we assume that *equal to perform*, which is to bear the same meaning, must be English, too." Here is a specimen that emphasizes Fowler's point: "This majority has even aided to make more psychologically youthful the image of a distinguished Democrat who ran for President on two occasions and may run again next year." Since "helped to make" is good English, the writer apparently assumed on the basis of analogy that "aided to make" was good English, too. This sentence, by the way, could also be written "helped make," illustrating again one of the exceptions mentioned in paragraph 1 to the normal use of *to* with the infinitive.

3. "Mr. Bowles devoted a large part of his talk today to insist that the Jeffersonian traditions no longer sufficed. . . ." At first reading this looks like the same error that was taken up in paragraph 2. But it is not. Here the writer mistook the "to" for the sign of the infinitive and at the same time invoked analogy—"used a large part of his talk to insist" is good English, therefore

234

why not "devoted . . . to insist"? But the "to" in the sentence is not the sign of the infinitive; it is merely the normal preposition following "devoted," as in "He devoted his time to music." Therefore, what is needed after the "to" is a noun or verbal noun (gerund), "insisting." The specimen is unusual, but the disregard of idiom is not.

INFLAMMABLE

See FLAMMABLE.

INFLUENCE (n.)

Takes preposition *over, upon,* or *with*.

INFUSE

Takes preposition *with*.

-ING

See NOUN ENDINGS.

INIMICAL

Takes preposition *to* or *toward*.

INNATE

Takes preposition *in*.

INNOCENT

This is something that defendants do not plead in court; they plead "not guilty." A sentence in a newspaper, "Dave Beck pleaded innocent today to a charge of grand larceny," prompted a lawyer to characterize the locution as an "absurdity." He argued that if a defendant were allowed to assert that he was innocent, he might be required to prove it, and it is fundamental in American jurisprudence that no man is required to prove his innocence. On the other hand, a plea of "not guilty" is merely a denial of an affirmative that the prosecution is obligated to prove. The news-paper locution arises from a desire to avoid a possible typograph-

235

ical error in which the "not" might be dropped from "not guilty," but that is insufficient reason to excuse an absurdity.

INNOVATION

By etymology and definition an *innovation* is a bringing in of something new. Therefore "new innovation" is a pleonasm, as in the sentence, "Seventeen U.S. companies have adopted another new innovation called vacuum melting." No "new."

IN NUMBER, IN SIZE

Both these phrases are usually wastefully redundant. For example: "According to Dr. Merle F. Walker . . . the inner core consists of a dense mass of stars equivalent in brightness to about 13,000,000 suns. Actually, he says, the stars are probably 'giants,' far larger than our sun and, hence, fewer in number." *Fewer* means smaller in number; hence, the *in number* adds nothing to the thought. Now an example of the *in size* redundancy: "Although small in size, the destroyer had a distinguished war record." There might be some point in the phrase if the sentence read: "Although small in size, the ship was large in glory." But as it stands, *in size* is, as it usually is, sheer waste.

IN ORDER TO

A wasteful locution. In the vast majority of instances *in order* may be deleted with no loss.

IN QUESTION

Another usually wasteful locution, *in question* often appears in writing almost as if it were the author's nervous cough. If the writer has devoted paragraphs to a bill before the Legislature and then writes, "Miss Stalcup took no direct position on the bill in question," or if he has been discussing a labor relations case and writes, "The case in question occurred at Bethlehem Steel," what purpose is served by the phrase? This is not to say that *in question* never is useful. If two or more things have been mentioned, the phrase is helpful in identifying which one is under discussion— which is what *in question* means. An example might be: "Several labor cases involving a similar issue have arisen at automobile plants, but the case in question occurred at Bethlehem Steel."

INQUIRE

Takes preposition *for, about, after,* or *into.*

INROAD

Takes preposition *into.*

INSENSIBLE

Takes preposition *to, from* or *of.*

INSEPARABLE

Takes preposition *from.*

INSIDE TALK

Unfortunately, all the words that describe the kinds of specialized language that fall within this classification have connotations that range from faintly to strongly disparaging. That is why the neutral label *inside talk* has been affixed to them. The subclassifications are these:

Argot: the speech of thieves and rogues, and, by derived meaning, the speech of any particular class of persons.

Jargon: originally meaningless, unintelligible speech, but now also the language of a science, sect, trade, profession, or the like.

Lingo: in contemptuous reference, the speech of foreigners or of a special class of persons.

Slang: current language below the level of standard usage employing new words or old words in new ways; a language that may or may not be peculiar to a particular class.

The reason that all these words have disparaging connotations is that outsiders dislike being outsiders. They envy or resent those who can speak and understand inside talk. And in some instances the very desire to keep outsiders out accounts for these languages: it is certainly the reason behind argot, it is often the reason behind slang, and it is sometimes the reason behind jargon. There is a tendency in specialized groups, for reasons of either establish-

237

ing a kind of mystic bond or asserting a kind of self-importance, to employ esoteric or pretentious words. It is difficult to see, for instance, what function is performed for the psychologist by *instinctual* that is not just as well performed by *instinctive*; what function is performed for the sociologist by *target ends* that is not just as well performed by *goals*; what function is performed for the pedagogue by *subject area* and *classroom situation* and *classroom teacher* that is not just as well performed by *subject* and *classroom* and *teacher*.

This is by no means to say that all inside talk, all jargon, is pretentious and useless. On the contrary, most of it is highly necessary. Those in specialized fields have need to communicate with one another in precise terms and with an economy of expression. A single word will often convey to a colleague what would require a sentence, a paragraph, or perhaps an even longer description to convey to a layman. The fact that the layman does not comprehend the single word does not indict it for use within its proper sphere.

With the onward march of education, however, the layman comes to comprehend more and more of the jargon of the specialties. In this way more and more useful words enter the language of the ordinary man and the language is enriched. But there is a danger here. It often happens that the layman does not exactly comprehend the specialized word or phrase he is taking over from the specialist, and the word comes into the language with an erroneous meaning so that thenceforth it becomes an ambiguous expression. In economics, for instance, the phrase *economy of scarcity* has a well defined meaning; it refers to a deliberate creation of scarcity to drive prices up. But during World War II one of our newspaper military analysts, who had heard but not understood the phrase, applied it as a description of mere shortages— of ammunition or ships or blankets or what not. The terms of psychoanalysis have suffered the most at the hands of lay writers and lay conversationalists. The cause is undoubtedly twofold: first, there is such an abundance of those terms; second, psychoanalysis has become fashionable in literature and conversation. Thus, *complex* is often used as if it meant a mere psychological peculiarity, *fixation* as if it meant an obsession, *exhibitionism* as if it meant showing off. And there are a host of other Freudian terms that are habitually misused because they are only half understood.

A pointed text for this particular sermon might be the following passage from Ngaio Marsh's *Death of a Peer:*

"What do you think of *me?*" asked Frid, striking an attitude. "Aren't I quite lovely?"

"Don't tell her she is," said Colin. "The girl's a nymphomaniac . . ."

"My dear Colin," said his father, "it really would be a good idea if you'd stick to the words you understand."

A final caution may be of value in a discussion of inside talk. In writing intended for general reading the use, whether by a specialist or by a layman, of jargon terms that are not commonly understood smacks of pedantry. If the writer believes that it is imperative to use such a term, he should at least explain it when it is introduced. It must never be forgotten that the function of writing is communication. *See also* **WINDYFOGGERY.**

INSIGHT
Takes preposition *into.*

INSPIRE
Takes preposition *by* or *with.*

INSTILL
Takes preposition *into.*

INSTRUCT
Takes preposition *in.*

INTEGRATE
Along with the adjective *integrated* and the noun *integration, integrate* took on a new meaning in the latter half of the 1950's. In its earlier and primary sense *integrate* means to unite

239

parts into a whole or to perfect a whole. In its later sense it means to eliminate segregation based on color. In accordance with BERNSTEIN'S SECOND LAW the new word has begun to overshadow, perhaps even to drive out, the older word. If a writer says, "The Salute to the President was an integrated show," or "The conference was called to consider the possible contribution of such experimental parks to the achievement of quality integrated education," only the context will disclose which meaning of the word is intended. A couple of decades ago such ambiguity would have been impossible. There is no doubt that the new meaning of the word is a necessity ("racially mixed" or "racially balanced" are cumbersome), but writers may have difficulty in finding a word to express the older meaning. Necessity may once again become a mother.

INTENT

Takes preposition *on* or *upon.*

INTENTION

Takes preposition *to* or *of.*

INTENTIONALLY

See ADVISEDLY, INTENTIONALLY.

INTERCEDE

Takes preposition *with* or *for.*

IN TERMS OF

Much present-day writing is peppered with the phrase *in terms of,* probably because it has a fine, learned sound. But often it is all sound, signifying nothing. The phrase, properly used, signals a translation from one kind of language to another. There is no suggestion of such translation in the following sentence: "He could not have been thinking in terms of the job he eventually was to take." All that is meant here is "about the job." Again: "Since Lee guarantees its fabrics for a 'lifetime,' this cost factor may prove thrifty when measured in terms of decades rather than years." Why not "measured by decades"? This latter example might be tenuously defended on the ground that there is actually a translation involved: a translation of one measurement of time into another. Even if the defense motion is granted, however, an additional consideration—that of terseness—enters the case. The question that should be asked is, Are these words necessary or are they merely a foggy phrase? *See* WINDYFOGGERY.

INTERNECINE

From the Latin root *necare* (to kill), *internecine* properly means deadly or characterized by slaughter. It does not, from its derivation, mean between brothers or members of the same faction. However, in accordance with BERNSTEIN'S SECOND LAW, *internecine*, in the sense of mutually destructive, is a word that the language needs. That sense has overshadowed the idea of *deadly*, for which the language has a plenitude of words. Thus, *internecine* has established itself at a point of no return.

INTERPOSE

Takes preposition *in* or *between*.

INTERPRETATIVE, INTERPRETIVE

Perhaps on the analogy of the irregularly formed and frowned-upon *preventative*, there are those who think that *interpretative* is likewise a gate-crasher. Not so. *Interpretative* is the proper form, although Webster finds *interpretive* also acceptable. *See* PREVENTIVE, PREVENTATIVE.

INTERVENE

Takes preposition *in* (dispute); *between* (disputants).

IN THE MIDST OF

Often a wasteful locution, as in, "In the midst of attacks on his defense policy, the President called for new funds for nuclear arms." The single word *amid* would suffice here. In general it is well to avoid *in the midst of* if a single word like *amid, in, within,* or *inside* will serve just as well.

241

IN THE NEAR FUTURE

A wasteful locution for *soon* or *shortly*.

IN THE VICINITY OF

Almost always a wasteful locution. It means *near*.

INTO

See IN, INTO.

INTRANSITIVE VERB

See LAY, LIE.

INTRIGUE

"The amusement device, capable of carrying two persons, rises a couple of inches from the floor and is said to intrigue both young and old." Dictionary or no, this is a use that is best avoided on at least two grounds. First, it is an erroneous borrowing from French, in which the word means puzzle; second, *intrigue* has become a fuzzy, all-purpose word to express meanings for which there are already perfectly good, precise words such as *mystify, enchant, interest, pique,* and *excite.*

INTRODUCE

Takes preposition *to* or *into*.

INTRUDE

Takes preposition *on, upon* or *into*.

INUNDATE

Takes preposition *with*.

INURED

See IMMURED, INURED.

INVENT

See DISCOVER, DEVELOP, INVENT.

242

INVERSION

The stylistic quirk of casting a sentence in reverse order or partly reverse order has acquired a certain vogue among writers who, lacking a style of their own, reach into a grab bag of tricks to give an illusion of style. "New this year was a torchlight parade by several thousand soldiers, coal miners, and others from the Place de la Bastille to the Place de la Concorde." Unless there is a valid reason for this kind of distortion, it is as pointless as a man's walking to work on his hands. There might, of course, be a valid reason in the example quoted. If the preceding sentence had recounted the happenings this year that were the same as those of previous years, there would be justification for emphasizing, "New this year. . . ."

Sometimes a different kind of reason arises. A newspaper writer in handling a list of casualties in an accident may decide, correctly, that he does not wish to begin his sentence with half a dozen names and wind up with "were injured." Under the influence of the inversion trick, therefore, he writes, "Injured were," followed by the list. But it never seems to occur to a writer under this spell that he could accomplish the same end and still have an uninverted sentence by writing, "The injured were" or "Those injured were."

But let us turn to examples in which no such reason arises. From an archaeological article: "Concealed was a chamber with two benches almost intact. . . . Recovered was a large two-handled vase, with a sculptured head of Hercules and the battle of the Amazons in relief." Here not only the sentence structure but also the natural emphasis is distorted. "Concealed" and "recovered" are not the ideas that call for emphasis, but rather the things concealed and recovered; these are what should have come first in the sentences.

Let there be no doubt as to the creator of this walking-on-the-hands school of writing: it is *Time* magazine, in whose pages the affectation has appeared continually. Here are two instances that glared at a reader within a dozen lines of each other: "Recalled he, in his 1946 book . . ."; "Explained another Cuban cor-

243

respondent. . . ." This type of thing may be reasonable in poetry
—"Quoth the raven, 'Nevermore' "—but in most prose, particularly when used often, it is a disturbing stylistic quirk.

INVEST

Takes preposition *with* or *in*.

INVOLVE

Takes preposition *in*.

IRONY

See RHETORICAL FIGURES AND FAULTS.

IRREGARDLESS

Illiterate.

ISOLATE

Takes preposition *from*.

-IZE

The suffix "-ize" is one of the devices that have helped the
English language grow. But it has also in some instances helped it
grow stuffy or grotesque. The suffix means, of course, to submit to
the action indicated by the root of the word (as in *burglarize* and
hospitalize) or to make similar to the thing indicated in the root
(as in *sterilize* and *slenderize*). Years ago Mencken noted the
tendency in the United States to manufacture new verbs by employing this device. He listed "such monstrosities" as *backward-
ize, respectablize, scenarioize, expertize, powerize*, and *manhat-
tanize*. Many such coinages quickly die an unlamented death. But
the mints are perpetually in business.

Commercial organizations are particularly eager to impress
their names on the language and so we get such words as *Simon-
ize, Sanforize*, and *Hollanderize*. Officialdom and business are
likewise quick to manufacture "-ize" words and they have given
us such expendable novelties as *concretize, finalize, definitize*, and
permanentize. Self-important people love important-sounding

words, and the "-ize" words seem to be one variety that satisfies their yearning. But the question that must be asked is not, Does this word sound important? but rather, Is this word necessary? That test will readily weed out a large proportion of the coinages that clutter the language. And when new ones appear, the proper view should be one of skepticism—a kind of damn-your-ize attitude. *See also* **WINDYFOGGERY.**

J

JARGON
See INSIDE TALK.

JEALOUS
Takes preposition *of.*

JEALOUSY
See ENVY, JEALOUSY.

JEER
Takes preposition *at.*

JOIN TOGETHER
Inclusion of *together* in this phrase makes for redundancy. Note how readily it could be deleted in the following sentence: "Two desolate isles off Staten Island are to be joined together." This is not to suggest that it must be deleted, still less to suggest a rewriting of the marriage rite: "What therefore God hath joined together, let not man put asunder." What is suggested is that when a writer is about to set down the phrase, he gather his thoughts (together) and ask himself whether the redundancy imparts strength or weakness. Most of the time he will find it imparts weakness.

Join takes the preposition *with* or *to.*

JUDGING
See DANGLERS.

JURIST
"A note was sent to Judge George Mullen, and the jurist replied. . . ." Despite journalistic usage, *jurist* is not a synonym for *judge.* A *jurist* is merely one versed in the law. Therefore,

although a *judge* is, or should be, a *jurist*, a *jurist* is not necessarily a *judge*.

JUST

As an adverb, *just* means precisely ("just right") or narrowly ("just missed the train") or only ("just a sip") or very recently ("just arrived"). *Just exactly* says the same thing twice; it is a redundancy to be avoided. *Just about*, as in "I am just about ready," would seem to be an oxymoron, or self-contradictory expression, since the words mean "precisely approximately." Still, the phrase is an idiom, one of those things that often defy logic.

JUST DESERTS

See DESERTS.

JUSTIFIED

Takes preposition *in*.

K

KEN

The word means scope of knowledge or range of understanding. It does not mean merely scope or range. The following is a misapplication: "The statement went on to declare that articles that 'once would have been considered outside of the *Post's* ken of interest' would start appearing with increasing frequency."

KIDNAP

"Two Seized in Boston Kidnap." *Kidnap* is a verb; what is needed here is a noun form, *kidnapping*. Likewise, the verb form will not do when an adjective form is required; this rules out *kidnap plot* and *kidnap ring*. The past tense and participle may be spelled *kidnaped* and *kidnaping* or *kidnapped* and *kidnapping*, but most of us prefer the double "p" spellings because of the similar-appearing word *napped* and to avoid the suggestion of a "naped" pronunciation.

KILOWATT

"The accord would allot to the Niagara Mohawk Power Company 445,000 kilowatt hours of power. . . ." No. The measure of productive capacity, which is what is wanted here, is the *kilowatt*. The "kilowatt hour," which is the amount of energy transferred or expended in one hour by one *kilowatt* of power, is used to measure production or consumption. The difference is akin to that between the capacity of a bucket and the amount of water that can be moved in it in a given period.

KILT

"The boy, wearing kilts, was given a place of honor near the altar." One boy wears one *kilt*, two boys wear two *kilts*. In other words, a *kilt* is not like pants, which should be obvious.

248

KIN

Despite some headline writers, *kin* does not refer to an individual, but to relatives collectively. If only one relative is involved, it is incorrect to write, "Gouger's Kin Offers 'Amends' to Charity." When used properly, *kin* is always plural.

KIND OF

Three uses of the phrase *kind of* (and *sort of*) may be distinguished:

1. To mean an approximation of, a quasi-something belonging to that class ("He is a kind of beachcomber"; "The dictionary is a kind of miniature encyclopedia"). In this sense, in which the phrase is standard usage, the meaning of the word *kind* is present but dim; we think not so much of any particular kind of the thing as of a loose characterization.

2. To mean *rather, somewhat,* or *in a sense.* Used in this meaning, the phrase is adverbial and may modify an adverb, an adjective, or a verb ("It is kind of late"; "I am kind of tired"; "I am kind of falling asleep on my feet"). Here the meaning of the word *kind* has all but vanished. In this sense, the phrase is casual usage and is not to be employed in serious writing.

3. To mean a species of a genus or, more broadly, a subdivision of a general category ("What kind of apple is that?"; "He got the kind of reception he deserved"). Here the meaning of the word *kind* is prominent, although in varying degrees. The use of the phrase in this sense is, of course, standard. But it is infested with booby traps, and for ages the authorities on usage have been busy either exploding them or putting up warning signs, depending on how they appraise the peril. Incidentally, the booby traps bring out rather sharply the distinction between spoken and written language, since most of the solecisms are common in speech but disapproved of in writing. Here, then, is a listing, with a verdict in each instance:

Kind of an apple. Kind of applies, as has been stated, to a subdivision of a broad category. You don't have a subdivision made up of one particular thing. Therefore you don't—or shouldn't—write, "Paula was a little uncertain what kind of a

249

place the White House was." Paula shouldn't be sounding her "a."

Those kind of apple. This construction need not detain us because it is unsound idiomatically and grammatically. But . . .

Those kind of apples is not disposed of as readily, particularly when a well-educated, well-spoken President of the United States tells his constituents, "If we want those kind of tests. . . ." There is an understandable yearning here for a plural modifier, since what is uppermost in the speaker's mind is "tests" rather than *kind.* Still, although that construction will persist in spoken language, the careful writer will avoid it as grammatically unsound and make it "tests of that kind."

Those kinds of apples. (Getting complicated, isn't it?) Although the singular for the generic class (apple) is preferred —and is almost invariable when the class is an abstraction ("those kinds of sculpture," "those kinds of composition")—the use of the plural cannot be regarded as a capital offense. We may be tolerant of "Mr. Crichton writes of his encounters with many sorts of persons." Likewise . . .

That kind of apples is acceptable. One may think of the apple category or of the category as made up of various classes of apples.

Much—perhaps too much—has been made in the two preceding paragraphs of the number of the noun following *kind of.* The determination can be made on these bases: If, as has been said, the noun is an abstraction, it is singular. For other words, either a singular or a plural may be used, depending on whether it is thought of as a category name or as members of the category. For instance: "It takes all kinds of people [category] to make up a world," but, "All kinds of persons [members of category] were in the audience"; "Various kinds of argument [category] were taken up in the course in logic," but, "Various kinds of arguments [members of category] broke out between the strikers and the police."

It may well be that in time all the *kind of* solecisms will become established in literary usage. If so, the traditional grammarians will find a way of saving their faces and their skins. They can always promulgate the notion—and here is a bequest to posterity from THE CAREFUL WRITER—that *kind of* is a compound adjective, a "nexus." ("Nexus," with a fine Jespersen ring to it, is guaranteed to quell any rebels.) Thus, if the President spoke of "those kind of tests," the grammarians would rally to his defense by proclaiming that *kind of* was a nexus to be construed as an adjective, just as if he had said "those dangerous tests." That, you see, would take care not only of the "those," but also of the plural "tests." All very neat, very tidy. But not gospel . . . yet.

KNOT

A common error is this: "The carrier *Wasp* is limping home at eight knots an hour." *Knot* is a unit of speed: one nautical mile an hour. Therefore "an hour" should never follow *knot*. The ship can travel "at eight knots" or "at eight nautical miles an hour." By the way, don't disabled ships ever do anything but limp? It's a limp figure of speech.

KNOW-HOW

See FAD WORDS.

KUDOS

From the Greek word meaning glory, *kudos* is an anything but glorious addition to English. Originally campus slang, it is now pseudo-literary. Let the Greeks have it back. It need hardly be added that the final "s" in the word is not the sign of a plural; there is no such thing as a *kudo*, as was thought by the author of a magazine ad who wrote, "Another Kudo for *Esquire*."

L

LACK

A *lack* is not a mere deficiency but rather a deficiency of something that is needful or desirable. Here is an inexact usage: "The lack of polemics between Moscow and Peking does not mean that a reconciliation is imminent." The lack in that sentence is of the word *absence*.

LACKING

Takes preposition *in*.

LADEN

Takes preposition *with*.

LADY

The social distinction between *lady* and *woman* has all but disappeared, and it has no place in the work of a practiced writer. *Lady* normally has no more justification than does *gentleman* in place of *man*. The social distinction between *lady* and *woman* not only has almost vanished but indeed seems to be in process of being reversed. Perrin recalls the woman looking for work who asked, "Are you the woman who wanted a lady to work for her?" And a *New York Times* classified ad called for a "young lady to assist in high-class men's shop." In speech, as a form of address to strangers, *lady* and *gentleman* usually are pretensions of the unlettered. It is the bus driver who says, "Lady, I can't change a twenty-dollar bill," and the unpolished waiter who says, "Would you like a cocktail, gentleman?" *Madam* and *sir* are the words for these situations. Yet in spoken language there remain uses for the other words. The lecturer's salutation is "ladies and gentlemen," and in ordering for your female friend in a restaurant you would say, "The lady will have the noodle soup."

LAG

Takes preposition *behind.*

LAMENT

Takes preposition *for* or *over.*

LATTER

A comparative form, *latter* refers to the second of two things, not to the last of any old number. It is frequently misused: "The agencies represented included the Port Authority, the Civil Aeronautics Administration, the Civil Aeronautics Board, the city's Department of Marine and Aviation, and the National Air Transport Coordinating Committee. The latter body, representing the air lines. . . ." Here you would have to say "The last named" or "The last of these," or repeat, at least in part, the name of the committee. Another misuse: "The program will include reports by Frank McGee and Wilson and Lee Hall. The latter two correspondents are a husband and wife team." The phrase "latter two" would be appropriate only if there were a "former two"—"Frank and Mabel McGee," for example.

Usually *latter* is used to avoid repetition, but repetition is not always undesirable. It clearly would be if it entailed an immediate second helping of "the National Air Transport Coordinating Committee." But it would be quite inoffensive if it meant merely writing, in the second illustration, "the Halls." And repetition is actually an advantage in some kinds of writing—news articles, for instance—in which the aim is to speed the reader on his way, because the use of *latter* compels him to shift into reverse and look back to see what *latter* refers to. That the reference may not be immediately apparent is evidenced by this sentence: "Although many a gifted leader adorns history, and the skein of history's crises is endless, it is only when the former is tested in the fires of the latter that true greatness gets its opportunity to rise."

LAUGH

Takes preposition *at* or *over.*

LAW BUSINESS

See OCCUPATIONS.

LAWMAN

In medieval England there was such a thing as a *lawman*, an officer with a specific function. In present-day America we are now discovering, especially in newspapers, that there are also *lawmen*, a vague group whose function seems to be enforcement of the law. "Mr. Cole said he was discriminated against by North Carolina lawmen because he is white." Mr. Cole undoubtedly meant policemen or sheriffs or F.B.I. agents or state constabulary or something else specific. Why the imprecise blanket word *lawmen*? Who needs it?

LAWYER

See ATTORNEY, LAWYER.

LAY, LIE

Lay is a transitive verb and never anything else except in the meaning of to deposit eggs ("The hen is laying") and in a few nautical terms (lay aloft). For those whose grammar lessons are far behind them or forever incomprehensible, let it be explained that a transitive verb is one that acts as a transmission belt, conveying action or influence from a subject to an object. The present tense is *lay* ("Watch as I now lay this book on the table"). The past tense is *laid* ("He laid his watch carefully on the desk"). The present participle is *laying* ("He is laying his plans for a medical career"). The past participle is *laid* ("He had laid his plans before entering college").

Lie is an intransitive verb and never anything else. An intransitive verb is one that confines the action to the subject; it does not transmit the action or influence to an object. The present tense is *lie* ("The Azores lie in mid-Atlantic"). The past tense is *lay* ("He lay in pain waiting for help"). The present participle is *lying* ("He is lying in bed"). The past participle is *lain* ("He had lain there for several hours").

The most common errors are, first, the use of the forms of

254

the transitive *lay* where forms of *lie* are required—"The pencil was laying on the table" (never, unless the pencil were depositing eggs) or "Women laid down in the roadway to halt the Soviet tanks" (No, down isn't laid; it comes off a duck)—and second, the use of *laid* instead of *lain* for the participle form of *lie*—"He had laid there for several hours."

These confusions are not infrequent, but the errors can only be classed as illiterate.

LEAN

Takes preposition *on, upon,* or *against.*

LEAVE, LET

Obviously we cannot, even if we would, reform the English language. What we can do, however, is to make the best and most precise use of the tools at hand. One way to do that is to let each word express a meaning of its own and not burden it with some additional meaning that is more exactly expressed by another word. For example, despite common usage (which the dictionary reflects), *leave alone* can have and should have a meaning different from *let alone. Leave alone* can and should exclusively mean to cause to be in solitude, and *let alone* can and should exclusively mean to allow to go undisturbed. Common usage, however, has given *leave alone* both meanings, to the detriment of precise expression.

Lest it be thought that the point is purely academic, observe the ambiguity of this sentence: "Something new was added when Durocher was seen to leave the third-base coaching line discreetly alone." What was meant here was not that Durocher walked away in solitude, but that he did not erase the white coaching line, as had been his custom. The phrase should have been *let alone.* Again: "What many in the West did not realize was that the Soviet Government generally left alone those who were working in the most important physical sciences." No doubt the scientists were accorded solitude, but the intent of the sentence was to say that they were undisturbed.

As to the substitution of *leave* for *let,* as in, "Leave us go to

255

lunch," it is an illiteracy. It has become a fashionable drollery even among the educated, but they are aware (it is to be hoped) that it is an illiteracy.

LEERY

Although based on a respectable word—*leer*, to look askance—*leery* is slang. "The State Department and the French and West German Governments have been leery of disengagement." Why not *wary* or *distrustful* or *chary* or *hesitant* (about)?

LEND, LOAN

Dictionaries and most other authorities sanction *loan* as a verb in American usage. Yet, probably because a British influence has been at work, most writers who observe the niceties seem to prefer *lend*, although some accept *loan* in financial contexts ("The bank loaned the corporation $3,000,000") and in art contexts ("Three of the paintings were loaned to the museum by Nelson A. Rockefeller"). If your ear is not offended by "Loan me your pen" or by "Friends, Romans, countrymen, loan me your ears," the authorities are right so far as you are concerned. The rest of us will continue to prefer *lend*, though we recognize that *loan* has a basis in both history and usage.

LENGTHY

A word that the language could have done without, *lengthy* has been with us a long time and is here to stay. Indeed, in accordance with BERNSTEIN'S SECOND LAW, it sometimes seems to be displacing the good word *long*. Yet its meaning—aside from the obvious one of long—is in some doubt. Both Webster and the Oxford indicate that it has the connotation of overlong or tedious or prolix. This would seem to accord with a tendency, in coining words, to use the suffix "-y" to suggest something distasteful or to be condemned—*catty, horsy, messy, garlicky, beery*, and the like. But *lengthy* is by no means uniformly used in this mildly pejorative way; in fact, sometimes it is used with pleasanter, friendlier connotations than *long*. A *long novel* is likely to be more of a bore than a *lengthy novel*; a *long prison sentence* often suggests a more

256

extended term than a *lengthy prison sentence*. To be sure, a *lengthy sermon* may conjure up a picture of more fidgeting than a *long sermon*, and *lengthy court proceedings* may suggest more motions, trial days, and appeals than *long court proceedings*. Or are these judgments all subjective? In any event they are enough to indicate that the meaning of *lengthy* is not at all sharp. Still the word works its fascination on writers, who occasionally use it even where it seems to have no pin-downable meaning at all. In a book review: "Thus in *Portrait of a Gentleman* we see a scoundrel—who has taken lengthy advantage of a girl—go blithely on his cheaply scandalous way." What does the word mean there—for a long time? repeatedly? continued? The best advice that can be given here about *lengthy* is in general to avoid it and say instead what you really mean—*overlong, tedious, prolix, rather long, very long, longer than necessary*, or even *longish*.

LESS

See FEWER, LESS.

LESSER

A double comparative (since *less* is already the comparative degree of *little*), *lesser* is a rather formal word for which there should be little use except in stock phrases, such as "the lesser of two evils," and in designations of flora and fauna, such as "lesser hemlock" and "lesser crested tern."

LEST

There are two different, yet quite similar, meanings of this word: (1) for fear that, and (2) so that . . . not. When we say, "The farmers prayed it would rain lest the crops be ruined," the meaning is either "for fear that the crops would be ruined" or "so that the crops would not be ruined." Therefore, *lest* is not followed by a *not* as if it meant merely *so that*, as it is erroneously in this sentence: "Presumably these precautions were taken lest early disclosure not affect the market." Of course, if the thing that is feared is itself a negative thing, the *not* is proper: "He was anxious lest his proposal not be accepted."

257

LET

See LEAVE, LET.

LEVEL (vb.)

Takes preposition *with* (a carpenter's plane); *at* (a target).

LIABLE

See APT, LIABLE, LIKELY. Takes preposition *for* (an act); *to* (a person).

LIBEL, SLANDER

Both words mean defamation, but in the eyes of the law there is a difference between them. *Slander* is oral defamation; *libel* is defamation by any other means—in print, in writing, in recorded speech, or by pictures, signs, or effigies.

LIE

See LAY, LIE.

LIKE, AS

Shorts are not acceptable dinner attire in most better-grade restaurants. There is no really logical reason for that, although restaurants could advance other kinds of reasons. But it takes a daring soul to defy the proscription. Similarly, the use of *like* as a conjunction ("In an experimental water tank, quartz crystals beamed sound like floodlights beam light") is not acceptable in better-grade writing, although there is no logical reason why it should not be. The story of *like* used in this sense is told succinctly by Curme:

"Instead of *as* we often find *like as* in older English: 'Like as a father pitieth his children, so the Lord pitieth them that fear him' (Psalms, CIII, 13). Here *like* is an adverb with the meaning *in the same manner. As* performs the function of conjunction. But early *like as* became felt as a unit, and later *as* began to disappear since *like* was felt as expressing clearly alone both the meaning and the function. The *like-as* clause has the great advantage over the *as* clause that *like* has a clear, distinctive meaning, while *as* has so many meanings that it is often difficult to discover what it means in the case in hand. Shakespeare, among other earlier writers, used *like* here as a short form for *like as*, just as *after, while*, etc., were used for older *after that, the while that*, etc., so that, just as the preposition *after* and the noun *while* have become subordinating conjunctions of time, the adverb *like* has become a subordinating conjunction of comparison, in accordance with sound grammatical analogies which have long been at work in English: 'Like an arrow shot From a well-experienc'd archer hits the mark' (*Pericles*, I, i, 163). Our grammarians have recognized *after, while*, etc., but still combat *like*. They demand the use of *as* here. *Like*, however, is widely used in colloquial and popular speech, since its vivid concrete force appeals to the feelings more than the colorless *as*."

That is the story. There is no logical reason why *like* should not be regarded as a conjunction; on the contrary, there are sound logical and historical reasons why it should be. And yet . . . yet . . . there are those objections by grammarians. Reasonable or unreasonable, they are a force in the language as it exists, as contrasted perhaps with how it should exist. The force has been exerted through generations of teaching and precept so that the objections are strongly entrenched. That does not mean that they are eternally entrenched. Indeed, there is every sign that popular usage will in time erode the fortress, particularly since the popular usage is finding its way more and more into print in the form of AD-DICTION: "Winston tastes good—like a cigarette should"; "Flattens hills like it flattens the floor." Perrin says (1942 edition): "If editors and publishers did not enforce the use of *as* instead of *like* according to the rule in their stylebooks, it is possible that *like* would become the dominant form, and it increasingly appears in print." The belief is well founded only in part. Not only editors but also most writers have an ingrained distaste for *like*, and do not merely adhere to a rule in their stylebooks. It will take more than a fiat by an authority on usage or an undiscriminating count of noses to bring about a change. The change is not here yet, and the serious writer who uses *like* as a conjunction still does so at his peril. Some eminent writers have appeared in the restaurant in shorts, but their eminence has perhaps protected them. The evidence—and it is significant—seems to be that far more eminent writers have avoided appearing in shorts.

Following are some specific cases and counsels concerning the troublesome word:

1. When *like* precedes a noun that is not followed by a verb, its use is unobjectionable: "He plays chess like an expert"; "She acts like a lady." In such constructions *like* is equivalent to a prepositional phrase, *similarly to*. Of course a gerund, which is a verbal noun, may follow *like*, as in, "Walking stimulates circulation like swimming." But the word after *like* must be a true gerund, not merely have the appearance of one, as in this sentence: "Again, it was a solid and desirable fact that the new Russian state did not look like withering away, as prophecy had foretold it should."

2. *Like* and *as* are not interchangeable. For instance, *as* usually cannot be used in place of *like* in constructions in which the verb is suppressed or its implied presence is not strong. Attempts to use it in that way are occasionally made by writers who apparently were frightened in infancy by the word *like*. One example: "He defied the ancient tradition that the chief spy, as his agents, should court anonymity." Another example: "A crowd of young adults raced up and down a Bronx street yesterday carrying marbles in spoons, jumping in potato sacks, and generally behaving as children." *As* is improper in both these sentences. Moreover, it sounds as hell.

3. *Like* cannot stand for *as if*, except for a few idiomatic phrases such as "The car looks like new" and "They cheered like crazy." But it is not proper to write, "He spent money like it was going out of style," or "The Russians advocated disarmament like they meant it."

4. Finally, one of the most prevalent misuses of *like* is in the comparison of things that do not permit comparison. These mistakes are errors of reasoning rather than of grammar. A few illustrations should make the point clear. Here is one: "Like ancient Athens, democracy flourishes in the United States." Here

"Athens" is apparently being compared to "democracy." Make it, "As in ancient Athens." Again: "He noted that, unlike past years, the French treasury was not getting ready to launch a loan." The "treasury" is neither like nor unlike "past years." Make it, "unlike what it did in past years." Still another: "Like a baseball pitcher's change of pace, Mr. Shirer has written a couple of juveniles since finishing *The Rise and Fall of the Third Reich.*" The comparison of a baseball pitch to Mr. Shirer won't stand up. Make it, "like a baseball pitcher throwing a change of pace." All these sentences illustrate the much belabored but ever valid point that the first requisite for good writing is clear thinking.

LIKELY

Idiom requires that when *likely* is used as an adverb, it be preceded by *very, quite,* or *most.* Without one of these words it is not acceptable, as in this sentence: "The Mississippi team likely will be less diversified on the attack." As an adjective it requires no companion: "It is likely to snow tomorrow"; "He is a likely lad." *See also* APT, LIABLE, LIKELY.

LIKEN

Takes preposition *to.*

LIKES OF

The phrase *the likes of* is a casualism that has no place in serious writing. Example: "The director, dapper in a tweed suit and smart bow tie, the likes of which are seldom seen in Moscow. . . ." Either make it singular—*like*—or omit the phrase altogether.

LIMITED

See INDEFINITELY.

LIMPID

Despite the sound of the word, it does not mean limp or frail; it means crystal clear. Therefore, it makes no sense in this passage: "By her acting she actually makes something stalwart

261

and inspiring of the limpid little thing who has played a decided second fiddle to her mother's favorite in the early scenes." For a similar misconception based on the sound of a word, *see* LIVID.

LINE
See OCCUPATIONS.

LINGO
See INSIDE TALK.

LINGUISTIC ANARCHIST
See PURIST.

LION'S SHARE
Not only overused but also misused, the phrase *lion's share* often appears in this kind of context: "Many factors played a part in the close election, in which the Democrats again won the lion's share of state constitutional offices." The *lion's share*, as conceived by Aesop, is all or almost all, not merely a majority or the larger part.

LITANY
A *litany* is a form of prayer in which clergy and congregation join in alternate responses, and by extension the word means a repetitive recitation. Somehow (by phonic association with *list*, perhaps?) the word is occasionally misused as if it meant a listing or history. Thus: "Upon this conclusion, Mark Rascovich has fashioned *The Bedford Incident*, an action-packed litany of a United States destroyer assigned to NATO defenses and its pursuits of a spying Soviet submarine. . . ." Whatever was in the writer's mind, the word is misused.

LITERALLY
Picture this in your mind, if you can: "The job of selecting the jury was carried out in a courtroom that literally bulged." And this: "But yesterday the United States Court of Appeals literally put the money in his pocket." What the writers of those

sentences were afraid of was that we would take them *literally*, but instead of escaping from the danger they plunged more deeply into it. *Literally* means true to the exact meaning of the words. What most writers (and speakers) mean when they use *literally* is *figuratively*, which is just about its opposite. When they do not intend to warn us against taking what they say *literally*, they use the word as a mere means of underlining a thought; usually the thought needs no underlining.

LITOTES

See RHETORICAL FIGURES AND FAULTS.

LITTLER, LITTLEST

Although occasionally used, both these forms are regarded as dialectal or perhaps as juvenile. When size is involved, the better forms are *smaller* and *smallest*; when quantity or importance is involved, the better forms are *less* (sometimes *lesser*) and *least*.

LIVE

Technical uses of the adjective *live* are so common these days that occasionally a writer is led to think it is interchangeable with the adjective *alive*: "About seven hours later he stepped into the hall to ask a maid what time it was. This was apparently the last time he was seen live." Oddly enough the adjective *live* is used almost exclusively attributively, that is, before the noun ("live lobsters," "a live topic," "a real live prince"). Only in a few specialized fields such as television, electricity, and gunnery is the word used predicatively ("The broadcast was live," "The trolley wire is live," "The aerial bomb was live"). In this respect the word behaves in an opposite manner to DRUNK, which is used predicatively.

LIVID

Does a person in a rage turn red or pale? On the answer to this question depends whether *livid* is used correctly or incorrectly in the following passage: "Provoo's face became livid. He leaned forward, banged his fist on the witness box, and

263

shouted. . . ." *Livid* means either black and blue or the color of lead. But perhaps by association with *vivid* or *lurid,* many people believe it means red or flaming. Here is a clear piece of evidence: "Lenin picked up the livid torch." It is difficult to visualize a torch that is either black and blue or ashen gray.

LO, THE POOR IDIOM

A French printer walked into the newsroom of an American newspaper in Paris at the beginning of his 10 P.M. shift. With hand extended (the ritual of the "shake-hand" is as inviolable a custom in France as the prandial *vin rouge*), and eager to display his newly acquired English vocabulary, he greeted each editor with a cheery "Good night." Logically, there is no reason under the moon why that should not be just as proper a salutation as "Good evening." Indeed, considering the hour, it might be expected to be even more proper. Yet anyone who knows English recognizes that it is not. Why is "Good evening" the correct salutation, whereas "Good night" is not only incorrect but not a salutation at all and is, rather, a phrase of farewell? The answer is idiom.

Idiom refers to that characteristic of a language whereby one form of expression is used rather than another that would seem to be just as proper logically or grammatically, or even more so. There isn't much sense, when you analyze it, in the phrase "Many a man has. . . ." But that is idiomatic.

A writer tampers with idiom at his own peril, and the peril is great. When he writes, "At that time *Sceptre* was all except invisible in the haze," he has flouted the idiom *all but.* When he writes "sharply at 8 A.M." or "sitting prettily" or "comes in handily," he is guilty of OVERREFINEMENT that violates the idiom that says these words do not take the "-ly" adverbial ending. When he writes about legislators trying "to bottle legislation" or an actor "mulling a bid"—rather than *bottle up* and *mulling over*—he betrays insensitivity to idiom and ignorance of the subject of VERB TAILS. When he writes, "The event is one of the methods the club raises money," he is misled by the analogy of the word "ways" (which can be used in this manner though "methods" cannot), and fails to discern that idiom can nullify analogy as well as logic and grammar. And when he writes, "His mother forbade him from playing chess until his marks improved," he has disregarded the idiom that dictates "to" after "forbid."

In addition to the type of idiom discussed thus far there is a large class of expressions, chiefly figurative or allusive and often in the cliché category, that are identified as idioms. These would include such phrases as on *all fours, clutch at a straw, cut and dried, split hairs, make head or tail of, put the cart before the horse, in the same boat,* and *up to snuff.* A collection of such expressions has been published by V. H. Collins in *A Book of English Idioms.* These phrases need give no trouble to a writer provided he is alert to the perils of the cliché. (*See* CLICHÉS *and* CURDLED CLICHÉS.)

But there is little guidance that can be given about idioms in general. They are something you grow up with and absorb with the air you breathe. The big dictionaries are some help because they often list idioms under the key word in the expression. The proper preposition to hitch to a verb—and this problem is a major category under the general heading of idiom—can often be found in dictionaries and books on usage (*see* PREPOSITIONS). But by and large (an idiom) the writer must play it by ear (another idiom). How good his ear is depends, of course, on the kind of English he has heard in his formative years and what he has seen in print.

LOAN

See LEND, LOAN.

LOCATED

To *locate* is to find or fix the position of something, usually with the connotation that an agent is doing the finding or fixing. Some object to *located* as a synonym for *situated,* as in this sentence: "The canyon is located about sixty miles northwest of the McMurdo Sound base." The objectors contend that with the auxiliary verb *is* the participle should be *situated,* not *located.*

Usage has probably overruled the objection, but often, as in the example cited, no participle at all is necessary: "The canyon is about sixty miles northwest, etc."

Locate has an additional meaning of to fix or set up in a particular place. It is used correctly in this sense in the following sentence, which also contains *located* in the controversial sense of *situated*: "Rockaway Park is located [omit altogether or perhaps change to *situated*] within fifteen minutes of Kennedy Airport, and this was a principal reason for locating [right] the lobster 'plant' and restaurant there." In the intransitive sense of taking up residence ("He located in Greenwich Village") the word *locate* is widely used in casual language, but is not regarded as standard in good writing.

LONGSHOREMAN, STEVEDORE

To most people these terms are interchangeable, but to waterfront people a *longshoreman* is a laborer and a *stevedore* is an employer of *longshoremen*.

LOST TO

The phrase *lost to* is occasionally subject to ambiguity because it can be used in two ways. One way is exemplified by this sentence: "If a freeway is built through the redwood forest, this great park will be lost to posterity." The meaning here is clear: The loser will be posterity. The second meaning of the phrase is illustrated by this sentence: "He lost his heart to Miss Jones." Again the meaning is clear: The loser is not Miss Jones, but *he*. Sometimes, however, the intention of the writer is not so easily detected: "Things have not yet developed to a point where Syria is irrevocably lost to the East." Would "the East" be the gainer or the loser? Again: "An Indonesian spokesman has said that Malaysia would be lost to the Chinese Communists if the United States did not take the initiative in efforts to reshape the new federation." Only special knowledge on the part of the reader or the context in which the sentence appears would make apparent whether "the Chinese Communists" would be the gainers or the losers. The phrase *lost to* requires special care in situations in which it can be read in two ways. If there is any chance of ambiguity, a different construction should be substituted: In the second example the wording might be changed to, "An Indonesian spokesman has said that the Chinese Communists might take over Malaysia if. . . ."

M

MADAM

The spelling is erroneous in this sentence: "An alleged madame and three women were arrested during the night raid on the apartment." The keeper of a bawdy house is a *madam*, not a *madame*.

MADE

Takes preposition *from, out of,* or *of.*

MAJOR

As an adjective in the comparative degree, *major* properly should not be used as a synonym for *important, weighty, serious, great, basic,* or *fundamental.* But by undiscriminating writers it often is. Not only is the word overused, but in addition it frequently is accompanied by qualifiers that should not attend a comparative: "*King John* is an extremely major work"; "The need for nuclear artillery in the European theater is more major than the need for planes"; "The total body technique in the treatment of cancer so far has been too major an undertaking to repeat." Strictly speaking, *major* means greater in importance (or in standing, size, value, quality, or the like) than others of the same kind. When we speak of a "major poet," we are, or should be, thinking of him in comparison with others in his field. No doubt it is uses like this that led to the belief that the word meant important or great. It should also be noted that since the word is a comparative adjective, it usually should not be preceded by *the*; one might speak of "a major poet," but not of "the major poet."

MANY

See FEW *and* A, AN (2).

MARGINAL

In economics *marginal* is a useful word meaning barely enough to yield a profit. No word, of course, need be restricted to the field in which it originated; if it serves a useful purpose outside that field, so be it. But if *marginal* is taken over merely as a FAD WORD to give an important sound to the simple notion of small or narrow, what is the gain? For example: "A marine expert said that the recent East Coast storms would have a marginal effect on prospects for game fishing there." Or: "Corruption in government is said to have been marginal here in comparison with other Asian countries." If *marginal* in each of these instances does not mean small or little, what on earth does it mean? And if it does mean small or little, why the pretentious word? *See* INSIDE TALK *and* WINDYFOGGERY.

MARRED

Takes preposition *by*.

MARTYR

As a noun, takes preposition *to*; as a verb, takes preposition *for*.

MASTERFUL, MASTERLY

The distinction in good current usage between *masterful* (imperious, domineering) and *masterly* (skillful, expert) is worth preserving. *Masterly* is never misused; *masterful* often is, as witness these examples: "In a masterful display of seamanship . . ."; "By masterful cut and manipulation of material so that it stands away from the bust. . . ." One way to remember the distinction between the words is to think of "-ly" as meaning *like: Masterly* equals *like a master*. Some misuses of *masterful* and *masterfully* may have their origin in the fact that *masterly* makes a reluctant adverb (*See* ADVERBS, RELUCTANT). Although it is an adverb as well as an adjective, and although there is another adverbial form of it—*masterlily*—neither is completely satisfactory. "He paints masterly" sounds just as odd as, "He paints masterlily." Each requires rephrasing into something like, "He paints in a masterly manner." This quirk should not, however, affect the maintenance of the distinction between the two words.

MASTERY

Takes preposition *of* (a subject); *over* (persons).

MATERIALIZE

As a fancy word for *happen, take place,* or *develop, materialize* is overpopular, as are most pretentious words. Properly it means to appear in substantial form, a form that can be apprehended by the senses, as in, "The expected profits never materialized." In the following sentence it is improperly, not to say absurdly, employed: "The accepted Pentagon estimates stress that the once-predicted missile gap did not materialize."

MATHEMATICAL TERMS

Mathematical expressions like *common denominator* may be useful in writing if they are short cuts that avoid circumlocution and carry the reader directly to the intended meaning. Thus employed, they are as serviceable as any other rhetorical figure. Sometimes, however, the less familiar mathematical terms like *geometric progression* or *coefficient* merely make a learned sound and compel the reader to go back over the ground to try to find his way out. When that happens, they are no short cuts to meaning. For example: "There is an inverse ratio between the length of time a plane has been around in regular service and the consternation its mechanical difficulties cause." A reader would not be likely to find that instantly clear. He would reread it and finally say to himself that it means, "The more time a plane has been in regular service the less consternation its mechanical difficulties cause, and vice versa." There, of course, is the answer: not only a clearer sentence, but also a shorter one. Leave most mathematical expressions to the mathematicians; they understand them.

MATHEMATICS

See -ICS.

MATINEE PERFORMANCE

" 'King Solomon's Daughter' will be given a special Sunday matinee performance. . . ." Omit "performance"; a *matinee* is a daytime, especially an afternoon, performance.

MAY

See CAN, MAY.

MAY, MIGHT

In grammatical terminology *may* is called the present tense and *might* the past tense, but this classification is more technical than real because both words apply to the present or the future. The past tense—*might*—has less to do with time than it has with furnishing the proper grammatical concordance. In the present tense we say, "He thinks he may go to Washington." In the past tense we say, "He thought he might go to Washington." (*See* SEQUENCE OF TENSES.)

Beyond this purely grammatical distinction, however, a distinction in meaning emerges in the ordinary usage of the words. *May* poses a possibility; *might* adds a greater degree of uncertainty to the possibility. This shade of difference appears in the following sentence: "Any broadcasting station that airs more commercials than the code allows may be fined, and in extreme cases its license might be taken away." Notice that no grammatical difference dictates the use of *may* in one instance and *might* in the other; it is rather a difference in intended meaning. If we say, "You had better get your tickets now or the house may be sold out," we suggest a real possibility; if we say, "You had better get your tickets now or the house might be sold out," the possibility is there but it is made to seem faintly more remote.

Occasionally, the flippant understatement of casual conversation may reverse these roles of the two words. The man at the cocktail party who says, "I might have one more drink," means he would like it pronto. But if he says, "I may have one more drink," he does not necessarily mean that he wants it immediately and he may be debating whether he wants it at all, but, hostesses

271

being what they are, he is probably going to get it before he can say "Hic!"

MAYORALTY

"He amassed a large plurality in last year's mayoralty primary." Why reach for the noun *mayoralty* to use as an adjective when the adjective *mayoral* is right at hand? Note also that the word should be neither written nor pronounced "mayorality."

MEAN, MEDIAN, AVERAGE

What *mean* does not mean is here illustrated: "Yesterday's mean temperature—the difference between the high and the low. . . ." *Mean* denotes the middle point; if the high is 80° and the low is 60°, the *mean* is 70°. *Median* is that point in a series at which half of the members of the series are on one side and half on the other. If five boys respectively weigh 100 pounds, 105 pounds, 110 pounds, 125 pounds, and 130 pounds, the *median* weight is 110 pounds. *Average*, statistically speaking, denotes the sum of a series divided by the number of members in it. The *average* weight of those five boys would be the total—570 pounds —divided by the number of boys—five—or, uh, 114 pounds. Nonstatistically speaking, *average* is commonly used to mean *ordinary* or *typical*.

MEANS

In the sense of financial resources, *means* is always plural ("His means are not sufficient to support a wife"). In the sense of agency through which an end is attained, *means* may be treated as either a singular or a plural ("All possible means are available"; "every means was tried").

Means takes the preposition *of, to,* or *for.*

MEANWHILE

Transitional words or phrases are often necessary to cover the crevices between unrelated or distantly related subjects treated in successive paragraphs. A favorite transitional word, particularly with newspapermen, is *meanwhile*. The word is all right if *meanwhile*—during the intervening time or simultaneously—is really meant. But if an article speaks of the commemoration of the Battle of Britain next Sunday and the next paragraph begins, "Meanwhile, a police court magistrate fined Lord Russell yesterday," the *meanwhile* has no pertinence. There may be a relationship of subject matter, but the time relationship, if any, is not identifiable. Likewise, if one paragraph of an article is devoted to a defendant's trial last spring and the next begins, "Meanwhile Judge Martinis will hear defense arguments today on the appeal motion," the *meanwhile* is meaningless. A meaningless transition word is like Scotch tape used to cover a broad gap. Not only is it transparent, but in addition it won't hold.

MECCA

"Although identified mainly with the Yiddish Art Theater, which was a Mecca for Jewish theatergoers on New York's Lower East Side. . . ." For Jews a Mecca yet! Which proves that a cliché can be explosive in the hands of the unwary. *See* CLICHÉS.

MEDDLE

Takes preposition *in* or *with*.

MEDIA

"In the debate over toll TV the mathematics peculiar to a mass media have tended to run away with common sense." Unless you suffer from the present-day AD-DICTION, the singular is still *medium* and the plural *media*.

MEDIAN

See MEAN, MEDIAN, AVERAGE.

MEDIATE

See ARBITRATE, MEDIATE. *Mediate* takes preposition *between* or *among*.

MEDIC, MEDICO

Neither is a serious word for one engaged in medical work. Any more, by the way, than is *doc*.

MEDITATE

Takes preposition *on* or *upon*.

MEET, MEET WITH

In the sense of coming into the company of, the word *meet* and the phrase *meet with* have distinct meanings. The distinction is brought out in the following passage: "Dr. James E. Allen Jr., State Education Commissioner, has been invited to meet with the members of the new city Board of Education on Thursday. . . . While the session with Dr. Allen is to enable him to meet the new board members, some members are known to be interested in hearing his views on the fitness of the Superintendent of Schools." In the first sentence the phrase *meet with* has the sense of joining the company of; in the second sentence *meet* has the sense of making the acquaintance of. Of course, *meet with* has other meanings, too: to *encounter* ("The expedition met with strange occurrences in the Antarctic") and to *suffer* or *experience* ("He met with an accident"). The point of all this is that *with* cannot always be lopped off the phrase *meet with*, though many other VERB TAILS can be amputated.

MEIOSIS

See RHETORICAL FIGURES AND FAULTS.

MENIAL

To speak of "porters, janitors, and other menial employes" is inappropriate unless the intention is to disparage them. *Menial*, although it had respectable enough beginnings (merely meaning pertaining to the household), now carries the connotation of something degrading. If you expect to get heat in your apartment next winter, you had better not refer to the janitor as a *menial*. (And you might get even more heat if you didn't call him "janitor.")

274

-MENT

See NOUN ENDINGS.

METAPHORS AND MIXAPHORS

Metaphor is a figure of speech in which a word or phrase implies a comparison or identity (as contrasted with *simile*, in which the comparison is made explicit by the use of "as" or "like"). Metaphor is just about as close as the average writer gets to creating poetry. The poet uses words, phrases, whole passages to evoke associations, connotations, pictures, and abstract ideas that could otherwise be expressed only by long and involved discourse, if indeed they could be expressed otherwise at all. Similarly, the metaphorist uses a word or a phrase as a compressed and colorful way of expressing a relatively elaborate idea. The metaphor is a kind of instant poetry; just add your own distilled water and drink. If we say, "She is a tigress," we have condensed into a single word the connotations of possessiveness, belligerency, alertness to danger, savagery, and whatever else you associate with a tigress, stripes excluded. Metaphor is a useful adornment of writing: useful because it permits communication of a complex thought in small compass, an adornment because it introduces color and imagery into what might be a commonplace statement.

If, however, the writer does not stick to the image he has set up, he is in danger of creating a mixed metaphor, known here for short as a *mixaphor*. In that event he has vitiated the usefulness of the figure by confusing the reader through a jumble of pictures, and has spoiled the adornment by shattering it. If, for example, he writes, "She is a tigress with her antennae on the alert for the grasping hand that might undermine the keystone of her existence," we get no picture of anything and are left with a sense of absurdity. This does not mean that a writer may not include two different pictures in a single sentence or a single passage; they must, however, be distinctly separate and it must be clear that the writer knows what he is about. He could write with impunity, for example, "She is a tigress in her office, but a lamb at home." Or, to take an actual instance, "One side of the Amer-

275

ican spirit is reaching for the moon (and planning to land on it), but another side is warming itself before the fires of national memory."

The mixaphor has on occasion trapped the greatest writers, but perhaps their very greatness has protected them. An obvious though little noticed Shakespearean example occurs in Hamlet's soliloquy: "Or to take arms against a sea of troubles." One does not reach for weapons to combat the sea, yet the discrepancy here is not obtrusive and the effect is certainly far from ludicrous. The same cannot be said, however, for the following exhibits:

"The internal strife gnawing at the country has not only mirrored the cold war but brought it to a hot focus from time to time."

"Yet the President has backed him to the hilt every time the chips were down."

"While Moscow is thus stoking up the cold war, however, Peking is playing it pianissimo."

"The root problems can be brought into pretty clear perspective by subjecting the angry torrent of words to the dissecting knife and exposing what lies beneath."

It will be noticed that it is the lulling lure of the CLICHÉ that leads into some of these pitfalls: *backed to the hilt, chips were down, brought into perspective, angry torrent of words.* Metaphors like these are so familiar, so trite, that they evoke pictures only faintly if at all, and the writer forgets that they are metaphors. These are almost the kind that Fowler calls "dead metaphors." But, as he points out, such metaphors are capable, under the stimulus of an affinity or a repulsion, of coming back to life: In "sifting of evidence" no picture of a sieve is evoked, but such a picture is evoked, and disastrously, in "All the evidence must first be sifted with acid tests." This resuscitation is one thing the writer must guard against to avoid mixing his metaphors. But in a larger sense he must re-examine his brief flights into poetry to be certain they have not stumbled on the quicksands of incongruity, if one may mix the metaphor. And one may not. *See also* RHETORICAL FIGURES AND FAULTS.

METHOD

For the solecism in, "The event is one of the methods the club raises money"—and similar errors—see ADVERBIAL FORCE IN NOUNS.

METICULOUS

The word does not mean careful or even very careful. Derived from a Latin root—*metus,* meaning fear—*meticulous* means timorously careful or overcareful. The misuses, arising from a desire to use the fancy word, are common: "In *Citizen Hearst,* a biographer of first rank presents a full-length word portrait, etched with meticulous detail . . ."; "The cannons appeared to be a high point in the visit for General de Gaulle; he examined them meticulously." It is not always possible to prove that a writer has misused the word, although there is often that presumption. An ad for a motor car speaks of "its handcrafted body and meticulous assembly." The manufacturers may well have been fearful of doing something wrong and thus were extra careful. If so, the word is properly used. But . . .

METONYMY

See RHETORICAL FIGURES AND FAULTS.

MIDNIGHT

It is odd that there should be confusion about a word that is as commonplace as *midnight,* but there is. For instance: "The picketing started at 10 A.M. Saturday and continued for fifteen hours. Shortly after midnight Sunday the crowd of white persons had grown to several thousand." It should be "midnight Saturday" (but, of course, the "Saturday" could be deleted). *Midnight* means twelve o'clock at night; it thus belongs to the dying day, not to the newborn one.

MIGHT

See MAY, MIGHT.

MILITATE

Takes preposition *against*. *See also* MITIGATE.

MINIMAL, MINIMIZE, MINIMUM

Minimize does not mean to belittle, depreciate, diminish, make light of, pooh-pooh, play down, or shrug off. It means to reduce to the least possible, that is, to a *minimum*. If a news article says that the Soviet Union paraded its scientific triumphs and played down its military might in an anniversary celebration, the headline states the situation improperly if it says, "Soviet Minimizes Its Armed Might in Annual Parade." A similar misuse is evident here: "Although Eastern bloc representatives tended to minimize the importance of the struggle, Yugoslav and Western sources said it was obvious the Soviet Union could not accept without a fight so direct a challenge."

The following is a correct use: "The Kennedy-Macmillan conversations . . . have been extremely friendly, which is another way of saying that they have avoided, or at least minimized [i.e., *held to a minimum*] the main issue." In the next example it would seem that the writer did not understand the meaning of the word completely: "But, he continued, these burdens must be faced even while city officials seek to minimize them as far as possible." The "as far as possible" is built into *minimize* and thus is redundant.

If a writer has an irresistible fondness for the sound of "mini-," there is a word available that means precisely what he usually has in mind when he misuses *minimize*. The word *minify* means to diminish, to lessen, to view or to depict something as less or smaller than it really is. The word is not used as much as it should be, but let us not minify it. Let it be noted also that *minimal* does not have the meaning of not much or just a little; it, too, involves the idea of a *minimum*, that is, the least possible.

MINION

Heavy-handed levity marks this use of the word: "This signal achievement gave Leo Durocher's suddenly inspired minions their sixth victory in a row." Thus employed facetiously to mean, one supposes, servants or creatures, *minions* is trite and unfunny. Used seriously, the word means either a loved one or such derogatory things as a servile dependent or a fawning favorite.

MINISTER (vb.)

Takes preposition *to.*

MINUS

In the sense of lacking or having lost, *minus* is a jocular casualism: "The professor fled from the burning house minus his pants."

MINUSCULE

Spelled so because it derives from the word *minus.* Not *miniscule.*

MINUTIAE

The singular, a rarity, is *minutia. Minutiae* is the plural and thus is incorrectly used in this sentence: "And how much minutiae was present to one's notice when the beaches were raked clean every morning by the lifeguards?" If the writer insists on using that word, the sentence would have to read, "how many minutiae were present, etc."

MISCONCEPT

Occasionally seen in headlines ("Soviet Misconcept of U.S. Imperils Parley's Success"), *misconcept* is a nonword—at least the dictionaries have never heard of it. *See also* CONCEPT.

MISHAP

See ACCIDENT, MISHAP.

MISQUOTATION

Well-known lines from literature are not always really well known. Often the sense is known but the actual words are not, as in *gild the lily.* Sometimes even the sense is not known, as in *God rest ye, merry gentlemen* instead of *God rest ye merry, gentlemen.* In any event, misquotations, whether of words or sense, are common.

There are those authorities who say we should be tolerant of them on the grounds that the erroneous versions sometimes have survived on their own merits or that they have equal validity with the correct versions or that to use the true form verges on pedantry. It may well be that there is merit in the form *A man convinced against his will is of the same opinion still;* it may have better cadence and a more modern flavor than *He that complies against his will is of his own opinion still.* There may be merit in *A poor thing but my own* as contrasted with *An ill-favored thing, sir, but mine own;* and in *Pride goeth before a fall* as contrasted with *Pride goeth before destruction, and an haughty spirit before a fall,* or *Pryde will have a fall; for pryde goeth before and shame cometh after.* But let us recognize that accuracy in a world of loose talk and confused thinking is a quality to be prized. The corollary to that statement is that the encouragement of inaccuracy, in whatever form, is to be abominated.

Let us also recognize that he who uses familiar quotations is usually employing clichés. If that is true, the employment of the correct form will remove some of the banality from the cliché; will, indeed, inject new life into it. Moreover, it will demonstrate that the user has first-hand and not second-hand familiarity with his quotation. Let him not worry about being accused of pedantry. People may say that a little learning (not knowledge) is a dangerous thing, but let him remember, in the words of the poet, that ignorance is not innocence but sin. *See also* CLICHÉS.

MISTRUSTFUL

Takes preposition *of.*

MITIGATE

A resemblance in sound causes *mitigate* to be confused by many writers with *militate.* "The fact that he is a Roman Catholic mitigated unfairly against him"; "Darkness, rather than stormy conditions, mitigated against spotting the tiny lifeboats." These uses are incorrect because *mitigate* means to moderate or

soften. The other word, *militate,* means to have effect against—
or, rarely, for.

MIX

Takes preposition *with* or *into.*

MIXAPHOR

See METAPHORS AND MIXAPHORS.

MOCK

Takes preposition *at.*

MODIFIER MISFITS

The best way to introduce the subject of misplacement and
erroneous relationship of modifying phrases is the way Copperud
does it in *Words on Paper*—to quote one of those mythical want
ads: "For sale: Piano by a lady going to Europe with carved legs."
The real-life examples are not so absurd; they go more like this:
"The new facilities will make it possible for babies to be born in
Roosevelt Hospital for the first time." There is no rule about the
placement of modifying phrases except perhaps the very general
one that they should be as close as possible to the things they
modify. Thus it should be "will make it possible for the first time
for babies to be born in Roosevelt Hospital." In the following
sentences the virgule (/) indicates where the phrase in *italic*
type should have been placed:

"Vasily Kuznetsov's face was impassive as he limped off
Franklin Field tonight after failing / to break his unofficial
world decathlon record *by a narrow margin.*"

"The first of these synthetics was produced / by German
scientists *between 1924 and 1927* who had been working on the
problem since their quinine supplies were cut off in World War
I." (Notice that the italicized phrase is not out of place as a
modifier but is out of place insofar as it separates the modifying
who clause from the thing it modifies—"scientists.")

"The Pentagon said Mr. McNamara had decided / to continue the present military program without using the additional

281

appropriated funds *after an intensive review*."

"Another African spokesman said that the President's address would not have the impact / it deserved *on Africa*."

"The Governor's proposal to give public money to private college students has raised one of the / most *potentially* troublesome political issues before the Legislature in some time." (It is not "most potentially" but "most troublesome." This sentence might well be recast, perhaps to read, "what is potentially one of the most troublesome political issues.") *For other errors of this type, see* ADVERBS, PLACEMENT OF.

Sometimes a modifying phrase relates to something that is nonexistent, as in this sentence: "His release Saturday night after being held hostage more than seventy-eight hours came. . . ." The phrase "after being held hostage" does not relate to "release" but to the nonexistent "he." The fault could be remedied by making it, "He was released Saturday night, etc." or "His release Saturday night after he had been held hostage, etc." A somewhat similar misfit is this one: "The seat was given up by Representative Paul J. Kilday to become a judge of the United States Court of Military Appeals." Did the "seat" aspire "to become a judge"? This is easily put right by writing, "Representative Kilday gave up the seat to become, etc."

Modifier misfits can be cured not by rules but by a second reading, a second thought to see that all is shipshape. *See also* ADVERBS, PLACEMENT OF *and* DANGLERS.

MONOLOGOPHOBIA AND SYNONYMOMANIA

A *monologophobe* (you won't find it in the dictionary) is a writer who would rather walk naked in front of Saks Fifth Avenue than be caught using the same word more than once in three lines. What he suffers from is *synonymomania* (you won't find that one, either), which is a compulsion to call a spade successively *a garden implement* and an *earth-turning tool*.

The affliction besets journalists in general and sports writers in particular. For instance: "Sugar Ray flattened Bobo in twelve rounds in 1950, outpointed him in fifteen sessions in 1952, and knocked him out in two heats last Dec. 9." Not content with the legitimate variables of the sentence—the manner of the outcome in each fight and the length of time it took—the writer makes what should be a constant also look like a variable. Thus, he leaves the reader to wonder whether a "session" or a "heat" is something different from a "round" and if not, what the hell?

Now avoidance of monotony caused by jarring repetition of a conspicuous word or phrase is desirable. A little touch of monologophobia might have helped the framer of this sentence: "The Khrushchev defeats, General Hoxha said, took place at the international Communist meetings that took place in Bucharest in June, 1960, and in Moscow in November, 1960." And a little touch of synonymomania undoubtedly would have been good for the writer of this one: "M. Gomulka's decision to join with the Polish 'liberals' could be decisive in deciding the fierce factional struggle."

But mechanical substitution of synonyms may make a bad situation worse. "Elegant variation" is the term applied by Fowler to this practice. It is particularly objectionable if the synonym is one that falls strangely on the ear or eye: calling a snowfall a *descent,* calling gold *the yellow metal,* calling charcoal *the ancient black substance.* Repetition of the word is better than these strained synonyms. Often a pronoun is a good remedy, and sometimes no word at all is required. Here is a pertinent sample of a synonymomaniac's obsession: "Somewhere among the thousands of skillful amateur wrestlers across the nation are sixteen outstanding grapplers who will win a place on the American team." Are "grapplers" something different from "wrestlers"? Why not use "ones" or let "sixteen" stand by itself, sacrificing "outstanding"?

Monologophobia has even given rise to bromidic constructions. Not infrequently we come across this kind of sentence: "It will be the third time in as many years that the dockers here will have had a chance to vote." What's wrong with the more direct and more precise form, "third time in three years"?

In the days of our forefathers Tom Swift almost never said anything; he usually *averred, asseverated, smiled, chuckled, grinned* (plainly or mischievously), *groaned, expostulated, ejacu-*

lated, declared, or *asserted.* Tom apparently has made his impress on news writing. The simple verb *say* never seems to be good for more than one inning; then writers or editors feel they must rush in all kinds of bush league relief pitchers. If Hemingway did nothing else for American literature, he reestablished the virtue and dignity of *say* and exposed the folly of the synonymomaniacs. But apparently a good many newspapermen haven't discovered him yet.

MONOPOLY

Takes preposition *of.*

MOOT

Errors that arise in the use of this word focus on the phrases *moot question* and *moot point. Moot* means arguable or subject to discussion, but the misusers think it means hypothetical, superfluous, or academic. Thus: "Jackie Robinson wondered if he had been elected to the Hall of Fame for his actual ability or for being the first Negro player. To those in the sport it seemed a moot question." The writer clearly did not think the question was open to debate; he thought it did not make any difference.

MORE THAN ONE

More than one, though technically plural, is regarded as singular. Thus, the following sentence is correct: "Mr. Hannah said that more than one charge of discrimination was involved." The reason for this is apparently what the grammarians call "attraction"—the verb is singular "by attraction" to the *one* and to the subsequent noun, "charge." If, less idiomatically, the phrase *more than one* was split apart and the attraction thus weakened, the verb would very probably be plural: "Mr. Hannah said that more charges of discrimination than one were involved." *See also* ALL BUT ONE.

MOST

Most as a shortening of *almost* is, like many another shortening, indigestible to the fussy. Although common in speech, where

it is folksy, the word is a misfit in a serious context like this:
". . . it seems to me that we should be in a clearer-headed condition than we now are in, postulating, as most all of us do, a
rational certitude that doesn't exist. . . ."

MOTIVE

Takes preposition *for*.

MUCHLY

See THUSLY.

MUSE (vb.)

Takes preposition *on* or *upon*.

MUTUAL

Properly speaking, *mutual* connotes interaction or rec-
iprocity between two or more persons or things. The meaning
"shared in common" dates to the late sixteenth century, but is
not now considered good usage. Therefore *Our Mutual Friend*
cannot be blamed for having introduced this sense of the word,
but by popularizing it Dickens certainly raised the same. (Footnote and special bonus for readers: The pun does not originate in
the novelist's name. *Dickens* as a euphemism for *devil* was also
in use in the sixteenth century, long before Charles of that name.
It appears in Shakespeare's *The Merry Wives of Windsor*: "I
cannot tell what the dickens his name is.") Because of Dickens's
popularization of that use of *mutual,* and because a suitable substitute is lacking, the tendency these days is to accept the phrase
mutual friend or *mutual acquaintance.* But the tolerance does
not extend to, "The two men's mutual interest in guns has provided an informal means of instructing youngsters." If Jones
respects Smith and Smith respects Jones, they have a *mutual*
respect. However, if Jones is interested in guns and Smith is interested in guns, they do not have a *mutual* interest, they have a
common interest.

MYSELF

See HIMSELF (HERSELF, MYSELF, ETC.)

N

NAB

A pet of headline writers ("Cops Nab Delinquent Drivers"), *nab* is slang despite the fact that it is ancient.

NATION

"He added that the two Balkan nations had high mountains and deep gorges." *Nation* denotes the community or people rather than the territory of a country.

NAUSEOUS

A thing is *nauseous* if it makes one sick to the stomach; the unfortunate victim of this malaise is *nauseated*. The common misuse of *nauseous* appears in this passage: "When he sits too long, turns his head too abruptly, or walks any distance, he gets dizzy, loses balance, and becomes nauseous." He doesn't become *nauseous* unless he turns other people's stomachs; he becomes *nauseated*. A person who feels sick is no more *nauseous* than a person who has been poisoned is poisonous.

NEAR-RECORD

When a wartime bomber pilot registered a *near-miss*, he really scored to some extent; the designation meant that his bomb had hit close enough to the target to cause damage to it. Under the influence of this word, however, others like it are sometimes used meaninglessly. For instance: "New York City registration, which ended last night, set a near-record." This is like saying, "The team scored three near-touchdowns." Just as nothing was scored by that team, so, in the registration, nothing was *set*. A somewhat similar example is this headline: "Near-Riot Is Averted at Hudson." What actually took place was, perhaps, a near-riot; what was averted was a full-fledged riot.

NECESSARY

Takes preposition *to* or *for*.

NECESSITY

Takes preposition *of* or *for*.

NEE

"Specifically, Jelke was convicted of inducing, enticing, and procuring Pat Ward, nee Sandra Wisotsky. . . ." *Nee* means born. You are born with only your family name; your given name is given afterward. The phrase might have been written, "originally named Sandra Wisotsky."

NEED OF, NEED FOR

"Dr. Alvin Eurich called yesterday for a replanning of medical education to meet the nation's growing need of physicians." The phrase *need of* opens a chance for ambiguity; it could suggest a need felt *by* physicians. A clean-cut instance of ambiguity would be this sentence: "The nation's pressing problem is the need of physicians." More doctors? Or less poverty among doctors? If the former is intended, *need for* will nail it down.

NEGLECTFUL

Takes preposition *of*.

NEGLIGENT

Takes preposition *of* or *in*.

NEITHER . . . NOR

"Premier Souvanna Phouma acted today to show that his government was dependent neither upon the young paratroop officer who brought it to power nor the support of pro-Communist leaders." Correlative conjunctions join equivalent elements. Therefore: ". . . neither upon the young . . . nor upon the support," or "upon neither the young . . . nor the support. . . ." *See* CORRELATIVE CONJUNCTIONS, LAW OF.

NERVE-RACKING
See RACK, WRACK.

NEW RECORD
See RECORD, NEW.

NIGHTLY
See DAILY.

NOISOME
Unrelated to *noisy*—but related by derivation to *annoy*—*noisome* means harmful, destructive, or offensive—and, more particularly, offensive to the sense of smell.

NOMINAL
See INDEFINITELY.

NONE
Miss Thistlebottom undoubtedly told you in grammar school that *none* always takes a singular verb. Although she was incorrect (the authorities agree almost without exception that *none* is more commonly a plural), she probably knew what she was doing, for the authorities are not altogether in agreement about when to consider *none* a singular and when a plural. Therefore, confronted with a collection of little monsters of varying degrees of understanding and judgment, she found it simpler to lay down a flat rule.

Similarly, newspapers with great numbers of reporters and copy editors who also have varying degrees of judgment find it simpler to lay down a similar rule—simpler and safer, too, because it spares them vituperative letters from Miss Thistlebottom's colleagues and former pupils.

Nevertheless, if a rule is needed, a better one is to consider *none* to be a plural unless there is a definite reason to regard it as a singular. One reason would be a construction in which it is followed by a singular noun: "None of the work was done in time for the opening"; "None of the food was served hot." Another reason would be the desire to emphasize the singular idea, but even in such an instance it would be better to achieve the emphasis by changing the *none* to *not one* or *no one*. For example, "Five persons were in the car but none [better: *not one* or *no one*] was hurt." Miss Thistlebottom's rule for considering *none* to be a singular does not have universal application in any event. For instance, you could not use the singular in a sentence like this: "The negotiations have been going on for two months, but none have succeeded." You couldn't possibly be thinking of a single "negotiation." Likewise: "France has maintained the principle that none of her forces is [make it *are*] permanently committed to European defense." There is no conception here of a single "force." The underlying fallacy in Miss Thistlebottom's reasoning is that since *none* is derived from *not one*, she thinks it always means that. But it doesn't. Sometimes it means *no amount* and most often it means *not any*.

NON SEQUITURS

Irrelevancies often result from a writer's desire to work in a piece of information and his incapacity to determine where it should go. This kind of gaucherie occurs most often in newspaper writing and, in that branch of writing, most often in obituaries: "Born in Des Moines, Mr. Tuttle joined Philip Ruxton in the business of making printing ink"; "Born in Frankfort, Ky., he was graduated from Centre College"; "Born in Brooklyn, N.Y., Mr. Friedman had been a trustee of Hebrew Teachers College." No wonder a reader wrote to the newspaper that printed these specimens, "Born in Waukegan, Ill., I get damn sick of the non sequiturs."

But the awkwardness is not confined to obituaries: "It was the second time that Mr. Emmerich, a stanch conservative who prefers to spend his spare time fishing and bird-watching, had been physically assaulted in connection with his actions to improve race relations"; "A young man of marked wit, intelligence, extravagant personal charm, and fine manners, Moulay Hassan is the target of bitter criticism from the Moroccan labor movement and the political left wing." The point to be noticed is that

289

if the pieces of information are to be linked in physical proximity, they should also be linked in meaning. "Born in Glasgow, he loved his mother" is disconcerting because it ties together two unrelated facts. But, "Born in Glasgow, he had no trouble learning to play the bagpipes" ties together two pieces of information that might well be related. If a couple of facts are in no way tied together, they should be kept as separate in writing as they are in real life.

NOR

The use of *nor* in the team of *neither . . . nor* is discussed under that heading and also under CORRELATIVE CONJUNCTIONS, LAW OF. By itself, *nor* may sometimes be substituted for *or* in a negative context to emphasize the negation. We may write, "He would not testify or even appear in court," or, to emphasize the second negative, "He would not testify nor even appear in court."

Nor is mandatory, however, if the negative has been walled into the first part of the sentence so that it does not carry over to the second part. It would not do to write, "He did not testify or even failed to appear in court." This kind of error is not uncommon: "In slimming the picture down to its present shape, we lost none of its main story line or sacrificed any scene that might have contributed to the delineation of character." Either make it "nor did we sacrifice" or alter the construction to "we did not lose any of its main story line or sacrifice. . . ." In both the following sentences the substitution of *nor* for *or* is the indicated remedy: "This policy has not yet been adopted by the six governments, or is early approval expected"; "Mr. Nixon had not expected a broadside attack from the Governor, or had the Republican National Committee." It should go without saying, but it will be said anyway, that *either . . . nor, neither . . . or, either . . . and,* and *neither . . . and* are all mistakes.

NOSTALGIA

By derivation *nostalgia* means a longing for home or, in short, homesickness. But it is used more often in an extended meaning of a pleasant-painful yearning for a past time or for something in a former time. That is the meaning here: "The book *For 2 Cents Plain* has another nostalgic meaning for us." It would be self-defeating as well as idle to attempt to restrict the word to the meaning of homesickness, because no other word in the language expresses the extended meaning. And if by the operation of BERNSTEIN'S SECOND LAW the new meaning should drive out the old, that would not be tragic; there still is the word *homesickness*, perhaps qualified by an adjective, to replace it. However, to pile on additional meanings, as in "Nostalgia for what has not happened is such sweet sorrow," is not excusable; all that was meant here was *yearning* or *longing*. Where there is real need for a word the language can be elastic; where there is no need for it the language should be firm.

NOT, PLACEMENT OF

Under close scrutiny, many constructions containing the word *not* make no sense, or at least not the sense intended. Examine, for instance, this heading for a book ad: "All saints are not simple . . . All saints are not lovable . . . This saint was both." When you zoom in on the first statement, you find it really says that there is no simple person to be found among saints. The second statement says that there is no lovable person to be found among saints. Then, in direct contradiction of these affirmations, we are told that there was one saint who was both of these things. Are the constructions therefore wrong? By no means. They are customary, idiomatic English. And this proves, once again, that idiom can pass through the hot blue flame of logic and emerge unsinged. This is not to say, however, that those who wish to be logical and precise will be unidiomatic if they write, "Not all saints are simple . . . not all saints are lovable." Idiom is on their side, too, and it is reinforced by reason. Therefore, the writer who prefers to say precisely what he means will write *not all*, yet will not scorn those who, without giving it a thought, write, *all . . . not*.

Not . . . but locutions, too, often produce apparent nonsense. Example: "The principal legal attack on the program has not been on constitutional grounds but on the ground that it is not authorized by any statute." Obviously there is an ellipsis after *but*—words are needed to fill out the clause. The only previously mentioned verb is "has not been" and that is what one would normally expect to be carried over. But this would make nonsense; what the reader is expected to supply is "has been." Does this mean that the construction is incorrect? Not at all. It, too, is idiomatic. Yet can it be gainsaid that the sentence would be better balanced and even stronger if the *not* were placed after the "been," where logic would insist on placing it?

On the other hand, sometimes logic must surrender completely to idiom because there is no other way out. Example: "Dr. Servatius did not press Eichmann for details of the Wannsee discussions, but only of 'the atmosphere.' " To move the *not* to a more logical position would require, "Dr. Servatius pressed Eichmann for details not of the Wannsee discussions, but only of 'the atmosphere.' " Not only is this version a little stiff, but in addition it does not mean precisely what the original sentence meant. The solution is to leave the *not* in its idiomatic position and to repeat the word "details"—"but only for details of 'the atmosphere.' " Many times troubles with *not . . . but* result merely from failure to maintain a proper parallelism, which in turn results from untidy thinking or lack of thinking at all. For instance: "Mr. Nixon has said that he cannot sanction a political campaign at this time because his fundamental duty is to think not of his own political interests but to carry out his duties as Vice President." Make it either "to think not of his own political interests but only of carrying out" or "not to think of his own political interests but to carry out."

Stress has been laid here on logic in the use of language, but it has also been pointed out that idiom can successfully defy logic. Fowler, although apparently granting that point, is unusually optimistic. "The older a language grows," he says, "& the more consciously expert its users become, the shorter shrift it & they may be expected to grant to illogicalities & ambiguities." The fettering phrase there is, "the more consciously expert its users become." Unfortunately, there is no evidence that as the

English language grows older its users are becoming more expert; on the contrary, there is evidence of the reverse. Fowler's view is that the *all . . . not* inaccuracy, like others of its kind, "will pass away in time." Alas, there is little reason to believe that either. The best that can be hoped for is a regime of containment. And every writer who takes the trouble to think about what he is doing and to become more consciously expert in the use of the language helps that cause.

NOT, SUPERFLUOUS

If a person thinks it is going to be cold tomorrow and tries to convey that thought by saying, "I shouldn't wonder if it wasn't cold tomorrow," he may be forgiven for not having said precisely what he intended to say. The dispensation is granted on the ground that a spontaneously uttered statement is not usually made with painstaking care. But similar forgiveness cannot be extended to an editorialist who writes, "In low spirits over recent events affecting his family, it would not have been surprising if the Governor had not reappraised his personal and political plans." The dangling modifier (*See* DANGLERS) at the beginning of the sentence should prepare us for a slovenly construction, and it is there. The second *not* produces an unintended DOUBLE NEGATIVE. What the writer intended to say was that it would not have been surprising if the Governor *had* reappraised his plans. Instead, he got himself tied up in nots.

NOT ONLY . . . BUT (ALSO)

Two points of interest concerning these correlative conjunctions are (1) their proper placement and (2) when to use *also* or its equivalent.

1. Correct placement of the *not only* (or *not merely* or *not alone* or *not entirely*) is simply a matter of maintaining a proper parallelism. This is true, of course, of all correlative conjunctions (*See* CORRELATIVE CONJUNCTIONS, LAW OF). In spoken language misplacements are extremely common because it is often difficult for a speaker to look ahead and see an evolving sentence in its entirety. In written language misplacements are almost as fre-

quent—but for this there is no excuse; it takes only a few marks
of a pencil to set things right. Specifically what is required is that
the part of speech or grammatical construction following the
not only be paralleled by the part of speech or grammatical construction following the *but*. It will be noticed that this requirement is not fulfilled in the following examples, in which a correct
form appears in parentheses:

"Mr. Koota said that Jackson not only knew Ruggiero but
also Anthony Anastasia" ("knew not only Ruggiero but also
Anastasia"; noun paralleled by noun).

"They hope to find out not only how the antibiotic attacks
disease microbes but also to learn how it produces its remarkable
growth effects" ("not only how the antibiotic attacks . . . but
also how it produces," omitting the redundant "to learn" and
paralleling a clause with a clause).

"Jehovah's Witnesses are not only denied freedom to have
an official central body, but to assemble and to worship as well"
("denied freedom not only to have . . . but to assemble"; infinitive paralleled by infinitive).

"A woman who recently drove through Algonquin Park with
her seven-year-old daughter said they not only saw a deer in full
daylight but the animal came up to take a snack from the little
girl's hand." (The ailment here calls for an unusual prescription
—inversion of word order to achieve parallel clauses: "A woman
. . . said not only did they see a deer . . . but the animal came
up.")

The placement of *only* by itself (*See* ONLY) permits devi-
ations from strict logic for reasons of idiom or of setting an early
signal of the intent of the sentence. No such reasons affect the
placement of *not only*, however, and the strict logic of parallelism
applies in all instances. At least it should apply. The unfortunate
truth is that either because of carelessness or because of ignorance
of the principle, *not only* is misplaced in at least half the sentences in which it appears. But neither carelessness nor ignorance
is an excuse in a court of law, nor is it in the court of language.

2. When is it necessary to follow the *but* by *also* or an
equivalent, such as *moreover, in addition, furthermore, to boot, as*

well, or *too?* The answer is, "Usually, but not always." When we wish to discard one element and substitute another we say, "Not A, but B." When we wish not to discard one element but rather to add another to it we say, "Not only A, but also B." The phrase *not only* customarily is equivalent to *partly;* and when it is, it should be followed by *but also.* It is not logical to say, "It is partly A, but B." It is logical, however, to say, "It is partly A, but also B." This is what is meant in most situations in which *not only* is employed. The following sentence—a not uncommon one —illustrates the use of *not only* in the sense of *partly;* the virgule (/) shows where the needed *but also* should have appeared instead of the insufficient *but:* "His theme was that Laos should be represented at the talks not only by Prince Souvanna Phouma's neutralists and the Pathet Lao political party, but / by the Royal Laotian Government and the political parties in Laos." The point becomes even clearer when the phrase *not exclusively,* which is equivalent to *not only,* is used. Note in the following sentence how necessary is the phrase *as well* (an equivalent of *also):* "A further point made is that surpluses are not exclusively the product of expenditure controls but of revenue-raising as well." To repeat the guide, when *not only* is equivalent to *partly,* the subsequent *but* should be followed by *also* or a comparable term, like *as well* or *in addition.*

Sometimes, however, *not only* introduces a moderate expression, which is then intensified by what follows the *but.* In such instances the *also* would not be appropriate. For example: "He is not only a painter, but a very good painter." This type of construction can be distinguished from the type discussed in the preceding paragraph by the fact that here, where the expression following the *but* is a mere intensifier, the accent falls heavily on some word following the *but.* In the example cited notice that the word *good* would be heavily stressed. Here are some additional illustrations, with the accented word set in *italics:* "Her successor and half-sister, Elizabeth, remained not only childless but *single*"; "Mr. Jack has completely reversed his stand on making Fulton Street a downtown crosstown artery—a project that he not only sponsored but was *championing* up to the moment the

Board of Estimate met to decide the issue"; "Such wars are not only admissible but *inevitable*"; "The humorous element is not only present but *dominant* in most of the erotic poetry of the Elizabethan period."

To sum up the discussion of the points in sections 1 and 2, there fortunately comes to hand a single passage that embraces both types of *not only* expression. The first one in the sentence is the intensifier variety; in reading it, remember that Berlin was one aspect of the "cold war front." The second is the "partly" type. Both examples have been *italicized*. "This speech will inaugurate a new flexible policy, *not only* for Berlin *but* for the whole cold war front; *not only* for the armed services *but* for the political and economic programs of the Government *as well*."

Finally, it should be said—and the foregoing passage makes it fairly clear—that the *not only . . . but* device can be overused. In simple, direct sentences like the one cited the *and* construction would be more forceful: ". . . for Berlin and for the whole cold war front; for the armed services and, etc." The *not only . . . but* approach might well be reserved for sentences in which *and* might be unclear or not immediately clear because of structural complexities.

NOT SO MUCH . . . BUT

Not A but B is a correct construction. But when the *not* is converted into *not so much* the construction must be converted into *Not so much A as B*. Following *as much* or *so much*, the correct conjunction is *as*. The following passage, therefore, is incorrect: "The idea is not so much that generalizations must be checked against instances, but [*as*] that generalizations as such are suspect, or even ex officio damned." In the following sentence the same error is compounded by a misplacement of *not so much*: "What frightens the 20,000 whites remaining in Leopoldville is not so much the spectre of dictatorship but of anarchy." The double error should be remedied thus: ". . . the spectre not so much of dictatorship as of anarchy." *See* CORRELATIVE CONJUNCTIONS, LAW OF.

296

NOT TOO

Litotes is a form of *meiosis* (*See both terms under* RHETORI-CAL FIGURES AND FAULTS). Neither is a fatal ailment in writing; indeed, properly used each can have a tonic effect. Specifically, litotes is a manner of expressing a thought by using the negative with its opposite, as in, "The Communist negotiators were not too certain what it might prove to contain." What this means, of course, is that they were uncertain or not very certain. (Incidentally, "very" is usually the word that "too" is substituting for in these expressions). Litotes, then, is a kind of understatement, sometimes useful to avoid immodesty or to avoid an overstrong presentation ("I am not too sure of my ground"; "I was not too excited about the play"). It is also used for purposes of sarcasm or humor. When used without reason, as it was in the sentence about the Communist negotiators, it smacks of a cliché. To put it another way, it's not too good.

NOUN ENDINGS

Many verbs have two noun forms—*abolition* or *abolishment*, *relaxing* or *relaxation*. Sometimes the meanings of the two are identical. When they are, the one to choose is the one in common use; the other will be conspicuous and perhaps irritating. For instance: "The Most Rev. Lord Fisher of Lambeth, retired Archbishop of Canterbury, had a few words of admonishment yesterday for statesmen and newspaper editors." *Admonition* is much the commoner word and the more graceful. Additional examples: "Rather than the blanket denouncements [*denunciations*] that might be expected, they were offering compromises"; "Mr. Brown said the typographers must not ignore advancements [*advances*] being made in the printing trade."

Sometimes the two noun forms have slightly different meanings. The job then, of course, is to select the one that fits the context. *Disarming* suggests a physical action, *disarmament* suggests rather a status or a process. Hence *disarming* would have been better in this passage: "The wounded detective, who has seven citations from the department, five involving the disarmament of

297

gunmen, was taken to the hospital." A similar illustration: "The secondary films were to be rushed by plane to a special laboratory in Los Angeles for development." It is not evident in dictionary definitions, but *developing* would be the better word for the processing of films. Fine points, perhaps, but worth -ment -tion -ing.

NOUNS AS ADJECTIVES

Any noun in English may be used as an adjective. In many instances the noun and the adjective are identical: a trusted *guide*, a *guide* flag. In other instances the noun is not normally an adjective but is sometimes used as one: *true* love, a *love* story. In still other instances the noun is used adjectivally as a nonce form: a *big brassiere* man from Texas. This kind of use is, of course, the darling of newspaper headline writers, who are compelled to crowd large ideas into small spaces: "Arms Parley Studies New Missile Ban." Finally, there are nouns that have their own adjective forms but that also may be used unchanged as adjectives: a *cloudy* day, a *cloud* chamber.

It is perhaps one of the strengths of English that its parts are so readily interchangeable. Yet a good writer will not use this license without some sense of responsibility. He will not, for instance, write, "The President carried on telegraphic and telephone conversations." He will not, in other words, use an adjectival form and a noun-adjective together. Nor will he, if he has any sense of style, write, "the medical chemistry research committee," but will prefer "the committee for research in medical chemistry." In general, two or more polysyllabic nouns used as adjectives are undesirable.

It is sometimes said that one should not use a noun as an adjective if an adjective form of that noun is available; for instance, that one should not say *freak* weather but rather *freakish* weather. The advice is correct provided the two words mean the same thing. But often they do not. If the adjective is one of quality rather than simple designation, it probably will not be the desired word. A *musical critic* is not the same thing as a *music critic*, and a *psychological teacher* is not the same thing as a *psychology teacher*. Here is a sentence by a writer who wanted to be sure he was right at least half the time: "Social editors in Havana fear that high society will suffer a mortal blow from the tax that the Government proposes to put on society pages." The word should be *society* in both places.

Although the use of nouns as adjectives is a useful tool of language, it is insidious, particularly in an age when headlines are so much a part of everyday life. "Have they caught the guy in the *bomb plot* yet?" one is likely to hear from a taxi driver or a barber. And even a President has been known to write in a state paper, "The United States continues to believe that conclusion of an adequately controlled *test ban agreement* is a matter of greatest urgency." The practice is that insidious. It will trap you if you don't watch out.

NOUNS AS VERBS

Does a person properly *author* a book, *chair* a meeting, or *contact* a friend? The issue raised by that question is whether and under what conditions nouns become acceptable verbs. To the first part of the statement the answer must be an unequivocal affirmative: Nouns do, by what is called "conversion" or "functional change," become verbs. The process has been going on since the thirteenth century, and without it our language would be a poor thing, indeed. According to Prof. Donald W. Lee ("Functional Change," *Word Study*, May 1950), the rate of such conversions up to the seventeenth century ranged from three every two years to eight a year. In our own times the rate must be even greater.

As to the conditions under which nouns become acceptable verbs, the answer is not so clear-cut. There are writers (and, of course, speakers) who delight in novelty and who attempt conversions regardless of whether there is any use for them. They are the ones who would *elevator* themselves to their penthouses, get *dinner-jacketed*, and go *theatering*. (*See* AD-DICTION.) The writer who has respect for the language will treat such antics with disdain. But he will not close his mind to the possibility that there is a continuing need for new words either to express succinctly new situations or to express old situations that otherwise require the expenditure of too much verbal effort. He may well accept *contact* in place of *get in touch with*, but reject *author* as a needless alternative to *write*. He may find that *pressure* as a verb is irreplaceable, but that *craft* as a verb is not. To him a ship need need not be *crewed*, but instead should be *manned* (also derived from a noun, but centuries old, well established, and completely adequate to its task).

One test, therefore, is the test of necessity: Does the word fill a need? The only other test is whether the word has established itself. This does not mean whether a large number of avant-gardists are using it, nor whether a large number of supermarket checkers are using it, but rather whether it is in normal use among speakers and writers of taste. If these tests seem to raise difficult barriers for a new word to surmount, that is as it should be. The language must grow and change, but it must change slowly and needfully.

NOUNS FROM ADJECTIVES
See ADJECTIVES AS NOUNS.

NOUNS WITH ADVERBIAL FORCE
See ADVERBIAL FORCE IN NOUNS.

NOW PENDING
Pending means hanging fire or continuing. Hence it is redundant to use *now* ahead of it, as in, "This suit is now pending in the Supreme Court." Omit *now*.

NUMBER
Anyone who can distinguish between one and more than one —and this class of the population should include all alumni of kindergarten, even those who majored in raffia work—might normally be expected to match a singular subject with a singular verb and a plural subject with a plural verb, and to match singulars and plurals in general. Curiously enough, however, errors in agreement between subject and verb are the most common ones

that writers make. So common are such mistakes that it is even more curious that the high priests of the let-'em-say-what-they-like faith, who seemingly subscribe to the odd theory that if a crime is committed commonly enough it becomes legal, have not yet decided that such mistakes are not mistakes at all.

Errors of number are, for the most part, not due to ignorance, because except for a very few categories there is nothing esoteric involved. The errors are due rather to carelessness and haste. This probably accounts for the fact that they are slightly more frequent in journalistic writing than elsewhere. The remedy, then, is simple and obvious—care. In the following divisions the principal blunders are categorized.

1. ERROR CAUSED BY COMPOUND SUBJECT. "Each boy's personal disposition and problem is quickly described"; "Some musicians protested, but the public and most of the profession was willing to go along." Avoiding this kind of error should be as easy and automatic as adding one and one. In each instance the subject embraces more than one thing, and the verb must be plural. The sole apparent exception—and it is only apparent— is a subject that contains two or more elements that apply to related ideas and actually add up to a single thought. For example: ". . . the waste and wear and dissipation of an uncontrolled birth rate and a high death rate is overcome by the lowering of both sides of the ratio at the same time." Here "waste, wear, and dissipation" are kindred concepts making up a single idea and therefore can take a singular verb. A subject of this kind, however, is exceptional; whenever there is doubt whether the subject is indeed of this variety, the safe course is to consider it to be plural.

2. ERROR CAUSED BY DISTRACTION OF INTERVENING WORDS. Here the writer is in the position of the golfer about to tee off whose eye is caught by a waving dandelion or by an ant crawling up a blade of grass; he takes his eye off the ball and flubs his stroke. Watch a couple of duffers in action: "Scientists say it is difficult to convert horsepower into pounds of thrust since the velocity [*the ball—keep your eye on it*] of the rockets [*the ant— forget it*] are [*swoosh*] not known"; "The complexity [*the ball*] of the building types [*waving dandelion*] needed today are

[*swoosh*] a reflection of the complexity of our society." Such hooks and slices are obviously avoidable if the writer will simply keep his eye on the ball.

3. ERROR INDUCED BY "ONE." Our golfer now thinks he is keeping his eye on the ball, but it is not a ball at all; it just looks like one. "Kwame Nkrumah, Africa's child and Ghana's father, is one of those men who was born a leader"; "It is also perhaps one of the few stories that does not overplay a brisk desire to keep distillers and brewmasters solvent." In neither instance does the *one* govern the verb; it is not the ball. This becomes evident if you turn each sentence around: "Of those men who were born leaders, Nkrumah is one," and "Of the few stories that do not overplay, etc., it is perhaps one."

4. ERROR WITH COPULATIVE, OR LINKING, VERB. A copulative verb (such as forms of *to be*) links elements of equal value. If the noun that precedes it and the noun that follows it are both singular or both plural, no problem arises concerning the number of the verb. However, if the copula links a singular noun and a plural noun, it is often difficult to decide which is the subject and whether, therefore, the verb should be singular or plural. For instance, is it correct to write, "Recommendations to the governments concerned is the fifth item of the truce agenda"? Or should the verb be "are"? Which is the subject—"recommendations" or "item"? Jespersen offers this key to such puzzlers: "The subject is comparatively definite and special, while the predicate is less definite, and thus applicable to a greater number of things." Using this key, we should have to decide that the subject of the quoted sentence is "recommendations" and that the verb should therefore be "are." No skilled user of English would disagree with this.

And yet the Jespersen key, good as it is, will not fit every lock. To take an extreme example, it will not fit this one: "It is junior officers in the Foreign Service who are doing some of the best work." You could not write "It are . . ." Examine, also, this sentence: "The only United States air aid being given to the United Nations operations are transport planes to ferry troops, equipment, and supplies." By the Jespersen standard the subject

—that which is "comparatively definite and special"—is "transport planes," and by this same standard the verb "are" is correct. But is not "the only United States air aid" the thing that is really being talked about? Is it not the real subject? Most skilled writers would say it is. Fortunately, in practice it is not necessary to debate this kind of fine distinction. A generally accepted rule of thumb is this: In the case of a copulative verb linking nouns of equal value, the first one should be regarded as the subject and the verb should be governed accordingly. Such a rule is completely reasonable since normal English construction places the subject first and the predicate second. A final example to drive home the point: "He may have a hard time showing that any bank deposits he holds is [make it *are*] money that he himself earned."

5. ERRORS CAUSED BY SENTENCE INVERSION. It is difficult to see why inverting the sentence structure should produce mistakes in the number of the verb, but it often does. Perhaps the answer is that a man standing on his head finds it hard to see things right. Examples: "Into each missile goes tens of thousands of parts, each of which must work perfectly"; "Just as the invention of writing was the key to the first organizational revolution, so is printing, the typewriter, the telephone, the radio, and television the key to the second"; "Recommended is the establishment of a new state agency to provide marital counseling, creation of a uniform civil marriage ceremony, and mandatory conciliation. . . ." Recommended also are not inverting the sentence like that. *See* INVERSION.

6. ERRORS FOLLOWING "THERE." This category is akin to the one concerning inversion. Error: "The article is focused on program content in television, a topic in which there appears to be almost as many views as there are people." When a series of items follows a verb after *there*, some writers favor a singular verb if the first item of the series is singular: "There is brisk action, dramatic Indian fights, much ruffling of young cavaliers, and a fine aristocratic swagger." However, a plural verb in such a construction would be unexceptionable; the singular verb might put the writer in the position of having to defend himself.

7. ERRORS OF PRONOUNS AFTER "ANYBODY," "EVERYBODY," "SOMEBODY," "NEITHER," ETC. Should it be, "Everybody who thinks they can write tries to do so"? The preference here is "Everybody who thinks he can write. . . ." *See* PRONOUNS.

8. ERRORS IN AGREEMENT OF NOUNS. "The prisoners were told to keep their yard clean." Fine; the prisoners share a single yard. "The prisoners were told to keep their nose clean." Pfui; the prisoners have more than one nose. This sounds elementary, doesn't it? But errors of the type exhibited in the second sentence are common: "Drivers who register after midnight tonight must provide proof that their car is insured." Only one car for all those drivers? It must be "cars." "Extra help for residents who have trouble with their state income tax is now being provided at the New York District Office." It must be "taxes" or "tax returns" (or perhaps "the state income tax").

There are instances, however, in which the thing possessed or shared by a number of persons or things is customarily stated in the singular. Let us examine this sentence: "Also in mild pursuit were several depositors whose curiosities had been piqued by the turn of events." You can almost hear the writer saying to himself that if the depositors possess individual shirts and wives, they surely must possess individual curiosities. Logically this is so: idiomatically it is not. It is difficult to frame a watertight rule; nevertheless it may be said that the noun remains in the singular when it applies to more than one person *but* (a) represents a quality possessed in common, or (b) is an abstraction, or (c) is a figurative word. Hence, all these would be proper: "The fliers plunged to their death"; "The men earned their living"; "The three were held prisoner" (abstract) or "as prisoners" (concrete); "The spectators held their breath"; and, "The depositors' curiosity was piqued." The use of plurals in such instances is a species of OVERREFINEMENT.

9. PROBLEMS WITH "EITHER . . . OR" AND "NEITHER . . . NOR." When these correlative conjunctions connect two plural nouns, the verb is plural; when they connect two singular nouns in the third person, the verb is singular: "Neither the teachers nor the students are happy about the new hours"; "Either the

President or the Vice President is expected to attend." When one noun is plural and the other singular, however, a difficulty arises: "Neither the students nor Mr. Reston were (?) was (?) optimistic about the chances of effective legislation."

Three ways out are available. The first two are frankly cowardly, but are recommended nevertheless. One is to find a noncommittal verb: "Neither the students nor Mr. Reston expressed optimism. . . ." The second is to change the construction: "The students were not optimistic, nor was Mr. Reston. . . ." The third way is to make the number of the verb correspond to the nearer of the two nouns: "Neither the students nor Mr. Reston was optimistic. . . ." Sometimes, as in the present instance, this third way is likely to call attention to itself and appear somewhat self-conscious. This is particularly true if the second noun and hence the verb are singular; if they are both plural, the reader pays less note because he is aware that the subject contained more than one noun, which would lead, grammar aside, to a subconscious expectation of a plural verb anyway. Thus he would accept the following sentence without a second thought: "Neither the tall, spare fisherman nor his friends deny that Mr. and Mrs. Morgan could rent their cottages for a better price." However, even a singular second noun and verb can be inconspicuous if the subject nouns are less naked and proximate than they are in the "students-Mr. Reston" example. Witness: "One reason that neither private building owners in the city nor even the municipal administration has moved ahead is that up to now there has been no firm guidance from Washington."

Other aspects of number are discussed under AS WELL AS, COLLECTIVES, PLUS, and WITH.

NUMERALS USED SUCCESSIVELY

When numbers of different categories appear one after the other they may, particularly if they are improperly set into type, cause confusion. Examples: "During 1958 7,724 Israelis emigrated"; "As of June 30, 870,266 were entitled to rations. . . ." A slight rewriting will always remedy this fault.

305

NUMERALS WITH COLLECTIVES

The general question to be raised here—and, it is hoped, answered—is exemplified by the specific question whether it is proper to say, as a headline did, "Twenty-five Troops Slain." "Troops" is a collective noun meaning a force of soldiers. You can use a numeral in front of it, as in "1,000 troops were sent to Vietnam." Yet you cannot—at least, should not—say, "Eleven troops were killed in Vietnam." The answer to this puzzle lies not in the size of the number, nor in whether it is exact or rounded. The answer lies rather in whether the context introduces the notion of individuals as contrasted with a group. Thus (using the identical figure) you could say, "500 troops paraded in Berlin," but not, "500 troops married German girls." The 500 troops on parade are thought of as a body of soldiers, but the 500 bridegrooms are thought of as individuals, *nicht wahr?* The same principle applies to such collectives as *police* and *clergy. See* **PERSONNEL.**

O, OH

As a vocative—that is, when used as a form of address—the word is O, always capitalized and not followed by any punctuation. The following, then, are wrong: "Oh, Lord God, we've been abused so long; we've been down so long; oh, Lord, all we want is. . . ." Make them: "O Lord God" and "O Lord." O in this sense appears almost exclusively in poetic or religious contexts.

As an exclamation or an utterance followed by a pause, the word is *oh*; it is capitalized only at the head of a sentence and it is followed by an exclamation point or a comma: " 'It takes her, oh, ten minutes to find it,' Miss Brennan laughed"; "Oh! spare us politics, dear uncle."

OBEDIENT

Takes preposition *to*.

OBJECT (vb.)

Takes preposition *to* or *against*.

OBLIGATE, OBLIGE

The more comprehensive of the two words is *oblige*. It says everything that *obligate* says, yet lawyers prefer *obligate* to denote the act of binding by duty or statute. The word might well be left to them. *Oblige* denotes that same kind of binding, and in addition it has the meaning of to put under a debt or to confer a favor. In this latter meaning *obligate* is not approved by careful users of the language; they frown, for example, upon "I feel obligated to him for what he did for my family." The use of *oblige* in the sense of to afford entertainment, as in the sentence, "The soprano will oblige with an encore," is a casualism, better left to masters of ceremony.

OBLIVIOUS

Strictly speaking, *oblivious* means, by its derivation, forgetful or lacking awareness of what one once knew. Although it is, of course, used in this sense, it is perhaps even more often used in the broader sense of unaware, heedless, unconscious, or impervious. Those who condemn the broadening of the word should ask themselves whether the language is in any wise damaged by this broadening. If *oblivious* in its primary sense had a unique meaning, we should have to conclude that there was actual damage. But since *forgetful* and *unmindful* convey the same meaning, we must find that *oblivious* is not entitled to special protective measures. On the other hand, in its broader meaning *oblivious* has even more synonyms, all of them more precise. The conclusion to be drawn from all this is that *oblivious* is a high-sounding word for which there is not great use—one that is better replaced by a more exact word. Those who wish to retain the narrow meaning will follow the word by the preposition *of*; others will follow it by *of* or *to*.

OBSERVANCE, OBSERVATION

An *observance* is a taking note of or acting in consonance with a tradition or duty or custom. An *observation* is a viewing, a regarding, a perceiving of something. Improper: "Dublin-born Maureen O'Hara joins host Andy Williams in observation of St. Patrick's Day Thursday night on Channel 4." To make the distinction even clearer: A little boy finds a vantage point for *observation* of a parade in *observance* of the Fourth of July.

OBSERVANT

Takes preposition *of*.

OBTRUDE

Takes preposition *on* or *upon*.

OBVIATE

The meaning of this word is to make unnecessary, but it is often misused to mean to remove or eliminate, as in this example:

"But any chance for such mediation appears to have been ob-viated by the attacks of Premier Castro."

OCCASION

Takes preposition *of* or *for*.

OCCUPATIONS

The words people use affectionately, humorously, or dis-paragingly to describe their own occupations are their own affair. They may say, "I'm in show business" (or, more likely, "show biz"), or "I'm in the advertising racket," or "I'm in the oil game," or "I'm in the garment line." But outsiders should use more caution, more discretion, and more precision. For instance, it is improper to write, "Mr. Danaher has been in the law business in Washington." Law is a profession. Similarly, to say someone is "in the teaching game" would undoubtedly give offense to teachers. Unless there is some special reason to be slangy or col-loquial, the advisable thing to do is to accord every occupation the dignity it deserves.

OCCUPIED

Takes preposition *by* or *with*.

OCCUR

See TAKE PLACE, OCCUR.

ODD

One use of *odd* is to indicate an indeterminate surplus over a given round number, as in "thirty-odd years ago." When it is thus coupled to a number a hyphen is used; otherwise you might produce the offensive ambiguity of "thirty odd Congress-men." Rarely, the word stands by itself, as in "1,300 and odd years ago" or "The load weighed 1,000 pounds odd." Since *odd* in-dicates an indeterminate surplus, which is usually just a few, a sentence like this one is absurd: "For the next three-odd years, the daybooks provided 'a safety valve for releasing corked-up pas-sions which might otherwise explode.'" If the writer meant three or four years, he should have said it that way; if he meant three years and a few months, he should have said it that way.

OF
See PREPOSITIONS, SUPERFLUOUS.

OF COURSE
See SIMPLE REASON.

OFFENSIVE
Takes preposition *to*.

OFFICER FOR POLICEMAN

Despite the dictionary, the feeling among the discriminating is that to speak of a policeman as an *officer* has a provincial flavor, much as has *counselor* for a lawyer or *parson* for a clergyman. But apart from that consideration, it is worthwhile to preserve the distinction between ordinary cops and officers, i.e., those of higher grade. It is true that police departments themselves use the word *officer* in referring to a patrolman; in New York, for example, there is a standard alarm that is sent urgently to scout cars to "assist an officer." It is also true that if a policeman is about to give you a ticket for passing a red light, that word is the only form of direct address that seems suitable: "But, officer, I am color blind." Nevertheless, *officer* still seems to have wisps of hayseed clinging to it.

OFF OF
See PREPOSITIONS, SUPERFLUOUS.

OLDER
See ELDER, OLDER.

OMPHALOSKEPSIS

A word meaning contemplation while gazing at the navel, *omphaloskepsis* would be of use only to a deipnosophist. And it has no more business appearing here than has DEIPNOSOPHIST.

ON

Headline lingo tends to insinuate itself into conventional language. Even a President has been known to speak of "test ban agreements" (*See* NOUNS AS ADJECTIVES). In headlines, space limitations often force the little word *on* into unaccustomed contexts—as in "President Defends Two Aides; Assails Question on Loyalty"—where the more usual word would be *about* or *concerning*. But that is no reason to inject *on* into a strange place in ordinary writing. The following instances demonstrate the growing prevalence of this tendency; the more natural word is parenthesized: "The Foreign Secretary, replying to a question on [*about* or *concerning*] whether he thought the threat of war over Berlin had been reduced, said . . ."; "Eighteen months ago the inter-American system applied diplomatic and economic sanctions on [*against*] the regime of the late Generalissimo Trujillo"; "Two other witnesses also were uncertain on [*about*] his part in the robbery." Headlinese is bad enough, though sometimes unavoidable, in headlines, but in normal writing it cannot be condoned.

ONE AND THE SAME

"The final proof that the mystery city and Morgantine were one and the same place was furnished by. . . ." Try omitting *one and* from this trite phrase and see whether it makes any difference in meaning.

ONE IDEA TO A SENTENCE

Marcel Proust and James Joyce undoubtedly never heard of such a dictum. How could they have heard of it? It was not set forth formally until 1954 and did not appear in print until 1958 (in *Watch Your Language*, written by the present author and published by Atheneum). Moreover, there was no need for them to hear of it. It was not intended as a guide for literary writing, nor for any kind of writing in which style or evocation of mood is a prime consideration. Yet it can contribute to both these objectives, as Hemingway, among others, showed. Examine, for example, this excerpt from the description of Robert Cohn in the opening paragraph of *The Sun Also Rises:*

He was Spider Kelly's star pupil. Spider Kelly taught all his young gentlemen to box like featherweights, no matter whether they weighed one hundred and five or two hundred and five pounds. But it seemed to fit Cohn. He was really very fast. He was so good that Spider promptly overmatched him and got his nose permanently flattened. This increased Cohn's distaste for boxing, but it gave him a certain satisfaction of some strange sort, and it certainly improved his nose. In his last year at Princeton he read too much and took to wearing spectacles. I never met any one of his class who remembered him. They did not even remember that he was middleweight boxing champion.

The one-idea-to-a-sentence dictum is designed, rather, for those kinds of writing in which instant clarity and swift reading, which are other ways of saying quick comprehension, are dominant desiderata. Such kinds of writing include the newspaper article, the complex technical article, and the article about a specialized field designed to be read by those who are not familiar with that field. When the problem of achieving clarity and swift comprehension was under study, a researcher noticed that one columnist-commentator had the reputation of being more understandable than his competitors. The researcher examined the man's writings to find out why. He found that the only major factor that appeared consistently was a shorter average sentence. Whether his diagnosis was correct or not, the finding was significant and he decided to test it. (A description of the tests appears in *Watch Your Language*, pp. 112-115.) In all the tests a correlation was found between average sentence length and comprehensibility. What was not noticed in the tests, however, was that all the sentences were not short, but rather that the *average* sentence was; in other words, a few sentences of three or four words offset some rather long sentences and pulled the average down. Still, although there were some rather long sentences, there were no complicated ones. This suggested a different diagnosis and led to the one-idea-to-a-sentence advice. It was found that in the clear, easily comprehended writing there was, almost without exception, just one idea to a sentence. Confining a sentence to a single thought will usually reduce the number of words. That is why there was a correlation between sentence length and comprehensibility. But the basic factor was, and is, "one idea, one sentence."

Formulas for good writing are usually ineffective and always distasteful to the writer. The notion that he should count the number of words in a sentence is as forbidding as the thought of counting the number of affixes, syllables, personal references, homely words, or anything else. Therefore, the one-idea-to-a-sentence advice should not be taken as a rule or a formula. For one thing, interesting writing demands variation in sentence length, as well as structure, and the one-idea guide may on occasion produce a jolting, monotonous concatenation of similar sentences. For another thing, it should be noted that there are instances in which two or more thoughts are as inseparable as Siamese twins. To take an extreme example, it would be nonsense to write: "The American flag is red. It is also white. It is blue, too." On the other hand, the reader is invited to judge whether in the appended two examples the one-idea-to-a-sentence version on the right is not easier to read than the cluttered, hard-packed version on the left:

The Egyptian revolutionary leader, long an advocate of better relations with the West, who risked his political future in signing a compromise agreement on control of the Suez Canal zone, in an interview expressed bitterness and disillusion over the results of his dealing with the West.	The Egyptian revolutionary leader has long been an advocate of better relations with the West. He risked his political future in signing a compromise agreement on control of the Suez Canal zone. But in an interview he expressed bitterness and disillusion over the results of his dealings with the West.

313

In a ten-page brief filed by their lawyers with the Securities and Exchange Commission and made public yesterday, two members of the American Stock Exchange charged by the Commission with a multi-million-dollar stock-market manipulation conceded that "the facts plainly justify sanctions" against them.

Two members of the American Stock Exchange charged with a multi-million-dollar stock-market manipulation conceded yesterday that "the facts plainly justify sanctions" against them. They conceded this in a ten-page brief filed by their lawyers with the Securities and Exchange Commission.

Aside from the natural-enough desire for economy of expression, what are some of the causes of overpacking of sentences? Following are a few of them:

1. The participial opening, dear to the hearts of journalists and especially sports writers: "Scoring four times in the opening period, Princeton downed. . . ."

2. The unnecessary inclusion of subordinate clauses. Often they are irrelevant to the statement being made and might better be included elsewhere. "Mr. Jones, who was born in Albany, N.Y., forty-nine years ago, said that the way to defeat communism. . . ." *See* NON SEQUITUR.

3. The unnecessary linking of coordinate statements by *and* or *but* or *as* or *while*. Often a new sentence is indicated. Although there are plenty of exceptions, a good guide is to reach for a period instead of a conjunction.

It is perhaps needless to point out, however, that a period cannot be dropped into the middle of a long sentence unthinkingly. Doing this will sometimes result in half an idea to a sentence: "He either will have to pitch Bronshaw in Brooklyn, where he doesn't like to work the left-hander." Is that a sentence? Is that an idea? Next sentence: "Or he will have to keep his ace southpaw idle until Milwaukee arrives at the home field next Tuesday." Other times a writer or an editor ineptly splits a long sentence, then finds himself holding a meaningless splinter like this: "The charge came after an assertion by District Attorney Hogan."

Underlying everything that has been said on this subject is the assumption that the writer is thinking intelligently about what he is doing. Without this all is in vain. For the thoughtful writer an excellent maxim, if repetition is not out of order, would be, "Generally it speeds reading if there is only one idea to a sentence."

ONE OF THE

Usually a wasteful locution. "One of the reasons" can usefully be compressed into "one reason."

For the grammatical error in the construction "He is one of the few great statesmen who has had no formal schooling," *see* NUMBER (3).

ONE OF THE . . . IF NOT THE

This common trap that authors write themselves into can be demonstrated by a single example: "It was described as one of the first, if not the first, joint essays on religion by representatives of the three major faiths." The plural "essays" fits well after *one of the first*, but does not fit at all after *if not the first*. One way out of the trap, but not a good one because it sometimes slightly alters the meaning, is to insert an "of the" ahead of the plural noun. The alteration of meaning that would result from placing "of the" ahead of "joint essays" consists in posing the assumption that there is or will be a body of such essays, which the writer clearly is not certain of. A better way out is to move the *if not* phrase to the end: "one of the first joint essays . . . if not the first." This kind of trap is not dissimilar to the type described under INCOMPLETE ALTERNATIVE COMPARISON: "A is as good, if not better, than B." *See also* IF NOT.

ONLY

Normally the proper positioning of *only* requires no more

315

than asking yourself, "What does it actually modify?" Thus a headline that says, "$35,000 Bond Thief Only Nets Paper," does not conform to the normal order; the *only* patently modifies "paper," not "nets," and so should adjoin it. An interesting exercise for developing *only* awareness was cited in the publication *Word Study*, distributed by G. & C. Merriam Company, as follows: "Eight different meanings result from placing *only* in the eight possible positions in this sentence: 'I hit him in the eye yesterday.'" Try it.

Once this awareness is developed, it becomes evident that the *only* is not in its normally proper position in the following statement: "The returning signal only becomes evident when the echoes are superimposed." Better: "becomes evident only when." Likewise it is not normally placed in this statement: "The difficulty with this type of system is that it can only provide a limited amount of power. . . ." Better: "that it can provide only." And the misplacement causes ambiguity in this sentence: "The decision affected only picketing at the Medical Center."

The words "normal" and "normally" have been prominent in the foregoing paragraphs. They are intended to underline the fact that there are abnormal yet proper placements for *only*. One abnormal placement is dictated by idiom, meaning that a normal placement would sound awkward and contrived. Example: "What is happening now can only be called a paperback-book explosion." The normal position for *only* here would be just ahead of "a paperback-book explosion," which is the phrase it modifies. But placed there, it sounds pedantic and unnatural.

Another "abnormal" placement, which is not really abnormal but only seems so, occurs when the *only* is a sentence adverb, that is, when it modifies an entire statement rather than a word or phrase. Example: "He only thought that he was being helpful." The *only* here is not intended to modify merely "thought," as would be the case if "thought" were heavily stressed. Nor is the meaning that his mental process was confined to a single idea, as would be implied if the *only* followed "thought." Rather the intention is to apply *only* to the entire

316

sentence, and a sentence adverb of this kind usually precedes the verb.

Still a third deviation from the normal placement of *only* occurs when it is the writer's desire to send up an early warning rocket to signal that there is a limitation on the statement that is being made. Normal positioning of the word would produce a sentence like this: "The new tickets will be honored by the participating airlines only if they are presented by the persons to whom they were issued." It is clear, correct, and idiomatic. Yet it might be improved by moving the *only* forward into the midst of the verb—"will only be honored"—thus alerting the reader quickly to the fact that there is a string attached to the sentence. Whether this is desirable will often be a matter for the writer's judgment. Opinions might differ on a sentence like this: "He said Brazil had abstained from voting in favor of sanctions against Cuba at the conference in Punta del Este only because she felt that the question must be settled by 'due process of law.' " Most writers would probably favor introducing the *only* ahead of "abstained," but none could maintain that the sentence is reproachable as it stands. Normal positioning of *only* is almost always defensible, but sometimes placing it elsewhere removes the need for a defense.

Only may be used as a conjunction in place of *but*, although this use is more appropriate to speech than to writing ("I would have attended the theater, only I caught cold the night before"). It should not be used, however, as Evans points out, in place of *except*, although it is so used by a distinguished professor of English in the following passage: "For this reason this dictionary does not use 'or' as a divider between synonymous or equivalent words —only when the members of the series are alternatives or when one member adds to another." Definitely a solecism, despite the eminence of the offender.

ONOMATOPOEIA

See RHETORICAL FIGURES AND FAULTS.

ON THE PART OF

A wasteful locution. It usually can be replaced with *by*. In the following example, "There was opposition on the part of the Councilman from Richmond," the phrase lengthens the sentence but does not add to it.

OPPONENT

See ADVERSARY, ANTAGONIST, OPPONENT.

OPPORTUNITY

Takes preposition *of* or *for*.

OPPOSITE

See CONVERSE, REVERSE, CONTRARY, OPPOSITE. *Opposite* as an adjective takes the preposition *to; opposite* as a noun takes the preposition *of*.

OPPOSITION

Takes preposition *to*.

OPTIMISTIC

Optimistic is no longer, as Fowler described it, a vogue word. Still it is overused and used in senses in which its meaning is strained and in which another word might be more serviceable. In its broadest meaning *optimistic* applies to a tendency to view things in the best possible light; it describes a general attitude rather than a manner of regarding an inconsequential individual happening. A baseball fan who says he expects the Yankees to overcome a five-run deficit in the last half of the ninth inning is better described as *hopeful* than *optimistic*. There are, of course, other ways of describing him, too, but that is irrelevant. Likewise, to say of a policeman's exaggerated estimate of the size of a crowd viewing a parade that "His total was optimistic" is definitely to misuse the word.

OR

See NOR.

318

ORAL VS. VERBAL

Although it is true that *verbal* means in the form of words, and has even taken over the specialized meaning of in the form of spoken words, it cannot be denied that much would be gained in the cause of precision if writers would use *oral* when they mean spoken words and *written* when they mean words committed to paper. *Verbal* might well be confined to those situations in which it is desired to distinguish communication by words from other forms of communication like gestures, smoke signals, and the light that shines from lovers' eyes. To speak of a *verbal agreement* may leave some doubt whether the agreement was made in a conversation or signed in a lawyer's office. Confronted with a choice between a word that can mean two things and another that can mean only one, are we not making better use of the tools of language if we select the precise word?

ORIGINATE

Takes preposition *in* or *with*.

ORTHOËPY

This item is merely a mischievous one that has no place whatever in a book that deals with written rather than spoken language. *Orthoëpy* is the study of pronunciation. But as far as the word itself is concerned, the OR*thoëpists* say it is pronounced OR*thoëpy*, and the or'THOëpists contend it is pronounced or*THOëpy*. Who shall decide, asked Pope, when doctors disagree? And about their own specialty, yet.

OTHER

Strictly speaking, *other* pertains to a thing distinct from a like thing already mentioned; for example, "one apple and the other apple" or "four boys and the other four." It is not incorrect—but not precise—to use it in the following way: "The pupil assignment bill was pictured by the Governor as providing the answer to the problem. The other four bills would. . . ."

It is preferable here to say, "the four other bills," since there has been no mention of a previous set of four bills to which these would seem to stand in comparison. *See also* ANOTHER.

OTHER (AND ELSE)

To write, "Florida has more birds than any state in the Union," seems to exclude Florida from the Union. What is needed is "any other state in the Union." Likewise, although it is proper to write, "He is better than anyone on the opposing team," it is improper to write, "He is better than anyone on the home team" (assuming he is a member of the home team). Make it, "better than anyone else on the home team." To state the case in general terms: When a thing is being compared with others of its own class it must, for purposes of the comparison, be set apart from the others. Hence, the word *other* or the word *else* is required.

On the other hand, when a superlative rather than a comparative is used, *other* is not included: "Florida has the most birds of any state in the Union." It pays to be other-wise.

OTHER THAN, OTHERWISE THAN

The simplest guide to follow, although it is subject to exceptions, is to use *other than* when the phrase modifies a noun or other substantive (since *other* is primarily an adjective) and to use *otherwise than* when the phrase is used adverbially. Thus this sentence is correct: "The Garden had no direct responsibility for the event other than furnishing the premises and the concessions." Here *other* clearly modifies "responsibility"—adjective modifying noun. On the other hand, this sentence is not correct: "Any attempt to change the status quo other than by negotiations would be worse." What is modified here is the infinitive "to change" and this calls for an adverb—*otherwise*.

At first glance the following sentence seems to be parallel with the one just cited, but it is not: "The Assistant District Attorney refused to discuss the case, other than to say he expected his inquiry might be long." Here the meaning is not an *other* way of discussing the case but rather an exception to the refusal to discuss. *Other than* can be justified in this instance as a preposition governing the infinitive "to say." But since the preposition "except" is right at hand, why not use it?

OTHERWISE

The lazy speaker or writer sometimes grabs for the word *otherwise* to finish a thought, much as he seizes upon "and so forth" or "and all that sort of thing" instead of setting forth clearly what he wishes to say. "The question of falseness or otherwise does not enter into the matter." *Otherwise* can be a noun, meaning a different way, but it is not often used as such. That meaning clearly would not fit in the sentence just cited. All the writer meant was "falseness or truth," and that is what he should have written.

OUTSIDE OF

In the sense of except for, *outside of* is a substandard casualism, as in the sentence "Health, education, and welfare are, outside of labor, the most controversial subjects in the American political arena today." As a mere synonym for *outside*, however, the phrase is acceptable: "He is a different man outside [or *outside of*] his office."

OVER, IN A COMPARISON

"Highway deaths are down eleven per cent in the state over the same period a year ago." If it is a reduction it is not *over*, it is *under*. Or it can be written *as against* or *compared with*.

OVERLAY, OVERLIE

See UNDERLAY, UNDERLIE.

OVERLY

An unnecessary and not especially graceful word, *overly* is a manifestation of the adverb syndrome, in which some people think a word cannot be an adverb unless it ends in "-ly." Dictionaries list several hundred words prefixed by *over*, such as *over-*

careful, overenthusiastic, and *overlearned,* but there will always be those who will insist on *overly careful, overly enthusiastic,* and *overly learned.* Which probably demonstrates that sometimes the "-ly" side is the windy side. *See* OVERREFINEMENT (5).

OVERREFINEMENT

There is such a thing, in writing and in other fields, as *overrefinement.* Usually it produces slight absurdity and sometimes outright crudity, as in the pose of the social climber who raises her teacup with her little finger stuck daintily out in the air. The vulgar extended finger evidences itself in many forms, listed herewith. Most of them are discussed in greater detail under the headings indicated.

1. AS FOR LIKE. Excessive timidity about the use of *like* (which rightly applies only to its employment to introduce a full clause) leads some writers to substitute *as* unnecessarily and erroneously: "They behaved as children." *See* LIKE, AS.

2. BETWEEN YOU AND I. Uncomprehending souls who have heard strictures about "It is me" tend to think of "me" as a naughty word, particularly when it is associated with "you," which they mistake for a nominative case. Thinking they are leaning over backward to be correct, they somersault onto their faces and come up with BETWEEN YOU AND I.

3. WHOM. If there is a verb anywhere near the pronoun *who,* our social climber leaps to the conclusion that the verb governs the pronoun and changes it to *whom:* "The police arrested a man whom they suspect committed the burglary." Perhaps half the time such a writer will be right. But if so, it will be sheer luck. *See* WHO, WHOM, WHOEVER, WHOMEVER.

4. NUMBER. Unnecessary and too literal pluralizing of qualities or things held in common by people is a kind of overrefinement that leads to an almost ludicrous extreme: "The audience held their breaths." *See* NUMBER(8).

5. THE ADVERB SYNDROME. One manifestation of this ailment is an insistence on using a word ending in "-ly" in the belief that an adverb must have that form: "He went directly to Washington." But there are many words that are adverbs either with or

without the "-ly," including *clear, direct, hard, high, laud, over, pretty, right, slow*. Nor do the two forms always mean the same thing. *Direct*, for example, can mean without any detours, and *directly* can mean without any delays. Another manifestation of the adverb syndrome is the tampering with idiom in the belief that only the "-ly" word will do: *sitting prettily, taking it easily, sharply at 8* A.M., and this unusual specimen, in which the suffix "-ly" converts a man into a dog: "Generally the defendant sits bored and indifferent when witnesses testify, but sometimes he snaps alertly and writes a quick note to his lawyer." *See* LO, THE POOR IDIOM.

6. PREPOSITION AT END. The misguided effort to avoid this supposedly wicked construction sometimes is a form of overrefinement that can look foolish: "The police haven't a clue by which to go"; "He hasn't a leg on which to stand." *See* PREPOSITION AT END.

A little learning, as the man said, is a dangerous thing.

OVERWHELM

Takes preposition *by* or *with*.

OWING TO

See DANGLERS *and* DUE TO.

OXYMORON

See RHETORICAL FIGURES AND FAULTS.

P

PACKAGE

This is a FAD WORD. That does not mean it should not be used. But, like all fad words, it should not be overused, and when it is used it should be used with discretion. Here is an admittedly unusual specimen of an indiscreet use in an article about new Western Union services: "W.A.T.S. provides subscribers with lower package rates for heavy users of long-distance service, based on six long-distance zones similar to those used in parcel post service." The conjunction of *package* and "parcel post" is unfortunate and momentarily confusing—almost an ACCIDENTAL PUN.

PANACEA

"We may see the day when that good old American cure-all, the pill, will be the panacea for mosquito bites." A *panacea* is a remedy for all ailments (and, you may rest assured, we will never see the day when there is one). Therefore, the word cannot be properly applied to a single affliction like mosquito bites.

PARAGRAPHS

A sentence quoted by Partridge from Alexander Bain probably says all that needs to be said about paragraphing: "Between one paragraph and another there is a greater break in the subject than between one sentence and another." A paragraph may be of one sentence or it may be of ten. An elementary-school teacher told her class that a paragraph could not contain only one sentence. When the impertinent pupils asked her why, she replied that obviously if it had only one sentence it would be a sentence, not a paragraph. That teacher deserves a sentence—and a long one.

Paragraphing is a visual device to show separations of subjects and to facilitate reading. Much depends on the subject, the typography, the purpose of what is being written, and the readers to whom it is addressed. A scientific paper designed to be read closely and slowly by a thoughtful audience may have longer paragraphs than a first-grade primer. In newspapers, where the narrow columns tend to elongate paragraphs and where the intent is to speed the reader who is pressed for time, paragraphs are shorter than they would be in a book. But even for newspapers it would be futile to lay down rules; the most that can be said is that for journalistic purposes a bread box is better proportioned than a telephone booth. That does not mean that in newspapers rhetorical units can be hacked to bits. The thing to remember is: "Between one paragraph and another there is a greater break in the subject than between one sentence and another."

PARALLEL

Takes preposition *to* or *with*.

PARENTHESES

See PUNCTUATION.

PARENTHESES TO EXPLAIN PRONOUNS

This is the "He (Jones) hit him (Smith)" affliction. Explaining a pronoun by using a parenthesized identification is occasionally unavoidable when a writer is dealing with someone else's quotations. But in his own writing it should very rarely be necessary.

An example of the fault: "Mr. Lane said that he was forwarding to United States Attorney General James P. McGranery a transcript of the testimony given before the commission on Friday by his (Lane's) administrative assistant." It is almost as if the sentence were addressed to two different readers—A, a stuffy soul, who cannot brook repetition of the name "Lane" and for whose benefit the pronoun "his" is used, and B, who would not understand to which person the "his" referred and for whose enlightenment the parenthesis is surreptitiously inserted in the hope that A won't notice it. Why not ignore A and simply say "Mr. Lane's"?

325

Here is another example, which goes to the absurd extreme of inserting three parentheses in a single sentence: "Corporal Brown testified that when Provoo enlisted his (Brown's) services in behalf of the Japanese, he got Provoo to agree that he (Provoo) would not ask him (Brown) to commit any traitorous act." The first parenthesis is rendered superfluous by the plain meaning of the words; the second and third could be eliminated by a simple reconstruction to make the sentence read, ". . . he got Provoo to agree not to ask him. . . ." With that change all the pronouns in the sentence would refer to the same antecedent, all would be tidy, and the parenthetical stumbling blocks would be removed. In a way, the use of identifying parentheses is a confession of inability to construct a clear sentence.

PARENTHETICAL PHRASES

Failure to recognize a parenthetical phrase often produces a sentence that goes awry. The error is illustrated by this sentence, fabricated for the occasion: "In 1776 President Johnson said that the American people were a sturdy folk." Obviously, in 1776 President Johnson wasn't saying anything. The error consists in not noticing that "President Johnson said" is a parenthetical phrase and that it should be set off by commas, with the "that" deleted.

Here are two real-life examples of the error from one story: "On Feb. 15 Mr. Hogan said that Fox, Ganz, and Berner went to the apartment. . . . In a nearby restaurant Mr. Hogan said that the detectives found the marijuana." A third example contains the same error, though it is not quite so obvious: "Right after the Oregon vote is counted, most of the leaders feel that their task would be greatly simplified were the General on the scene in the United States."

It should also be noted that the verb of the parenthetical phrase, since it is merely part of an interpolation, does not govern the other verbs of the sentence. The following sentence demonstrates the point: "While Mr. Truman was serving as chairman of the Senate committee investigating war contracts, Mr. Cooper said that he had been lent to the committee by the

Washington Police Department." What this sentence literally says is that Mr. Cooper made his statement at the time Mr. Truman was chairman of the committee. But such, of course, was not the writer's intention. He erred by failing to recognize that "Mr. Cooper said" is parenthetical. Those words should be enclosed in commas, the word "that" should be deleted, and the following verb—which is not governed by "said" but is on the same level as "while Mr. Truman was serving"—should be changed to "was lent." *See also* SEQUENCE OF TENSES.

Here is a different kind of poor parenthesizing: "The Prime Minister is elected, not as a United States President is by a nationwide vote, but is chosen by the party that wins a majority in the House of Commons." Lift out the parenthetical clause enclosed in commas and you find that the sentence has run off the rails and piled up in wreckage. Correct it in one of two ways: (1) "The Prime Minister is not elected as a United States President is, by a nationwide vote, but is chosen, etc."; (2) "The Prime Minister is elected, not as a United States President is— by a nationwide vote—but by the party, etc."

PARLIAMENTARIAN

"Recent communications from Washington to the French Government were offensive to French dignity, the Premier told parliamentarians of his own Independent party today." A *parliamentarian* is, properly, an authority on the rules and usage of parliamentary assemblies. Members of parliaments may or may not be *parliamentarians*, and a *parliamentarian* may or may not be—and often is not—a member of a parliament.

PARONOMASIA

See RHETORICAL FIGURES AND FAULTS.

PARSON

See OFFICER FOR POLICEMAN.

PART

Takes preposition *from* or *with*.

PARTAKE

Essentially *partake* means to take a share in or of with others, although in common use it can also mean to take a portion of alone, as in "He partook of a well-prepared dinner." Used this way, however, it is a rather overformal word. In the sense of take part in, it is ordinarily replaced by *participate*. "Through television many young people will then be able to partake in one of the best educational programs that Leonard Bernstein has yet put together." *Participate* would be better here.

Partake takes preposition *of* or *in*.

PART AND PARCEL

"The Indian attitude now is that Kashmir is part and parcel of India." Strike out *and parcel* in this legalistic cliché and see if it makes any difference in meaning.

PARTIAL

Takes preposition *to*.

PARTIALITY

Takes preposition *to, toward,* or *for*.

PARTICIPATE

Takes preposition *in*. *See also* PARTAKE.

PARTICIPLE

See SEQUENCE OF TENSES *and* GENITIVE WITH GERUND.

PARTICIPLES AS ADJECTIVES

Participles are often used as adjectives: the *growing* plant, the *burned* child. But perfect (or past) participles—those ending in "ed," "d," "t," "en," or "n"—are not employed as adjectives indiscriminately. It is proper to speak of *the wrecked plane,* but not altogether acceptable to speak of *the crashed plane.*

Sounds like a puzzler, doesn't it? The answer seems to be that it is transitive verbs that are normally used this way, rather than intransitive verbs. A plane that has been wrecked (transitive verb) is *a wrecked plane*, but a plane that has crashed (intransitive verb) is not *a crashed plane*. If you smoke you are not *a smoked man*, but if you smoke a herring it is *a smoked fish*.

There are, to be sure, exceptions to this principle, but they seem to be idiomatic uses of long standing. For example, *escaped prisoner* and *escaped convict* are well established, though a bear that broke out of a zoo would not usually be referred to as *an escaped bear*. *Confessed spy* is another that has gained approval. And there are others such as *retired schoolteacher, grown man, determined woman,* and *well-read youth. Crashed plane* appears in newspapers so often that it probably will win full acceptance in time, but it has not quite done so yet.

PASSIVE VOICE
See ACTIVE VOICE AND PASSIVE VOICE.

PATHETIC FALLACY
See RHETORICAL FIGURES AND FAULTS.

PATIENT
Takes preposition *in, with,* or *of*.

PATRON
Patron for *customer* is a piece of commercial ostentation. But most businesses—from shoe stores to jewelry shops—put on such airs. One is reminded of that old tree surgeon who fell out of his patient.

PAUNCH
See BELLY.

PECULIAR
Takes preposition *to*.

PENDING
See NOW PENDING.

PEOPLE, PERSONS

The use of *people* preceded by a numeral used to be verboten, especially in newspaper offices. From that prohibition it is only a short jump to considering *people* to be a naughty word. This idea produces such odd locutions as, "Mr. Arsenault thinks persons in Quebec should know more about the problems of the island's Acadians" and "Millions of persons around the world switched on radios and television sets to hear President Kennedy." Or, to take an even more extreme example: "Old drawings found in an attic here are adding laurels to a deceased artist whose prime job had been to make persons laugh." That usage would make several *persons* laugh, but the artist's job was to make *people* laugh.

The only rule has to be a general one, its application often dependent on the writer's ear: Use *people* for large groups; use *persons* for an exact or small number. At one end of the scale "one people" is unthinkable, "two people" only a little less so, and "fifty people" acceptable. At the other end of the scale, "millions of persons," although not unthinkable, is hardly a common usage, but "4,381 persons" is quite proper. *See also* INDIVIDUAL.

PER

"The Soviet shoe industry produced about three shoes for each person." (And this in a planned economy?) The phrasing is the kind of absurdity that results from a too literal interpretation of the advice not to mix Latin and English. "Per person" would have been the natural phrasing; *per* in the meaning of "for each" is natural and desirable in any statistical or economic context. Otherwise such abnormalities as these result: "Rents a room range from $25 to $41"; "Belgium is rated third, with a yield a cow a year of 3,760 kilograms of milk." On the other hand, *per* is decidedly out of place as it is used in commercialese ("Please make the shipment as per my previous letter") or as it is sometimes introduced into student writing ("He returned to Washington per automobile").

PER CENT

From the Latin *per centum*, this phrase used to carry a period, as would any other abbreviation; but present usage dispenses with the period. *Per cent* means in a hundred or out of a hundred (and there's a paradox for you); five per cent means five in a hundred or five out of a hundred. Like *fraction*, it is sometimes misused to mean a small portion, but it should be remembered that there are such things as ninety-eight per cent and 300 per cent. Another misuse, technically, is illustrated by this sentence: "The council's board is made up of forty per cent Catholics, forty per cent Protestants, and twenty per cent Jews." Very strictly speaking, this phraseology probably means that the Catholics on the council are forty per cent Catholic and sixty per cent something else. An improvement would be, "Of the council's board forty per cent are Catholics, forty per cent Protestants, and twenty per cent Jews."

PERFECT

See INCOMPARABLES.

PERFECT INFINITIVE

See SEQUENCE OF TENSES.

PERIOD

See PUNCTUATION.

PERMEATE

Takes preposition *into* or *through*; *permeated* takes preposition *by*.

PERSEVERE

Takes preposition *in*.

PERSONAL FRIEND

"Mr. Driggs had been a personal friend of the late Orville Wright." Sovereigns may have nonpersonal friends, but usually not we commoners. The "usually" is inserted there because occasionally there is an exception: "Mr. Hughes is a long-time business friend of several Atlas executives and is a close personal friend of Mr. Odlum." The adjective *personal* is necessary in that context, but normally it is tautological.

PERSONIFICATION

See RHETORICAL FIGURES AND FAULTS.

PERSONNEL

Personnel is a collective noun, referring to a body of soldiers, workers, or whatnot, but it does not apply to individuals. Therefore it is improper to write, "Three military personnel and some civilians came with Mr. Long to Galveston." In this respect the word is similar to *police*. As a collective, *personnel* may take either a singular or a plural verb—a singular when it is thought of as meaning a body, a plural when it is thought of as soldiers, employes, or members of a staff. *See* NUMERALS WITH COLLECTIVES.

PERSONS

See PEOPLE, PERSONS.

PERSUADE

Takes preposition *to*. *See* CONVINCE, PERSUADE.

PERSUADED

Takes preposition *by* or *of*.

PERTINENT

Takes preposition *to*.

PERVERT

Takes preposition *from*.

PHANTOM APPOSITION

"He is an amateur diplomat, a quality shared by many of

his noncareer predecessors in this post." It is one thing to have a whole clause or even a sentence as the antecedent of a relative pronoun (*See* WHICH), but here we have a noun in apposition to an unexpressed idea that the reader must extract from an antecedent phrase. The reader is thus forced to do the work the writer should have done. "Amateur diplomat" is not a "quality." Make it either "His forte is amateur diplomacy, a quality, etc." or "He is an amateur diplomat, as were many of, etc."

PHASE OUT
See FAD WORDS.

PHONY
Phony is slang and therefore inappropriate in this context: "The counsel for the defendant conceded that an alleged interview with Miss Taylor that led her to sue for libel was a phony." Despite the abundance of synonyms for the word, both noun and adjective—*fake, sham, spurious, bogus, counterfeit, charlatan, imposter*—its prospects for a long life are unusually good, perhaps because it often has a flavor—a scornful flavor—that the synonyms do not possess.

PINCH HITTER
As a synonym for substitute or replacement, the phrase is a weary cliché. In addition, its use usually does not conform to the original intent of the word. In baseball, where the word originated, a pinch hitter is a player sent in to bat because his manager believes he will do a better job under the circumstances than the man being replaced. In this sense a tenor hastily inserted into the cast to replace a singer who is indisposed is not a "pinch-hitting tenor"; he is not expected to do even as good a job as the missing star, much less a better one. The word can, by extension, be used this way, but why do it?

PIQUED
Takes preposition *at* or *by*.

333

PIVOTAL

That which is *pivotal* is something on which an issue turns; it is something crucial. To say, "The election race in Illinois, pivotal state with its twenty-seven electoral votes, is close," is to suggest that the whole election turns on Illinois. If so, well and good. But if not, the writer should select one of many words that might suit his meaning more exactly: *important, vital, essential, critical.*

PLACE, USED WITH ADVERBIAL FORCE

See ADVERBIAL FORCE IN NOUNS.

PLEASED

Takes preposition *at, by,* or *with.*

PLENTY

"The Weather Bureau forecasts 'earmuff weather' for New Year's Day—no rain or snow but plenty cold." Whether *plenty* is being used here as an adjective or an adverb, it is a casualism. Good writing would demand *plenty of,* or a different phrase altogether.

PLUNGED

Takes preposition *in* (despair); *into* (water).

PLURALS

What follows is a miscellany of quirks concerning the formation of *plurals.*

1. The word *general* is either an adjective or a noun. When it is used as an adjective in a compound title, the plural is formed by adding "s" to the noun, as *postmasters general, attorneys general, consuls general.* In military titles general is a noun and therefore it is the element that takes the "s," as *lieutenant generals, adjutant generals.* Similarly the noun in *court-martial* is *court*; therefore, *courts-martial.*

2. Plurals of proper names ending in "y" are normally formed by adding "s," as the two *Germanys* (not Germanies),

the three *Marys*, the *Fogartys*, the two *Kansas Citys*. There are a few, but very few, exceptions to this rule, such as *Mercuries*, the *Two Sicilies*, the *Rockies*, the *Alleghenies*, and the *Ptolemies*.

3. Names ending in "s" form their plurals by adding "es," as the *Joneses*, the *Jameses*. Use of an apostrophe rather than the "es," as in, "The J. R. Crews' have been married forty years," borders on the illiterate.

4. Plurals of foreign words that have been taken into English vary. On one hand we have *alumni, beaux, data, strata*, and *phenomena*. On the other hand, we have *stadiums* and (usually) *curriculums, indexes, appendixes*. The choice of the foreign or the Anglicized plural will sometimes rest with whether the word is being used as a technical one in a specialized field or in an everyday setting. In the latter case the vote should normally go to the Anglicized form.

5. A few plurals seem almost unreasonable: *mongooses, still lifes, talismans*.

6. There is sometimes confusion about whether to use the singular or the plural after the prepositions *between* and *from*. This problem is discussed under BETWEEN AND FROM.

PLUS

"The determination of the French Army to win at least one war, plus the political manipulation of hardly more than a few hundred rich French-Algerian settlers, have lost North Africa to the West." No. The verb should be singular—"has." *Plus* is a preposition meaning with the addition of, not a conjunction equivalent to *and*. *See also* NUMBER *and* MINUS.

POINT

For *Up to a point, see* DEGREE.

POINT OUT

See EMPHASIZE.

POLITICKING

The word must have a "k," as must *politicked*, in the same

335

way that the past tense and participial forms of the verb *picnic* must have a "k." *Webster's Third New International* gives the present tense as *politick*, but *Webster's* (no relation) *New World* gives it as *politic*. The vote in this quarter goes to the *New World*. Thus, the forms of the word, which means to campaign or pursue political activities, are: present tense, *politic*; past tense, *politicked*; participle, *politicking*. See ARCING, ARCKING.

PORTMANTEAU WORDS
See CENTAUR WORDS.

POSSESSED
Takes preposition *of*, *by*, or *with*.

POSSESSIVES
Undoubtedly we are witnessing these days a reversion in part from the prepositional genitive—*the specialty of the day*—to the simple " 's" genitive of olden days—*the day's specialty*. This reversion was rather wryly forecast twoscore years ago by Fowler. His teeth were set on edge at that time by such possessives as *Ontario's Prime Minister*. Most of us today have somewhat less sensitive teeth. The reversion, however, is not a complete one and probably never will be. Whereas we may be able to accept *Ontario's Prime Minister*, we still cringe at a form like this: "Until recent years they wore dresses of black bombazine, a fabric unheard of since the century's turn."

The distinction that used to be made, and still is to some extent, is that the prepositional genitive is associated with things, whereas the " 's" genitive is associated with animate beings. At no time, however, was this distinction an ironclad rule. Curme cites the example "A book's chances depend more on its selling qualities than its worth." He points out that to take the " 's" genitive "the thing must usually have some sort of individual life like a living being, but this idea of life may be very faint. It is faintest when the name of a thing is used as the subject of a gerund [*See* GENITIVE WITH GERUND], where it is often not felt

at all." There can be a suggestion of animation, of personification, in *Ontario's Prime Minister*, just as there is in *death's door*,
Love's Labour's Lost, or the *storm's fury*. The " 's" genitive is
often used with inanimate things for poetic effect: *April's breeze*,
mountain's rim, *river's trembling edge*. It is used also in familiar
phrases such as *for pity's sake* and *duty's call*. And these
days we do not grit our teeth at the *nation's well-being*, *yesterday's newspaper*, the *sun's warmth*, the *ship's propeller*, a *year's
study*, a *day's journey*, or *states' rights*, although we may well grit
them at the *table's top* or the *century's turn*. For use of the apostrophe in possessives, *see* PUNCTUATION.

POSSIBILITY

Takes preposition *of*.

POSSIBLE

Knowledge of the meaning of *possible* is common, but so
are the misuses of the word. Briefly, it means capable of happening or of being done, attained, achieved, or the like. One common
misuse is that of the after-dinner speaker: "Our thanks go to the
committee for making this affair possible." Ridiculous. The affair
was always possible; what the committee did was to transform
the possibility into reality.

Another misuse perhaps arises from the stereotyped phrase
"as possible," indicating a maximum effort. Although it is all
right for you to say to the dentist, "I'll be as brave as possible,"
it is not all right for him to say, "I'll try not to hurt you any more
than possible." He does not mean *possible*; he means *necessary*.
Still another misuse is following *possible* with a pleonastic
"may," as in this utterance: "I think it is quite possible that we
may be on the threshold of setting up new methods for dealing
with each other on international problems." The "may be"
should be converted to "are." It should go without saying that it
is entirely proper to precede *possible* with "may," as in, "It may
be possible to set up new methods. . . ." Here there is no redundancy but rather a conjecture as to the possibility.

A form of redundancy that crops up in newspapers occasionally is this one: "A possible suspect in the North Brunswick mass murders was picked up here today." If a man is a suspect, he is possibly the criminal. Delete *possible*. Finally, there is the darling of police reporters, the *possible fracture*: "The victim suffered fractured ribs, a possible fractured jaw, and contusions and abrasions [that means *bruises and cuts*] of the face and body." It may be finical to point out that all fractures are *possible* and that suffering a *possible fracture* is something like setting a *near-record* (*See* NEAR-RECORD). It is also apparent that the *possible fracture* is as well entrenched in the press as the *alleged thief* (*See* ALLEGED, ACCUSED, SUSPECTED). Still it is difficult to resist the temptation to point out that it is just as easy to write *possibly* as it is to write *possible*. But the pointing out is done without much hope. *See also* FEASIBLE FOR POSSIBLE.

POSTPONE
See DELAY, POSTPONE.

POT-BELLY
See BELLY.

PRACTICABLE, PRACTICAL

What is *practicable* is capable of being done; what is *practical* is what is capable of being done usefully or valuably. It may be *practicable*, for instance, to convert the nation's railways into airways for electronically guided, low-flying, safe, all-weather jet planes, but the plan may not be *practical*. (Incidentally, did anybody ever investigate to determine whether it really is *practical?*)

PRACTICALLY, VIRTUALLY

Practically means, in the strictest sense, in practice or for practical purposes. No question about its use arises when it is contrasted with *hypothetically* or *theoretically*—as in, "Hypothetically communism seems sound, but practically it doesn't work."

However, by a very easy extension *practically* is also used to mean as good as. In this sense it impinges on the meaning of *virtually*, which denotes almost, as good as, or in effect. Thus the two words have come to mean just about the same thing, and sometimes their meanings can be kept separate only by the closest study of the context. For most situations the words are *practically* (for practical purposes) indistinguishable, as well as *virtually* (almost or in effect) indistinguishable.

Both Partridge and Evans quote an example from Sir A. P. Herbert concerning an appropriate use of *practically*: You may say that a family is *practically* extinct when its sole survivor is a childless old man who is dying. The family is, for practical purposes, extinct. That is quite true. But let it be noted that you could also properly say that the family is *virtually* (i.e., almost or in effect) extinct. On the other hand, if there is only enough coffee in the house for one more meal, it would not be altogether proper to say, "We are practically out of coffee." As a practical matter you are not out of coffee because there is still some left; however, you are *virtually* (almost) out of coffee.

Much ado about very little? Undoubtedly. If after thought you find it almost impossible to draw a distinction in any given context, don't fret. The words are just about interchangeable now, and half a century from now they most likely will be completely so.

PRECEDENCE
Takes preposition *of*.

PRECEDENT (adj.)
Takes preposition *to*.

PRECEDENT (n.)
Takes preposition *for* or *of*.

PRECIPITATE, PRECIPITOUS
These two words spring from the same root, but usage reserves *precipitous* for physical characteristics ("a precipitous

339

cliff") and *precipitate* for actions ("a precipitate departure" or "precipitate changes"). Incorrect: "The NBC position was that precipitous reforms in publicity releases rather than on the air were not very meaningful." Here is a mnemonic device: Think of the "s" in *precipitous* as standing for "steep" and the "a" in *precipitate* as standing for "abrupt." There is also the adjective *precipitant,* which is close in meaning to *precipitate;* it denotes rash, hasty, abrupt.

PRECLUDED
Takes preposition *from.*

PREDESTINED
Takes preposition *to* or *for.*

PREDICATE
The verb *predicate* is one that most writers should have no occasion to use in a lifetime. It is used fairly often, however, and in most instances loosely or erroneously: "The other defendants were discharged because their convictions could be predicated only on wiretap evidence." In good usage *predicate* is not synonymous with to base upon or found on. It means to affirm one thing of another: "In his logical argument he predicated the inherent greed of man." Does that sound like the kind of verb you would have much use for? Then why not forget it? Incidentally, the books all warn against misusing *predicate* for predict, but this misuse of the word seems to be the only one that is not at all common.

PREDICT
See PROPHESY.

PREFACE (n.)
Takes preposition *of* or *to.*

PREFERENCE
Takes preposition *to, over, before,* or *above.*

PREFER . . . THAN

The normal preposition following *prefer* is *to* or *over*—"I prefer bourbon to Scotch" or "I prefer bourbon over Scotch." A difficulty arises, however, when an infinitive follows *prefer*. You cannot say, "I prefer to drink bourbon to to drink Scotch." One way out is to substitute "rather than" for "to"—as in, "I prefer to drink bourbon rather than to drink Scotch." This is undoubtedly pleonastic because the sense of "rather" involves preference. Still it is also undoubtedly idiomatic, and idiom often overrides reason.

If the redundancy offends you, however, there are other escape hatches: You can substitute "would rather" for *prefer*, or you can change the infinitive to a participle, making it "I prefer drinking bourbon to drinking Scotch." Or, as was clear at the outset, you can give up "drinking" altogether.

PREGNANT

Takes preposition *with* or *by*.

PREJUDICE

There are two things to be noted about this word. One is that although *prejudice* means a preformed judgment either for or against, it is most often used to mean a judgment against. It is used, that is, in a pejorative sense unless something in the context indicates otherwise—as in "I have a prejudice in his favor" or "I may be prejudiced, but I like abstract expressionism." The second thing to be noted is that the word is often used loosely—too loosely—in condemnation of someone with whom a writer disagrees. In addition to denoting a preformed judgment, *prejudice* means an opinion derived from extraneous considerations or one that is not reasoned. A book reviewer writes, for instance: "The book is not helped at all by Mr. Adams's use of Copey as a clothesline for airing his own prejudices about crackpot theorists of education. . . ." For all the reviewer knows, Mr. Adams may have spent a lifetime working out his ideas and may have formed his judgments quite reasonably. If so, his ideas are not *prejudices*. *See also* BIAS.

PREJUDICIAL

Takes preposition *to*.

PREMISE

"He was serving a sentence for breaking into a premise in an attempted robbery." In logic alone can you have *a premise*; in legal matters the word is used only in the plural. And that means also that you cannot speak of *a premises*. One is reminded, although Heaven alone knows why, of Sidney Smith's remark on seeing two lower-class English women arguing across a back fence: "They will never agree. They are arguing from different premises."

PREOCCUPIED (adj.)

Takes preposition *with* or *by*.

PREPARATORY

It does not mean prior to or before. "As the former Far Eastern commander reviewed his service in the Orient preparatory to leaving for Paris. . . ." The review in no sense prepared him for his departure; all the writer meant was that one event preceded the other.

Preparatory takes the preposition *to*.

PREPOSITION AT END

For years and years Miss Thistlebottom has been teaching her bright-eyed brats that no writer would end a sentence with a preposition if he knew what he was about. The truth is that no good writer would follow Miss Thistlebottom's rule, although he might occasionally examine it to see if there was any merit in it. There will be no mention here of the boy who whined, "What did you bring that book for me to be read to out of up for?" Nor will there be any mention of Winston Churchill's complaint about arrant nonsense (or pedantry), "up with which I will not put." But those two bromides state the case for and against Miss Thistlebottom.

It is well to consider that a sentence ending with a preposition is sometimes clumsy, often weak. For instance: "He felt it offered the best opportunity to do fundamental research in chemistry, which was what he had taken his Doctor of Philosophy degree in." The end of a sentence is a conspicuous point and therefore can be a strong point. The end of the sentence just quoted is like the last sputter of an engine going dead.

Sometimes, however, a preposition can itself provide strength at the end of a sentence. This occurs when the preposition carries the real import and the verb has a rather low charge; in such instances heavy stress—perhaps the heaviest stress of the sentence —falls on the preposition, and idiom demands that it appear at the end. Examples: "He didn't know what he was getting into"; "I found this tool but I don't know what it is for"; "He didn't know what it was all about."

Instances like these are not usual, however. In most sentences ending with prepositions, the stress falls not on the preposition but on the word preceding it. And yet the sentences are still good. Why? Because they are idiomatic and have been constructed that way from Shakespeare's "We are such stuff as dreams are made on" to today's "Music to read by." They are a natural manner of expression. Examine a handful: "It's nothing to sneeze at"; "Something to guard against"; "You don't know what I've been through"; "He is a man who can be counted on"; "I'm not sure what the cake was made of." Surely there is nothing amiss with these idiomatic constructions. Woe to Miss Thistlebottom if she tries to "correct" them. She won't have a leg on which to stand.

That last sentence implies the caution that should go forth to the writer: If by trying to avoid ending a sentence with a preposition you have seemed to twist words out of their normal order and have created a pompous-sounding locution, abandon the effort. Indeed, there is no reason to make the effort at all, unless the sentence sounds like the final sputter the engine has come to. Like that one.

PREPOSITION PILE-UP

Preposition pile-up is exemplified by this sentence, manu-

343

factured for the occasion: "The rocket will rise to from between about 100 and 200 miles to between about 700 and 800 miles." Such clumsy constructions most often arise when a range is being specified. Most often only two prepositions pile up, and it is easy to eliminate one of them. For instance: "Under the new plan industry would pay taxes on between twenty and thirty per cent of its investment income." It can be changed to "taxes on twenty to thirty per cent."

Sometimes the word *at* used superfluously causes preposition pile-up: "Most of them are priced at under $10"; "I was surprised to find the average attendance ranging at between 500 and 1,000." When it is recalled that *at* denotes a specific point, it is obvious that the word is not only excess baggage in the two sentences cited, but also erroneous, since no exact point is being referred to but rather any point within the specified bounds. The phrase *at about* ("The crowd was estimated at about 1,000") is open to the same objection, but here the remedy is to drop the *about. See* ABOUT.

PREPOSITIONS

Is it dissimilar *from* or dissimilar *to?* Is it enjoin *to, from, against,* or what? These are questions that cannot be answered with rules. The proper preposition is a matter of idiom; and idioms, if they do not come "naturally," must be either learned or looked up. An attempt has been made in these pages to provide a place where they can be looked up. Rather than make a listing, it has been deemed more serviceable to include the idioms in the alphabetical places where the key words of the teams fall. It should go without saying that no compilation of this sort can be complete or should pretend to be complete. Moreover, not every word listed is followed by every preposition possible. For instance, a great many of the words could be followed by a *to* infinitive or a *by* phrase; these prepositions are not included, however. Likewise *about* and *over* are generalized prepositions in the sense of "concerning" and can be placed after many words; they, too, are not included in most instances. If a desired idiom cannot be found here or in an unabridged dictionary (and dictionaries do not in all instances provide this kind of information), the only thing to do is to consult three knowing friends and get a consensus.

PREPOSITIONS, SUPERFLUOUS

Prepositions are sometimes used redundantly: circle *around*, *from* hence, *from* whence, request *for*, out *of* (when direction is meant). The *out of* fault usually appears in this manner: "Mr. Lumumba slipped out of the side door of his official residence." This would seem to mean that he had been in the door—not the doorway—and that he emerged from it. Make it "out the side door." *Out of* is not, of course, incorrect per se; *out of a job, two out of three, out of charity* are all wholly proper phrases. The preposition *of* gives trouble also in the phrase *off of*, which must be characterized as a low casualism: "He borrowed $5 off of me"; "The doctor took the patients off of barbiturates." Either change *off of* to *from* (first sentence) or delete *of* (second sentence).

PREREQUISITE (adj.)

Takes preposition *to*.

PREREQUISITE (n.)

Takes preposition *of*.

PRESENT (vb.)

Takes preposition *to* or *with*.

PRESENTLY

Presently originally meant now, but the Oxford designates that meaning as obsolete. Since the Oxford was printed, however, the old meaning has been revived by writers who apparently think it has a more important sound than *now*. Nothing is gained by blurring the word and giving it two meanings. *Presently* is better reserved for *before long, forthwith, or soon*.

345

PRESIDE

Takes preposition *over* or *at*.

PRESUME

See ASSUME, PRESUME. *Presume* takes preposition *on* or *upon*.

PRESUMPTIVE, PRESUMPTUOUS

Presumptuous is almost never misused; *presumptive* often is. *Presumptive* means founded on a presumption or affording a basis for a supposition, and it is chiefly a lawyer's term. *Presumptuous* means taking excessive liberties, presuming too much, arrogant. The confusion of the two words is exemplified here: "Mr. Nehru said it would be presumptive of him to suggest to the United States that it should end nuclear tests." Mr. Nehru meant he would be presuming too much, hence *presumptuous*.

PRETENTIOUS PLURALS

Most nouns have a plural form, and almost any noun is capable of having one. The only argument to be made here is against the use of a plural for pretentious effect, for the scientific sound of it, and sometimes regardless of whether the plural signifies two or more things that can actually be differentiated.

What used to be the *value* of, say, a course in literature is now the *values* of it. A *specific* used to be a general term for a trait, or a medical term for a precise remedy for an ailment; now in the plural it is a haughty substitute for *details* or *specifications*: "the specifics of the de Gaulle plan." In addition we are beset by *attitudes, learnings, skills, strengths*, and—uttered by teachers, no less—*knowledges*. If the pedagogues are what formerly were called teachers of English, they now profess to be giving instruction in something dubbed "language arts"—that is, they teach reading, spelling, writing, listening, speaking into a microphone, and, if there is any time left over, grammar. But *language arts* certainly has a more imposing ring than plain "English."

As was said at the outset, there is no quarrel with plurals as such—that is, legitimate plurals—but when a writer finds himself

346

using *correlations, experiences, materials,* or *techniques,* he should ask himself whether he is using the exact word or merely making an important sound. *See also* INSIDE TALK.

PREVAIL

Takes preposition *on, upon, with, against,* or *over.*

PREVENT

The form "Immigration officials could not prevent him entering the country" is widely disapproved. (*See* GENITIVE WITH GERUND.) Better is "prevent his entering" or "prevent him from entering."

PREVENTIVE, PREVENTATIVE

Most authorities agree that the form *preventive* is preferable.

PREVIOUS

See SIMULTANEOUS.

PRINCIPAL, PRINCIPLE

The noun that means a basic truth or a determined course of action is *principle.* The noun or adjective pertaining to the head man or to the first or foremost is *principal.* If you need a mnemonic device, you might relate the ending of *principal* to the beginning of *a*lmighty or *a*ll-important.

PRIOR TO

A faddish affectation for *before.* Would you say *posterior to* in place of *after?*

PROCEED

A fancy word for *go, walk, travel,* or *move.* Considering that from its very derivation (*pro,* forward, and *cedere,* to move) *proceed* means to go forward, there is almost a contradiction in logic in this example: "The trio of happy Hibernians had then proceeded back to the sheriff's office." A worse example: "He threw his car into reverse and proceeded out of the garage."

347

PRODIGAL

Takes preposition *of*.

PRODUCTIVE

Takes preposition *of*.

PROFICIENT

Takes preposition *in* or *at*.

PROFIT

Takes preposition *by* or *from*.

PROGENITOR

A *progenitor* is an ancestor, a forefather, not an originator or inventor. The word is misused here: "Yale and Harvard, twin progenitors of the American game of football, play for the eightieth time today." Yale and Harvard may (or may not) have devised the American game, but its *progenitors* were, perhaps, Rugby or association football.

PROHIBIT

Takes preposition *from*.

PROLEPSIS

See RHETORICAL FIGURES AND FAULTS *and also* EX POST FACTO CONSTRUCTION.

PRONE

Tracing its origin to *pro*, meaning forward, *prone* denotes a face-down position, not merely a horizontal one. It is opposed to *supine*, a position in which one lies face upward.

PRONOUNCE

Takes preposition *on* (thing); *against* (person).

PRONOUNS

Pronouns and their reference words ("antecedents" or

348

"principals," if you like) often cause trouble. This discussion concerns the main categories of difficulty. In addition, however, particular words and problems are examined elsewhere in the vocabulary—for example, under BOTH, EACH, EITHER (3), NONE, THAT AND WHICH, WHAT. What this means is, in short, that if you don't find what you are looking for here, look elsewhere. Following, then, are the categories:

1. WRONG OR AMBIGUOUS REFERENCE WORD. "She was one of ten chicks Mr. and Mrs. Sherry purchased some time ago when they were six weeks old." When who was six weeks old? Keep in mind that pronouns have an affinity for the nearest noun. That does not mean, however, that the nearest noun always and inevitably governs. For instance: "Secretary of State Dulles told Foreign Secretary Eden that he had a 'bad habit'—doodling." The sentence is reasonably clear despite the fact that the noun nearest to *he* is "Eden," to which it is not related. The sentence would be beyond any quibbling doubt if "told" was changed to "confessed to." Proximity of a pronoun to its antecedent is, to be sure, an aid to meaning. Still, clarity in the use of pronouns is not a mere matter of geographical position but rather one of meaning and context. It is the job of the careful writer to spot ambiguities and, having spotted them, to decide whether to make a change of words or to make a change of construction to clear up the trouble.

2. IMAGINED, BUT NOT ACTUAL, REFERENCE WORD. "The broad-spectrum antibiotics have so simplified pneumonia therapy that it is now frequently treated at home." When the writer set down *it* he had "pneumonia" on his mind, but "pneumonia" is serving here as an adjective; the only noun is "therapy," which, of course, is not what the *it* refers to.

3. NO REFERENCE WORD AT ALL. "Dr. Barnes expressed his views before executives of city councils of churches. It was one of a number of meetings of. . . ." Perhaps the writer thought he had said "a meeting of executives" but he hadn't, and the *it* is left stranded. Here is another instance involving an absent-minded writer: "As a magistrate, he stirred some interest by holding invalid the arrest of persons for merely sleeping in the sub-

way. The police still do it, however." The police still do what?

4. CONFUSION OF ANTECEDENTS. "A carelessly playful lion failed to look before he leaped at the circus in Madison Square Garden last night, knocking down his trainer instead of jumping over his head." The word *his* appears in two parallel constructions and would be expected to refer to the same antecedent. But no—one refers to the lion and the other to the trainer. As a general thing, the same pronoun should not be used successively to refer to different antecedents unless the differentiation is made sharp and clear. Incidentally, the next category indicates how the difficulty in the lion sentence might have been averted.

5. IT AND SHE. (*a*) *Animals*. Is an animal a *he*, a *she*, or an *it*? There is no generally accepted rule, but in some quarters the guide that is followed is to use *he* or *she* if the animal has a name and thus is personalized, so to speak; otherwise to use the pronoun *it*. (*b*) *Ships*. Sailors like to personalize their ships and, for reasons that one can adduce according to his bent, think of them as females. Landlubbers could well do likewise and refer to ships as *she*. But, once committed to the feminine pronoun, the writer should stay with it and not vacillate, as the writer of this caption did: ". . . the German U-505, as she was carried early yesterday to Chicago's Museum of Science and Industry, where it will be set up as a memorial." (*c*) *Countries*. Here again there is no generally accepted rule. A serviceable guide is to use the feminine pronoun in referring to a country except when the name includes a common noun. Surely countries have sufficient individuality and personality to be dignified by personification, even if they do not always act like normal, decent people. Thus, "France will state her position"; "Russia massed her troops." But, with names including common nouns, *it* is more appropriate: "The Soviet Union declared it would attend"; "The United States drafted its note." There are, however, exceptions: "Guatemala, he said, is so small that a soldier could march across her in one day." She may be small, but she doesn't have to be downtrodden. The feminine pronoun should not be used when the reference is to the country as a physical, geographical domain rather than an abstract entity. The following illustrates a different kind of ab-

350

surdity: "The Premier agreed that France was 'the sick man of Europe,' but he denied she was decadent." You may or may not accept the rule suggested here that nations should be considered to be feminine, but one rule you must accept is not to be ridiculous. Substitute "the nation" or "the country" for *she* in the sentence cited.

6. PRONOUN AFTER "ANYONE," "ANYBODY," "EACH," "EVERYONE," "EVERYBODY," "NEITHER," "NO ONE," "NOBODY," "SOMEONE," "SOMEBODY." The problem here is typified by the sentence "Give everyone credit for having the courage of their convictions." The essence of the problem is that all the words listed above are singular in form but often plural in connotation—yet in English many of our pronouns do not have common number, that is, a form that is equally at home with a singular or a plural antecedent. In a sentence like the one cited, therefore, we have to make a hard choice between a singular pronoun or a plural pronoun or else we must change the antecedent. The use of *their* in such contexts is common enough in spontaneous, casual speech, and even occurs occasionally in the work of reputable writers. Yet the writer of craftsmanship and taste will reject the grammatical inconsistency of the combination of a singular noun and a plural pronoun. He will examine the possibilities available. They are either to use *his or her* or to use simply *his*. The first alternative is stilted and is to be shunned except when the issue of sex is present and pointed, as in, "The pool is open to both men and women, but everyone must pay for his or her towel." Commonly, however, the word to be used is *his*, as the nearest approach in this imperfect language of ours to a neutral pronoun in such a situation. Therefore: "Give everyone credit for having the courage of his convictions." There are rare instances in which even this possibility is not available. For instance: "And so everybody took their guitars and songs, their poetry and perambulators, their high-bouncers and dogs, and went peacefully home." Changing *their* in each instance to *his* or even *his or her* will not solve the problem. The solution here is to recognize the imperfection of the language and modify the wording—just as we do when we find ourselves in a situation in which we require the non-exist-

351

ent past tense of *must*. The thing to do is change the antecedent, making it "they all," "the crowd," or "the visitors." This is no ignominious defeat because nothing has been lost; it is rather a facing of the facts of syntax.

7. SWITCH IN PERSON OF PRONOUN. This error is a kind of swapping of horses in midstream—usually an abrupt change from third person to first person in the same clause. "I wonder if you will entertain the same admiring attitude toward the writer of this letter, who at the age of seventy-one is returning to face my [make it *his*] accusers under the McCarran Act." What is involved here is inconsistency of point of view. Another and similar example: "I was a middle-aged man whose doctor had told me I [make it *him he*] must rest."

8. PRONOUN PRECEDING ANTECEDENT. This is not a serious fault unless the reader is kept in suspense too long, e.g.: "Pummeling his opponent to a pulp and showing the strength he had acquired in weeks of intensive training, during which he had obviously picked up some fine points of boxing, Artie (Kid) Alonzo scored a quick knockout. . . ." Fowler says: "The pronoun should seldom precede its principal." To which one might add, maybe that is why the "principal" is called an "antecedent." Regarding the sentence quoted, *see also* ONE IDEA TO A SENTENCE.

9. CASE OF PRONOUN. The problem of *It is I* versus *It is me* displays how sharp the cleavage between written and spoken English can sometimes be. There can be no doubt that formal grammar demands the nominative case (*I*) of a pronoun joined to the subject of the sentence by a copulative, or linking, verb. But there can also be no doubt that speakers of the language, as contrasted with writers, often tend to think of the position after the verb as the place where an object usually appears and, hence, to use the objective case for a word in that position. Therefore it is not unusual to find in spoken language (and sometimes in written language, too) such sentences as, "He did it, not me"; "I'm sure it was him"; "There will only be us two at dinner." Although all these (including *It is me*) are common, and most of them even acceptable, in spoken language, they are not acceptable in what

should be the more precise field of written language. Curme, who certainly cannot be classed as a linguistic mossback, has this to say on the subject: "The plain drift of our language is to use the accusative of personal pronouns as the common case form for the nominative and accusative relations. . . . It is to be hoped that all who are interested in accurate expression will oppose this general drift by taking more pains to use a nominative where a nominative is in order. . . . It is gratifying to observe that this careless usage, though still common in colloquial speech, is in general less common in our best literature than it once was."

The converse of the misuse of the objective case where the nominative is called for is also fairly prevalent in spoken language: "Between you and I"; "Four years of hard work are required for he who seeks a degree"; "Let's you and I go to the theater tonight." In each instance the objective case is required. Such errors are often committed by those who have been made gun-shy by *It's me,* and the blunders are usually a form of OVER-REFINEMENT. *See also* WHO, WHOM, WHOEVER, WHOMEVER.

PROPHESY

Although *prophesy* is a synonym for *predict,* it has the connotation of inspiration or occult knowledge. It is not appropriate in a context like this: "In reviewing gains from the joint American-Canadian hydroelectric generating plant at Massena, N. Y., Mr. Moses prophesied even greater savings for users of current from the Niagara Falls plant." Nor would a meteorologist of the United States Weather Bureau enjoy being called a *weather prophet;* here the term suggests aching corns, rheumatism, and mysterious intuitions. The weather man is a *predicter* or *forecaster. Predict* means to infer from information or foretell on the basis of facts. Occasionally *prophesy* is the suitable word: "This golden age, the Mayor prophesied, would be 'one which will find public and private effort and enthusiasm dovetailing to produce maximum benefits to those who live, work, and seek recreation in our city.' " The Mayor was speaking of a vision rather than of a picture based on information.

353

PROPITIOUS

Takes preposition *to* or *for*.

PROPORTIONS

"A building of huge proportions"; ". . . super-tankers whose proportions exceed the present facilities of the canal." Strictly speaking, *proportions* expresses a relationship of one part to another, or of parts to the whole. Except in informal usage it has nothing to do with size. A better word in the examples cited would be *dimensions* or *size*.

PROPOSITION

As a noun, *proposition* means a well delineated proposal. Its use to mean a project, affair, or enterprise is a casualism. Casualisms in serious writing are fine in their place; they may be useful to lend a particular flavor to what is being related, or to convey a thought for which no other word is suitable (FIX, for example, to mean an unethical prearrangement). But aside from these exceptions they tend to turn sweet water brackish. If you read that "West Berlin's isolation and the loss of its historical hinterland have kept it a shaky proposition from the businessman's viewpoint," the conversational misuse of *proposition* seems out of place in writing that is not conversational. Surely freshness in writing need not depend on the man in the street's use, or misuse, of language.

As a verb, *proposition* is even lower in the linguistic scale. It is a slang word meaning either to approach someone with a proposal, usually improper or illegal, or to ask sexual favors.

PROTAGONIST

From a film ad: "A study of mores, sometimes severe, always caustic . . . the relations of one protagonist to another." From a theater review: "The main protagonist of the play is one Nick Bellino." From a news article: "Inejiro Asanuma . . . an influential protagonist of closer ties between Japan and the Communist world." The word *protagonist* comes from the Greek *protos* (first) and *agonistes* (actor) and, as could be surmised

354

from this derivation, it means *the* (not *a*) leading character. That makes the first two of the foregoing citations wrong. In the third example the assumption seems to be that the first part of the word *protagonist* is related to the prefix "pro," meaning for, in behalf of, partisan of; the word therefore is used as if it meant proponent or champion. This, too, is erroneous. The error undoubtedly arises from thinking of the word as if it were the opposite of *antagonist*, of which there can be any number. The things to remember are that a *protagonist* is a one-of-a-kind character and that the word does not inherently indicate that he is for or against anything.

PROTEST

Takes preposition *against*.

PROTOTYPE

It's a first model of something; therefore it is tautological to write, "The prototype models, which will be shipped to the Los Alamos Scientific Laboratory. . . ." Make it "the prototypes," deleting "models."

PROVEN

"The effectiveness of the treatment was proven." *Proven*, a Scottish participle of *prove*, has spread and is not uncommon in this country. But the regular form, *proved*, is to be preferred. The participial adjective *proven* is used in some technical areas, as "a proven oil field."

PROVIDE

Takes preposition *with*, *for*, or *against*.

PROVIDED

See DANGLERS.

PROVIDED, PROVIDING

Both words, though originally participles, have long histories of use as conjunctions. But those of us who were tutored by

Miss Thistlebottom are conditioned to recoil from *providing*. There is no reason for this; still we recoil. The words should not be used as a mere synonym for the more general word *if*; they imply a stipulation or condition of some kind. Thus, you would say, "Guests may have meals in their rooms if they prefer," but you would not say, "Guests may have meals in their rooms provided [or *providing*] they prefer." You could correctly say, "provided [or *providing*] they pay for the service."

PUBLICIST

"Publicist Found Dead." The man referred to in the headline was a press agent. *Publicist* originally referred to an expert on public law, and then was more loosely applied to those who wrote on public issues. Despite the dictionary, need we debase the word still further to gratify those who strive to make the poorer seem the better?

PUNCTUATION

Punctuation marks are the traffic signs and signals placed along the reader's road. They tell him when to slow down and when to stop, and sometimes they warn him of the nature of the road ahead. Traffic engineers do not always agree on what signs should be used and where they should be placed, and neither do writers or editors. In fact, about the only things writers and editors do agree on in the matter of punctuation are that a period is placed at the end of a declarative sentence (except in headlines and advertising copy) and that a question mark is placed at the end of a sentence that genuinely asks a question.

Much of punctuation is arbitrary. Some of it is necessary to sense, as will appear in the section below on commas. Some of it is closely involved with grammar. The general tendency these days is to eliminate as much punctuation as possible, especially commas. But to carry this tendency to the extreme of trying to eliminate virtually all punctuation, as some suggest, is ill advised, to say the least. Where punctuation is used to prop up weak prose it might well be eliminated, but so might be the weak prose. Where punctuation is used to make things clearer or to facilitate reading it justifies itself, and to suggest eliminating it makes no more sense than to suggest eliminating a man's arms because they spoil the clean aesthetic lines of his body. Cadence, mood, and style all depend to some extent on punctuation, and they, too, make punctuation desirable. The listing that follows by no means constitutes a punctuation manual; rather it is a directory of the points that often bother, or at any rate should bother, the writer.

APOSTROPHE

1. In measures of time and space the genitive form is used: *two weeks' pay, forty hours' practice, a hair's breadth.* Occasionally words of this kind are used as an adjective-noun combination, and the apostrophe is then superfluous. In "a full-credit eight weeks' summer school" there is no genitive relationship between "eight weeks" and "school," any more than there is between "full-credit" and "school." It should be "full-credit eight-week(s) summer school." Similarly, in "fifty pounds pressure" there is no genitive relationship, and no apostrophe is needed. But these instances are exceptional.

2. In a plural noun used to modify another noun the normal practice is to use the apostrophe (*drivers' licenses, ladies' girdles*), but there is a tendency these days to accept the omission of the apostrophe in many instances: *teachers college, boys club, parents association.* That such forms are not logical is demonstrated by the fact that the apostrophe is usually deemed mandatory for nouns with irregular plurals: *men's club, children's hospital.* Yet the illogical form is widely accepted, though hesitantly. Unless the form without the apostrophe is an official title—as it is in *Governors Island* and *Teachers College of Columbia University* —a writer cannot err by following the normal practice of using the apostrophe. Of course, it is important to put the apostrophe in the right place, as this letter writer did not: "We are attaching to this letter the Board of Superintendent's full report." Needless to say, no such board has only one superintendent. Likewise it makes a difference whether you write, "She went to the little boy's room" or "She went to the little boys' room."

3. In possessives the normal practice is to add " 's" to the

noun: *John's, woman's, cat's.* When a proper noun ends in "s" the normal (but not universal) practice is also to add " 's": *James's, Thomas's, Jones's.* However, what is universally avoided, where possible, is a triple sibilant. If there are two sibilants in the name to begin with, the added "s" is omitted: Mr. *Moses' house, Texas' junior Senator, Jesus' wounds.* This practice of avoiding a triple sibilant applies also to some common nouns: *for goodness' sake, the rhesus' spryness, for conscience' sake.* Sometimes the triple sibilant cannot be avoided: *Texas' senior Senator, the Moses' son, Xerxes' second bridge.* Plurals of nouns ending in "s" form the possessive by adding merely an apostrophe: *girls', ladies', wives'.* Possessive personal pronouns never take an apostrophe: *its,* not *it's; theirs,* not *their's; hers,* not *her's.*

Even if the style of a publication calls for omission of "s" in the possessive of a name ending in a sibilant (*James', Jones'*), the "s" is added if the final letter, which in other circumstances might have an "s" sound, is silent: *Giraudoux's, Malraux's, François's.*

When it is desired to indicate the possessive case for two coordinate nouns, each takes " 's" in written prose—*John's and Jane's love affair*—although in spoken language it is common practice to indicate the possessive only for the second noun—*John and Jane's love affair.*

The use of the possessive case with lifeless things is discussed under **POSSESSIVES.**

4. In plurals of figures, letters, decades, years, and the like, " 's" is in favor: *three 4's, four A's, the '20's* (or, of course, *the Twenties*), *the 1800's* (or *the Eighteen Hundreds*), *B-52's, LST's, the non-U's.* Plurals of words cited as words rather than as concepts also are indicated by " 's": "There are too many *and's* in that sentence." On the other hand, if it is the sense of the words rather than merely the words as patterns of letters that is meant, no apostrophe is used: "There are too many ifs in your proposal."

5. In contractions the apostrophe replaces an omitted letter or letters: *don't, rock 'n' roll, wouldn't've.* Some writers are so timid that they think they are using contractions when they are in fact using whole words. Thus, they write, *'though, 'till,* and

'round, all of which without the apostrophe are card-carrying members of the English language.

COLON

The colon heralds fulfillment of a promise implied in what precedes it. It is sometimes equivalent to *for example,* but more often to *that is* or *this is what that means.* The colon is used when the sentence is intended to come almost to a dead stop. For example: "Two things are essential to success: ambition and hard work." However, when the sentence is not intended to be interrupted the colon is not used—more specifically it is not inserted between a verb and its object or a preposition and its object: "Two things essential to success are [no colon] ambition and hard work"; "Success is a combination of [no colon] ambition and hard work." The word immediately after a colon is capitalized only if what follows is a complete statement: "We stand at a great divide: We must trade or fade."

The colon is used to introduce quoted matter. The comma may be used for this purpose if the quotation is a single sentence or, at any rate, brief—"She said, 'No, I won't.'" But longer quotations require a more formal introduction—"The report of the Senate committee said:" (Followed by a paragraph, two paragraphs, or twenty paragraphs of quoted matter).

COMMA

The comma indicates the briefest pause of all punctuation marks. Some commas are mandatory, as in a series; others are optional and are inserted at will by the writer in the interest of clarity. The tendency these days is to use a minimum of commas. And if a writer feels the need to use a multitude of commas in a sentence, it is likely that the sentence is confused and requires recasting. Such a one is the passage cited under *Alliteration* in RHETORICAL FIGURES AND FAULTS: "In all such ways have the needs of men, the passions of people, and the pride of nations conspired, performing their earthbound best, to conceive a revolution, within and among themselves, to match in menace and in mystery, the assault on sky and space." Actually, in this con-

359

voluted sentence the last four commas do nothing to clarify the sentence and indeed make it jerkier than it needs to be. On the other hand, commas are sometimes indispensable to meaning. Prof. Maxwell Nurnberg of New York University, in an amusing article that appeared in one of the University's publications, offered pairs of sentences to bring out this point. Here are three samples:

a) What's the latest dope?
b) What's the latest, dope?

a) The Democrats, say the Republicans, are sure to win the next election.
b) The Democrats say the Republicans are sure to win the next election.

a) Do not break your bread or roll in your soup.
b) Do not break your bread, or roll in your soup.

Grave issues of law have hung on commas. Indeed, recently Michigan discovered that its state constitution inadvertently legalized slavery. Section 8, Article 2, read: "Neither slavery nor involuntary servitude, unless for the punishment of crime, shall ever be tolerated in this state." It was decided to move the comma after "servitude" and place it after "slavery."

Now for some comma categories.

1. WITH NONRESTRICTIVE TERMS. A restrictive, or defining term, is one that the preceding noun cannot do without because the term (word, phrase, or clause) pins it down or delimits it. A nonrestrictive term is one that merely provides additional or parenthetical information; it usually could be omitted without affecting the basic sense of what is being said. Example of a restrictive term: "Updike writes in the almost too brilliant story 'Lifeguard' that. . . ." Here "Lifeguard" defines or identifies the story that is being spoken of; it cannot be omitted. Example of a nonrestrictive term: "In a brilliant story, 'Lifeguard,' Updike writes. . . ." Here the name of the story is not essential to what is being said; it could be omitted without destroying the thought. The restrictive term is not enclosed in commas, whereas the non-

360

restrictive term is. In general, commas are used to set off incidental or parenthetical matter. Notice how the omission of a comma in the following sentence affects the meaning: "The luncheon was in honor of the three new Council representatives from Australia, Cuba, and Yugoslavia." As the sentence stands the meaning is that three new representatives are replacing three old ones. The intended meaning is that representatives of the three countries are new to the Council. The names of the countries are incidental or parenthetical; they are a nonrestrictive term and should be set off by a comma (perhaps even a dash) after "representatives." Another, and simpler, example: "The President was accompanied by his wife, Lady Bird." The name is a nonrestrictive term and expendable. Unless the President is a polygamist the comma is mandatory.

A common comma fault is what amounts to a reverse of the use of the comma with a nonrestrictive term. The fault is the use of commas with a restrictive or defining term, where none are indicated. Example: "A rejected suitor shot himself in the apartment of the entertainer, Beverly Aadland, early today, the police said." This punctuation suggests that Miss Aadland is the one and only entertainer. The name is a defining term and should not be set off by commas. On the other hand, it would be correct to write, "the apartment of an entertainer, Beverly Aadland."

Kindred situations in which the comma is necessary to convey the proper meaning appear in the following two sentences: (1) "Mrs. Anna Roosevelt Boettiger, only daughter of the late President Roosevelt, disclosed today plans for her third marriage to Dr. James Addison Halstead." Surely she is not marrying the same man for the third time. A comma is necessary after "marriage." (2) "Mayor Wagner has decided to seek a third term with Paul R. Screvane and Abraham D. Beame as running mates." Anyone not knowing the facts would be justified in assuming that Screvane and Beame were Wagner's running mates the first two times. This was not true, however. Therefore a comma is required after "term."

More on restrictive and nonrestrictive expressions appears under THAT AND WHICH.

2. IN A SERIES. Should it be "The colors are red, white and blue" or "The colors are red, white, and blue"? The answer is either; the authorities do not agree and never will agree on whether a comma should or should not precede the "and." The only rule is that once you have made your choice you should follow it consistently. The no-comma school does use a comma before the "and" in one situation: where semicolons are required to separate the previous members of the series. For instance: "The executive committee is made up of the president of the club; the secretary, who is a paid officer; the treasurer, who must be a certified public accountant; the first vice president, and a specially elected member." The semicolons are required because commas have already been appropriated for a different function: to set off subordinate clauses.

3. FOR PARENTHETICAL PURPOSES. Commas are used to enclose parenthetical phrases interpolated into a sentence. "As the lips and skin of the mask are in natural colors, the inventor says a very lifelike illusion is created." The inventor does not say it because the lips and skin are in natural colors; the illusion is created because the lips and skin are in natural colors. "The inventor says" is a parenthetical phrase and should carry commas fore and aft.

Sometimes the reverse of this error occurs: "This morning, some sources said, the total death count might reach more than 400." There is no parenthetical phrase here, as is proved by the use of "might" (governed by "said") rather than "may." Therefore both commas should be removed. *See also* PARENTHETICAL PHRASES.

4. FOR PHRASES WITH A COMMON TERMINATION. Sometimes two or more phrases have a common element, only one of which is expressed: "It is the best, if not the only, book on the undertaker's art." A common error is failure to insert the second comma. Sometimes a writer will neglect to insert both commas: "His achievements had not saved him from suggestions that he was at bottom only a Southern as distinguished from a national politician." Commas are necessary after "Southern" and "national."

362

A closely related situation is one in which an explanatory phrase appears in a sentence: "It recommended that population exposure to radioactive materials that cause somatic or bodily damage be limited to. . . ." There is no one-or-the-other meaning intended by the words "somatic or bodily damage"; the words "or bodily" are intended to explain "somatic." Therefore: "somatic, or bodily, damage."

5. BETWEEN COORDINATE CLAUSES. When the clauses are long and especially when they tend to go different ways (introduced by *but, not,* or *nor,* for instance), a comma is used to separate them. Examples: "The school was founded five years ago, but a first grade was added for the first time last year"; "The estates and clubs run by the British Civil Service were closed to her, and once on an excursion she and her party were given sandwiches to eat on the grass outside."

6. WITH SUBORDINATE CLAUSES. A subordinate clause, or even a long phrase, that precedes the principal clause is followed by a comma. Examples: "If the people of the United States are interested in not wasting public money, they must make efforts to see that such funds are properly administered"; "Because of the demand for passage that has grown up in the past week, the authorities have decided to put two packet boats a week on the Algiers-Marseilles run next week."

7. WITH INTERPOLATED WORDS OR PHRASES. Parenthetical elements like *of course, indeed, incidentally, nevertheless, as a matter of fact, actually* are usually set off by commas, but there is no general agreement about this. The word *too,* meaning also, is customarily set off by commas when it is in the middle of a sentence, although such a separation is not quite so frequent when *too* appears at the end of a sentence.

8. MISCELLANEOUS ERRORS:

a) *Comma masquerading as a series punctuation mark.* "A French administration spokesman announced today the arrest of five alleged slayers, three Europeans and two Moslems." Question: How many were arrested? As the sentence is punctuated, the answer could be either five or ten. When a comma setting off an appositive is capable of being mistaken for a series comma, it is mandatory to use a dash or a colon. In this instance a dash or a colon should appear after "slayers."

b) *Comma used in place of a colon.* "The Governor has another major message for the Legislature this week, the long awaited summary of his recommendations on higher education." This construction calls for a colon after "week." *See* COLON *above.*

c) *Comma used in place of a semicolon.* "Not only can he cook, he also prepares the family meals on occasion." The pause after "cook" is almost a full stop and calls for a stronger signal than a comma. If there were a "but" after "cook," however, the pause would be reduced and a comma would be sufficient punctuation. Sometimes in one of these *not-only-but* constructions the writer actually makes a full stop: "The Wahabis not only dominate women. They also maintain an absolute prohibition of alcohol."

DASH

The dash is a much used, often overused, piece of punctuation. Some writers almost seem to wish that dashes came in various strengths so that they could be used to enclose thoughts within thoughts within thoughts. Unless the dash is employed to indicate a breaking off of the thought ("I think you should not —but who am I to offer you advice?") or to mark a summing up at the end of a sentence ("Ambition and hard work—these are the ingredients of success"), it usually appears in pairs, performing the same function as parentheses: "Winners of Art Festival Awards in each of seven categories—painting, music, dance, theater, architecture, literature, and fashion—will be honored." When dashes do appear in pairs, the reader's expectation is that they are marking off a parenthetical statement, and it is not wise to disappoint that expectation as the writer of this sentence did: "The Weather Bureau made official what everybody had guessed —that this January was the coldest in a long time—since 1948." Taken separately, these uses of the dash are proper enough, but taken together, they are confusing. A colon after "guessed" would be an improvement. Perhaps more confusing is the sprinkling of dashes through a sentence like this: "Physicists at Columbia University are delving into the mysteries of the forces within the nucleus of the atom—source of atomic energy—with a powerful new tool—a beam of mesons—the sub-atomic particles believed to serve as the 'cosmic cement.' " A comma substituted for every dash except the one after "tool" would greatly clarify matters. Another example of a rash of dashes: "Nearly all tape machines have some indicator—a 'magic eye' tube, or better—a meter—that is supposed to tell you when the recording volume is set properly." Substitute a comma for the dash after "better."

As a footnote it may said that the present-day tendency is not to use any other punctuation mark together with the dash. In former days it was customary to write "Item:—" or "Dear Sir:—" and sometimes to follow a dash with a comma. These practices are now considered to be redundant punctuation.

EXCLAMATION POINT

The exclamation point (or "screamer" or "astonisher," as it is sometimes called in newspaper offices) is used sparingly in most writing because the statements that require it—those containing a strong emotional charge—are themselves relatively rare and because omitting the mark often produces a kind of understatement that is strong in itself. A general writing fault is to use the exclamation point needlessly; a specific one is to use it in a context like this: "It was bound to happen sometime! A bull got into a china shop here." A commentary appropriate to this usage appears in *The King's English,* by the Fowler brothers:

"When the exclamation mark is used after mere statements it deserves the name, by which it is sometimes called, the mark of admiration; we feel that the writer is indeed lost in admiration of his own wit or impressiveness."

Like other punctuation marks, the exclamation point is often indispensable to convey proper meaning. For illustration, if a man comes home sossled at 2 A.M. and says to his wife, "Evenin', precious; how's my li'l honeybunch?" her monosyllabic reply may have three meanings, depending on punctuation: (1) "Well." (She's feeling well, thanks.) (2) "Well?" ("I'm waiting for an explanation, buster. And don't call me honeybunch.") (3)

365

"Well!" ("You're a fine spectacle, you miserable creature!")

An example of an emotionally charged sentence requiring an exclamation point would be, " 'Hang the traitors!' the crowd shouted."

Since the exclamation point indicates strong feeling and often is intended to raise eyebrows, it is a favorite of the advertising fraternity. The most matter-of-fact statements often carry exclamation points intended to introduce a note of excitement: "Wheatlets are edible!" or "At last! Toothpicks at a price you can afford!!" And, of course, the words "Now!" and "New!" are never unattended by exclamation points. But those are tricks of salesmanship and bear no relationship to general writing.

HYPHEN

The world of the hyphen is anarchic. Such rules as there are tend to break down under the pressure of exceptions. The result is that in many instances the use of hyphens may be left to the taste and judgment of the writer.

Hyphens are necessary evils. They should therefore be used only when necessary. One such necessity is to avoid ambiguity. For example, if the sentence says that "The President's plan provides for nursing home care," what is meant: care at home by nurses or care in a nursing home? In this instance it was the latter that was intended, and the meaning could have been made unmistakable by writing "nursing-home care." Sometimes it is not ambiguity but absurdity that needs to be avoided. Here are two situations in which hyphens can eliminate absurdity: "They have enabled the five-inch gun crew to iron out kinks in its fire control system." One more hyphen is needed to make that crew man-size. (Incidentally, some writers would put a hyphen between "fire" and "control," but hyphenating a compound adjective is optional.) "The former President will speak to small business men." Since it is not small men that are being spoken of, "small-business men" would be preferable.

This "small-business men" example demonstrates acutely the anarchy that the hyphen introduces into the language. Most dictionaries give "businessman" as a solid word, but in order to

366

speak of a man who operates a small business it is necessary to violate that spelling and divide the word. Similarly, "self-conscious" is hyphenated in most dictionaries, but Webster II gives "unself-conscious," an atrocity, whereas Webster III makes it "unselfconscious," despite the fact that without the prefix its form of the word is "self-conscious." And here is a real puzzler: "Hence the large number of ex-public schoolboys in every Labor Cabinet." "Public school" is clearly two words. "Schoolboys" is just as clearly one word. The "ex-" has to be attached to the first word. Therefore, the version in the foregoing sentence would seem to be orthodox. Yet it adds up to nonsense. There is no rule about what to do with this kind of combination. But since "school" is more closely related here to "public" than it is to "boys," would it not make sense to break up "schoolboys" (as we did "businessmen") and write "ex-public-school boys"? However, a writer is free to adopt this form or reject it. (*See also* EX-.)

In the use of hyphens a distinction must be made between phrases used adjectivally before a noun and those used adverbially or adjectivally after a noun. It is correct to write "a fifty-four-to-twenty-eight Senate vote" or "a coast-to-coast tour." But the hyphens are not correct when these same words appear in adverbial phrases, as "The Senate voted, fifty-four-to-twenty-eight, to table the bill" and "The ex-President will stump coast-to-coast for Mr. Kennedy." Other examples of erroneous hyphens: "It has achieved wide acceptance by word-of-mouth" (but "word-of-mouth advertising" would be correct); "If you're partial to gabardine but want it light-in-weight, you'll prize this new suit" (but "a light-in-weight suit" would be correct, albeit clumsy).

Adjective phrases consisting of an adverb and a verb are usually hyphenated ("a well-dressed man"), except when the adverb ends in "-ly" ("a sharply cut version of *Henry* V").

The suspensive hyphen is used to show that one element in a phrase is to be linked to a later one. Missing links are evident in this sentence: "The change in Administration attitude is reflected in pre and post satellite letters." A hyphen is required in "post-satellite." "Pre" is not a word in itself but a prefix; therefore it too requires a hyphen—a suspensive hyphen. Hence it should be "pre- and post-satellite letters." Another example of a missing suspensive hyphen is this sentence: "The University of Michigan has taken considerable risks in designing a series of single or two-volume studies of individual nations." Make it "single- or two-volume studies." In both instances if you do not like the appearance of the suspensive hyphen you can get around it by inserting the missing words: "pre-satellite and post-satellite letters" and "single-volume or two-volume studies." A similar but slightly different situation is presented here: "The paintings include land and seascapes." Since a hyphen cannot be used after "land" ("landscapes" is not a hyphenated word), you would have to write it in full—"landscapes."

The locked-in hyphen occurs when it is the first element rather than the last that is intended to be applied to both. Example: "The measure was killed in a well-timed and executed maneuver." One solution is to repeat the hyphen: "a well-timed and -executed maneuver." This solution has been resorted to in the following instances: "mass-produced and -distributed radiation meters"; "the best-actor, -actress, and -director categories." But it is an awkward solution. A smoother way out is to repeat the missing element: "a well-timed and well-executed maneuver"; "mass-produced and mass-distributed radiation meters."

One generalization that might be drawn about hyphens is that compounds tend to solidify as they age. In the interval between Webster II and Webster III, for example, *pin-up* has become *pinup*, *nimbo-stratus* has become *nimbostratus*, and *sawtooth* has become *sawtooth*.

PARENTHESES

When explanatory matter, comments, or asides not intended to be part of the main thought are dropped into a sentence, they may be set off either by dashes or by parentheses: "In the last general election in Britain, the Conservatives won for the third time in succession—an almost unprecedented achievement—on the slogan 'You never had it so good' "; "The middle class qualities (I refrain from saying virtues) that the aspiring, climbing members of the working class display are rewarded in the world."

Parentheses have one slight advantage over dashes in this kind of interpolation: They signal clearly that an interpolation is coming; indeed, when you see the first mark you know for sure that a second lies somewhere down the line. The dash, on the other hand, is used for other purposes (*See* DASH *above*) and the signal may not be quite so clear, especially if the interpolated matter is long.

Partridge and Fowler each point to a different kind of error that may attend the use of parentheses. Errors they are, without doubt, but they are not as common as the two authors would lead you to believe. Nevertheless, they will be included here simply to make sure that all exits are guarded. Partridge points to the danger of losing the thread of grammatical sequence and cites a sentence that begins as follows: "But the present Exhibition, arranged by him in connexion with the Jubilee of the British School of Athens (though the results of the discoveries at Knossos itself naturally still form the main theme on an amplified scale), the object has been to supply as far as possible the materials for a general survey of the Minoan culture in its widest range, etc." The fault here obviously lies in the fact that if you remove the parenthetical matter you do not have a grammatical sentence—any more than you do with the parenthetical matter included. A kind of reverse side of this coin is the parenthetical interpolation that lacks a grammatical coherence of its own: "Those who stayed heard about the preservation of eyesight, Frederick the Great, Victor Hugo, and how to make fried oysters, Roquefort cheese dressing, and potlikker (waving a wastebasket in the air to represent the pot)." No conceivable subject for the participle "waving" appears in the sentence. The form here employed —and the writer may have had this in mind—is a convention that is recognized in certain specialized forms of writing such as court records and stage directions: "Q. Do you recognize this letter? (holding up Exhibit B.)"

Fowler's warning concerns a parenthesis that is irrelevant to its sentence, and he quotes this example: "In writing this straightforward & workmanlike biography of his grandfather (the book was finished before the war, & delayed in publication) Mr Walter

369

Jerrold has aimed at doing justice to Douglas Jerrold as dramatist, as social reformer & as good-natured man." "The very worst way of introducing an additional fact," says Fowler, "is to thrust it as a parenthesis into the middle of a sentence with which it has nothing to do."

There is some evidence that the use of parentheses has become more common in modern writing, particularly in critical and expository writing. Parentheses seem almost to have become a mark of "sophisticated," knowing style. They do have their uses in simplifying sentences that otherwise would be encumbered with ponderous subordinate and coordinate clauses and in permitting the use of pointed asides that might otherwise seem overemphatic. But, like every other stylistic device, they can be overdone.

See also PARENTHESES TO EXPLAIN PRONOUNS *and* PARENTHETICAL PHRASES.

PERIOD

The period is the red light that brings the reader to a halt—in fact, it is known as a full stop. Aside from certain technical uses such as to indicate abbreviations (*Dr., T.V.A.*) and ellipsis, in which three are used (. . .), the period is employed to mark the end of a statement. That all sounds simple enough to preclude doubts as to how to use this form of punctuation. Yet doubts do arise. First, let us examine a rather rare specimen: "Surrounded by a score of youngsters, playing, running, wrestling, screaming, shouting—'Patsy, he stepped on my ping-pong ball.' 'Patsy, there's a piece of this game missing.' 'Patsy, watch my schoolbooks.' 'Patsy, who's this guy?'—he stood yesterday in one of the green-walled recreation rooms." Since a period indicates a full stop, you cannot use it in the middle of a sentence. You cannot have a full stop and at the same time keep the sentence running. The solution here is to end the quotations with either commas or semicolons. Next, let us examine the doubts of a high school English teacher, who apparently was not alone in her doubts because she wrote, "We have been discussing this point at school and would like your opinion." She wanted to know

370

whether, if a sentence ends with an abbreviation, you use one period or two—that is, one period for the abbreviation and another for the full stop. The answer is you use one period; you would write, for example, "The teacher who asked this question is the holder of a Ph.D." If a sentence ends with an ellipsis, however, four periods are used—three to indicate the ellipsis and one to mark the end of the sentence: "The people of the United States adopted the Constitution in order to form a more perfect union. . . ."

QUESTION MARK

The question mark appears after a direct question, but not after an indirect one. A direct question is presented in this sentence: "The question is who is telling the truth." Properly punctuated, it would read, "The question is, Who is telling the truth?" In the form of an indirect question, which would take no interrogation point, a similar sentence might read, "He asked the jury to decide who had been telling the truth." Occasionally writers will misplace the question mark: "What program should the West offer they ask?" Obviously the question mark should be placed immediately after the question: "What program should the West offer? they ask." This form of sentence raises an additional matter of punctuation. A phrase of attribution is usually set off by a comma or commas: "The West has drafted a program, they said"; "They asked, What program should the West offer?" The question that arises is whether the question mark in the middle of the sentence should be followed by a comma. Most authorities believe not; the question mark displaces all other marks. A few publications and publishing houses, however, use the comma in conjunction with the interrogation point. *The New Yorker*, for instance, uniformly prints sentences like this: "When asked 'Where's your line?,' he would simply tap the envelope in a confident, one-up way." That form, however, is the preference of the few. If it does nothing else it illustrates how much of punctuation is determined by taste and individual choice.

QUOTATION MARKS

To the do-it-yourself sign painter and poster letterer, quotation marks are a fascinating and irresistible mystery. There is no accounting for the way in which these artists reach for quotation marks at the slightest, even at no, provocation: "Special 'Mother's Day' Dinner"; "Prices Slashed for Our 'Fire Sale' "; " 'No Trespassing.' " And the card that graces (or graced) the knick-knack shop in Palm Beach: "Brow 'z' ers Always Welcome." Somebody had something cute in mind, but what?

Actually the legitimate uses of quotation marks are fairly few: to enclose the exact phraseology of spoken or written language that is being cited; to set off titles of books, chapters, and the like, when italics are not so used; to mark a word or phrase being used in a special way, and sometimes to disclaim responsibility for the words of someone else.

Illustrations of the overuse and abuse of quotation marks are easy to come by. "The little guests were warned not to pick so much as one 'sprig' of this Christmas decoration." What, one may ask, is a sprig if not a sprig? A newspaper article said, "The watchdog committee is trying to determine whether there was a political fix in the case," but another article in an adjoining column spoke of an offer "to 'fix' a wage dispute." The latter article also referred to "a man with an 'in' to the Detroit teamster chief" and to "charges of 'planting' a former Secret Service agent on the Senate committee's staff." If it is necessary to use slang in writing that otherwise conforms to so-called standard English —and there is no gainsaying that the word "fix," at least, qualifies as necessary since there is no synonym—the slang should be used without the apology of quotation marks. When it is desirable to descend to the vulgate level to select a slang word or phrase, the writer should descend, not condescend.

A different abuse of quotation marks is the practice of breaking into and out of quotations several times in one sentence: "He added that the Communist acceptance of the United Nations plan for the repatriation of ill and disabled war prisoners through an about-face' was 'no surprise,' in view of the previous 'gestures' apparently made 'deliberately' to show progress toward 'easing the situation.' " Quoting a pungent or significant word or phrase to point up what a speaker said is all to the good. But to quote a collection of nondescript items, as in the cited sentence, is pointless and, what is worse, annoying to the reader.

Finally, a technical point about quotation marks: When successive paragraphs of quoted matter are printed, opening quotes (they look like 6's) are used at the beginning of each paragraph, but closing quotes (9's) appear only at the end of the final quoted paragraph. *See also* QUOTING IN FRAGMENTS.

SEMICOLON

The semicolon is almost equal to a full stop; it is used, as in this sentence, to separate contact clauses—that is, clauses that are not linked by a conjunction. The semicolon is also used to separate long, involved coordinate clauses: "No doubt the Secret Army Organization can, and will, slaughter innocent Moslems (women and children included), assassinate Europeans who oppose it, and explode more bombs; but these acts will just be the mad gestures of killers who know they are doomed, or of despairing French military officers selling their lives dearly for a cause that was wrong and is now hopeless." Sometimes, as has been noted under COMMA(2), the semicolon is used in series when the comma has been appropriated for use within members of the series. What the semicolon is not used for is to cover up the faults in a sentence out of control, as in this instance: "The concern owns vast cacao, coffee, and palm plantations; a construction company that has built half the roads and new buildings in the territory; it imports machinery and equipment from all over the world and is constantly seeking to diversify and expand." Often the semicolon is serviceable in places where the comma does not provide a sufficient pause. In the following sentence, semicolons in place of commas would lengthen the stops and lend more dignity to the phrases: "The cathedral is really new, it opens out and up, it soars and glows and conveys its message . . . in amazingly simple terms." As with other marks of punctuation, the use of the semicolon is sometimes decided on stylistic grounds and is a matter of the writer's taste.

PUNISH

Takes preposition *by* or *with* or *for*.

PUNISHABLE

Takes preposition *by*.

PUNS

Only a bad pun is the lowest form of humor. A good one can hold its head up in the company of the best wit. The trouble is, How can you tell the difference? It's largely a matter of taste and opinion, but here are three suggested tests: First, both of the double meanings in the play on a word should be appropriate; second, the reader's reaction should not be a wince followed by a sickly smile, but rather a double take followed by a pleased smile or—if you're lucky—by a guffaw; third, since the basis of humor is incongruity and unexpectedness, the pun should have an element of surprise—it should not be obvious, it should not be just lying there begging to be picked up.

At the risk of outraging contrary opinions—and the risk is formidable when you are dealing with puns—an example of good and bad will be cited. The first is the opening sentence of a news story about a streetcorner Kris Kringle who had imbibed too much and fell afoul of the police: "A Santa Claus carried his load a bit too far yesterday." The second example is a headline, which will have to speak for itself if it can: "Middies to Have One Bell of a Time Today for Wringing Out Cadets on the Gridiron."

The pun is, of course, an ancient tool of the writer's trade. Shakespeare, in the opening scene of *Julius Caesar*, presents a cobbler who professes to be "a mender of bad soles" and says he meddles "with no tradesman's matters, nor women's matters, but with awl." Shakespeare had a penchant for that sort of thing, and so have had other writers before and since. One of the sparkling puns of all time must surely be George S. Kaufman's, "One man's Mede is another man's Persian," and another was F. P. A.'s comment on Spain's "putting all her Basques in one exit." But there have been plenty of good writers who did not have a taste, or perhaps a talent, for the play on words. No good writing has ever

374

suffered for want of the gifts a good pun could bestow, but neither has any good writing ever suffered for its presence.

PUPIL

It is not proper to speak of admitting "a limited number of Negro students to previously all-white elementary schools." Those who attend elementary schools are *pupils*; those who attend higher institutions of learning (high schools may be included among these) are *students*.

PURGE

Takes preposition *of* or *from*.

PURIST

In English usage, as in most other human affairs, it is wise to avoid extremes and follow a reasonable middle course. The extremists in matters of usage are, on the right, the purists and, on the left, the new-day linguistic anarchists. According to Bergen Evans (in his sometimes fascinating book *Comfortable Words*), "A purist is one who applauds a female performer by shouting 'Brava! Brava!' while leering with contempt upon the vulgar mob ignorantly shouting 'Bravo!'" A linguistic anarchist, on the other hand, may be defined as a devil who can cite Scripture and the latest count of noses to advise the populace that it is quite correct to say, "The pencil is laying on the desk," but wouldn't dream of saying it himself because he knows better.

PURPORT

As a verb, *purport* is a useful journalistic word because it means to profess, to give the appearance of, to imply or to convey the idea of, and it permits the entry of a faint doubt into what is being said without flatly affirming or denying—that is, it is a neutral word with a slightly unneutral overtone. When a newspaperman writes of "a manuscript that purports to be the original of a Jefferson letter to a slave," he is not taking sides and expressing any opinion as to the manuscript's authenticity, yet he is

375

leaving quite open the possibility that the manuscript is not authentic.

Fowler and Evans both set forth two restrictions on the use of the word. Evans states them clearly this way: "Purport cannot be used in the passive, since its significance is already passive—standing for, 'is supposed, is represented to be.' Also the subject of purport may not be a person; it must be a thing or a person considered as a phenomenon." A violation of the first restriction would be, "A manuscript that was purported to be the original of a Jefferson letter." A violation of the second restriction is this sentence: "Occasionally the announcers purport to dedicate parts of the program to specific American soldiers."

PURPOSEFULLY, PURPOSELY

Of these two, which overlap in meaning, *purposefully* is weightier and less common. *Purposely* means by design or intentionally, not accidentally. *Purposefully* means infused with purpose, with a definite goal in mind. A writer will sometimes use *purposefully* simply because he thinks it is a fancy word: "General de Gaulle had kept his own Algerian policy purposefully obscure." If all that is meant is "not unintentionally," as seems to be the case here, then the word should be *purposely*.

See also ADVISEDLY, INTENTIONALLY.

PURSUANT

Takes preposition *to*.

PURSUIT

Takes preposition *of*.

PUTTING TWO AND TWO TOGETHER
See DANGLERS.

Q

QUALIFY
Takes preposition *for* or *as*.

QUALITATIVE
Qualitative contrasts with *quantitative* and has nothing to do with high quality or excellence. It relates to the kind or constituents of the subject being described. The writer of the following ad had an erroneous notion about the word: "Richard K. Doan's program reviews—terse, incisive, qualitative—appear daily . . . in the *New York Herald Tribune*."

QUERY
Misuse of this word is not common, yet it crops up occasionally in newspaper headlines: "U. S. Citizen Dies in Haitian Prison; Beaten During Police Query, Embassy Says." A *query* is a question, not a questioning. *Inquiry* was meant.

QUESTION (n.)
Takes preposition *on, about, as to, concerning,* or *of*.

QUESTION MARK
See PUNCTUATION.

QUESTION WHETHER
When *question* is followed by *whether*, there is a common tendency to insert *as to* between them. Sometimes this insertion is tolerable, but usually it is not. *As to* is equivalent to *about*. When you write *the question*, what follows should be the question itself in indirect form: "The question whether we should accept Mr. Khrushchev's proposals of 'peaceful coexistence,' then, is the question whether we should accept what have always been our own demands when they take the form of an offer

from our opponents." Both those uses are correct: they state the questions under discussion.

This one, however, is improper: "Concerning the question as to whether or not the United States should retain the Philippine Islands after the Spanish-American War, Miss Leech quite rightly states that it was a highly controversial issue." Here again the question is stated in indirect form, but the *as to* suggests that the *whether* introduces what the question is *about* rather than what it *is*. Delete the *as to*.

When instead of *the question* we have *a question*, the insertion of *as to* is defensible though not necessary. *The question* suggests that the question is already of general knowledge or that an immediate appositive clause is going to identify it, but *a question* permits the writer either to tell what it is *about* (*as to*) or to state it immediately in direct form with no intervening words. Either of these forms is proper: "This posed a question as to whether the Communist party, once in power, could live up to its contention," or "This posed a question whether the Communist party, etc." If a noun is used after *question*, either *as to* or *of* may precede that noun: "It raises a question as to [*of*] the moral standards of those who think such rules are necessary or desirable."

Although *as to* can be, and most often should be, eliminated after *question* as a noun, the verb *question* sometimes introduces another complication, illustrated by this sentence: "Señor Nunez was questioned whether Cuba intended to establish diplomatic relations with East Germany." It might seem that *questioned* is here exactly synonymous with *asked*. That is not true, however, as becomes evident if the sentence is turned into the active voice. Whereas you would write, "Newsmen asked him whether . . . ," you would not write, "Newsmen questioned him whether. . . ." *As to* or *about* or *concerning* is necessary before *whether*. Or, of course, you might write, "Newsmen asked him the question whether . . . ," but that would be using words wastefully.

QUIETEN

A favorite of British writers, *quieten*—as a form of the verb *quiet*—verges on an affectation when used by American writers.

QUIT

Some words have overtones that a dictionary definition does not always catch. Most dictionaries define *quit* as meaning to leave or go away from. Often, however, the word suggests a renunciation, even a huffy one. Therefore, when a professor is retiring, the headline "Historian to Quit Yale Post in June," though technically correct, is not altogether satisfactory because it seems to indicate a sharp departure. The exigencies of headline writing being what they are, however, it is too much to hope that it will always be possible to observe this nuance.

QUITE

The meanings of *quite* are completely ("He was quite wrong") and positively ("Mink eyelashes are quite the fashion"). It follows that something should not be termed *quite complete* since the phrase involves a redundancy. Still less can something be *quite similar* to something else because the phrase presents two contradictory ideas: *similar* means nearly like, and the phrase would thus mean "completely nearly like." The expression *quite all right* presents superficially a redundancy similar to *quite complete*, but there is a difference. Both Fowler and Evans take note of the seeming redundancy, Fowler condemning it as "a foolish pleonasm" and Evans excusing it on the grounds that grammar is not logical and that in any event the phrase does not commonly mean that things are all right but rather that things are *not* all right. Actually the redundancy is only apparent, not real, because the notion of *all*—i.e., the complete sum—has virtually disappeared from the phrase *all right*, and so the phrase *quite all right* suggests no repetition of an idea.

The use of *quite* to mean rather, as in "The girl was quite pretty," is an inoffensive casualism, as are such phrases as "quite an exploit" and "quite a little." *See also* ABSOLUTELY.

QUIZ

Quiz denotes an informal questioning to test a person's

knowledge. It is best restricted to the campus and the television screen. Certainly it should not be applied to anything as formal and solemn as a cross-examination in court, as in the headline, "Eichmann Calm as Quizzing Ends."

QUOTA

Quota means something more than mere number; it denotes the part assigned to one or given by one. A misuse: "While it is true that Westerns and mysteries and flame-covered fiction make up a large percentage of the American paperbacks, we also have a substantial quota of the finest titles that have in this way been made possible for the mass reading public." All that is meant here is number.

QUOTED AS SAYING

Some journalists have a peculiar fondness for the locution illustrated by the following sentences: "I'm sorry but we don't serve colored here,' they quoted her"; "There's absolutely no truth in it,' the paper quoted Mr. Paar"; " 'Nothing,' the general was quoted." There is little more justification for this bobtail construction than there would be to write, "the general was reported" or "the general was described" or "the general was cited." The clause cries out for completion: "the general was quoted as saying." Or, if the difference in time between the saying and the quoting is significant, "the general was quoted as having said." The journalists are intent on saving words, as journalists always must be, but here the pseudo-economy produces un-English.

QUOTE FOR QUOTATION

The noun *quote* for quotation is a casualism, unsuitable for serious writing. It is inappropriate in this passage from the review of a new dictionary: "One interesting feature of some of the entries consists of quotes from contemporary notables." *Quotes* for quotation marks is acceptable as INSIDE TALK among writers, editors, printers, and readers of this book.

QUOTING IN FRAGMENTS

Introducing a partial quotation that causes an abrupt switch in the same sentence from third person to first person is by no means incorrect. But it is often clumsy. For instance: "He said, however, that there was no need to do so because he had already 'expressed myself fully.' " Another example: "Dr. Jonas E. Salk, who developed the vaccine, preferred to remain in 'my role as an investigator.' " In sentences like these the quoted matter should be carefully examined to determine whether a quotation is indeed necessary; if it is, the writer should select only the significant words. In the first example it hardly seems necessary to quote the rather ordinary phrase. In the second, the "my" could be eliminated from the quoted matter. There is nothing wrong with either sentence except a lack of grace.

What is not permissible, however, is to try to remedy the lack of grace by modifying the quoted words to make them fit the syntax of the main sentence. That is what was done here: "Mr. Truman smilingly conceded that he 'feels more kindly toward newspapermen now that one is about to become a member of his family.' " Obviously the word he used wasn't "feels" unless he said: "Mo'nin' y'all. Ah feels more kindly toward newspapermen, etc." The solution, of course, is to begin the quotation with the word "more." Likewise, "his" should be "my."

R

RACK, WRACK

The verb *rack* comes from a word denoting a frame, and means to spread out, strain, or torture by stretching. The verb *wrack* comes from a word denoting wreck, and means to wreck, ruin, destroy. This etymology explains why the word is *nerve-racking* rather than *nerve-wracking*; something that is *nerve-racking* does not wreck the nerves, it merely strains or tortures them. It likewise explains why the spelling in this sentence is incorrect: "The issue has wracked Polish intellectuals since 1956. . . ." Still further, it explains why you *rack* your brains rather than *wrack* them—you strain or torture them, you don't ruin them.

The phrase *rack up*, a sports page favorite, is also related to the idea of a frame. It comes to us from the poolroom, where the score is kept with counters on an overhead kind of frame, usually a wire. Thus a score can be *racked up*, and even a victory can be *racked up*. But there is a tendency these days to go even further: "The Indians racked up Jim Coates for six runs on six hits." Really, that is racking the meaning too far.

RACKET

See OCCUPATIONS.

RAISE, REAR

At one time a war raged (and some skirmishes still go on) against the use of *raise* to describe what parents do to children. The battle cry was, "You raise pigs, but you rear children." However, in this country at least, the war is over; we *raise* both pigs and children, and some parents will testify that you can't always tell the difference.

RAISE, RISE

The verb *raise* is exclusively transitive. Such intransitive uses

382

as the following are obsolete: "Half the spectators involuntarily raised from their seats"; "Specially designed saw teeth cut away paint so that windows raise and lower with ease." The intransitive verb is *rise*.

As to the nouns, both words are in good use, although *raise* is applied primarily to an increase in pay, so much so that "pay raise" is redundant. If *rise* is to be used for a wage increase, however, *pay* or *wage* in front of it is mandatory. That is, you wouldn't say, "I got a rise out of the boss." *See also* BOOST.

RANGE

Takes preposition *through*, *with*, *along*, or *between*.

RATHER THAN

If we start from the premise that in this phrase *than* is a conjunction, modified by *rather*, an adverb, we must conclude that grammatically the elements linked by the conjunction should be parallel. The following sentences, then, would clearly be wrong: "The draft decrees will be submitted to the council in such general terms as to disguise rather than explaining [*explain*] their real import"; "Just as many expanding families move to larger quarters elsewhere, so should the colleges consider moving rather than try [*trying*] to expand"; "This suggested that C.F. & I., if it moved upward, might do so only on a selective basis rather than following [*follow*] United States Steel's across-the-board increase"; "He issued secret orders to each regional commander of the Paris camp to report all resources in his district which must be destroyed rather than fall [*be allowed to fall*] into the hands of the enemy."

So much for the technically proper grammar of the construction. There is an unmistakable trend in usage, however, toward treating *rather than* in some constructions as a prepositional group. This is especially true when the words are used to indicate *instead of* or *to the exclusion of*, a meaning slightly different from the more literal meaning, which denotes a preference but not an exclusion. Thus, we get the idiomatic, though not entirely grammatical, constructions exemplified in the following sentences: "Commander Carpenter explained that he had gotten into the raft rather than waiting [grammatically *waited*] in the capsule because the capsule was listing badly"; "The projectile-like fins have given way to more discreet blades that sweep into the sideline of the long car rather than dominating [grammatically *dominate*] it as last year."

The meaning *instead of* and hence the prepositional nature of the phrase is almost invariable when the *rather than* comes first in the construction: "Rather than raising prices on all steel products, each company has acted selectively"; "The evidence referred to by Mr. Askwith, rather than supporting his conclusion, leads to the opposite conclusion." The dominance of idiom over grammar is strong in both examples; "rather than raised" in the first one and "rather than supports" in the second would be impossible. *See also* PREFER . . . THAN.

RAVISH

Headline: "Elm Beetle Infestation Ravishing Thousands of Trees in Greenwich." Insex? Keep your mind on your work, buster; the word you want is *ravaging*.

That item appeared in *Watch Your Language* and prompted a Mrs. Harold J. Richards to pen her agreement. It is well known, she wrote, that only God can make a tree.

RE

See ANENT.

RE-

Often attached to words needlessly (sometimes properly and sometimes improperly), the prefix "re-" is almost a sign of insecurity, of fear that the reader or listener will not understand that *again* is meant. A teacher testifies that his pupils will often say *recopy* when they mean *copy* (sometimes they say, "I'll copy it over," which comes to the same thing). Likewise they say, "Would you repeat that again."

Similar redundancies have crept into standard English. The

word *reiterate* is an example. *Iterate* means to say or do a second time or often; *reiterate* means, therefore, to say or do over and over again, and the only excuse for it is that *iterate* is not in general use. *Redouble* does not mean anything different from *double* (except in bridge), yet one never *doubles* his efforts, he always *redoubles* them. *Echo* does not necessarily mean a single return of a sound, yet if more than one round trip is to be spoken of, the meaning is nailed down by the use of *re-echo*. *Duplicate* and *reduplicate* both mean *double* (or *redouble*). *Vamp* and *revamp* both mean *refurbish*. In recent years real estate men have taken to speaking of *reconverted* buildings, which differ in no way from *converted* buildings. And one member of the tribe, referring to the amount of new construction in an area of New York, exclaimed, "There's a terrific re-renaissance going on there."

An even more peculiar use of "re-"—again apparently introduced out of fear of misunderstanding—crops up in the photographers' trade: a picture is never *touched*, but it is often *retouched*. There is nothing wrong with most of these "re-" words; it is merely interesting to note how, in the cause of explicitness and emphasis, the language is formed and re-formed.

REACTION

Anyone who has ever seen those printed slips on which the Busy Big Executive votes for one in a list of candidates ranging from "For your information" through "Please give necessary attention" to "What's your reaction to this?" will recognize how deeply dug into the language the word *reaction* is. So it is probably futile to point out that the word properly belongs to the world of science, where it refers to a response to a stimulus—and a somewhat mechanical response at that, rather than a considered one. It is probably also futile to point out that instead of mechanically picking up the word *reaction*, a writer would do better to pause, think, and choose the word he really means: *opinion, reply, response, attitude, feeling, impression, view*.

REAR

See RAISE, REAR.

385

REASON

Takes preposition *for.*

REASON . . . IS BECAUSE

However common this construction may be in everyday speech, it is disapproved for shaped writing. Since the meaning of *because* is *for the reason that,* the construction is a redundancy. This becomes evident if *for the reason that* is substituted for *because* in the following sentence: "The reason the astronaut's hand would not burn is because there are so few of the 100,-000,000-degree atoms in space." Eliminate either *reason* or *because.*

REBELLIOUS

Takes preposition *against, to,* or *toward.*

REBUFF

Rebuff is a word much used in headlines, but it should be used with care. Often headline writers employ it to denote a mere rejection: "President Rebuffed on Tax Program." However, the word means not simply to repulse, reject, or refuse, but to do so curtly, brusquely, or in the manner of a snub.

RECEPTIVE

Takes preposition *to* or *of.*

RECKON

The use of *reckon* to mean guess, think, or suppose is regarded by most authorities as dialectal or casual. They disapprove such uses as this one: "He reckoned the play would have a favorable reception." Implicit in the word *reckon* is a counting or calculation, and the safest course is to restrict it to uses in which there is some suggestion, even remote, of a computation. *See also* CALCULATE *and* FIGURE.

Reckon takes the preposition *on.*

RECONCILE
Takes preposition *to* or *with*.

RECORD, NEW
New is almost always superfluous with *record:* "By stroking five home runs in his trips to the plate Musial established a new major-league record." If he established a *record*, it had to be a *new* one. The only occasion on which *new* might be appropriate would be an instance in which a direct comparison was being made with a previous *record*.

RECUR, REOCCUR
Basically these words mean the same thing: occur again. Still, a writer with a feeling for words senses a difference. *Recur* is the more common word, yet here is a sentence from a writer who deliberately chose *reoccur*, and with reason: "The image of French stability and internal strength for which General de Gaulle has fought will now be clouded by the realization that he has had to fight an internal rebellion that could reoccur even if put down now. . . ." *Reoccur* suggests a one-time repetition. *Recur* suggests repetition more than once, usually according to some fixed schedule, as in "the recurring phases of the moon," although it can also apply to a one-time repetition. It is the ability to feel a fine distinction such as this and to choose the word that precisely expresses the thought that marks the writer of competence and taste.

REDOLENT
Takes preposition *of*.

REFERENCE
See ALLUSION, REFERENCE.

REFLEXIVE PRONOUNS, REFLEXIVES
See HIMSELF (HERSELF, MYSELF, ETC.)

REFUTE

"Hodding Carter, editor and publisher of *The Greenville Delta Democrat-Times,* refuted today a suggestion that he belonged to a Communistic group." *Refute* means to disprove. The newspaper printing the sentence had no evidence of that, and probably did not mean to say that. What it did mean to say was that Mr. Carter *denied, disputed, answered, countered, contested, challenged,* or *rejected* the suggestion.

REGARDLESS

The word must be followed by a preposition, and the preposition is *of.* It is a solecism to write, "Regardless how much torment of troubled souls is potentially packed into Eugene O'Neill's *Long Day's Journey Into Night,* the final test of this great drama is in how it is presented and played." *See also* IRREGARDLESS.

REGIME

In the governmental sense *regime* means the system of rule or administration rather than the incumbency of a particular politician or group. Thus, the United States has a *democratic regime,* but did not have a *Wilson regime.* Under the influence of headline writers, however, who understandably prize the six-letter *regime* above the fourteen-letter *administration* or the ten-letter *government,* the word has insinuated itself where it does not belong. Thus we read: "Observers in London regard the uprising as the most serious threat to the Prime Minister since his regime [*government? group? party?*] gained power." Even the State Department occasionally falls into error: "We have likewise emphasized the fact that we cannot accept any control by the East German regime in our rights of access to Berlin."

REGRET (n.)

Takes preposition *at* or *for.*

REGRETFULLY

The word is sometimes misused for *regrettably,* as in the

388

following sentence: "Spike heels, regretfully, proved the undoing of some women at the World's Fair." *Regretfully* conveys the idea of feeling regret. *Regrettably*, the word needed here, means unfortunately. *See* HOPEFULLY.

REJOICE
Takes preposition *at* or *in*.

RELATION, RELATIVE
Whether you use *relation* or *relative* to denote a kinsman probably depends on what you learned in elementary school or at your mother's knee. Both are sanctioned by dictionaries. Still there are those of us who favor *relative* as having a less bucolic flavor, but perhaps we are under the influence of elementary school or Mom. If, in defiance of "those of us," your preference runs to *relation*, you still cannot use it this way: "Samuel Clark, who is no relation to Dick Clark. . . ." If you wish to keep *relation*, you will have to say "no relation of." If you wish to keep "to," you will have to say "not related to."

RELATIVELY
Like *comparatively*, the word *relatively* should, strictly speaking, be used only when there is an expressed or clearly implied comparison. The following is a poor use: "United States military sources expressed shock that a plane carrying the President would have twenty-six persons aboard, a relatively heavy load." Relative to what? There is no typical plane or load.

RELISII (n.)
Takes preposition *for* or *of*.

REMAND BACK
A redundancy, as in this sentence: "The Appeals Court remanded the case back to the trial court." *Remand* means to send back. Delete *back*. A similar redundancy is this one: "In sixteen ballots taken in the Assembly Mr. Wellington Koo and Mr. Kuriyama see-sawed back and forth." Omit *back and forth*.

389

REMIND

It should not be used intransitively, as in, "Lincoln White reminded that the Department on Jan. 16 had announced that all United States citizens desiring to travel to Cuba must obtain passports specifically endorsing such travel." Since *remind* means to recall to one's mind, it must be followed by an object that has a mind.

REOCCUR

See RECUR, REOCCUR.

REPEL

See REPULSE, REPEL.

REPENT

Takes preposition *of*.

REPLETE

Takes preposition *with*.

REPLICA

A *replica* is a facsimile or almost exact copy, with the additional meaning in fine arts (in which field it finds its proper use) of a copy made by the original artist and hence of equal value. Therefore this use is improper: "A replica of the original home of the society at Clos de Vougeot in Burgundy was made in spun sugar by the hotel's pastry chef." And this use, found in an ad, is absurd: "A solid walnut replica of a seventeenth-century electric clock." There are so many words that convey the meaning usually intended—*model, copy, reproduction, miniature, duplicate, counterpart*—that *replica* should be restricted to its rare proper job.

REPRISAl

Takes preposition *for* (an act); *against* or *upon* (the perpetrator).

390

REPUGNANCE

Takes preposition *to, against,* or *for.*

REPULSE, REPEL

"Some students were repulsed by the thought of going into debt for an education." Perhaps because it is associated with *repulsive,* some assume that *repulse* means to disgust. To be *repulsed* is to be beaten or driven back. The desired word in the quoted sentence is *repelled,* which is the only one of the two that carries the idea of aversion. The distinction between the words can be seen in this sentence: "She repulsed the suitor because he repelled her."

REQUEST

The verb is not idiomatically followed by *for,* as it is in this example: "The President has requested Congress for both these powers." Although the verb *ask* is so followed, the analogy is misleading. Make it either "has asked Congress for" or "has requested Congress to grant."

RESEMBLANCE

Takes preposition *to, between,* or *among.*

RESENTMENT

Takes preposition *against, at,* or *for.*

RESPECT

In respect takes preposition *of* or *to; with respect* takes preposition *to.* By itself the noun *respect* takes preposition *for.*

RESPONSIBILITY

Takes preposition *for.*

RESTRAIN

Takes preposition *from.*

RESULT
See AS THE RESULT OF.

REVEL
Takes preposition *in*.

REVENGE
See AVENGE, REVENGE.

REVEREND
If it is borne in mind that *reverend* is an adjective, not a noun, a couple of its misuses will be avoided. For instance, it is a gaucherie to use it as a form of address or as a synonym for a person, as in, "Good morning, reverend," or, "I saw the reverend this morning." Further, as an honorific *reverend* should always be preceded by *the*: "the Reverend James A. Smith." Still further, placing the honorific before a surname with nothing in between is frowned upon: "the Reverend Smith" should be "the Reverend Mr. Smith" or "the Reverend Dr. Smith" or "the Reverend James A. Smith." Finally, recalling that *reverend* is an adjective, one should not, strictly speaking, pluralize it by writing, "the Revs. John Smith and James Robinson."

REVERSE
See CONVERSE, REVERSE, CONTRARY, OPPOSITE.

RHETORICAL FIGURES AND FAULTS
The writer's bag of tricks contains an assortment of devices that help him to make his points effectively and to lift his prose from the stodgy level of a mere succession of words. Chief among these devices are figures of speech. There are a great number of them, many with Greek-derived names that are harder to fathom than the figures they describe. It is of little importance to know the names, but it is of some importance to know when and how the figures can be useful and when and how they can betray the writer into absurdity. The catalogue that follows, which is by no

means complete, attempts to provide some guidance to the tricks and the traps.

ALLEGORY

An *allegory* is a metaphorical narrative (*see* METAPHOR below) in which the surface story and characters are intended to be taken as symbols pointing to an underlying, more significant meaning. *Pilgrim's Progress* and *The Faerie Queen* are usually cited as outstanding examples of the category. The dangers inherent in allegory are (a) obscurity, which may prevent the reader from deriving any meaning at all from the story, (b) unskillful presentation, which may lead the reader to derive the wrong meaning, and (c) obviousness, which makes employment of the device unnecessary.

ALLITERATION

Alliteration is repetition of sounds at the beginnings of words or in accented syllables. Most commonly the sounds are those of consonants. Charles Churchill's line about "apt Alliteration's artful aid" is in itself far from apt. His alliteration, if any, is visual rather than aural, since the four "a" sounds are all different. True alliteration may range from comic abominations like "Peter Piper picked a peck of pickled peppers" to the subtle music of Shakespearean lines like "Sleep dwell upon thine eyes, peace in thy breast! Would I were sleep and peace, so sweet to rest!"

These days alliteration is more common in poetry than in prose, although even in poetry there are those who scorn it as outdated. In prose, as in poetry, it can heighten effect, help create an intended atmosphere: "The carpet of dead leaves has taken on a moist tinge of mahogany, of maroon." Some prose writers are so addicted to alliteration that they almost automatically employ it, even in ordinary expository writing where it serves no purpose and indeed may divert attention from the substance to the form: "In all such ways have the needs of men, the passions of people, and the pride of nations conspired, performing their earthbound best, to conceive a revolution, within and among themselves, to

match, in menace and in mystery, the assault on sky and space.
. . . And against America, an appointed antagonist awaits."

Needless to say, alliteration, because of the strong hold it fastens on the memory, is a favorite device of the advertising profession, which wants the public to keep ever in mind that "Progress is our most important product," that one should always say "Make mine Martin's," and that "You'll love its full, fascinating flavor; treat your taste to a change today."

ALLUSION

One way of making a point more understandable, often more colorful, is to link it to a literary character or situation or to a proverb or topical saying. This is the rhetorical device known as *allusion*. It can be useful provided it really helps the reader and does not serve merely to display the author's erudition, as it often does. It is one thing, for example, to allude to the labors of Hercules, but quite another to allude to the suicidal tendencies of Armida. The test of a serviceable allusion is whether it would be meaningful to a reader of some education. If it would not be, forget it.

ANALOGY

Analogy makes a comparison of similarities in two things. It is an admirable device for explaining the complex in simple terms. Trying to clarify the workings of a fusion bomb for the layman would be quite difficult if the writer confined himself to scientific language, but by resorting to analogy he can say: "The process is like the lighting of a cigarette in a high wind when one has only one match. It is not enough to light the match—one must be able to shield it against the wind long enough for the cigarette to be lighted." Compare METAPHOR and SIMILE.

ANTICLIMAX

Climax denotes an ascending by steps; *anticlimax* is the reverse. In writing, climax is normally expected in a progression. Anticlimax is a fault unless it is invoked for humorous effect: "A gentleman, a scholar, and a good judge of liquor."

394

ANTITHESIS

The juxtaposition of contrasting elements, *antithesis* is among the commonest and most effective of rhetorical devices. An example from Pope: "The learn'd is happy nature to explore, the fool is happy that he knows no more."

CHIASMUS

A heightener of dramatic or oratorical effect, *chiasmus* is the inversion in the second of two parallel clauses or phrases of the structure of the first. It is most simply illustrated by the nursery rhyme line, "Old King Cole was a merry old soul and a merry old soul was he." Chiasmus is quite common in the Bible: "We have made a covenant with death and with hell are we at agreement" (Isaiah). It also appears in other elevated writing: "The will is free: strong is the soul" (Matthew Arnold).

CLIMAX

See ANTICLIMAX.

DYSPHEMISM

Dysphemism is almost the opposite of *euphemism*. It means the use of a disparaging or offensive term to describe something inoffensive or even grand. To speak of a navy destroyer, as sailors do, as a *tin can*, or of one's mother as *the old lady*, or of a mansion as a *shack* is to use a dysphemism. Obviously, the figure is a popular one in the coining of slang.

EUPHEMISM

Euphemism is the use of a mild term to avoid what is deemed to be an unpleasant one, as *pass away* for *die*. A discussion of this subject appears in the vocabulary proper. Not to be confused with euphemism (and, indeed, not even a rhetorical figure) is *euphuism*, a precious, elegant literary style that was used in Elizabethan days, but happily has gone out of fashion.

EXAGGERATION

Exaggeration probably appears nowhere but here as the

designation of a rhetorical device. Most authorities are content to speak of *hyperbole*, which means exaggeration to intensify what is being mentioned. Someone has said, according to Macaulay, that hyperbole "lies without deceiving." When we say, "I'm eternally grateful" or "His Cadillac is as long as a Pullman car" we are indulging in hyperbole. We don't expect anyone to take what we say literally; we are lying but not deceiving. Hyperbole is usually thought of as an isolated expression inserted into speech or writing to heighten the effect. Exaggeration, however, may be thought of as a consistent manner of writing, usually employed to produce humorous results. It makes of hyperbole not an occasional indulgence but almost a way of life. It is most evident in the work of writers for *The New Yorker* and their imitators, although *The New Yorker* did not originate the manner.

Here, for example, is A. J. Liebling telling of his reporting days on *The New York World-Telegram* when an economy drive began: "Reporters using the subways were required to bring in signed notes from the platform guards before submitting a voucher requesting reimbursement of their nickels." And again: "The awful sensation of working for a grain and feed store in an automotive age afflicted the New Yorkers on the staff—I never left the city room without taking off my jacket and slapping the lapels to dislodge hayseed. . . . The shop was continually cluttered with bright boys shipped in and out of the woods for eight and a half days of big-town polish so they could go back to the Sierra Nevadas as managing editors with New York experience. Out of the five dollars a week they would get out there they would repay Scripps-Howard, fifty cents at a clip, for the round trip on the Greyhound bus."

Or here is James Thurber reminiscing about the Riviera edition of *The Chicago Tribune* in the 1920's: "We went to work after dinner and usually had the last chronicle of the diverting day written and ready for the linotypers well before midnight. It was then our custom to sit around for half an hour, making up items for the society editor's column." There follow some examples of such items. Then: "It is true that the languorous somnolence of our life was occasionally broken up. This would happen about one night a week, around ten o'clock, when our French composing room went on strike." Such a style makes for easy, comical reading, and it is enlightening too, provided the reader understands that everything is not to be taken as literally true, that he must keep his saltcellar handy. All this is not exaggeration to intensify the effect; it is exaggeration deliberately used to afford humor. As such it is regarded here as a separate rhetorical device.

HYPERBOLE
See EXAGGERATION.

IRONY
Irony is a gentle form of sarcasm in which the written or spoken words carry an implication quite different from—often opposite to—what appears on the surface. It is a form of humor, unless its bite is so sharp as to wound. Its message is usually addressed to the knowing. An example from *The New Yorker*: "In order to drum up public support for a campaign to keep the subways tidy, the Transit Authority and the Young Men's Board of Trade hit upon the striking idea of attaching a special carpeted car to a regular train and serving champagne to the press in it. The public was excluded. Doubtless the public will resolve, as one man, never to litter the subways again, if only to protect itself against some greater fatuity by the men who deal in public relations. Indeed, we see larger possibilities in this method of proceeding by contraries. *The Times*, for example, might consider soliciting contributions for its annual work of charity by publishing a list of the city's Hundred Most Enviable Bankers. Other charitable organizations might vie with one another to discover the most overdeveloped child from an underdeveloped country. . . ."

LITOTES
A form of MEIOSIS, the figure *litotes* is a kind of understatement in which an affirmative is expressed by using the negative of its opposite, *not bad* for good, *far from correct* for incorrect. *See* NOT TOO in the main vocabulary.

397

MEIOSIS

Meiosis is the opposite of HYPERBOLE—it is an understatement, a making less of something, rather than an exaggeration of it, as when the father comments on the son's straight "A" record in college by saying, "That's pretty fair," or when the adolescent emits a wolf whistle at a striking girl and then remarks, "She's okay."

METAPHOR

Metaphor is a figure of speech in which a comparison or identity is implied: "She is a tigress." *See* SIMILE, and METAPHORS AND MIXAPHORS in the main vocabulary.

METONYMY

Substitution of the name or an attribute of one thing for the name of another is the figure of speech known as *metonymy*. Examples: *"Have you read O'Neill?"* (meaning O'Neill's works); *the White House* (meaning the Administration or the President); *the great unwashed* (meaning the lower classes). Compare SYNECHDOCHE.

MIXAPHOR

A mixed METAPHOR. *See* METAPHORS AND MIXAPHORS in the main vocabulary.

ONOMATOPOEIA

Onomatopoeia denotes the suggesting of the sense by means of the sound of words. Some words in themselves imitate by sound the things they describe: *bang, buzz, moo, hiss, sizzle.* In addition, however, the writer may skillfully put together words that suggest by their sound the picture, the tone, the feeling of what is being described and in such writing the style is onomatopoeic. The passage quoted under ALLITERATION is in full as follows: "The carpet of dead leaves has taken on a moist tinge of mahogany, of maroon. You no longer crush it underfoot with a dry, metallic crunch; it rather yields resiliently with the muffled

sound of seaweed at low tide. The deep, stagnant, brooding stillness of October—a cathedral stillness—has been succeeded all
of a sudden by the fervent chirping of birds calling to each other"
(*Sylva*, by Vercors).

OXYMORON

A figure consisting of seemingly contradictory words, *oxymoron* has the startling effect of a paradox. *Conspicuously absent*
is an example from ordinary prose, and Elizabeth Barrett Browning's *thunders of white silence* is an example from poetry.

PARONOMASIA

This is a fancy word for pun. *See* PUNS in the main vocabulary.

PATHETIC FALLACY

The *pathetic fallacy* is no fallacy at all, although Ruskin,
who coined the phrase, thought it was. It consists in ascribing
human attributes or characteristics to lifeless things. This has
always been a poetic device. Here, for instance, is Shelley: "See
the mountains kiss high Heaven/ And the waves clasp one another;/ No sister-flower would be forgiven/ If it disdained its
brother. . . ." The device is a writing fallacy only if it is overdone or if its attributions are ludicrous. Compare PERSONIFICA-
TION.

PERSONIFICATION

Whereas the PATHETIC FALLACY ascribes human characteristics to inanimate things, it does not quite make persons out
of them. *Personification*, however, takes that extra small step.
It is a figure of speech in which abstract ideas or lifeless objects
are regarded as persons and often are named as if they were
persons. Again from Shelley: "Thy brother Death came, and
cried,/ Wouldst thou me?/ Thy sweet child Sleep, the filmy-
eyes,/ Murmured like a noontide bee,/ Shall I nestle near thy
side?/ Wouldst thou me?" Personification is not so common as

399

it once was in poetry, and it is rare in the prose of today's writers.

PROLEPSIS

Prolepsis is a rhetorical figure whereby an adjective applied to a noun foretells a coming event by referring to it as if it had already taken place. The soldier in Browning's "Incident of the French Camp," when addressed by his chief with the words "You're wounded!" responds by saying, "Nay, I'm killed, Sire!" and then, suiting the action to the word, "Smiling, the boy fell dead." The use of *killed* is an illustration of prolepsis. The figure of speech, not a common one, is unobjectionable so long as it does not descend to absurdity, as it does in such instances as "The dead man fired four shots at the police." This ill-advised extension of the figure is termed in these pages the EX POST FACTO CONSTRUCTION.

SIMILE

Like METAPHOR, the figure known as *simile* draws a comparison. But whereas metaphor implies the comparison by substituting one thing for another or attributes of one thing for another, simile makes the comparison explicit by using *as* or *like* or *as if*. A metaphor would be, "She is a tigress"; a simile would be, "She is like a tigress." Simile is extremely common not only in poetry and prose, but also in everyday conversation: "He works like a beaver"; "He is as strong as an ox"; "The children were as good as gold."

SYLLEPSIS

This one is usually not a serious figure of speech. It involves using a single word to link two thoughts, each of which gives a different meaning to the linking word. In the sentence "She left in a Cadillac and a huff," the word *in* is first used to denote a spatial relation and then to denote an abstract situation. A bromidic construction nowadays is this type of sentence: "Twenty years and 400 pages later the hero marries the heroine." That, too, is a form of *syllepsis*, the linking word being *later*, which in its first application means more subsequent in time and in its second application further advanced toward the end. Syllepsis is sometimes used to achieve a humorous effect and sometimes, alas, it is produced by faulty writing. Compare ZEUGMA.

SYNECHDOCHE

In *synechdoche* the part is made to stand for the whole, as in referring to workmen as *hands*, cattle as *head*, intellect as *brains*, royal status as *purple*. Sometimes the line of separation between *synechdoche* and METONYMY is obscure.

TMESIS

See entry in main vocabulary.

TRANSFERRED EPITHET

If the poet speaks of *the angry sea* or *the hasty days*, he is using the device known as *transferred epithet*: the association of an adjective with a noun to which it would not normally be linked. This device is not dissimilar to PATHETIC FALLACY. As a poetic device, transferred epithet is a useful ornament, and it is often serviceable in ordinary prose as well. But the journalistic urge to compress, to shorten, to be breezy, which inevitably has its effect on other kinds of writing, occasionally produces some dubious uses of the device: "A brief visitor to Paris"; "Premier Castro spends incredible hours before the microphone"; "Three out of five fires are caused by a careless cigarette or a careless match." If a transferred epithet creates an immediate feeling of incongruity or ludicrousness, it is best avoided.

ZEUGMA

Like SYLLEPSIS, the figure known as *zeugma* uses a single word to link two thoughts, but in syllepsis the relationship of the linking word to both ideas is correct, whereas in zeugma the relationship is correct for one idea but not for the other. A fabricated example of zeugma might be, "He sat munching his sandwich and his beer," in which *munching* fits with "sandwich" but is out of place with "beer." An actual example from fiction is, "Something odd in the behavior of the pair held his attention and his curiosity." The term zeugma is often used to refer to syllepsis, but as here distinguished it obviously is a writing fault, which syllepsis is not.

RICH

Takes preposition *in.*

RID

Takes preposition *of.*

RISE

See RAISE, RISE.

ROB

You wouldn't think a grown-up literate would misuse this word, but every once in a while it happens. Headline: "Bronx Payroll Robbed." Film review: "They joined forces, if not all their talents, to rob all the money of a modern Nevada gambling town. . . ." *Rob* means to steal from. If you think of *rob* as standing for Relieve Of Booty you'll never fall into the illiterate usage.

Rob takes the preposition *of.*

ROBBER, THIEF, BURGLAR

A news story reporting that a diplomat from Ghana in Washington was robbed at knife-point by three men referred to the rascals as *thieves.* They were not. It may be useful to draw the distinctions between the classes of larcenous lads. A *robber* is one who does his dirty work by the use or threat of force. A *thief* is one who does it secretly or stealthily. A *burglar* is one who breaks and enters premises with felonious intent. A *bandit* is one who . . . shucks, forget it; the word is too glamorous for the ordinary run of criminals, and it is overused in any event.

ROBOT

See FRANKENSTEIN.

ROOFTOP

What would a *rooftop* be, anyway? Use *housetop* or just plain *roof*.

ROUND

See BULLET.

'ROUND

Forget the apostrophe. In the phrase *year round*, for example, *round* is not a contraction of *around* but is a preposition in its own right. *See* ALL ROUND.

ROW

As a three-letter word, the noun *row* is a great temptation to headline writers trying to label a dispute: "South Africa Row on Defense Grows"; "Attlee Suffers in Row With Rebel Leader." To begin with, *row* is a casualism and not a serious enough word to describe the serious situations to which it is usually applied. To end with, it overstates the situation most times because it means a noisy quarrel or a brawl.

SAME

See SUCH.

SANITARIUM, SANATORIUM

The words are used pretty much interchangeably these days, *sanitarium* being the commoner form. If there is a distinction to be made it is that a *sanitarium* is a kind of general hospital and a *sanatorium* is more in the nature of a health resort where certain natural assets are good for what ails the patient but also where specific treatment is offered.

SATIATE

Takes preposition *with.*

SATURATE, SATURATED

Takes preposition *with.*

SAVE

As a synonym for *except* it is fancy and out of place in most present-day writing. Certainly it is out of place in journalistic writing like this: "Those who were nurses earned an average of $66 a week, more than those in any other profession save chemists, mathematicians, and statisticians." The word might well be left to the poets and to the occasional writer whose taste tells him that on the lofty literary plane on which he finds himself the word is appropriate.

SAVINGS

The use of *savings* as a singular noun is a solecism. "It would mean a reduction of about twenty-five motormen and conductors with an annual savings of $150,000." Dropping the "s" (or the "an") makes the difference between literacy and illiteracy.

SAY AND ITS SYNONYMS

One mark of an unsure writer is that he seems to tire quickly of the word *say*, and to feel that he must turn to a synonym: " 'I'm going for a walk,' said Tom. 'So am I,' averred Dick. 'You can come with me, then,' rejoined Tom. 'Okay,' Dick stated." It isn't always that the words are misused, but rather that they become conspicuous by their very variety, their needless variety. (*See* MONOLOGOPHOBIA.) Sometimes, however, they are actually misused. As is true of most synonyms, those for *say* are not exact equivalents. *Say* means to express. Here is what some of the synonyms mean: *affirm* is to declare as true; *assert* is to express strongly or positively; *asseverate* is to assert seriously; *aver* is to express with confidence; *declare* is to express explicitly, particularly in a formal or public way; *state* is to express in detail or to recite. It is well to discriminate among these shades of meaning or, failing that, to stick to *say*.

SCAN

See SCRUTINY.

SCARCELY

See HARDLY.

SCARED

Takes preposition *at* or *by*.

SCIENTIST

In an age that worships science everybody wants to be one of the high priests, and the congregation is constantly setting up false gods. The man who invents a self-sharpening lawn-mower or the man who calculates what percentage of cars coming off an assembly line will have one wheel missing likes to be called a *scientist*, and unfortunately there are many writers who will gratify his wish. Those who by investigation originate, develop, and systematize knowledge—that is a broad definition—may be termed *scientists*, though it would be more informative to designate even these people more specifically as *physicists, chemists,*

405

geologists, biologists, or what have you. Those who apply the scientist's findings are *engineers* or *technicians*—or perhaps *experts* or *specialists,* to take two more titles of the new aristocracy.

It should be pointed out in passing that *engineer* is also a badly mishandled term, and the engineers themselves resent your calling the man who replaces a tube in your television set "a television engineer." The short of the whole matter is that the widespread quest for status threatens to dilute solid, rather exact designations. It should be resisted.

SCRUTINY

Since *scrutiny* means careful or minute inspection, it is redundant to speak of "close scrutiny" or "careful scrutiny." Adverbs of similar meaning should, of course, be omitted when the verb *scrutinize* is used. *Scan,* in its primary meaning, is a synonym for *scrutinize:* to examine closely. But, paradoxically, in its more prevalent modern use it means to view hastily and superficially, as to *scan* the headlines.

SCULP, SCULPT

The humorous (but not very) words *sculp* and *sculpt* are BACK FORMATIONS from *sculpture.* One of the troubles with them is that they are used by the unknowing when no humor is intended: "The memorial was sculpted by Frederick Wellington Ruckstull." There is a perfectly good verb *sculpture* and that is what should be used.

SEARCH

In search takes preposition *of.*

SEASONABLE, SEASONAL

Seasonable means appropriate to the season or timely. When you write, "The weather was seasonable for the Fourth of July," you mean that the weather was in keeping with that time of year. *Seasonal* means associated with or connected with seasons, as in "Despite a seasonal rise, farm employment was below the level of September a year ago."

SECURE

Obtain and *get* are too homely for some people, and so they turn to *secure* as a more important-sounding variant. But *secure* does not mean, or should not be used to mean, precisely the same thing as *obtain*. The connotation of the word is the notion of obtaining with sureness and certainty. Thus, it is inexact usage to say, "He went to the store to secure a package of cigarettes," but it is exact to say, "Seats at the concert were not reserved, so we went to the hall early to secure good locations."

SEEING AS HOW

See how.

SEEM

See can't seem.

SELF-CONFESSED

"Here in New York the self-confessed slayer of Eileen Fahey was arraigned. . . ." Except in certain totalitarian countries, no one else can do your confessing for you. The idea of *self* is implicit in *confessed*. Therefore, write "confessed slayer."

SELF-DEPRECATING

One can *depreciate* (belittle) oneself, but cannot normally *deprecate* (protest against, disapprove of) oneself. *See* depre- cate, depreciate.

SELF-MADE

"Hong Kong still has to find adequate housing for 500,000 refugees, who live in self-made shacks." Admittedly this is a rare specimen, but what one writer has done another may also do. A *self-made* man is a man who has made himself. But a *self-made* shack. . . ?

Then again there was the sentence in a newspaper story, "But the bulk of Mr. Getty's fortune is self made." Smart money, eh? Maybe that's what is meant by "an independent income."

407

SEMI-
See BI-.

SEMICOLON
See PUNCTUATION.

SENIOR CITIZENS
One of the latter-day EUPHEMISMS, this is a term that could well be left to those who feel a need for it. There are plain words to say the same thing, e.g., in descending order of harshness, *the aged, the old, the elderly*, and, perhaps, *the older*.

SENSATIONAL
See ATOMIC FLYSWATTERS.

SENSIBLE
Takes preposition *of* or *to*.

SENSITIVE
Takes preposition *to* or *of*.

SENSUAL, SENSUOUS
Of these two words *sensual* is the coarser. It applies to gratification of the animal senses and has overtones of lewdness. *Sensuous* applies to enjoyment produced by appeal to the senses. Thus, *sensuous* music might stimulate *sensual* desires.

SEPARATE
The word is necessary in a sentence like this: "President Sukarno held separate meetings with his nine ministers." But it is excess baggage in a sentence such as, "Dr. Teller offered thirteen separate suggestions," where it contributes nothing to the meaning. Even worse is its appearance in this trite combination: "They stressed that forty-eight separate and distinct projects were involved." Try eliminating either adjective—better, both—and see whether there is any difference. *See also* DIFFERENT.

408

SEQUENCE OF TENSES

If a melody in a major key is transposed to a minor key, it is not just the first few notes that are modified; almost every phrase that follows undergoes change. Something similar happens in grammar: The verb in a subordinate clause is adjusted to the verb in the main clause. To take a simple example, "He says he is hungry" becomes, when turned into the past tense, "He said he was hungry." Unhappily, the problems that arise are usually not that simple, as any newspaperman will testify.

Journalism is peculiarly sensitive to the sequence-of-tenses question because for the most part it is recording the past—and not exclusively the immediate past, but successive layers or planes of past time. To a lesser degree most writing—fiction, history, scientific reports—is also dealing with the past and must face the grammatical questions involved in that kind of narration. Yet conventional books on grammar and syntax treat the subject skimpily, often nebulously.

It is not possible to set down a comprehensive, rigid set of rules concerning tense usage because writers differ in some of their ideas about it and often are capricious in their own composition. It is possible, however, to consider the more common problems that arise, and to suggest how they can be met.

1. The conversion of "He says he is hungry" to "He said he was hungry" is a conversion to what is called the *normal sequence*.

2. To this normal past-tense sequence there are exceptions. When the subject matter of the dependent clause concerns something that is a timeless truth, or is characteristic, or is habitual, the present tense is retained. The *exceptional sequence* (or, as Fowler terms it, the "vivid sequence") is used in such sentences as these: "The child did not know that dogs bite"; "The teacher told the class that the earth revolves around the sun." But there are exceptions even to these exceptions—instances in which the force of the normal sequence is irresistible: "I never knew you were a musician"; "When were you first told you were an adopted child?"

3. A simple past event is recorded in the *past tense:* "The

409

police reported the accident." An event prior to a simple past event is recorded in the *past perfect tense:* "The police reported that a car had swerved off the road." Still earlier events are also recorded in the past perfect tense (because we have no past-er tense than that): "The police reported that a car had swerved off the road after its steering gear had broken."

4. Sometimes these verbs of indirect discourse are used even when the actual governing verb has been omitted, though implied. It is a favorite device of conservative British journalism. A report of a Parliamentary debate will give the Prime Minister's views in this fashion: "No, he did not think there was any cause for alarm. If the country kept its defenses up and its alliances intact, all would be well." The "he said" is invisible, but it exerts its influence just the same. The device is even more common in fiction: "Her very vagueness frightened her, for life and death, rightly understood, were ominous dreadful words and she would never understand them. Life, as she had been taught in her youth, was meant to be pleasant, generous, simple. The future was a clear space of pure, silvery blue, like the sky over Paris in good weather. . . ." Again, the "she thought" is not expressed, but it governs every other verb.

5. The purpose of using the past perfect tense, of course, is to indicate that the event referred to is antecedent to another past event. If the subordinate clause includes a time element that itself indicates this priority, the past perfect becomes unnecessary and, in the view of some writers, even redundant. Proper usage would be: "A close friend reported Jones said last week that he would be elected." Although "had said" would not be wrong, "said" is preferable.

6. When the "he said" phrase appears anywhere but at the beginning of the sentence, the verbs in the other clauses are not affected by it; they remain in the same tense as in the original direct quotation. In such a position the "he said" phrase does not govern the sentence; it is a mere parenthetical interpolation. (*See* PARENTHETICAL PHRASES.) Hence this sentence is proper: "Jones is sure, he said, that he will be elected." But for exceptions to this primarily daily-newspaper approach see paragraphs 7 and 11.

7. To the foregoing paragraph there is this exception: When a statement is unequivocally associated with a particular time in the past, the tense used must indicate this. Although it is correct to use the present tense—that is, the tense of the original direct quotation—in such a sentence as, "He is sick and tired, he said, of graft in the police department," it is necessary to use the past tense in one like this: "He was sick and tired, he said, and asked to be excused from testifying." Another example of a statement associated with a particular time in the past: "He was glad, the speaker said, to see so many friendly faces."

8. Phrases such as *according to* and *in the opinion of*, when used in past-tense contexts, may be regarded—but do not have to be regarded—as equivalent to "he said." When they appear at the beginnings of sentences they may govern the subsequent verbs; when they appear anywhere else, however, they are considered to be mere parenthetical interpolations and do not govern the verbs.

9. The *present perfect tense* in a sense straddles the past and the present; it speaks of actions that are thought of as not wholly over and done with but closely associated with the present. For the purpose of tense sequence the present perfect is regarded as equivalent to the present tense, so the tense of a subordinate clause governed by the present perfect remains unchanged. This construction is incorrect: "The United States repeatedly has declared that the presence of Allied garrisons in West Berlin was [make it *is*] not a negotiable issue."

10. The tense of the dominant verb in a sentence does not necessarily and indiscriminately govern every other verb in the sentence. Sometimes clauses are interpolated or added almost as if the writer were taking you aside and revealing information quite outside the context of the rest of the sentence. In such sentences the verbs of these clauses go their own way. Example: "George M. Haskew, water engineer, said the main reservoir of the Plainfield Water Company, which supplies [not *supplied*] many communities in that area, was full for the first time since early June."

11. When future time is indicated in a subordinate clause,

special problems arise. One involves the time at which the sentence will be read. It would be quite proper for a newspaper to write: "Secretary of State Dean Rusk said he expected to discuss Berlin with Andrei A. Gromyko next week when they go to Geneva to sign a Laos accord." The Geneva meeting will still be in the future when the newspaper reader picks up his paper. However, if the same sentence was written for a monthly magazine or a history book, the verb "go" would be just as impossible as the phrase "next week." The verb would have to be "went." When the time of reading is not at issue—and it usually is not for the newspaper writer—the exceptional sequence ("go" in this instance) is preferable to the normal sequence ("went"). There are indeed occasions when the exceptional sequence will prevent ambiguity. Here is an ambiguous sentence: "Some believed that the same issue would be raised again when the name of Japan was presented this year." Does everything in the sentence refer to the past, or does some of it refer to the future? "Is presented" would have made the meaning unmistakable. Then there are some writers who seem to be so intimidated by the sequence-of-tenses idea that they modify a completely independent verb to make it conform to another verb that does not govern it at all. For example: "Tactical moves in the Senate apparently assured a showdown on civil rights legislation before this session of Congress adjourned [make it *adjourns*]." Another example: "Belgium presented to the United Nations today a detailed plan for the withdrawal of Belgian troops from Ruanda and Urundi within three months after the two African territories became [make it *become*] independent July 1." Another special problem of sequence in connection with future time arises when it is desirable to make certain that the clause containing the future element will be understood to be part of what a speaker or author was saying, rather than something contributed by the writer of the sentence. This is a relatively rare situation, but it does occur: "A South Vietnamese rebel leader said today that the aim of his movement was to form a coalition government with a neutral policy after the present administration had been overthrown and United States forces had withdrawn." Obviously to write "has

412

been overthrown" and "have withdrawn" would be to suggest that those things were surely going to happen rather than that they were thoughts in the mind of the rebel leader.

12. The *perfect infinitive* (containing the word "have") is used to denote action prior to something else. Thus it is improper to write, "She was the first woman ever to have completed the Channel swim." Delete "have" and make it "to complete." The construction "to have completed" would be correct only if a subsequent action was expressed; for example, ". . . to have completed the Channel swim before reaching the age of twenty-five." A similar solecism is the "doubling up" of the expression of past time by the use of the perfect infinitive: "He would have liked to have selected Mr. Gerosa's replacement [make it *to select*]"; "The comments of Senator Mahoney and others indicated that the Senate would have refused to have removed the Commissioner [make it *to remove*]."

13. The tense of the verb in a clause introduced by "after" is normally the past perfect ("After he had left, she wept"), but the simple past tense is acceptable. Likewise if a participle follows "after," it normally would be a *perfect participle* ("After having passed through customs, the travelers proceeded"), but here again the *present participle* ("passing") is acceptable.

14. Whether to use the present participle or the perfect participle sometimes constitutes a puzzle. Do you say, "Locking the door, she went out," or "Having locked the door, she went out"? In this instance you would say, "Locking the door, she went out." The test is whether there is a significant interval between the events. If there is, use the perfect participle; if there is not, use the present participle. You would not say, "Finishing his pie, the Ambassador rose from the table." There has to be an interval or the Ambassador would be guilty of an unlikely breach of etiquette. On the other hand, you would not say, "Having fallen ten stories, the workman crashed to his death on the pavement." What is being described there is a continuous sequence. If there is an interval between two events, it may or may not be regarded as significant. Thus you might write either "He was quoted as saying" or "He was quoted as having said."

413

SERIES OUT OF CONTROL

A normal series, or enumeration, follows the pattern "1, 2, and 3." A series out of control, or, as Fowler dubs it, a bastard enumeration, would be "1, 2, and A." Hence, a normal series would be, "He likes reading books, listening to music, and seeing plays," whereas a series out of control would be, "He likes reading books, listening to music, and he doesn't go out much." Such solecisms occur when a writer embarks on a series and then, out of carelessness or forgetfulness (which are about the same thing), or out of ignorance of how a conjunction should be used, abandons the series and turns to something else. If it is kept in mind that a conjunction connects equivalents (*reading, listening*, and *seeing*, for example), the error should not be difficult to avoid. It is surprising how common the mistake is—probably the most common writing fault extant after disagreement between subject and verb (*See* NUMBER).

Look at these: "The home side struggled along with weak pitching, anemic fielding, and what hitting they did lacked authority"; "The seniors, wearing chemises, rolled-down stockings, and revealing rouged knees, performed . . ."; "The owners pay fines, protest that rehabilitation of the old dwellings would be prohibitively costly, and the situation remains unchanged in most cases"; "The production models will have a speed of sixty-five miles an hour, a range of 150 miles, and carry 300 pounds." In addition to carelessness, the fault in all these instances is undoubtedly traceable to the fact that some writers would rather kick their grandmothers than be caught repeating a word—in the examples cited the word *and*, which should be inserted between the first and second items in the series.

SERVICE

As a verb, *service* is greatly overused when *serve* would serve better. Perhaps because Americans think *serve* suggests something menial, perhaps because *service* has become a piece of commercial jargon widely disseminated by the advertising profession —and perhaps because of an unthinking preference for the bigger word over the smaller—*service* has almost come to displace *serve*. There is a role for *service*: when it is used to mean provide maintenance, repairs, inspection, and the like. It is properly used here: "The company received a long-term contract to install and service all the city's parking meters." Obviously *serve* would not do in that context. But *service* is just as obviously out of place in these sentences: "The West Shore Railroad services both states"; "Dr. Walsh estimated that the hospital ship would spend eight months in Indonesia, servicing that country and perhaps others."

SET, SIT

For most practical purposes *set* is transitive only—that is, it transfers action to an object—and *sit* is intransitive. You *set* the plate on the table, you don't *sit* it there. There are a few inconsequential exceptions: The sun *sets* (intransitive) and the hen *sets* (intransitive); one *sits* oneself at a table (transitive) and *sits* a horse (transitive). Normally, inanimate objects do not *sit*, but there are exceptions here, too: the setting sun may be said to *sit* on the horizon, and the satellite may be said to *sit* atop the rocket booster.

SEVERAL

The word means more than a couple but not a great many. This use is not right: "Several hundred persons soon will be approached on the question of staggering their working hours. The responses, which will be sought from 1,400 to 1,800 of those employed in Manhattan's central business district, will be tabulated within the next month." Fourteen hundred is too many hundreds to be called *several*.

SEWAGE, SEWERAGE

Sewerage is the system, including *sewers*, for the disposal of waste matter and surplus water. *Sewage* is what passes through such a system.

SHALL AND WILL

Miss Thistlebottom probably taught you that to express simple futurity in a declarative sentence you should use *shall* in the first person and *will* in the second and third persons, whereas to express determination you should simply reverse that order. However, never in all history was greater determination expressed —in violation of that rule—than in Winston Churchill's defiant declaration of June, 1940: "We shall not flag or fail. We shall go on to the end. We shall fight in France, we shall fight on the seas and oceans, we shall fight with growing confidence and strength in the air; we shall defend our island, whatever the cost may be. We shall fight on the beaches, we shall fight on the landing grounds, we shall fight in the fields and in the streets, we shall fight in the hills; we shall never surrender."

Perhaps you, too, have forgotten Miss Thistlebottom's prescription. If not, this is as good a time as any to do so. *Will* has just about taken over the field in declarative sentences. *Shall* seems to lend a faint touch of formality to what is being expressed, as in the Churchill statement, and so is not entirely extinct. But no one could brand a writer a culprit for ignoring Miss Thistlebottom's rules, any more than he could convict a writer who followed them. The usage in America, at least, has simply left the rules behind, and there has been no detectable loss in precise expression.

SHAMBLES

The original attraction of this much-misused word may have lain in the fact that the writer could startle his public by using an obviously plural word with a singular article—*a*. In any event, writers are still under its spell and seem not to care what the word means. A *shamble* was originally a bench, then a bench for displaying meats, then by extension an abattoir. In a figurative extension the plural means a scene of slaughter. But it does not mean merely a wrecked or littered place, as in this sentence: "The dormitory of the New Jersey State Prison Farm was a shambles."

For some writers the word seems to have lost all trace of its original meaning. Witness: "Is it rationally defensible that . . . we should risk a thermonuclear war which not only would leave that very city a heap of shambles, but in addition would spell the end of Europe?" Heap of shambles, indeed! Clearly, in that writer's mind the word meant nothing more than ruins. It may be that *shambles* is succumbing to BERNSTEIN'S SECOND LAW, but possibly it can still be rescued.

SHOW

In the sense of to appear, *show* is a sad casualism. "Mr. Dix failed to show for questioning." Interestingly, the original slang expression was *show up*, but perhaps because this was not terse enough or tough enough for the present-day slang slingers, it was bobtailed into *show*. (*See* VERB TAILS.) Now the word has been consecrated by the aviation industry: A prospective passenger who reserves space on a plane and fails to *show* is a *no-show*, and he is as out of favor as the word that describes him.

SHOWED

The past participle of *show* is commonly *shown*. The following must be classed as a rarity: "Critics said that Mr. Gregory had showed himself to be an ultraconservative."

SIC

Fowler says that *sic*, Latin for so or thus, "amounts to Yes, he did say that, or Yes, I do mean that, in spite of your natural doubts. It should be used only when doubt *is* natural." Surely there could be no doubts, natural or otherwise, about the slogan described in the following passage: "The Automobile Merchants Association of New York and the Brooklyn and Long Island Automobile Dealers Association will open a drive next Friday under the theme 'You Auto Buy—Now!' (sic)." The word *sic* should never be used to clobber the reader into seeing the point of a joke. An additional item about its use is this: Many writers think an exclamation point is necessary after *sic*, sic: *sic!* It isn't; the word is not supposed to say, "Can you beat this!" or "Golly, gee!" or anything like that; it means merely "That's what the man said (or wrote)."

417

SIDESWIPE

Sideswipe seems to have been originally a railroading term based on the word *swipe,* meaning a swinging blow. *Swipe* is slang, however, so apparently a few generations ago some finicky people, reluctant to give up a word so useful, especially to newspaper people, decided to make it respectable and transformed it into *sidewipe.* The "purified" form has an artificial sound, however, and *sideswipe* is now the commonly accepted word.

SIMILAR

Takes preposition *to.*

SIMILE

See RHETORICAL FIGURES AND FAULTS.

SIMPLE REASON

The phrase "for the simple reason that" is best avoided because it suggests a superior attitude toward the reader. "Shipping sources said here that they welcomed the lower air rates agreed on in Cannes, France, for the simple reason that heightened interest in travel to Europe was bound to benefit all means of transportation." The writer seems to be saying, "The reason is simple; why didn't you think of it yourself, you halfwit?" Sometimes the reason is not simple at all, and the phrase creates the suspicion that the writer is trying to suggest the superiority of his intellectual grasp. Incidentally, from the point of view of lean prose the phrase requires five words to say what can be said in one—*because.*

The words *of course* can have the same patronizing flavor, as in, "Clebsch was, of course, the greatest German mathematician of the nineteenth century." Can that statement be accepted as a matter of course by most readers? On the other hand, *of course* can on occasion be helpful to a writer in establishing an attitude of confidence in the reader's intelligence or comprehension or in establishing a bond of sympathy or kinship: "Einstein's Theory is, of course, difficult to understand in all its ramifications." When to use the phrase and when to avoid it are matters of judgment.

418

SIMULTANEOUS

A common, if mild, solecism is illustrated in this sentence: "Now, simultaneous with the continuing anti-Malaysia agitation, Jakarta is pressuring the three major oil companies in Indonesia." It is not the immediately following phrase that is modified by *simultaneous*, but rather the verb, "is pressuring," and thus an adverb is required—*simultaneously*.

Similar constructions occur with *previous* and *doubtless*, but both these words are adverbs as well as adjectives, whereas *simultaneous* is an adjective only. It is perfectly proper to write, "Previous to the continuing anti-Malaysia agitation, Jakarta was pressuring . . . ," or, "Doubtless, Jakarta is pressuring the oil companies to win concessions." But *simultaneous* will not do. If *simultaneous* is used as an adjective—after a copulative verb, for example—it is proper: "Jakarta's pressure was simultaneous with the anti-Malaysia agitation."

SINCE

1. REDUNDANT "UNTIL." *Since* means from some time in the past until the present; therefore an *until* phrase used in conjunction with it is out of place. Wrong: "Sewanee had not fielded a baseball team since 1922 until this spring." Make it "from 1922 until this spring," or "between 1922 and this spring," or simply "since 1922."

2. TENSES WITH "SINCE." Because *since* covers past time up to the present, it requires a verb that does the same thing, and this means the present perfect tense. (The verb of the clause introduced by *since*, however, is in the simple past tense.) Wrong: "There has been no definite agreement on any one of the many issues that kept Laos divided since a ceasefire was declared in the civil war last year." Make it "have kept."

For an error combining since *and* ago, *see* AGO, SINCE.

SINUS

An example of ignorant spoken language creeping into print:

419

"U. S. Ambassador to India John Kenneth Galbraith, undergoing treatment for sinus. . . ." A *sinus* is a bodily cavity, so to speak of "treatment for sinus" is like speaking of "treatment for leg" or "treatment for heart." What the Ambassador was being treated for was *sinusitis* or a *sinus infection* or perhaps a *sinus condition. See also* VIRUS.

SIT
See SET, SIT.

SIZE
See PROPORTIONS.

SKIRT AROUND
"The tanker, the 1,900-ton *Pianetta*, was expected to skirt around submerged obstacles." Delete *around*; the word *skirt* means to move *around*.

SLANDER
See LIBEL, SLANDER.

SLAVE
Takes preposition *to* or *of*.

SMALL IN NUMBER
See IN NUMBER, IN SIZE.

SO FAR AS
See AS FAR AS.

SOLICITOUS
Takes preposition *of*, *for*, or *about*.

SOLUTION
Takes preposition *of* or *to*.

SOME

When used before a figure, *some* means approximately or more or less. Therefore this usage is ridiculous: "Some 35,683 attended the races at Aqueduct." And this one is redundant: "The President has made a happy gesture in gathering at the White House some thirty-odd leading figures in the sports world." *See also* ABOUT *and* ODD.

SOMETIME, SOME TIME

Sometime means at a point of time; thus, "The statements were made sometime last month." When the *some* is intended to be an adjective modifying *time* and producing the equivalent of *a short time* or *a long time* or *an indefinite time*, the term is written as two words. These, therefore, are incorrect: "Statements made sometime ago by the Atomic Energy Commission . . ."; "For sometime now, Wallachs has been giving away little woven labels, for shirts, that say 'Please—No Starch!' "

SONIC WRITING

Writing by sound (or by ear) is not necessarily sound writing. The sonic writer is first cousin to the coiner of the CURDLED CLICHÉ; his trouble is a combination of carelessness and faulty reproduction of tonal elements. The reporter who hears an interviewee say, "It strains credulity," and, unfamiliar with the phrase, reproduces it as, "It's strange credulity," is a sonic writer. The fault is, to be sure, not common, but neither is it rare. The following examples give evidence:

"Both Senator Mahoney and Speaker Heck have also featured in speculation." It almost sounds right, but the desired word is *figured*.

"He was tearing in rickety-split, when he saw he couldn't make the catch." Japanese accent? The word is *lickety-split*.

"He finds the West Berliners worrying these days, if not about shoes and ships and ceiling wax, then about pigeons and asparagus." If there's floor wax, why not ceiling wax? But no. Let's stick to *sealing wax*.

"It all points up the growing awareness of the fact that

421

language barriers are among those that must be raised if the world is truly to become one." Raising those barriers would only raze more hell.

"Before serving two years in the Army, Grim had only a spattering of minor league experience." Maybe the rookie made a splash, but still the word is *smattering*.

"Obviously, no sensible American President will unlease a suicidal holocaust unless the concession demanded is huge. . . . A defeat-crazed leader . . . might still unlease the Doomsday Bomb." One *unlease* in a semi-learned journal might suggest a printer who had slipped his leash, but two of them suggest a sonic writer.

"Among his colleagues Mr. Woodward is known for being an avaricious reader." Undoubtedly a subconscious combination of *avid* and *voracious* rather than the word *avaricious* itself, which has a quite different meaning.

"There is a rather widespread reluctance to enter the listings against Mayor Wagner." This one looks like a subconscious combination of *enter the lists* and *take to the hustings*.

"The clear-cut policy of N.B.C. to cover the news and worry about the consequences later is imminently appealing." *Eminently*.

These errors do not arise from ignorance. In virtually every instance if the writer's attention were directed to the mistake he would smile sheepishly and reach for his pencil. The errors do arise, however, from the similarity of sound and the thoughtlessness it induces. Thoughtlessness, it need not be added, is an enemy of good writing.

SOONER

An adjective or an adverb in the comparative degree is followed by *than*, except when used by the sufferers from AD-DICTION in Madison Avenue, where a cigarette is merely smoother, a detergent is merely sudsier, a coffee is merely coffee-er, and an analgesic works merely faster—but not *than* anything.

It should come as no surprise, then, that *sooner* should be followed by *than*. Yet a common solecism is to substitute *when* for *than,* as in this example: "No sooner had the inquiry been announced when it became known that eighty-nine Eastern and Western railroads were appealing. . . ." The error arises from thinking of *no sooner* as if it were *scarcely* or *hardly.* (*See* HARDLY.) Incidentally and irrelevantly, when we say *no sooner* we usually actually mean *a little sooner.* And a little sooner is an Oklahoma baby. Where does that leave us?

SOPHISTICATED

In an extended and amusing passage in *Comfortable Words,* Evans traces the mutations of what he terms "one of our most erratic words." Successively it has meant wise, oversubtle, adulterated, corrupted, worldly wise, and highly complex. Its latest meaning is refined, not in the social sense but in the sense of an advanced stage of development. Thus we have *sophisticated* second- and third-generation missiles, and a President has told us that assessment of the country's budget problems "requires a more sophisticated view than the old and automatic cliché that deficits automatically bring inflation." These new meanings of the word are not so far removed from the old as might appear. An underlying element has always been the notion of change from original condition, or complication of the artless state. Such alterations sometimes have had bad associations and sometimes good ones. At present good has triumphed over evil, but no one knows what the next mutation will bring.

SORT OF
See KIND OF.

SOUGHT
Takes preposition *after* or *for.*

SPARING
Takes preposition *of.*

SPATE
Literally, a *spate* is a kind of flash flood. By extension, it

means a quick, overwhelming torrent of whatever it is that is being spoken of. In this sense it is a FAD WORD, much overused. Sometimes it is misused, as in this sentence: "A spate of books on the Civil War has been appearing in the last several years." All that is meant—or needed—here is a *large number, a great many*, or, if you will, an *outpouring*.

SPEAKING OF
See DANGLERS.

SPECIAL
See ESPECIAL, SPECIAL.

SPECIALIST
See SCIENTIST.

SPELL OUT
Spell out is a tired old work horse that deserves a rest. "The full details of Consolidated Edison's purchase plan were spelled out at a public hearing"; "The Government refused to spell out details behind the indictment"; "Mr. Rockefeller did not spell out the details of his proposal"; "This has been clearly spelled out in news dispatches." *Spell out* means to explain clearly and to provide the details. If you must use the cliché, at least spare us the details.

SPIRAL
A *spiral* keeps going round and round but has no sense of up-and-down direction unless the writer gives it one. It is not enough to write, "Prospects for ending the sixty-five-year ban on the sale of precolored oleomargarine in this state spiraled today." The word should be escorted by "upward" or "downward" or, still better, should be replaced.

SPLIT INFINITIVE
There is nothing wrong with splitting an infinitive ("He is going to about make the grade") except that eighteenth-

and nineteenth-century grammarians, for one reason or another, frowned on it. And most grammar teachers have been frowning ever since. The natural position for a modifier is before the word it modifies (*See* ADVERBS, PLACEMENT OF). Thus the natural position for an adverb modifying an infinitive should be just ahead of the infinitive and just after the *to* (usually designated the "sign of the infinitive").

That is what reason has to say on the subject. But reason and logic are not always the determining considerations in usage. As the permissivists are so fond of telling us, what the language should be cannot always stand up in the face of what the language is. In this instance what the language is has been profoundly shaped by those dead grammarians and their heirs and assigns. For better or worse, their taboo against the split infinitive is a linguistic fact of life, which a writer ignores at his own risk. Does that mean the risk should never be taken? By no means.

Reasonable or unreasonable, the unsplit infinitive must be accepted as today's norm; it is what readers as well as writers have been taught is correct. Stylistically there is sometimes much to be said for the unsplit infinitive, particularly if a long phrase intervenes between the *to* and the infinitive: "He intended to, without speech-making or fuss and feathers, take his place on the rostrum." But in addition it is unwise to appear to be going out of one's way to defy the current norm, as in this sentence: "Specialists were unable to definitely identify representative specimens from the site." Here the writer might have said "could not definitely identify" and thus have avoided attracting undesired attention. Again, "Congress tightened up quarantine laws to allow the Department of Agriculture to thoroughly search cargoes from abroad." The "thoroughly" could be placed after "abroad" or dropped altogether.

There are those, of course, who would not permit a split infinitive in any circumstances. And, on the other hand, there are those who would greatly relax the taboo. Curme, for instance, in an unusual display of ardent advocacy, says that "the split infinitive is an improvement of English expression," and then, to show how common it has become, lists three and a half pages of examples ranging from Burns to Herbert Hoover "taken from the author's much larger collection." The compilation is impressive, but naturally a similar compilation of unsplit infinitives would run into volumes that no library on earth could contain. Nevertheless, Curme's contention that the split infinitive is often an improvement and his observation that it is becoming more common cannot be disputed.

Starting from the premise that the unsplit infinitive is the current norm, let us examine when it is preferable to depart from it:

1. When avoiding the split infinitive produces ambiguity. "The Thanksgiving Day setback was sure to defer further American hopes of keeping pace with the Soviet Union in lunar exploration." Does "further" modify "defer" or "hopes"? All would be clear if it read "to further defer." Here is an infinitive properly split to avoid a similar ambiguity: "It would be a blessed day indeed if the public could be persuaded to quietly denounce poor service and tip truly according to conscience."

2. When avoiding the split infinitive is almost impossible. "Rumania's Communist rulers expect the nation's industrial output to more than double in the next five years"; "The Governor has decided to all but give up on his minimum wage bill"; "He refused to so much as listen to the prisoner's appeal."

3. When avoiding the split infinitive produces clumsiness or artificiality. Just as splitting an infinitive can invite unwelcome attention, so the obvious taking of evasive action to avoid splitting one can also be undesirably conspicuous. "The Premier proceeded to admonish sharply the ten die-hard Opposition speakers." A reader can only wonder why "sharply" is in that position. Another unnatural placement: "The objective is apparently almost to double coffee consumption in the Soviet Union in the next three years." Only fear of the taboo prevented these writers from saying the natural things: "to sharply admonish" and "to almost double."

Sometimes a writer will cringe in terror before an imagined taboo. When an infinitive contains an auxiliary—a part of the verb *to be* or *to have*—even the most hair-splitting anti-infinitive-splitter does not contend that an adverb cannot stand before the main verb. Complete sanction is given to such a construction as "His aim in life was to be constantly improving"; this, says Curme (and he speaks for the overwhelming majority), "does not seem to be generally felt as a split infinitive." Yet an occasional timid soul (this one was a teacher of English, no less) writes: "The college girl has indeed done admirably, considering that she is pulled in one direction by this force, in another direction by her desire properly to be educated." The natural sequence —"to be properly educated"—is also the approved one.*

The issue of the split infinitive has been undergoing a gradual change. It may well be that fifty years from now the taboo will be dead. But for the present the careful writer will in general observe it and when necessary disregard it. He will disregard it not defiantly but boldly—boldly in the sure knowledge that he knows what he is doing and can convince the discriminating reader of that fact, boldly because he is aware that to do otherwise would be to fall into ambiguity or awkwardness.

SPONDEE

See FOOT.

SPOONFULS

From a recipe: "Now throw in two tablespoons full of chopped parsley and cook ten minutes more. The quail ought to be tender by then." Never mind the quail; how are we ever going to get those tablespoons tender? The word, of course, is *tablespoonfuls,* no matter how illogical it seems. One dictionary contains the entry *spoonsful,* but this is not generally accepted.

STALEMATE

A technical term that, like GAMBIT, must be handled with care, as it was not in this sentence: "The stalemate that settled

* In the example just given, "educated" would usually be regarded as a verb, different from "informed" in the sentence "To be fully informed, read *The New York Times.*" This distinction is discussed under VERY.

427

on the Congo seemed to be lifting." Chess nuts will tell you that a *stalemate* is as final as checkmate, and it cannot be eased, broken, lifted, or anything else except, perhaps, avoided.

STATE
See SAY AND ITS SYNONYMS.

STATISTICS
See -ICS.

STEP UP
See FAD WORDS.

STEVEDORE
See LONGSHOREMAN.

STICK UP FOR
"President Tito had never ceased to insist that he would stick up for his independence." A juvenile casualism, it means to defend, champion, or side with; and since it means these things, why not use one of them or something like it?

STILL AND ALL
It is a dialectal expression. "Granted that on occasion the mere presence of TV can impart a theatrical flavor to an event deserving of serious reportorial study, still and all the Fourth Estate cannot altogether ignore the larger issue." The phrase crops up sometimes in speech, but it is inappropriate in careful writing. And incidentally, it is wasteful of words: Why not just *still?*

STOMACH
See BELLY.

STRAITJACKET
It should not be spelled *straightjacket.* A *straitjacket* is not a jacket that is straight—i.e., without curves or angles—but one that is confining, which is the sense of *strait.*

428

STRANGLED

"Rubinstein was found strangled to death on Jan. 27, 1955"; ". . . the Broadway Butterfly, who was strangled to death in 1924. . . ." Delete *to death* in each case. That's what *strangled* means.

STRATA

"Around the death of Mr. Kennedy has sprung up a mystique. In part it reflects the deep guilt feelings which afflict so wide a strata of our contemporary society." *Strata* is a plural noun. The singular is *stratum*. *See also* AGENDA, DATA, *and* MEDIA.

STREAMLINED

The word is usually a meaningless jazzer-upper. "A streamlined program of teacher training designed to attract persons into the profession was outlined yesterday." Unless the plan was to cut down wind resistance in training teachers, what was intended here was *new, novel, improved, more efficient, less cumbersome, shorter,* or some other more precise substitute for the fuzzy *streamlined*.

STREET

For the number of this noun following *between* and *from*, *see* BETWEEN AND FROM.

STRESS

See EMPHASIZE.

STRIVE

Takes preposition *for, with,* or *against*.

STUDENT

See PUPIL.

STUNNING

See ATOMIC FLYSWATTERS.

SUBJECT

Takes preposition *to* or *of*.

SUBJUNCTIVES

The subjunctive mood of a verb is the form associated with condition, command, wish, doubt, desire, possibility, and the like. Most authorities agree that the subjunctive as a form evidenced by an identifiable verb change is vanishing in modern English.

There are certain exceptions. One is the use of the subjunctive for poetical or rhetorical effect: "Would I had wings!"; "Philosophers must deal with the question of the meaning of life, if indeed it have any at all." These uses, it will be observed, lend an archaic flavor to writing, and unless that is desired they should be shunned. Another exception is the use of the subjunctive in certain frozen phrases: "The public be damned!"; "Far be it from me . . ."; "Lest it be thought . . ."; "God forbid"; "Come what may." A third exception is the use of the subjunctive after verbs connoting command or request: "The attorney insisted that the prisoner be admitted to bail"; "The Senator urged that the bill allow certain exemptions." A fourth exception is the use of *were* in some contexts expressing conditions or wishes: Bryant cites as examples "If I were you, I would not do that" and "I wish I were in Europe," then adds: "Even here the tendency today is to use the indicative *was*, the *were* being principally a literary idiom." This final observation is open to great doubt; "if I was you" would be classed as illiterate, and "I wish I was in Europe" is only a mite better, perhaps because of the influence of "I wish I was in Dixie."

The fourth exception includes a use of the subjunctive that is very much alive and kicking: in expressing conditions that are not true or are merely hypothetical. Most writers have no difficulty with such conditional constructions. They write almost instinctively, "If I were king"; "If the Congo were not an underdeveloped country, its political troubles would not be so acute." Difficulties do arise, however, from making the unwarranted assumption that *if* always introduces a condition that is contrary to fact and thus should always be followed by a subjunctive. *If* may introduce clauses of supposition or concession, as well as conditions that are not true or are hypothetical, and in such clauses the verb is usually in the indicative, not the subjunctive, mood.

In the following incorrect examples the proper word is *italicized:* "If these efforts be [*are*] successful, our example will be noted and emulated in other Northern communities"; "He repeated his denial at a news conference when asked if he were [*was*] 'prepared to die for another's crime' "; "The Egyptian declared that if there were [*was*] more trouble the U.A.R. would 'exterminate Israel.' " (This previous example also involves a question of SEQUENCE OF TENSES.) "If many Japanese may be [*are*] hazy as to the religious significance of Christmas, the merchants seem to have missed nothing of the Western techniques in pursuing the commercial aspects of the holiday"; "The State Department press officer said that if there were [*was*] any 'distortion' it was Dr. Halperin's own."

As if and *as though* normally introduce unfactual or hypothetical statements and so should be followed by the subjunctive mood, not the indicative as in this sentence: "Justice Frankfurter issued a dissenting opinion that looked as if it was going to stop on page 5. . . ." A sentence containing an *as if* may be thought of as an elliptical version of a fuller construction, which in this instance would read, "Justice Frankfurter issued a dissenting opinion that looked as it would look if it were going to stop on page 5. . . ." In the fuller construction *was* is impossible, and it is equally impossible in the sentence cited. The same holds true for this one: "Though visibly exhausted from a long day in the Senate, he addressed the almost empty chamber as if every member was (make it *were*) in his place." *See also* AS IF, AS THOUGH.

A not-uncommon error is to have an inconsistency of moods in the *protasis* and the *apodosis*. If you suffer from this affliction, don't see a doctor; just read on. The protasis is the condition: "If your grandmother had wheels. . . ." The apodosis is the consequence: ". . . she'd be a trolley car." Notice that both parts are couched in the subjunctive. Here are typical errors: "If you paid

431

$100, we don't believe you can beat these suits." (The "paid" is a subjunctive, equivalent of "were to pay." But the "can" is indicative; it should be "could.") "If the program is implemented, it would represent the greatest expenditure of school building funds over such a period in the history of the city." (Here there are two possibilities: change the "would" to "will," on the assumption that the protasis is suppositional; or change the "is" to "were," on the assumption that the protasis is subject to serious doubt or is hypothetical.) "Counterforce strategy means that in nuclear war we would hope to attack only military installations, not cities, provided an enemy observes similar rules." (The apodosis—which comes first in this sentence—is subjunctive; therefore the protasis should also be subjunctive: "observed" or "were to observe.")

SUBSEQUENT TO

A wasteful locution. It means *after*. *See also* PRIOR TO.

SUBSTITUTE

Here is a common solecism: "He wanted to substitute bird-hunting sprees on Christmas with a more conservation-minded practice." Fowler devotes almost two full pages to what is, for him, an angry discussion of this error. But the point to be made —which he never makes—is simply this: If you find yourself about to follow *substitute* with any preposition other than *for*, it is just about certain you are wrong. In the quoted sentence *replace* should substitute for *substitute*.

SUCH

As a pronoun, *such* is best avoided in at least two kinds of contexts. One is the kind in which *same* would be the word chosen in legalistic or business English: "For those who fancy such, the tripe is first-rate." *Same* and *such* are equally nondescript when used in this manner. The other context is one in which *such* means *the like*: "The party feasted on hot dogs, hamburgers, and such." Both must be classed as casualisms, to be used only with semihumorous intent.

432

Sometimes *such* is used adverbially, although the word is not an adverb. We say, "He is such a bright boy that he should be advanced more rapidly." The *such* here does not mean *the kind of* (adjective), but rather the degree of brightness (adverb). We may, of course, bow to those who would put strict grammar ahead of idiom and change it to "He is so bright a boy," but there is no need to do so. However, if the phrase is "such difficult problems," which we would have to change to the stilted "problems so difficult," we are justified in telling the critics to go climb the tree they are trying to put us up. *See also* THAT, RELATIVE PRONOUN.

SUFFER

Takes preposition *with* or *from.*

SUFFIXATION

If *suffixation* has an unpleasant sound, that is what is intended, because it describes a mostly unpleasant process. This is the process, more widespread today than ever before, of coining new words by using real or imagined suffixes. It is indulged in usually by advertisers bent on novelty or by merchants bowed in ignorance.

A classic instance is the development of "-burger" as a suffix. In the beginning there was *hamburger,* beefsteak prepared as it was prepared in the German city of Hamburg, i.e., chopped. Some roadside etymologist got the idea the word designated something containing *ham* prepared in *burger* style, whatever that was. He decided to call his meat patties *beefburgers.* He wasn't really saying anything different from *hamburgers,* but apparently he and his customers thought he was, and so *hamburgers* became *beefburgers.* The new designation caught on (though the old one did not disappear). Thus, "-burger" made its debut as a suffix suggesting something chopped. From there it was a mere hop, skip, and gulp to *cheeseburgers, nutburgers,* and *what-have-you-burgers.*

Then there is "-cade," which never was a genuine suffix either. The word *cavalcade* (originally from the Italian *cavalcata*) means a procession on horseback. When newspapers began to

433

refer to automobile processions as *cavalcades*, the purists howled. The news writers, supposing that the "caval" part of the word referred to horses (which it did) and the "cade" part to a procession (which it did not), obliged the purists by inventing *motorcade*. The purists were not obliged, but the word was and is useful. We now have, in addition, *aquacade*, which presumably was thought of originally as a procession of swimming events.

New inventions and new situations require new words, and suffixation helps meet the need. The earliest days of radio brought us the word *broadcast* in a new meaning: disseminate in all directions by wireless. Came then television and with it the need for a new word. The new word turned out to be *telecast*, which does not mean anything substantially different from *broadcast* (since the "tele-" part of *television* simply denotes the idea of distance), yet the association of *telecast* with *television* was sufficient to convey the meaning. The suffix "-cast" has also been made to do duty in designating a particular kind of program—a *newscast*.

Sometimes a suffix is employed to lend an important sound to a commonplace thing. The suffix "-orium" makes a swimming pool into a *natatorium* and a filling station into a *lubritorium*. The day may yet come when a used-car lot will be christened an *autotorium*.

No discussion of suffixation would be complete without mention of the two most common and most ridiculous word endings: "-rama" and "-thon." The "-rama" class began with two legitimate words, *panorama* and *cyclorama*, which include the Greek *horama*, meaning a view. The first sign of proliferation came with the word *Cinerama*, which still contained the legitimate notion of view. From there on, however, "-rama" became a form of AD-DICTION used not to mean anything related to a view but to suggest something smashing, spectacular, or huge. A *camerarama* turned out to be a sale of cameras. An air-conditioner dealer advertised a *trade-o-rama*. Robert E. Morseberger in *The New York Times* Book Review (Feb. 26, 1961) listed the following discoveries, among others: *cleanorama* (a spectacular cleaning spree), *tomatorama, beanarama, bananarama* (sensational sales of tomatoes, beans, and bananas), *bowlarama* (twenty bowling alleys with automatic pin setting), and *teasarama* (a panoramic display of feminine contours).

The ending "-thon" began with the word *marathon,* denoting a long-distance foot race. The endurance idea of the word apparently suggested itself to a press agent who found himself promoting an endless dancing contest in the dizzy Twenties, and he dubbed it a *danceathon.* That did it. From then on "-thon" became a suffix denoting long distance or long time, and up cropped such words as *walkathon, talkathon* (usually substituted for *filibuster* in describing a certain kind of Senate debate), *telethon* (long-distance long distance?) and *sale-a-thon* (sale prices effective all week). And there is no end in sight to this wordathon.

More recently there has been a flood of "-in" words. The torrent began with the union tactic of the *sit-in,* and the civil rights campaign swelled it with such coinages as *stand-in, lie-in, wade-in, swim-in,* and (getting further and further away from the original notion) *stall-in, dump-in, pray-in,* and *school-in.*

It is unfortunate that the process of suffixation is so prolific and that it breeds so many bastards. But that is true of human reproduction, too. Yet in both instances good and useful offspring often emerge and it would be ridiculous to condemn either process. What we can do in the case of suffixation, however, is to practice birth control.

SUITABLE
Takes preposition *to, for,* or *with.*

SUPERIOR
Takes preposition *to.*

SUPERLATIVES
1. WITH TWO THINGS. The boxing referee who confides to the gladiators in the ring, while four million literates and illiterates listen in by television, that he wishes them "Good luck, and may the better man win" may be grammatically correct but he is guilty of OVERREFINEMENT. His offense is trying to improve on idiom.

There are a few idioms in which the superlative is used when only two things are being compared: "May the best man win"; "In the bout he got the worst of it"; "Put your best foot forward" (although Shakespeare wrote in *King John*, "Nay, but make haste; the better foot before," and in *Titus Andronicus*, "Come on, my lords, the better foot before"). Unless you are Shakespeare, idioms should not be tampered with.

But aside from such constructions, the general precept is that the comparative degree is used when two things are involved, although spoken language often uses the superlative. Thus, the following sentences should be corrected as indicated: "The worst [*worse*] of the two power failures knocked out four of the five Brooklyn-bound BMT subway lines"; "The new cards were presented to Miss Josephine and Miss Margery; Miss Josephine, as the oldest [*older*], again received No. 1"; "The report on the hypothetical satellite is perhaps the least [*less*] surprising of the two."

2. TEN BEST OR BEST TEN? Webster says that "in good usage" superlatives precede numerals used in a collective sense ("The best ten pictures of the year," where you are thinking of a group of ten that is best) and follow those used distributively ("The three worst pictures of the year," where you are thinking not of a group of three but of three individual films).

This seems to be a rather precious distinction and one that is not generally observed. The tendency is rather to put the numeral first—"the ten best pictures." (*But compare* OTHER.) A letter writer attempts to make an even finer point about this usage; he objects to "the ten best pictures" on the ground that if the pictures vary in quality only one can be the "best." There is no validity to this argument because a superlative does not necessarily apply to only a single thing: we commonly say "one of the finest painters of the fifteenth century" or "among the worst examples of architecture," using the superlative to describe a plurality of things. It is well to observe fine distinctions, but if we begin to create them where they do not exist we run the danger of becoming tongue-tied—or typewriter-tied.

436

SUPINE

See PRONE.

SUPREME

See INCOMPARABLES.

SURPRISE, ASTONISH

You won't catch this book retailing that bromidic tale about Noah Webster (or was it Dr. Samuel Johnson or neither?) who, when his wife said she was *surprised* at catching him dallying with the maid, replied, "No, madam, it is I who am surprised; you are astonished." Nevertheless, the tale makes a point worth noticing about the two words, whose meanings tend to overlap these days. Both words convey the idea of wonder, but *surprise* contains the added ingredient of the unexpected. It is well to hold that distinction in mind.

SURPRISED

Takes preposition *at* or *by*.

SUSPECTED

See ALLEGED, ACCUSED, SUSPECTED. *Suspected* takes preposition *of*.

SUSTAIN

In the sense of suffer, *sustain* is a favorite of newspapermen: "Six Greek Cypriotes have died of injuries sustained in last night's fighting north of Nicosia." Aside from the perhaps trivial objection that if they died they obviously did not *sustain* (i.e., bear without yielding) their injuries, the word *sustain* suggests an effort to find a fancy synonym for *receive* or *suffer* or *incur*, any one of which is more exact.

SWAP

A casualism, *swap* is inappropriate in a serious context like this: "The next step is to complete the arrangements for the swapping of war prisoners."

SWOOP
>*See* ZOOM.

SYLLEPSIS
>*See* RHETORICAL FIGURES AND FAULTS.

SYMPATHETIC
>Takes preposition *with, to,* or *toward.*

SYMPATHY
>Takes preposition *with, between, for,* or *toward.*

SYNECHDOCHE
>*See* RHETORICAL FIGURES AND FAULTS.

T

TACTICS
See -ICS.

TAKE
See BRING.

TAKE PLACE, OCCUR
"The crash took place at about 8 A.M. as the three-car train neared Catanzaro." Although dictionaries define *take place* as meaning to come to pass or occur, usage seems to favor confining it to that which is prearranged or scheduled. *Occur* (or *happen*) is used for that which is spontaneous or accidental. Therefore a crash does not *take place* and a commencement does not *occur*.

TAPS
"At the end of the ceremony 'Taps' was sounded and the eulogies were read." Three things should be noted about the word *taps:* Since it is not the name of a musical composition but a military signal like, for instance, reveille, (1) it is not enclosed in quotation marks, (2) it is not capitalized. Moreover, (3) it is a plural noun. Therefore: ". . . taps were sounded."

TARGET
A FAD WORD. "The Wage Board has set Thursday as the target for completing its work." That use is innocuous enough except that there are other, more normal, ways of saying the same thing. But when *targets* are "raised" or "lowered" or "achieved" or "passed," the combination of FAD WORD and MIXAPHOR becomes unbearable.

TARGET ENDS
See INSIDE TALK.

TASK FORCE

See FAD WORDS.

TAX

Takes preposition *with* or *for*.

TECHNICIAN

See SCIENTIST.

TELL

1. Dictionaries class as dialectal or colloquial the phrase *tell on*, used in the sense of to betray or bear tales against, as in, "The case was finally solved because a man who had received $2,000 from the swindle told on the man who had received $98,000." Whether it is dialectal or colloquial, the phrase surely sounds juvenile, just a step above *snitch on*.

2. *Hear tell*, in the sense of it is said, is likewise a casualism, perhaps a regionalism, not suitable for serious writing.

TEMPERATURE

Colloquially, *temperature* is used as if it meant *fever*, that is, a temperature in excess of the normal 98.6°. It is even used in this way by some doctors and medical authorities: "Massachusetts General Hospital issued the following bulletin: 'Everett has no temperature.'" It is doubtful that *temperature* used thus is, or ever was, a euphemism for *fever*. More likely it is a layman's short cut (though a longer word), just as SINUS is often used for *sinusitis*. The careful writer (and physician) will use *fever* or "rise in temperature" or "a temperature of 102°" when referring to the abnormal condition.

TEMPORIZE

Takes preposition *with*.

TENDENCY

Takes preposition *to* or *toward*.

440

TENSES

See SEQUENCE OF TENSES.

TERRIBLE, TERRIFIC

See ATOMIC FLYSWATTERS.

THAN

Normally *than* is construed as a conjunction; thus, the pronoun following it should be in the same case as the antecedent, as in, "No one is more aware of the state's needs than he," and, "The people trusted no one more than him." Occasionally failure to follow this guide can lead to ambiguity. Take the sentence "He understands animals better than her." The construction is correct if the meaning is that he does not understand her as well as he does animals, but incorrect if the meaning is that he understands animals better than she does. An exception to the general rule—and it is an idiomatic one—is the expression *than whom*. We say, "Pascal, than whom there was no greater French genius, lived in the seventeenth century."

For other than *problems, see* DIFFERENT, HARDLY, PREFER . . . THAN, SOONER, *and* RATHER THAN.

THANKS TO

Oddly, this phrase may be used properly in three ways. First, it may be used to express the meaning that appears on the face of it—to convey gratitude, as in, "Thanks to you, I got the job." Second, it may be used to express an opposite meaning— a sarcastically bitter, scornful attribution of blame, as in, "Thanks to you, I lost my job." Third, it may be used in a neutral way to express mere causation, as in, "Yet the sky is crowded, thanks to the tremendous speed of modern aircraft," or, "Thanks to a President from Massachusetts, the Supreme Court is about to enter one of its rare periods without a Justice from Massachusetts." In this versatility *thanks to* contrasts with the verb *credit*, which should be, but not always is, used only in favorable contexts. *See* CREDIT.

441

THAT, CONJUNCTION

It is difficult to give precise guidance on when the conjunction *that* may be omitted and when it should be used. The reason is that in the vast majority of instances the inclusion or exclusion of *that* is optional and a matter of idiom—in short, how it sounds to one speaking English as a native tongue. In general you cannot go wrong if you include it. It is completely proper to write, "He was sure that the home team would win." On the other hand, in simple, comprehensible-at-a-glance sentences like that, the conjunction could just as well be omitted.

There are two situations, however, in which the inclusion of the word seems to be definitely indicated. One is a sentence in which a time element intervenes between the verb and the clause. The following sentence, for example, would have been better if *that* had been inserted after "today": "President Adib Shishekly announced today opposition elements had attacked government troops." Note that in sentences like that one there is a chance of ambiguity in addition to a slight awkwardness; the *that* could be understood either after "announced" or after "today." The other situation calling for the inclusion of *that* is one in which the verb of the clause is long delayed; it is then advisable to use the *that* to signal the start of the clause. This was not done in the following sentence: "We know you do not wish to make misleading statements in the Bulletin and request the statement in the February issue regarding Ball State Teachers College offering a course in footwear application be clarified." Insert *that* after "request" and see how much easier to read it all becomes. In the following sentence, also containing a delayed verb in its clause, notice how the reader is led off on a false scent and is forced to backtrack: "The Army disclosed today a document that 'apparently contained secret information' on the Army's roles and missions has been discovered 'in the hands of unauthorized persons.'" Inclusion of *that* after "today" is definitely needed.

Here is another undesirable omission of *that*: "Mr. Brownell said a District of Columbia grand jury returned the indictment last Oct. 13, but that the District Court had kept it sealed pending the arrival of Mr. Onassis." When you have *but that* or *and that* introducing a second clause, it is surely preferable to insert *that* ahead of the first clause. A matter of balance. *See also* AND WHICH.

THAT, RELATIVE PRONOUN

1. After *whatever*, the use of *that* is not only superfluous but unidiomatic as well: "The Council appeared to be engaging the Duvalier Government in a war of nerves to bolster whatever opposition to it that may develop." As an adjective, *whatever* means *any . . . that*. The idea of *that* is already included in the word, and should be deleted from the sentence.

2. Following *such* with the pronoun *that* is a not-uncommon error: "Deputy Police Inspector Johannes Spreen told the luncheon meeting that Central Park was 'clean' and that such fear of it that existed was 'largely psychological.'" With one exception, a defining clause following *such* is introduced by *as*, not by *that*. The exception is a clause of result: "Her fear was such that she fainted."

THAT AND WHICH

It is natural, it is normal, to say, "This is a car that can go," or "It's the kind of book that I like," or "Oatsies are a breakfast food that peps you up." Yet although the relative pronoun *that* is natural to *say* in such constructions, it does not always seem to be natural to *write*. There are writers who have the notion that the relative *that* is colloquial (which it is in the sense that it is natural in spoken language), whereas the relative *which* is literary. That is a mistaken idea. Jespersen has put his finger on one cause of the error: "*Who* and *which* reminded scholars of the Latin pronouns and came to be looked upon as more refined or dignified than the more popular *that*." To this day there are those who seem to feel that *which* is more stately.

Fowler has identified another cause of the error: "It is a fact that the proportion of *thats* to *whichs* is far higher in speech than in writing; but the reason is not that the spoken *thats* are properly converted into written *whichs*, but that the kind of clause properly begun with *which* is rare in speech with its short

443

detached sentences, but very common in the more complex & continuous structure of writing, while the kind properly begun with *that* is equally necessary in both."

What kinds of clauses are "properly" begun with *that* and what kinds with *which? That* is better used to introduce a limiting or defining clause, *which* to introduce a nondefining or parenthetical clause. Getting away from the grammatical jargon, we might take this as a guide: If the clause could be omitted without leaving the noun it modifies incomplete, or without materially altering the sense of what is being said—or if it could reasonably be enclosed in parentheses—it would be better introduced by *which;* otherwise, by *that.* For example: "The Hudson River, which flows west of Manhattan, is muddy." (A nondefining clause; it could be omitted or parenthesized.) But: "The river that flows west of Manhattan is the Hudson." (The clause defines "river" and could not be omitted.)

Nowadays the use of *that* to introduce a nondefining or parenthetical clause is quite uncommon; we would not be likely to write, "Hollywood, that has been the film center of the world, is being challenged by foreign studios." *Which*, however, as has been noted, appears not infrequently to introduce defining clauses, where *that* would be more natural: "I found myself wondering what was the quality in him which interested me." Neither of these "improper" uses can be condemned on the ground of ambiguity; the meaning in each instance is perfectly clear. There can be rare instances of uncertain meaning, however. The New York Public Library, seeking to get rid of obsolete and worn-out books, was puzzled about its powers because of a directive that read: "The New York Public Library will arrange for the disposal of the above books, which have no net salvage value, by destruction, by removal. . . ." The clause after "books" was what worried the library. Did it merely describe all the obsolete books or did it restrict the disposable ones to those having no salvage value? The library decided that the clause was merely parenthetical, but a good case could be made out for the intention of the directive to specify only a certain kind of book—in which case omission of the commas and substitution of *that* for *which* would have made the meaning unmistakable. It should be noted parenthetically that a nondefining or parenthetical clause is always enclosed in commas. Then the punctuation, at least, clarifies the meaning even if the choice of pronoun does not.

But how about an even rarer instance in which punctuation is lacking—a wireless message? Here is an actual one from a New York company to a Paris subsidiary: "Although management will pay for deductions each month employe will receive a bill from the management for those deductions which must be paid in dollars." What is meant—that all the deductions must be paid in dollars, or that employes will be billed for whatever deductions must be paid in dollars? The latter was the intended meaning, and *that* instead of *which* would have made it instantly clear.

Here is another instance of uncertain meaning, this one by the editor of a dictionary: "There are many different degrees of standard usage which cannot be distinguished by status labels." The absence of a comma suggests the editor meant the clause to be restrictive. But can one be sure? And would not the use of *that* have made it certain?

The preference expressed here for the use of *that* for the defining clause and *which* for the nondefining does not rest so much on any ground of clarity, however, as on the ground of doing what comes naturally. Oddly enough, despite ample evidence that the relative *that* is preferred for the defining clause by speakers of the language, the structural linguisticians, who normally contend that the spoken language is *the* language, and who set great store by counts of mass noses, take up no cudgels in this cause. They are perfectly free, of course, to use *that* and *which* indiscriminately. No one ventures to lay down a rule on the subject, not even Fowler—he merely expresses a wistful wish. Yet it is all very curious.

Often there are two relative clauses modifying a noun. Sometimes both are defining, in which case *that* would be proper for both: "A parking ticket is a summons that is affixed by an officer of the law and that a motorist is obliged to heed." Sometimes one is defining and the other nondefining: "The essays include Dr. Blackett's article that appeared in *The New Statesman*, 'The Real Road to Disarmament,' and which received considerable criticism." Since the two clauses are not precisely parallel it would be better not to link them with "and." In this instance, as in many similar ones, the "and" could be simply deleted. Following is a legitimate linking by "but": "The Kashmiris would view it as a last resort to win that part of the state that is held by India, but which they consider rightfully theirs." Conceivably the second clause could have been regarded as defining also, and could have been introduced by *that*.

Let it be noted that there are two exceptions to the use of *that* to introduce a defining clause. One is a situation in which the demonstrative *that* and the relative *that* come together, as in this sentence: "The latent opposition to rearming Germany is as strong as that that has found public expression." Idiom dictates making it *that which*. The second exception is a situation in which the relative follows a preposition: for example, *of which*, not *of that*.

A final note should mention the point—usually the only point—about these relative pronouns that Miss Thistlebottom taught you in elementary school: *Which* normally refers to things, *who* to persons, and *that* to either persons or things. The point is elementary and needs no elaboration.

THE

A simple enough word, *the* usually provides no problems except when it is not present. That problem is discussed under ARTICLES, OMISSION OF.

A minor puzzle: We say "translated from the Russian" but not "translated into the Russian." Instead, we say "translated into Russian." Why? The answer to this mystery seems to be that there is an ellipsis, not of the word "language" (otherwise "translated into the Russian" would be correct), but of the word "original" or "version." We translate something "from the Russian original" but not "into the Russian original." Actually, the word *the* is not necessary even in the first instance.

446

THEORIZE

Takes preposition *about*.

THIEF

See ROBBER, THIEF, BURGLAR.

THIS

In recent years there has been a lava-like spread of the word *this*: "This is murder"; "See that bearded guy across the room? Well, this is a real painter." Here* is a little-noticed casual usage that has pervaded the spoken language so widely and so relentlessly that it looks as if it* might ultimately become a standard idiom. *This*, which has always referred to something present or near, is rapidly supplanting *it* and *that* even where no proximity is indicated. This is linguistic progress?

The foregoing paragraph, in substance, was an incidental part of a manuscript written for magazine publication. The magazine editor telephoned to talk about it. He liked the article in general, but he wanted to eliminate that* paragraph. His end of the telephone conversation went something like this: "I don't get the point. Where's the error? This seems to me to be perfectly good English. People have always talked like this. As far as I can see, this is a perfectly good idiom. In general this is a fine article, but I think I'd cut out this paragraph." When he had finished, it was gently suggested to him that one reason he detected nothing wrong with the use of the word *this* was that he himself had used it almost half a dozen times in a minute or so. He subsided and the paragraph stayed in.

The distinction between *this* and *that* may be stated as follows: *This* refers to something nearby either in space or in thought; *that* refers to something at a distance—great or small—in space or in thought. Normally, if an idea has already been stated and we are pointing back to it we use *that*: "All men are created free and equal. That has always been basic in the American philosophy." An acceptable exception, however, is an instance in which we gather what has been stated previously and

---

* For this word the new idiom would inevitably substitute *this*.

bring it back into the present for summing up or re-examination or drawing a conclusion: "All men are created free and equal. Obviously Negroes are men. This leads to the conclusion that Negroes must enjoy the same rights as others." When allowance has been made for that exception, it may be said that generally *that* is used to refer to what has already been stated and *this* to what is about to be stated. As to spatial relationships, there should be no difficulty in making the distinction between the two words: "This is a great book that I am reading, but that one on the table is trash."

How comes it that *this* has begun to usurp the functions of *that?* A good guess is that the neologism is traceable to Yiddish. In Yiddish no distinction is made between *this* and *that;* the word *dus* covers both ideas (the word *dorten* is used to indicate spatial separation, but it is an adverb meaning there, rather than a pronoun or an adjective). Another clue indicating Yiddish paternity is the word order of some sentences in which the *this* is prominent—"This is progress?" rather than the normal English order, "Is this progress?" The neologism perhaps was borrowed from New York's East Side by young intellectuals as a kind of slang, exported to Hollywood's intellectuals, and re-exported back to Broadway and Madison Avenue, whence it has spread country-wide in stronger form than mere slang.

For some time the all-pervasive *this* was used only in speech, but since spoken language often has an effect on written language, it is now beginning to appear in print as well. "Dr. Dalton has just begun a search of human bone marrow cells to see if the telltale structures are present. If he finds them, this would be impressive proof indeed." (The expletive *it* should be substituted for *this;* the pronoun *this* is used improperly in any event since its antecedent is an adverbial clause instead of a noun clause.) "The time might come when strategists may reckon that Israel's means of retaliation might be so paralyzed by an Arab assault that the only safe policy would be for a first strike, not a second strike. This is virtually what happened at the time of the Suez war." (Change *this* to *that*.) "One speaker held the floor yester-

448

day. This was Mr. Mongi Slim." (Make it *That* or *He.*) "The tendency in Congress is to respond to every Soviet threat by increasing our military strength. This won't be enough." (As was noted earlier, *that* generally should be used to refer to what has already been stated.)

If the* *this*-substitution were a normal slang phenomenon, there* would be no cause for concern; we could simply batten down the hatches and wait until it blew itself out. But it* does not have the look of normal slang. For one thing, rather than abating, it seems to be insinuating itself more and more into the language of both the knowledgeable and the know-nothings. For another thing, when a normal piece of slang subsides and dies it leaves the language unaffected, whereas the ground lost by the spread of the *this* neologism will be difficult to regain. If the distinction between *this* and *that* becomes blurred, as it is becoming, how is it to be brought back into sharp focus short of a vast, almost impossible task of re-education? That* is where the danger lies. It is the danger of losing a sensitive and useful discrimination between words, and suffering the consequent impairment of communication, for no other reason than the desire of smart alecks to be smarter alecks. This is worthwhile? Surely not. As Shakespeare put it: "O, that* way madness lies; let me shun that*; No more of that*."

THOUGH, ALTHOUGH

These two words mean the same thing and are employed interchangeably with two exceptions: (1) only *though* can be used in the idioms *as though* and *even though*, and (2) only *though* can be used adverbially in a final position, as in, "He said he felt fit; he looked a little pale, though." *Though* is the more commonly used of the two, except at the beginning of a sentence.

THOUGHTFUL

Takes preposition *of*.

* For this word the new idiom would inevitably substitute *this*.

449

THRILL (vb.)

Takes preposition *to, at,* or *with.*

THRONGED

Takes preposition *with.*

THUSLY

Thus is an adverb. Thus, the word *thusly,* which is a casualism, is a superfluous word; it says nothing that *thus* does not say. There is no more reason for it than there would be for *so-ly.* *Muchly* is another superfluous word of the same kind.

TILL

See UNTIL, TILL.

TIME, USED WITH ADVERBIAL FORCE

See ADVERBIAL FORCE IN NOUNS.

TINKER

Takes preposition *with.*

-TION

See NOUN ENDINGS.

TIRED

Takes preposition *of, from,* or *with.*

TMESIS

From a Greek word meaning a cutting, *tmesis* refers to the slicing of a word or sometimes a phrase to insert something between the parts, as in *abso-goddam-lutely.* It is usually either a humorous device, as in the foregoing example, or perhaps a gesture by the unlettered of their disrespect for the long word, as in one cited by John Moore in *You English Words:* the *prole-bloody-tariat.* Here is another sanguine coinage, this one from Kingsley Amis in *Take a Girl Like You:* "He got the formula off a barman in Marrakesh or some-bloody-where." The device is also used more prosaically in a phrase like *what person soever* (in place of "whatsoever person") and *how often soever,* written by Samuel Johnson; or like *brave men and true* (in place of "brave and true men") or like *something entirely else.* Another from Moore is the *'Ouse of Bloody Commons.* There's that bloody again; one would almost think that where there is tmesis there has to be blood. Some writers, like James Joyce and E. E. Cummings, have employed tmesis to achieve psychological or poetic effects, but it is by no means a common literary device.

TOGETHER WITH
See WITH.

TOLERANCE
Takes preposition *for, of* or *toward.*

TOP
Whatever excuse headline writers may have for using *top,* a three-letter word, day in and day out does not apply to the insistent, faddish use of the word by other writers. One would think that such words as *chief, main, foremost, important, principal, highest, first,* and *leading* had been cast into outer darkness. We have *top posts, top educators, top echelons,* even "a top leader of Cuba's counterrevolutionary organization" (presumably to distinguish him from a bottom leader or a middle-position leader). In a news magazine we read of a forest ranger's "top worry of the day," but that is probably a result of the magazine's having tired of the designation "No. 1." To top it all, we read in a newspaper of a "top slum block," meaning, of course, the first of the worst. Now there is nothing wrong with the word *top* used as an adjective. And there is nothing wrong with using it occasionally. What is wrong—and this applies to any FAD WORD—is to succumb to the infection of an epidemic. Here is an effective immunization shot: Try putting *top* at the bottom of your list of synonyms for a little while, and see if the fever doesn't subside.

TOPSY

"In the absence of such reorganization, the city's court structure as a whole has just 'growed,' like Topsy"; "Like Topsy, that Government-held surplus of farm commodities 'just keeps growin'.'" Once and for all, Topsy's exact words, punctuated variously in different editions and in different books of quotations, were: "I 'spect I grow'd." No "just," no "jes'," no "growin'," no nuffin'. Anyway, Topsy, Queen of the Clichés, should drop dead. *See* CLICHÉS.

TORMENTED

Takes preposition *by* or *with*.

TORTUOUS, TORTUROUS

Tortuous primarily means winding or twisting and, by derivation, not straightforward, devious. Insert an "r" and the word comes close to *torture* in both sound and meaning. *Torturous* denotes involving or producing pain or torture.

TOTAL

See INCOMPARABLES.

TOTAL OF

The phrase *a total of* is excusable when used to avoid starting a sentence with a numeral: "A total of 712 deaths were recorded over the three-day holiday." In almost all other situations it is a wasteful phrase that, in the interest of terseness, should be omitted. In some situations, where the writer wishes to indicate a summing up, or to emphasize the "totality" of separate items, the phrase is justified, even necessary: "During the holiday there were 140 deaths from drowning, 402 from auto accidents, and 170 from miscellaneous causes, a total of 712."

TOWARD(S)

In the United States the favored form is *toward*; in Britain, *towards*. *See also* UPWARD(S).

TRAGEDY, TRAGIC

In supercharged writing, particularly in lurid journalism, there is a tendency to use these words loosely to apply to almost any kind of misfortune, small or great. Thus, the loss of a pet hamster becomes a *tragedy* for the stricken owners. In the Aristotelian sense a *tragedy* concerns the downfall of a highly superior person caused at least in part by some fault inherent in him. Although the word need not be restricted to that type of situation, it is well to use it only if something great or heroic is involved in the misfortune. Otherwise the word loses its majesty and power.

TRANSITIVE VERB

See LAY, LIE.

TRANSMUTE

Takes preposition *to* or *into*.

TRANSPIRE

The nontechnical meaning of *transpire* is to be emitted as a vapor, hence, to leak out or become known. But the unknowing, particularly those who tend to reach for the fancy word, think it means to happen or take place, and they write, "The treaty looked to the appointment of a governor for the territory, but this never transpired." A really remarkable misuse of the word is this one: "Since little transpires that does not leak out, the Vatican itself is somewhat embarrassed." The meanings of words may be and are changed by needful usage and sometimes even by ignorance. But a needless and even harmful change such as this one should be resisted by those who know better. The change is needless because there are enough words to convey the desired meaning: *happen, occur, turn out, take place*—and yea, even *come to pass*. The change is harmful to the language because there is no other word that expresses the meaning that would be lost. The proper meaning—escape from secrecy—is almost as much to be valued and preserved as is the proper meaning of DISINTERESTED.

453

TREAT

Takes preposition *of* (a subject); *with* (an enemy).

TRIGGER

Although *trigger* has been a verb for a long time, no one ever spoke of *triggering* a rifle or a pistol, and the word is still not used very widely in that sense. But with the advent of the hydrogen bomb (*triggered* by an atomic bomb) the word came into fashion with, shall we say, a bang. "High official sources think the impending arming of West Germany may have triggered the fall of Soviet Premier Malenkov"; "The drift away from support of the pacts in France triggered by the defeat of Premier Mendès-France . . ."; "It happened to coincide with a phase of pondering on the wisest uses of enormous wealth, which in turn had been triggered off by the appearance of the sad face of Mr. J. Paul Getty on my television screen. . . ." (Notice in the last example the curious coupling of the crisp *triggered* with the soggy and superfluous VERB TAIL *off*.) There is nothing wrong with these uses of *trigger* except that every Thomas, Richard, and Henry is indulging in them. Perhaps this notice will trigger a return to such solid words as *cause, produce, signal, start,* and *begin. See* FAD WORDS.

TRIO

There is a tendency, especially in newspaper writing, when three persons are involved in a story, to refer to them as a *trio:* "The trio were honored for the part they played in the hazardous transfer by lifeboat of two injured crew members." The word *trio* denotes a set of three or three individuals with at least some kind of loose organization. It does not mean any old three individuals. If there had been two persons in the story, would the writer have said the *duo,* or if there had been five would he have said the *quintet?*

TRIVIA

The only trouble this word gives concerns its number: "As operated now, Congress blocks more laws than it passes and trivia

454

rather than substance dominates debate." The word is a plural, as in, "My, how the grammatical trivia mount up in this book!"

TROCHEE

See FOOT.

TROVE

"A pre-Inca trove was found in Peru." Know what a *trove* is? It's something that's found.

TRUCULENT

Here is another word whose primary meaning has been significantly modified. Dictionaries and books on usage tell us that *truculent* denotes marked by savage or barbarous ferocity, cruel. It is difficult to find the word used in this sense. Some of the good books go on to say that it is erroneously used to mean mercenary or base. It is even more difficult to find this misuse—so much so that one is led to wonder if the books have not been borrowing from one another. The "misuse" that is most common gives *truculent* the meaning of challengingly, sulkily, and disagreeably pugnacious or aggressively defiant: "President Syngman Rhee continued yesterday to manifest a truculent, unbending attitude toward an armistice agreement." What shall be said about this manifestation of BERNSTEIN'S SECOND LAW? There is no reason to resist it, even if it were possible to turn back so strong a tide, first because the "proper" meaning is rarely employed, second because it is unnecessary in view of the sufficiency of other words that say the same thing, and third because there is no other word that signifies what this "misuse" of *truculent* does. *However, see* TRANSPIRE.

TRUE

Takes preposition *to* (form); *with* (a line or edge).

TRUST

Takes preposition *to* or *in*.

TRY

As a noun, *try* is used in such conversational phrases as "nice try" and "give it a try" and occasionally in such a slangy headline as "Actress in Suicide Try." For serious writing, however, it has not achieved respectability.

TRY AND

Used in place of the standard *try to*, as in "try and be good," the combination of *try* with *and* is generally acknowledged to be characteristic of spoken language, i.e., colloquial.

There can be no doubt that in a few locutions it has a faintly different meaning from *try to*, which denotes merely an essaying of something. It can add a heartening tone, as in "try and be brave," or a note of determination, as in, "I will try and practice every day." On still rarer occasions it can be the only possible wording. If A says he is going to punch B in the nose, the spoken challenging response is "Just try and do it"; if a pugnacious X claims Y's seat at the football game, Y's challenging response is "Try and make me move." In either situation *try to* would not suit the intended meaning; it would not be idiomatic.

When allowance has been made for these exceptional uses— to express essaying coupled with encouragement, determination, or challenge—the careful writer will cling to *try to* as the proper construction in the overwhelming number of situations. He will not write, "Mr. Smart decided to try and get Ernest Hemingway to write for the publication," nor, "Soviet workers were urged to try and talk 'believing' comrades into becoming atheists." It should be noted that whether the locution is *try to* or *try and*, only one action is contemplated: When we say "try and be good" we do not mean two separate things as the *and* would suggest; we do not mean *try* to be good and *be* good. Therefore the *try and* idiom is not parallel, as one authority declares, with "go and find one" or with "come and get it." In these instances two actions, albeit closely related, are indeed contemplated. It is in no sense a casualism to write, "There are things about Hawaii that make a person wish he could pack up tomorrow and go and live there."

The point being made here is that the *go and* and *come and* idioms are standard and logical, whereas the *try and* idiom is substandard (except in the few uses already indicated) and illogical.

TUMMY
See BELLY.

TURBID, TURGID
Often confused, these words have nothing in common. *Turbid* means muddy or clouded. *Turgid* means inflated, grandiose, bombastic.

TYPE
The noun *type* has in recent years been teaming up with other words to emerge in the guise of an adjective, as in "V-type engine." But the metamorphosis is not complete and probably never will be. Although "V-type engine" has a perfectly proper sound, "high-type man" remains a vulgarism. Between these two extremes there are gradations that are not so easily labeled; for instance, "a series of character-type comedies" or "a New Deal-type candidate." Since the combination seems to have originated with technicians, this origin may offer us a clue to the propriety or impropriety of the usage. Perhaps it may be said that the *type* compounds should be used as adjectives only when the reference is technical or at least highly specific ("O-type blood," "cantilever-type bridge"), and that at all other times *type* should remain a noun ("high type of man," "comedies of the character type"). That guide should hold for the next half century, anyway.

As a postscript it should be noted that there are some illiterates who omit *of* even when the uncompounded *type* is clearly a noun: "The Tibetan terrier is the type dog that . . ."; "The coach said he would welcome more of that type hitting." Would you say "that breed dog" or "that kind hitting"?

U

UNANIMOUS
See INCOMPARABLES.

UNDERLAY, UNDERLIE
Whereas *lie* is exclusively intransitive (*See* LAY, LIE), when it is prefixed by *under-* or *over-* it becomes exclusively transitive. Another oddity about *lie* is that when it is made into *underlie* or *overlie* its meanings are in most instances interchangeable with *underlay* and *overlay*. However, you could not write, "The principle that underlays his action"; it would have to be *underlies*. When there is doubt about which form to use, a serviceable test is to break the word apart and move the *under-* or *over-* to a prepositional position. Thus, "The principle that lies [not *lays*] under his action." In geological contexts the *-lie* forms seem to be preferred: "A stratum of shale underlies the sandstone"; "The sandstone is underlain by shale."

UNDER WATER
Fused into a solid word, these two make an adjective, as in "underwater photography." But the solid word is improper in this sentence: "A tugboat lying twenty-five feet underwater was lifted off the harbor bottom." Make it *under water*.

UNDER WAY
See WAY, NAUTICAL.

UNFAVORABLE
Takes preposition *for, to,* or *toward*.

UNINTERESTED
See DISINTERESTED.

UNIQUE
See INCOMPARABLES.

UNKNOWN

In the interest of precise expression it is well not to use *unknown* if a more exact word like *unascertained* or *unidentified* or *undisclosed* will better convey the meaning. "It is reported that the Shah and his Queen will be in Rome only a few days, after which they will continue their journey toward an unknown destination." The word is not used incorrectly here, but it is not precise. The destination would be truly *unknown* if the Shah were framing the itinerary for the journey beyond Rome as he went along. What was meant, however, was that the destination was not made public. Similarly, an unclaimed body should be that of an *unidentified* man rather than that of an *unknown* man.

UNLESS AND UNTIL
See IF AND WHEN.

UNPALATABLE
Takes preposition *to*.

UNPRECEDENTED

The older the world grows, the less likelihood there is that an event in normal human affairs is *unprecedented*. Baseball, for example, is a normal human affair, but the writer of the following sentence discarded caution: "The Cardinals plan to go ahead with the day-and-night double-header against two different rivals, believed to be unprecedented in the major leagues." The very next day he found himself compelled to write: "Meeting two different rivals on the same day had not been done in the National League since 1883." *Unprecedented* is a favorite word of the "gee-whiz" school of newspapering, but its careless use is by no means restricted to journalism.

UNTIL, TILL
With both these words available and legitimate, you would

think everyone's needs would be well taken care of. But no. There are always some writers who seem to find these versions too uncomplicated, and insist on "Open Thursday nights 'til 9 p.m." or "Make no move 'til you see Valiant" or even ". . . All day 'till my temples throb and thrill. . . ." There was once a *til* (no apostrophe), but it is now obsolete in American English. *Till* and *until*, however, are both alive and kicking; use one or the other.

UP UNTIL

Although there is nothing grammatically wrong with the phrase *up until* or *up till*, the writer should always ask himself, "Is this *up* necessary?" The answer will always be, No. The *up* may be discarded as excess baggage. *Up to* and *up through* are something else again.

UPWARD(S)

As an adverb, *upward* is the favored form in the United States. As an adjective preceding a noun, *upward* is the only acceptable form—as in "an upward [not *upwards*] trend in the market." *See also* TOWARD(S).

UPWARD(S) OF

The phrase means, as should be obvious, more than. But there have been perverse souls since the early seventeenth century who have thought it means less than. This meaning, along with the meaning approximately, is labeled by Webster "erron. & dial.," and that characterization does not seem unreasonable.

USED TO

The verb *use*—in the sense of accustomed or normally—sometimes takes a final "d" and sometimes not. In the regular past tense the word is *used*, as in "He used to love scrapple." With the auxiliary *did*, however, the word is *use*, as in "He did not use to like scrapple." The phonetic similarity of the two forms occasionally produces this kind of error: "This moving and haunting little film has an uncommon personal quality, a concentration upon the fate of the individual such as we didn't used to get in Soviet films." This is just as illogical as "He didn't went to school." It should be added, however, that employing *use* in this sense, though common in conversation, lacks grace in writing.

USEFUL

Takes preposition *in, for,* or *to.*

V

VARIANCE
Takes preposition *with*.

VARIED, VARIOUS
Between these words there is a shade of distinction. *Varied* means made different, made various, or variegated. *Various* means different, distinct, diverse. You would not speak of *varied* parts of the country, nor should you write, "The exhibit includes a six-screen seven-projector movie by Charles Eames that explains *varied* science fields." In each instance the indicated word is *various*.

VARIOUSLY
"The woman was described variously as Mrs. Lumumba or the wife of Georges Grenfell, a member of Mr. Lumumba's Cabinet." When only two things are at issue, *variously* does not apply; the word refers rather to several things. What the writer obviously had in mind was that the description of the woman came from *various* sources, and he should have used some such phrase to communicate his meaning.

VARY
Takes preposition *from*.

VAULT
There is a tendency, especially in newspapers, to use *vault* imprecisely. For example: "The vaults are to the right of the lobby. One is inside the other. The outer one is two feet by four feet, the other a foot square." A *vault* is a permanent part of a building and is generally a space big enough to walk into. The things referred to in the foregoing example were undoubtedly *safes*.

VENAL, VENIAL

It is unfortunate that two words that look so much alike should be so unalike in meaning. *Venal* means corruptible or purchasable. We speak of a *venal* politician or a *venal* press. The word traces to the same root as *vend*, meaning to sell. *Venial*, which derives from a root meaning forgiveness, denotes capable of being forgiven, excusable, and therefore minor. Mnemonic device: "A politician who's *venal* lands in a house that is penal; we can be much more genial if the sin is trifling and *venial*."

VENGEANCE

See AVENGE, REVENGE.

VERBAL

See ORAL VS. VERBAL.

VERBS, CANTILEVERED

See CANTILEVERED VERBS.

VERB TAILS

Verbs there are that love a tail—an adverb or a preposition. To take an example, the verb *break*, in addition to going it alone, loves to team up with tail words to express *break in, break out, break away, break down, break up, break off,* and even *break in on.* The tails are often necessary; they may give the verb a completely different meaning from its original one. Sometimes, however, they are merely excess baggage, adding nothing to meaning: for instance, *continue on* or *close down.* In still other instances they are clearly excess baggage but are so idiomatic that one would not dream of amputating them. Who would tell anyone but a dog to *sit* rather than *sit down?* We thus have three categories of verb tails: necessary, usually unnecessary, and unnecessary but idiomatic.

1. NECESSARY. These are the ones that definitely modify the meaning of the verb. Here are some examples: *bottle up; break in, etc.* (see foregoing paragraph); *beat down, off, up; burn down, up; check in, out* (of a hotel); *clamp down; conjure up; face up*

463

to; ferret out; go on; head in, off; hear out; hold up; lock up; meet with; mull over; shrug off; simmer down; single out; sit in; sleep in; sum up; tear up; thresh out; visit with; water down; wind up; write up; wrap up. There are, of course, hundreds of others, but these will suffice to show that dropping the adjuncts to the verb in such instances modifies the meaning or leaves the verb incomplete.

2. USUALLY UNNECESSARY. The verb *check* seems to attract more hangers-on than any other, and most of the time the dependents can be cut off. One meaning of *check* is to confirm or verify, but some users seem to feel that the word needs company to convey this meaning and so they say *check into, check on, check out, check over,* and *check up.* In writing, the appendages can almost always be dropped with no loss of meaning and some gain in conciseness. A man used to *head* a committee; now he often *heads up* a committee. A fugitive used to *hide;* now he frequently *hides out.* People used to *win* or *lose;* now they often *win out* or *lose out.* What is gained by these expansions? Nothing immediately apparent. There are a few borderline combinations, no doubt. For instance, *end up.* There is no need for the appendage in the sentence "The picture begins on a sad note but it ends up happily." But there is need for it in the sentence "If a boy cheats in school he will end up a criminal."

3. UNNECESSARY BUT IDIOMATIC. There is no discernible difference between *hurry* and *hurry up* or between *slow* and *slow down (up)* or between *speed and speed up.* Yet there are situations in which you would not wish, for reasons of either cadence or idiomatic flavor, to drop the adjunct. In such situations keep the adjunct, but keep it only in such situations; if there seems to be no real reason for it, drop it.

One peculiarity of verb tails is the shifting tendency to add them or subtract them, for no apparent reason except perhaps to create a new vogue or to appear a little ahead of the vanguard. The process of addition has already been noted in the variations of the word *check* and in the expressions *head up* and *hide out.* The process of subtraction is equally operative. A man used to be *framed up,* but now he is *framed.* In slang terms an enterprise used to *fold up*, now it merely *folds*. The noun form *fade-out* has now been replaced on occasion by *fade* (". . . at the fade it looks as if Bertha has acquired a samurai") and no doubt this will affect the verb form as well. When a person put in an appearance he *showed up*, but now he merely *shows* (whence the airline jargon *no-show*). It is to be expected that the television commentators who now say, "That wraps it up for now," will one day say, "That wraps it for now." Obviously there is no rational reason for any of these mutations, nor do they follow any pattern except the generalized pattern of restless change. But perhaps when language—and particularly colloquial language—ceases to change it will be dead. *See also* FACE UP TO, MEET, MEET WITH, *and* VISIT WITH.

VERDICT

"Supreme Court Justice Hofstadter handed down a verdict of guilty." Impossible. A *verdict* is a finding by a jury, not a finding by a judge. Judges render *decisions, judgments, rulings, opinions*—almost anything but *verdicts*.

VERITABLE

Like *literally*, this word is sometimes used by writers for unnecessary emphasis, as if they were saying, "I really mean it." The only difference is that whereas *literally* is usually misused for *figuratively*, *veritable* is used correctly, though superfluously and perhaps a trifle ostentatiously. "At one point he had to worry about more than 700 horses, not counting the veritable menagerie of less domesticated beasts." A collection of beasts is indeed a menagerie. What does *veritable* add to the thought?

VERSUS

The abbreviation *v.* is used in legal citations: "Marbury v. Madison." In all other areas the word is usually spelled out, but if it is necessary to employ an abbreviation (in titles or headlines, for example) the customary form is *vs.*: "The Yankees vs. the Senators," "The President vs. His Critics."

VERY

Do you say "I am very interested" or "I am very much interested"? This is the crux of an issue that has set grammarians at pens' points for decades. But the issue is scarcely worth more than a few drops of ink and certainly no drops of blood.

At bottom is the contention that *very*, originally an adjective, is not a full-fledged adverb, although it is a partly fledged one. A true, card-carrying adverb should be able to modify a verb, yet we cannot say, "I very appreciate your invitation," nor, using the past participle after a passive verb, "Your invitation was very appreciated." The grammarians making that contention argue further that, as an intensive, *very* may properly be applied to an adjective denoting a quality (*very late*) but not to a verb denoting an action (*very delayed*). All this sounds reasonably simple. But the principle is difficult to apply because past participles tend to take on the coloration of adjectives and often actually have become adjectives, e.g., *interested, pleased, respected, neglected*, and a host of others. Application of the principle therefore assumes that speakers and writers can draw the fine distinction in individual cases and that their hearers and readers can do likewise. Many such words would set even grammarians to quarreling, so it is manifestly unreasonable to expect the general run of users to call every play correctly. What, then, to do? The advice here is not to boggle at using *very* except when the word it modifies is clearly a verb or at least its verbal nature is not entirely concealed. Here is an example of a participle that clearly retains its verb form: "The astronaut was commended." (The intensified form would have to be "very much commended," not "very commended.") The verbal nature of a participle often is not entirely concealed if it is followed with a "by" phrase, as in, "The flight was delayed by bad weather." (The intensified form would have to be "much" or "very much delayed," not "very delayed.") Webster III cites the example "towns were very separated from one another," but it is likely that most good writers would not accept this usage; they would feel that the verbal tone of "separated" is much stronger than the adjectival tone. On the other hand, to take another borderline case, most writers would accept "He felt very encouraged," though they might be happier with "very much encouraged." And—to answer the question posed at the outset of this discussion—"I was very interested" is unexceptionable; "interested" is an adjective in any man's dictionary.

An aside on the word *very*, which has nothing to do with the foregoing dissertation: Inexperienced writers tend to use the word too much. Often its use is self-defeating; the writer intends to intensify what he is saying, but instead weakens it. He may write, "Hemingway's prose is very lean and very strong," not realizing that he would express his thought more forcefully if he wrote, "Hemingway's prose is lean and strong." If the word *very* seems to be necessary to strengthen what has been written, the writer should re-examine his original selection of words. Strong words usually need no such prop.

VEST (vb.)

Takes preposition *in*.

VIA

The word means by way of (in a geographical sense), as in, "They flew to Paris via London," not by means of, as in these two incorrect sentences: "The severest type of attack would entail simultaneous, accurate, dispersed delivery, via missiles or bombers, of nuclear weapons"; "The Soviet Union and its satellites are cutting a swath from the north of Africa to its center via economic and cultural agreements, scholarships, free travel, diplomatic offensives, radio broadcasts, and exchange trips."

VIE

Takes preposition *with*.

VIEW

With a view takes preposition *to*; *in view* takes preposition *of*.

467

VIRTUALLY

See PRACTICALLY, VIRTUALLY.

VIRUS

"The shortstop retired after an inning and a half because of an attack of virus." This is like saying "an attack of germ" or "an attack of bacterium." Since *viruses* seem to be with us—perhaps too much with us—these days, we may as well straighten out the terminology pertaining to them. You could speak of a *virus attack*, or an *attack of a virus*, or a *virus infection*, but not of an *attack of virus* as if *virus* were a disease. There are those who say, "He has a virus," which may be technically correct in the sense that he has a *virus* in his body but is actually incorrect because what these speakers mean is that he has an ailment, which they are designating *a virus*. See also SINUS.

VIS-À-VIS

This phrase from the French, meaning literally face to face, carries the same idea in English. As a preposition, it means face to face with, confronted with, or even in comparison with, but not regarding or concerning, as the writer of the following sentence thought: "Let us consider the Supreme Court's decision vis-à-vis segregation in the schools." As a noun the word means opposite number or partner.

VISIT WITH

Like MEET WITH, this phrase has its own standing. But the difference between *meet* and *meet with* is much greater than that between *visit* and *visit with*. *Visit with* encompasses more than the mere paying of a call; its emphasis is on the social converse that accompanies the call. So much so, indeed, that *visit with* as a casualism is sometimes applied to the social converse without the physical presence, as in this sentence: "Mr. Truman called his daughter in New York and later visited on his bedside telephone with his sister, Miss Mary Jane Truman of nearby Grandview."

468

VOID (DEVOID)

Takes preposition *of*.

VULGATE

Linked etymologically with *vulgar*, which these days suggests coarseness or lack of refinement, *vulgate* does not have the same base connotation. Aside from its technical uses with reference to the Bible, it means merely ordinary or colloquial speech. *See* CASUALISMS.

VULNERABLE

Takes preposition *to*.

WAIT

See AWAIT, WAIT.

WANT (n.)

Takes preposition *of*.

WANTING

Takes preposition *in*.

-WARD

The suffix "-ward" denotes direction to or motion toward. Therefore the words "to the" preceding a "-ward" word are tautological. Examples: "The fountain would have to be moved a little to the westward." (Either omit *to the* or change *westward* to *west*.) "Two programs for diverting surplus waters of two northern California rivers hundreds of miles to the southward have been proposed." (The same remedy is indicated.)

WARN

To *warn* is to give notice of an impending unpleasantness; further, the word *warn* suggests acceptance of the reality or probability of the impending event. Such being the case, the word does not have the objectivity required in a context like this: "Warning that the United States is preparing a new world war directed against the Soviet Union, Nikita S. Khrushchev has called on the Moscow party organization to. . . ." To be completely objective, *warn* should not be used when what is involved may be a charge, or merely somebody's pipe dream. In the instance cited, "saying" would be a good neutral word. Footnote: *Advance warning*, like ADVANCE PLANNING, is tautological and a wasteful locution.

WARY

Takes preposition *of*.

WASTEFUL LOCUTIONS

Some word groupings are as usual and inconspicuous as the buttons on the sleeve of a jacket, and just as useless. This criticism is not aimed at CLICHÉS, many of which, although usual and inconspicuous, are definitely useful. It is aimed at locutions that employ three or four words to do the work of one or two: *at the present time* for *now; in order to* for *to; in the course of* for *in, during,* or *while.* There is nothing grammatically or logically wrong with these phrases. But stylistically they are inert. Moreover, in the kinds of writing in which terseness is mandatory— news writing, for instance—they are intolerable. Above all, they suggest that the writer has been operating unthinkingly, that he has been setting down words automatically. This is never to be countenanced. Instead of a listing here of humdrum profitless phrases, many appear in their alphabetical places in the vocabulary, and this sermonet applies to each.

WAY

Takes preposition *of* (manner, method).

WAY, ADVERB

Used in place of *away* in the sense of far, *way* has not gained complete literary acceptance, although it appears occasionally in serious writing: "The children are sophisticated and knowledgeable way beyond their father"; "In the fast-moving world of theoretical physics, Fuchs is considered way out of date"; ". . . the United States is way ahead of Russia." *See also* WAYS.

WAY, NAUTICAL

The phrase is *under way* (two words), not *under weigh*. Its only connection with *weighing anchor*, whence the misspelling arises, is that a ship must *weigh* (lift) *anchor* before it can get *under way*. The phrase is *under way* whether it concerns a ship, a sprinter, or a Presidential campaign.

471

WAY, USED WITH ADVERBIAL FORCE
See ADVERBIAL FORCE IN NOUNS.

WAYS

This word is fine in a shipyard, but not as a measure of distance. To say, "He was a long ways from home," is to stray a long *way* from good English.

WAYS AND MEANS

Except as the name of a governmental committee, the phrase is a wasteful locution. Pick one word or the other.

WEAN

Writers sometimes use *wean* as if it meant raise, rear, or bring up. "The new Yankee first baseman was weaned on stickball"; "Frequently a person met at some social gathering will tell me in a confidential tone, 'I was weaned on *The Nation*.'" *Wean* means, primarily, to end dependence on mother's milk; in a derived meaning it denotes to reconcile to deprivation of some desired influence. No doubt some of those who use the word loosely know what it means and are simply taking a long hop, skip, and jump from deprivation to substitution. But the suspicion is that most of those who use the word loosely are in the dark about its true meaning. For those who wish to avoid the suspicion, the safest course is to follow *wean* with the preposition *from*, or to substitute for *wean* what they really mean—something else like *raise, rear, bring up, nourish,* or *suckle.*

WEIRD

See ATOMIC FLYSWATTERS.

WHAT

The pronoun *what* may be either singular or plural, just as ALL may be. The duality gives rise to a multitude of errors. The errors seem to be of two kinds: first, those that are traceable to the inability of some writers to believe that the word can be anything but singular, and second, those that occur when the *what* governs more than one verb in a sentence. Avoidance of both types of error requires, at a minimum, deciding what the word means or stands for in the context. Usually it stands for either *the thing that* or *the things that* in the broadest sense. Here is an error made by one of the singular fellows: "A long, T-shaped conference table has six manikins dressed in what appears to be six different dresses." Make it *appear;* "dressed in what" is equivalent to "dressed in things that" or "dressed in garments that." Another example: "Tass published this morning the texts of notes to the United States, Britain, and France calling upon them to halt what was described as 'provocative acts' in West Berlin." (Make it *were described;* "things that, or acts that, were described.")

In the second type of error—those that occur when the *what* governs more than one verb—the penchant for the singular also seems to play a part: "What looks like two supersize golden bird cages were erected overnight." The writer was unable to believe that *what* could be anything but singular, but then could not bring himself to carry his conviction to the bitter end and write "was erected." Here *what* stands for *things that* and governs both verbs, which accordingly should be "look" and "were erected."

In this second type of error a contributory cause is the frequent presence of a copulative verb, which creates uncertainty in the writer's mind about which element is the subject and which the predicate. He will write: "Most cant and jargon are local and temporary. What persists are the exceptionally apt and useful cant and jargon." If the sentence were inverted to read, "The exceptionally apt and useful cant and jargon are what persists," all would be well. But as it stands the subject of the copulative verb "are," by normal standards, is the first element—"what persists" (*See* NUMBER, [2]). The writer evidently decided that the *what* here stands for *the thing that* and made the first verb singular; but the *what* also governs the second verb, which thus should be *is*. Here is a similar example: "Thomas did write some of the very best poetry of our time, and Pollock actually did do some of its very best painting. Their reputations as such are not inflated. What is inflated, and exaggerated and distorted, are the accompanying interpretations." The "is" should be changed to "are."

Determining just what the word *what* stands for in a sentence is not always simple, and there is sometimes room for disagreement. Viewed in one light it may stand for *the things that*; viewed in another light it may stand for a more abstract notion like *the element that* or *the quality that*. There is a possibility of such a disagreement in the following sentence, although there can be no disagreement that the two verbs must be brought into line: "What governs our lives are automatic reflexes and the rote of bare utility." Does the *what* here stand for *the things that*? If so, the first verb should be "govern." Or does the word stand for *the determining factor that*, or some such notion? If so, the second verb should be "is." In the following sentence similar alternatives are presented: "What is more striking than the material comparisons of the two thoroughfares are the contrasts in atmosphere and attitudes." Here it might well be contended that *what* stands for *the feature that*, and if that contention is accepted the "are" should be changed to "is."

WHATEVER
See **THAT, RELATIVE PRONOUN.**

WHEN, AS, AND IF
See **IF AND WHEN.**

WHEN AND WHERE
One school kid will say, "Addition is when you add two and two." Another will say, "Addition is where you add two and two." Both are using a juvenile construction. Most authorities agree that the construction is undesirable, but they do not agree on why this is so. One advances the theory that *when* (and presumably *where* also) cannot be used to join a clause to a noun—there must be two full clauses. It is perfectly proper, however, to say, "Noon is when the sun is directly overhead," and "Home is where Affection calls." Perrin says rightly that the objection to the *when* and *where* clauses as used by juveniles is

stylistic rather than grammatical, and comes from their overuse in amateurish definitions. He might have gone a step further and said that the stylistic objection arises from the use of *when* and *where* in situations where their meanings do not apply. *When*, for instance, has a temporal meaning, and it does not apply in a sentence like this: "The 'hard-ticket policy' is when they up the price of admission to a $3.50 top and sell reserved seats to performances that are given only twice a day." That kind of sentence is not suitable in mature writing.

WHENCE

See FROM HENCE, FROM WHENCE.

WHERE

Where, used as a conjunction in place of *that*, is a casualism that is common in conversation but is out of place in writing of almost any kind. The newspaper writer who composed the following sentence was undoubtedly striving for folksiness, but hayseed got mixed into it, too: "We see where one of The Experts said the other day . . . that play with a toy gun gives a child 'a sense of power and freedom.' " The next step down is to write, "We see as how. . . ."

For comments on the construction "Addition is where you add two and two," *see* WHEN AND WHERE.

WHEREABOUTS

Unlike *headquarters*, which is usually plural, *whereabouts* is singular. The reason? Well, *headquarters* contains a noun—*quarters*—that is in the plural, but *whereabouts* does not; it is an amalgamation of an adverb and a preposition with an old adverbial "s" tacked on. Thus, the word may sound like a plural, but it is not one. There is one situation, however, in which it may be considered a plural—when it refers to the places in which two or more persons or things may be. Example: "Herr Ulbricht and other leading members of the party have dropped out of sight; their various whereabouts have been unspecified for five days."

475

WHETHER

See QUESTION WHETHER, DOUBT, *and* IF,

WHETHER OR NOT

Usually the *or not* is a space waster; e.g., "Whether the terrorist statement was true or not was not known." When, however, the intention is to give equal stress to the alternatives, the *or not* is mandatory: "The game will be played whether it is fair or not." The following sentence fairly cries out for the *or not:* "The union feels that the shortcomings of the machinery the law provides for dealing with major strikes have already become so clear that Congress is likely to consider alternative remedies, whether the law is upheld in the Supreme Court." One way to test whether the *or not* is necessary is to substitute *if* for *whether.* If the change to *if* produces a different meaning—and it would do so in the second and third of the foregoing examples—the *or not* must be supplied.

WHICH

The use of *which* to refer to the whole idea of a preceding clause is frowned upon by the ultrafinicky, but may be regarded as permissible if it is not ambiguous. It tends to be ambiguous when the *which* follows a noun, as in this sentence: "Laboratory animals don't catch the disease, which hampers research." It would be better to make it *which fact,* or to reconstruct the sentence. Here is another example, in which the reader might have to hesitate a moment to determine what the *which* referred to: "The two ships will then try to force a passage through the ice to the coast, which has never been achieved before." Changing *which* to *something that* or *a thing that* would remove the momentary confusion. Other remarks about *which* appear under THAT AND WHICH and AND WHICH.

WHILE

Properly, *while* is used to mean during the time that ("He had the radio playing while he read"). Acceptably, though with

476

less universal sanction, *while* is also used in the sense of *although* or *but* ("While he is a brilliant student generally, he has no feeling for mathematics"). Incidentally, in the sense of *although*, the *while* clause precedes the main clause. Improperly used, in the judgment of most stylists, *while* sometimes is made to serve as a weak substitute for *and* or for a semicolon. ("Mr. De Sapio is the leader of Tammany and Democratic National Committeeman, while Mr. Prendergast is the Democratic State Chairman.") In this sense of *and*, it is branded as "journalese" by nonjournalistic critics—and not without some justice, because newspapermen, under the spur of MONOLOGOPHOBIA, sometimes use it to avoid repeating *and*, as: "Aboard the Indonesian boat were one two-inch mortar, four machine pistols, three Bren guns, twenty-eight rifles, and three radio receivers, while it carried food for twenty days." It may be unduly restrictive to suggest that *while* be confined to its temporal meaning, but it is safe. *See also* AWHILE *and* WORTHWHILE.

WHO

See THAT AND WHICH.

WHO, WHOM, WHOEVER, WHOMEVER

The proper use of *who* and *whom* sometimes requires a bit of grammatical analysis. It is understandable, therefore, that the spontaneous speaker, unable to take the time for the analysis, will occasionally err. The transgressions of the writer, however, are not so easily overlooked.

The errors in spoken language arise chiefly from two causes. One is the tendency to regard a noun toward the beginning of a sentence as being in the nominative rather than the objective case; this produces such solecisms as, "Who did you wish to see?" The second is the fear of committing such solecisms; this leads to OVERREFINEMENT, as in, "Whom shall I say is calling?" It may well be that in the spoken language the first type of error is on the way to becoming standard, and that in the written language also it may ultimately become admissible. Let it be noted, however, that for centuries impatient linguists have been busy burying *whom*, but it refuses to play dead. The second type of error is condemned not only by the old guard but also by the new guard, who are, of course, intent on getting rid of *whom* except for a few inescapable uses. One such inescapable use, it may be pointed out here, is a situation in which the pronoun directly follows a preposition: "For whom the bell tolls"; "to whom it may concern." Another inescapable use is in the phrase "than whom" (*See* THAN).

The most common misuse of *whom* for *who* occurs in relative clauses in which another verb diverts attention from the verb that governs or is governed by the pronoun. For instance: "William Z. Foster, whom Federal Judge Ryan ruled is not physically fit now to be tried, is in prison." Here the *whom* should be *who*. A simple way to determine this is to turn the clause into a straightforward sentence, substituting a personal pronoun for the relative pronoun. In this instance you would get: "Judge Ryan ruled he [*he*, nominative; therefore *who*, also nominative] is not physically fit." On the other hand, *whom* would be correct if the sentence had read, "William Z. Foster, whom Judge Ryan declared not physically fit . . . ," because the straightforward sentence would read: "Judge Ryan declared him [therefore, *whom*] not physically fit." Here are other examples of misuses, with the proof of the error—the straightforward sentence—given in parentheses: "One purge victim whom the President apparently believed was innocent of wrongdoing was Amelito R. Mutuc" (the President apparently believed *he*—therefore, *who*—was innocent). "The French actor plays a solemn, vagrant man who suddenly turns up in her town outside Paris and whom she suspects is her husband, missing since World War II" (she suspects *he*—therefore, *who*—is her husband). The following passage reverses the error: "Mr. Kelleher, who Mr. Sherman blamed for printing a million duplicates of the Hammarskjold stamp misprints . . ." (Mr. Sherman blamed *him*—therefore, *whom*).

When a preposition precedes a *who* (or *whom*) clause, many writers find themselves in trouble. They jump to the conclusion that the relative pronoun is the object of the preposition,

478

whereas it is the entire clause that is the object; the pronoun may or may not be in the objective case depending on what its function is within the clause. "The disputants differed diametrically as to whom they thought might turn out to be the violator." Here the whole clause is the object of the prepositional *as to* and within this clause the pronoun is the subject and should be the nominative *who*. Following is a similar error involving the word *whomever*: "He called on the party to close ranks behind whomever was nominated." The pronoun *whomever* is not the object of the preposition *behind*; the object is the entire clause, and within that clause the pronoun is the subject of *was nominated*—therefore, *whoever*. In the sentence that follows, however, *whomever* would be correct: "The sentiment here plainly is against the Yankees and for whoever the Yankees happen to play." The whole clause is, of course, the object of the preposition *for*, but within that clause the pronoun is the object of the verb *play* and therefore should be *whomever*.

As a concluding item, it should be noted that the relative pronouns *who* and *whom* follow the person and number of their antecedents. Illustrating the correspondence of person is this passage: "Many married reservists complain of the inequities of sacrifice. Why should I, they write, who have [not *has*] already served two years or more be asked to serve again?" Illustrating the correspondence of number is this sentence: "Mr. Trumbo is one of the writers who have [not *has*] been officially barred." This point is discussed under NUMBER, (3).

WHOSE

In elementary school Miss Thistlebottom may have insisted that *whose* should refer only to persons; if she did, forget it. Since *which* has no genitive of its own, it is only fair to let it borrow *whose* when the loan is useful to avoid clumsiness. It is nonsense to compel one to write, "The car, the carburetor, brakes, and steering wheel of which need overhauling, is to be sold at auction." No one in his right mind would approve that. And never forget that banner "whose broad stripes and bright stars" have inspired us all these many generations.

WIDOW

To say, "Mrs. Franklin D. Roosevelt, widow of the late President," is to indulge in a redundancy. Say, "widow of the President."

WIN

As a noun, *win* is a needless casualism. Just how needless is illustrated by this example of MONOLOGOPHOBIA: "A victory for Mr. Macapagal would be a win for the more progressive forces in the Philippines." Would not repetition of "victory" have made for better balance and better rhythm? The noun *win* should be left to the sports-page headline writers, who probably popularized it in the first place.

WINDYFOGGERY

In nature wind and fog do not normally coexist. In language, however, they sometimes do, and the greater the wind the more impenetrable the fog. This linguistic condition may be thought of as *windyfoggery*. It embraces gobbledygook, that wordy, involved, and often unintelligible language usually associated with bureaucracy and big business. But it also includes the self-important circumlocution of ordinary orators, the pretentious pseudoscientific jargon of the pseudosciences, and the monumental unintelligibility of some criticism of those arts that do not readily accept the bridle of plain words.

There have been many translations into windyfoggery of well known pieces of simple writing—passages from the Bible, from Lincoln, from Shakespeare—and there have been many parodies in windyfoggery of ordinary thoughts. One illustration will bring out the point. Prof. Lionel Trilling of Columbia takes the statement "They fell in love and married" and translates it thus: "Their libidinal impulses being reciprocal, they activated their individual erotic drives and integrated them within the same frame of reference." A contrived example, to be sure; but is it much different from writing, "improved financial support and less onerous work loads," when one wishes to say, "more pay and less work"? Or is it much different from writing, "The supervision of driver and safety education at the state and local levels should be assigned to personnel qualified by virtue of their adequate personal characteristics and specialized training and experience in this field," when all that is being said is that good teachers are needed?

Turn now, if you will, to art criticism. This is the kind of thing you sometimes find: "Motherwell seems to have several kinds of courage; one of them is the courage to monumentalize the polymorphous-perverse world of his inner quickenings; he is the architect of a lyrical anxiety where Gorky was its master scrivener; the liquefied tick of Gorky's id-clock becomes in Motherwell the resonant Versaillean tock, the tall duration of a muralizing necessity that strains to leap its pendulum's arc while carrying a full weight of iconographic potency."

Pseudoscientific writing occasionally includes this sort of observation: "A factor analysis of the scale scores has yielded six attitude clusters that make sense intuitively and that resemble factors found in other job satisfaction studies." Or this type of definition (this one is a definition of reading presented by a professor of educational psychology): "A processing skill of symbolic reasoning, sustained by the interfacilitation of an intricate hierarchy of substrata factors that have been mobilized as a psychological working system and pressed into service in accordance with the purpose of the reader." Let us mobilize our substrata factors and proceed.

Dr. William B. Bean, who in the *Archives of Internal Medicine* often tilted a lancet at the writing operations of his fellow healers, has passed on the story of a New York plumber who had cleaned out some drains with hydrochloric acid and then wrote to a chemical research bureau, inquiring, "Was there any possibility of harm?" As told by Dr. Bean, the story continues:

"The first answer was, 'The efficacy of hydrochloric acid is indisputably established but the corrosive residue is incompatible with metallic permanence.' The plumber was proud to get this and thanked the people for approving of his method. The dismayed research bureau rushed another letter to him saying, 'We cannot assume responsibility for the production of a toxic and noxious residue with hydrochloric acid. We beg leave to suggest to you the employment of an alternative procedure.' The plumber was more delighted than ever and wrote to thank them for reiterating their approval. By this time the bureau got worried about what might be happening to New York's sewers and called in a third man, an older scientist, who wrote simply, 'Don't use hydrochloric acid. It eats hell out of pipes.' "

Windyfoggery may result from sheer pomposity. It may result from a kind of wistful desire to make learned sounds. It may result from an incapacity for direct, clear thinking. Or it may result from incomplete knowledge of one's subject, which leads one to wrap a paucity of information in a plethora of words. Jargon may be useful for communication between members of the same profession (*see* INSIDE TALK). But windyfoggery, which often is jargon gone wrong and blanketed in blurriness, is not useful to any purpose.

-WISE

A cartoon in *Punch* showed two parent owls and a baby owl sitting on a branch, and the caption had one of the parents saying, "How's he shaping up wisewise?" If ridicule could kill, that cartoon should have had the "-wise" fad lying lifeless at our feet. But perhaps the circulation of *Punch* is not sufficiently large, for the fad thrives.

The suffix "-wise" can have three distinct meanings. The first, related to wisdom, denotes knowledgeable about, as in *pennywise, weatherwise, worldlywise.* The second denotes in the characteristic way or in the manner of the root word, as in *clockwise, sidewise, otherwise.* In this sense it is synonymous with and sometimes interchangeable with "-ways." The third meaning—and this is the fad meaning—is with respect to or concerning, as in coinages like *jobwise, sanitationwise, flavorwise.* The first two meanings are old and respectable; the third, though apparently old, fell into disuse and has been revived.

Tacking "-wise" onto a noun has a smart, efficient-sounding effect, and the devotees of the practice no doubt imagine that they are achieving a telescoping economy of language. They compare "Colorwise, the new printing method is superior to the old" with "So far as color is concerned, the new printing method is superior to the old," and conclude that they have made a gain in directness. But it does not occur to them that they could attain equal directness and greater grace by saying, "The new printing method reproduces color better than the old." They write, "Saleswise, the new candies are doing very well," when they might better write, "The new candies are selling very well." They write, "Mr. Carraway recalled that the most popular plan in the Senate votewise was the one providing for forty-one Senators and 144 House members," when they might better write, "Mr. Carraway recalled that the plan that got the most votes in the Senate, etc." They write, "Newswise, the survey suffers from the fact that . . . ," when they might better write, "As news, the survey suffers from the fact that. . . ."

The wiseacres go on and on coining "-wise" words. As Strunk observes, "There is not a noun in the language to which '-wise' cannot be added if the spirit moves one to do so. The sober writer will abstain from the use of this wild syllable." It may be that there is an occasional context in which a "-wise" word performs more efficiently than another locution. If so, the word will provide its own justification and there should be no hesitancy in using it. If, however, its use is simply a form of fad-following, forget it. And, if all goes well, the fad, like all fads, will ultimately fade. *See also* FAD WORDS.

WITH

With is a preposition, not a conjunction. Therefore when it is used in the sense of association or addition, the phrase it introduces does not make an otherwise singular verb plural. "The new tax ruling with its many exceptions and qualifications are [make it *is*] difficult to grasp." The same principle applies, of course, to *along with* and *together with*. Here is an unusual example in which the writer assumed incorrectly that the *with* produced a plural: "Ada Everleigh, who with her sister rose to notoriety at the turn of the century as madams of Chicago's swankiest brothels, is dead at the age of ninety-three." Grammatically

483

speaking, "madams" should be "a madam," but then the rest of the sentence would not track, nor would the meaning be quite intact. What is required here is a reconstruction: "Ada Everleigh, one of two sisters who rose. . . ."

WITH THE EXCEPTION OF
A wasteful locution. Use *except* or *except for*.

WITH THE RESULT THAT
This wasteful locution usually means *so*.

WITNESS
From dictionary definitions it is difficult to detect a significant difference between *see* and *witness*, except that *witness* seems to pertain to something of more than ordinary importance. Yet it is evident that there is a real difference when one reads a sentence like, "Certainly, I have never witnessed such a religious leader." It is clear to anyone whose ear is attuned to English that the word is there misused. Likewise something is wrong with a sentence that says, "They have witnessed Cardinals, Archbishops, and Bishops get to their feet and express diametrically opposite views." The point seems at first consideration to be that you can *witness* a thing but not a person. But even that statement requires further refinement if you conjure up a sentence like, "He witnessed the Grand Canyon." What is *witnessed* is an event, an occurrence, an action, perhaps even a situation, but not either a "thing" or a person. *Witness* is no ordinary synonym for *see* or *watch*, and some care is required in its use.

WOMAN
See LADY.

WORST COMES TO WORST
"He observed that if worse came to worse and France did not finally ratify the treaty arrangement. . . ." Idiom sometimes has a way of flying in the face of logic. Admittedly *worst comes to worst* is not logical; nevertheless it happens to be the idiom,

and has been so at least since the days of Thomas Middleton (1570-1627).

WORTHWHILE

Dictionaries differ on whether the word is hyphenated or solid (the preference here is for the solid word). But either way no distinction in spelling is made, whether the term is used as an attributive adjective—"a worthwhile project"—or as a predicate adjective—"the project is worthwhile." *See also* AWHILE.

WORTHY

One of outstanding worth was once called a *worthy*. In present-day use the word is most often employed humorously and even faintly disparagingly ("The worthies of the Board of Aldermen have seen fit to . . ."). In accordance with BERNSTEIN'S SECOND LAW, the word now has become almost out of place when used in its original sense, as in this sentence from a book review: "It is fun to make the acquaintance of such worthies as Samsi-Adad, first of the Assyrian conquerors; Gandash, chief of the Kassites, and Pu-Sarrumas, King of Kussara." The same review, by the way, used the words *celebrities* and *personages*, and these, too, are becoming victims of devaluation.

WORTHY

Takes preposition *of*.

WRACK

See RACK, WRACK.

XMAS

The "X" stands for Christ, which in its Greek form, *Christos*, begins with the letter *chi* (χ). The word, which incidentally should never be pronounced "exmas," is used in commercial messages, but is inappropriate in any kind of more serious writing.

YCLEPT

Denoting called or named, *yclept* is the past participle of the verb *clepe*. As a serious word it is archaic; as humor it is archaic hat.

YE

The word means the, and, believe it nor not, that is the way it is pronounced—*the*. So "Ye Old Coach House" is nothing different, except visually, from "The Old Coach House."

YEARN

Takes preposition *over, for, after*, or *toward*.

YIELD

Takes preposition *to*.

YOU

In the sense of *one*, the word *you* can convey directness and informality in writing: "The scientists have never demonstrated that if you lower blood cholesterol by change in diet, you also decrease the risk of heart attack and hardening of the arteries." Like any other writing device, this one should not be overdone. In particular it should be avoided if it suggests that the writer is talking down to the reader ("You had better get your tax return into the mail by tonight") or if it might seem so personal as to be offensive ("You won't have a hangover tomorrow if you skip some of those nightcaps tonight") or if it is far-fetched or unnatural ("If your pet ostrich has shingles, you ought to see a veterinarian").

ZEAL

Takes preposition *for* or *in*.

ZEUGMA

See RHETORICAL FIGURES AND FAULTS.

ZOOM

Aside from its meanings connected with sound and camera, *zoom*, originally an aviation term, denotes rapid upward motion. Both the following sentences are therefore incorrect: "Melville zoomed down the incline in 2:15.2, a full second ahead of Tommy Burns of Middlebury"; "At least twelve large hawks are making their homes atop city skyscrapers and zooming down to snatch pigeons." Both writers may have had in mind the word *swoop. Swoop* is usually down; *zoom* is always up.

Theodore M. Bernstein, assistant managing editor of *The New York Times*, joined *The Times* as a copy editor immediately after his graduation from the Columbia University School of Journalism in 1925.

During World War II he headed the foreign news desk, in charge of all war news; and in 1952 he was appointed to his present position. In late 1960 Mr. Bernstein went abroad on temporary assignment to serve as founding editor of the International Edition of *The Times*, published daily in Paris and distributed throughout Western Europe and the Middle East.

This busy and distinguished editor has also been a teacher; for twenty-five years he was a member of the faculty of Columbia's School of Journalism, holding the rank of associate professor when he retired from teaching in 1950. His first book—*Headlines and Deadlines*, written with Robert E. Garst—was published in 1933, with a revised edition issued in 1961. *Watch Your Language* was published in 1958, and *More Language That Needs Watching* followed in 1962. These last two books evolved from *Winners & Sinners*, a bulletin on better writing composed by Mr. Bernstein and circulated, since 1951, to reporters and editors of *The Times*.

Mr. Bernstein was born in New York City. He and his wife, Beatrice, make their home in Greenwich Village.